Two week loan

Please return on or before the last date stamped below.
Charges are made for late return.

LF 114/0895 UNIVERSITY OF WALES, CARDIFF, PO BOX 430, CARDIFF CF1 3XT

A Corpus of Formal British English Speech

A Corpus of Formal British English Speech: The Lancaster/IBM Spoken English Corpus

Edited by Gerry Knowles
Briony Williams, L. Taylor

LONGMAN
London and New York

Addison Wesley Longman Limited
Edinburgh Gate
Harlow, Essex CM20 2JE
United Kingdom
and Associated Companies throughout the world

Published in the United States of America
by Addison Wesley Longman, New York

First published 1996

ISBN 0 582 05639-X Csd

British Library Cataloguing-in-Publication Data
A catalogue record for this book is available from the British Library

Library of Congress Cataloging-in-Publication Data
A catalog record has been applied for

Set by 8
Printed in Great Britain by Bookcraft (Bath) Ltd.

Contents

Editor's acknowledgements

The Spoken English Corpus (SEC) project was supported jointly in 1984–5 by the Humanities Research Fund at Lancaster University and by IBM (UK) Ltd, and subsequently by IBM UK Ltd. IBM not only provided financial support, but actively participated in the project.

The editors wish to thank the many people at Lancaster and IBM who contributed to the project, or to the publication of the corpus. The project would not have begun at all but for the continued help and support of Geoffrey Leech at Lancaster and Geoffrey Kaye at IBM. The publication of the corpus in its present form was made possible by Peter Alderson, who later took over as Speech Research Manager at IBM. The text was made ready for publication thanks to the work of Nick Campbell, former research fellow at IBM, Matthew Peters, programmer at IBM, and of students at IBM, in particular Ashley Groombridge.

Without the speakers who produced the texts, there would of course be no spoken corpus at all. The University Orator, Colin Lyas, kindly reproduced two of his Degree Day speeches as M05 and M06. Heather Kempson and Rita Green, at that time MA students, produced the dialogue J06. These three texts were recorded in the Media Services Unit at Lancaster University.

The majority of texts in the corpus were obtained from the BBC, and we wish to thank Norma Jones of BBC Sound Archives for her help in organising contracts, contacting speakers, and providing information during the three years of the project.

Thanks are also due to all those who gave free permission for their work and/or speech to be included in the corpus:

Elizabeth Bell (*Story Time*); Louise Botting (*Money Box*); James Cox (*News*); John Carlin (*From our own Correspondent*); Alina Dadlez and Decca International (extracts from *Betjeman Reads Betjeman*); Isabelle Dean (*Time for Verse*); Paddy Feeny (*Review of the Year*); Dr Robert Fox (*Science and Belief in 18C France*); Susan Hampshire (*Week's Good Cause*); David Henderson (*The Reith Lectures III*); John Hollis (*Listening and Reading*); Martin Jarvis (*Morning Story* and *Time for Verse*); Juliet Johnson (*Money Box*); Catherine Kneafsey and Oxford University Press (extracts from *Streamline English Series*); Doris Lessing (author of *Through the Tunnel*); Colin Lyas (*Nelson Mandela* and *Tom Stephenson speeches*); Christopher Poole (*Review of the Year*); Brian Redhead (*Week's Good Cause*); Diana Ruault and Open University Educational Enterprises Ltd. (OU programmes – *Modern Art, Science and Belief in 18th Century France, Development of Fractions*); Graham Seal (author of *What shall we do if it rains?*); Simon Taylor (*Review of the Year*); Janet Trewin (*News*); The Met Office (*Weather Forecasts*).

Special thanks are due to Molly Price-Owen of BBC World Service Sport for her help with the *Review of the Year* extracts.

The following samples were obtained with the permission of the BBC and are covered by a contract with them covering copyright permission:

A01	In Perspective
A02–A12	From our own Correspondent
B01–B04	News
C01	The Reith Lectures III
E01–E02	Daily Service
F01–F03	Money Box
F04	Review of the Year
G01	Story Time
G02	Listening and Reading
G05	Morning Story
H04–H05	Time for Verse
J01	Review of the Year
K01–K02	Week's Good Cause
M02	Motoring News
M03	Weather Forecast
M04	Programme News
M07	Travel Roundup
M08	Weather Forecast
M09	Programme News

In addition to the copyright agreement with the BBC, permission to use material was obtained from any individuals not employed by the BBC,

The Open University Educational Enterprises Ltd gave permission for the inclusion of samples D01–D03.

Oxford University Press gave permission for the inclusion of *Streamline English* material, texts G03, G04, J02, J03, J04, and J05.

Decca International gave permission for inclusion of the samples of John Betjeman's work, texts H01, H02, H03 and M01.

Publisher's acknowledgements

We are grateful to the following for permission to reproduce copyright material:

The BBC for extracts from their programmes *In Perspective* (Radio 4), *From our own Correspondent* (Radio 4), *News* (Radio 2, 3 and 4), *Daily Service* (Radio 4), *Money Box* (Radio 4), *Review of the Year* (BBC World Service), *Motoring News* (Radio 4), *Weather Forecast* (Radio 4), *Programme News* (Radio 4), *Travel Roundup* (Radio 4); The Commonwealth Society for the Deaf for *This Week's Good Cause* (Radio 4 25.1.87); David Henderson for *The Reith Lectures III* (Radio 4 20.11.85); Heather Kempson and Rita Green for their dialogue J6; Jonathan Clowes Ltd, London on behalf of Doris Lessing/HarperCollins Publishers, Inc for an abridged and complete form (see page 262) of the short story 'Through the Tunnel' from *The Habit of Loving* by Doris Lessing. Copyright 1954 Doris Lessing/Copyright 1955 by Doris Lessing. Originally appeared in The New Yorker. Copyright renewed; Colin Lyas for two of his Degree Day speeches M05 and M06; John Murray (Publishers) Ltd for the poems 'Eunice', 'Felixstowe: *or* The Last of her Order', 'Harrow-on-the-Hill' and an extract from *Summoned by Bells* by John Betjemin; The Open University for 'Modern Art: Berlin Dada', 'Science and Belief' and 'Development of Fractions'; Oxford University Press for extracts from *Streamline English* by Bernard Hartley and Peter Viney (1978); the author's agent on behalf of the author for 'Lion at School' from *The Lion at School and Other Stories* by Philippa Pearce (Viking Kestrel). © 1971 Philippa Pearce; Graham Seal for an extract from his short story 'What shall we do if it rains?'.

We have unfortunately been unable to trace the copyright holder of the item K01 (*This Week's Good Cause*) (Radio 4 18.1.87) and would appreciate any information which would enable us to do so.

Introduction

The Lancaster/IBM Spoken English Corpus began in September 1984 as part of a research project into the automatic assignment of intonation undertaken by members of the Unit for Computer Research on the English Language at Lancaster University in collaboration with the Speech Research Group at IBM UK Scientific Centre. The first task for the project was to collect samples of natural spoken British English which could be used as a database for analysis and for testing the intonation assignment programs. The result is a machine-readable corpus of approximately 52,637 words of contemporary spoken British English.

The original design of the corpus was determined by the need to provide data for research into speech synthesis. As a result, unlike most other corpora currently being used in the computational linguistics field, the SEC exists in various forms. The texts are made available not only in standard orthographic form, but in different versions with a range of special annotations. For instance, in order to study prosodic patterns in the corpus, the texts were transcribed prosodically. A grammatically annotated version was produced using the CLAWS system (Constituent-Likelihood Automatic Word-tagging System) developed at Lancaster, which made possible an analysis of the syntax of spoken texts, and of the connection between syntax and prosody.

However, whatever the original motivation for compiling a corpus, it quickly becomes an object of interest in its own right. New users find it valuable for applications for which it was not designed. For example, the SEC has been used profitably by MA students at Lancaster whose main interest is in English Language Teaching. For most of these users the corpus has been compiled in an appropriate form, e.g. the orthographic texts present the texts in the manner required for concordancing. There are also users who need to make their own independent analysis of the data. They may wish to make a kind of annotation not yet carried out, e.g. phonemic transcription, or check the prosodic transcriptions. For such users copies of the original recordings are available. These were produced mainly by IBM UK Scientific Centre using equipment of sufficient quality to make the tapes suitable for instrumental analysis.

The corpus contains an interesting range of speaking styles. It is impossible in a corpus of 52,000 words to include samples of every style of spoken English; emphasis has been placed on collecting a sizeable sample of the type of spoken English suitable as a model for speech synthesis. This explains the relatively high proportion of prepared or semi-prepared speech produced by trained broadcasters. Small samples of highly stylised speech of the kind used in sermons or poetry reading have been included: these are examples of what might traditionally be regarded as 'good speaking', but are in fact quite inappropriate as models for speech synthesis by computer. These have proved of considerable interest for the study of prosodic style.

An important attribute of a modern corpus is that it is computer-readable: a corpus tends to reside on a hard disk rather than a bookshelf. In presenting the corpus in this book form, we have taken into account the needs of established corpus linguists, and of those who are not yet familiar with corpora. Anyone who has the corpus on disk can make hard copies of most of the files; but without a special font to print the prosodic symbols, the prosodic texts will be either unprintable or unreadable. For this reason the prosodic version has been chosen for publication. It is also the case that despite a rapidly growing literature on prosody and intonation, it is still difficult to find prosodically transcribed texts of naturally produced speech. It is hoped that this book will be of use to those who are unfamiliar with corpora but need access to prosodically transcribed material.

The original compilation of the SEC was completed by 1987. Since then the corpus has been analysed from several different points of view. Some of the early findings have been published (Knowles et al. 1996). But it is far from finished. Work so far has essentially involved an extension of techniques designed for written corpora (see e.g. Garside et al. 1987). The current aim is to develop a new methodology specially for spoken corpora. This will involve digitising the speech waveforms, conversion of the corpus texts into a speech database, and the development of annotation methods to relate the texts to the phonetic information in the waveforms.

Prosodic characters

The prosodic transcription was based on the system used by O'Connor & Arnold (1973) with some modifications:

- no distinction was made between symbols for onsets and nuclei
- the distinction between high and low variants was extended to all tones
- high and low were defined not with respect to the pitch range, but to the immediately preceding pitch level

These are discussed further below.

The following set of 15 special characters was used:

|	Minor tone-group boundary
||	Major tone-group boundary
‸	Caret
ˋ	High fall
ˎ	Low fall
ˊ	High rise
ˏ	Low rise
ˉ	High level
ˍ	Low level
ˇ	High fall rise
ˬ	Low fall rise
ˆ	Rise fall
·	Stressed but unaccented
↑	Up arrow
↓	Down arrow

Table 1. Tonetic stress marks

Some notes on the interpretation of these characters are necessary:

(1) Stressed and accented syllables:

An accented syllable has an independent pitch movement associated with it, the 'tone'. Tones are marked with iconic symbols representing the pitch movement.

Syllables which are perceived to be stressed but not accented (i.e. they are prominent but have no independent pitch movement) are marked with a dot.

Unstressed syllables are left unmarked.

The pitch of all unaccented syllables is predictable from the tone marks on neighbouring accented syllables.

(2) Pitch direction:

The terms *fall*, *rise*, and *level* describe pitch movements which begin on the vowel of the accented syllable (or in the case of a falling diphthong, on the first element of the diphthong). Any pitch movements before this point are ignored in this terminology.

Most of the pitch movement of a fall is completed on or soon after the accented syllable, leaving a slight drop over the tail of the tone group. A rise might start almost level, with a marked increase in slope towards the end of the tone group.

The level tone is not strictly level except possibly in special styles in which it is intoned. Any rising or falling is insufficient for the tone to be classed as a rise or a fall.

(3) Simple and complex tones:

Simple tones move in only one direction up or down. Complex tones change pitch direction: fall-rise and rise-fall.

The fall of the fall-rise is completed quickly, and the completion of the rise is delayed to the end of the tone group. The rise of the rise-fall is completed quickly on the accented syllable, and the fall is completed as soon as possible thereafter.

A phonetic variant of the fall-rise is the 'shallow fall': instead of falling to low and rising again, the pitch movement is cut off before it reaches low.

(4) High and low:

A distinction is made for all tones between a high and a low variety. A high tone begins higher than the preceding pitch level, and a low tone begins lower than the preceding pitch level.

(5) Up arrow and down arrow:

These are used to indicate significant changes of pitch which are not sufficiently marked by the tone symbols. The up arrow indicates a rise in pitch and the down arrow a drop in pitch.

When used in conjunction with tone marks they indicate a rise or drop in pitch which is significantly greater than that indicated by the high or low position of the tone mark alone.

Used alone, on an unstressed syllable, the arrow marks a pitch pattern which is not predictable from neighbouring tone marks. At the beginning of a tone group, the arrow indicates that the pitch contour begins significantly above or below its expected level towards the bottom of the pitch range.

For further details of the system, see (Knowles et al. 1996) especially chapter 3, 'The formulation of an intonation transcription system for British English'.

The composition of the corpus

In line with the conventions used in the Lancaster-Oslo/Bergen (LOB) corpus project (Johansson et al. 1978, 1986), each text is assigned to a category [A..M] and identified by number within that category. In addition, each text is given an absolute number to indicate its position in the corpus as a whole. For example H03 is the third text in category H, and is also text no. 34.

Figure 1 on page 7 lists the categories, and gives the total number of words in each category, and this figure expressed as a percentage of the 52,637 words in the whole corpus.

Breakdown into categories

Category A - Commentary

A01	In Perspective
A02-A12	From our own Correspondent

Texts in this category include news reports on events happening around the world. They are more informal than those in category B. *In Perspective* covers a religious topic, the reports *From our own Correspondent* all deal with overseas news events:

A02	The PNC meetings in Lebanon
A03	Westmorland and Sharon suing *Time* magazine
A04	The conflict in El Salvador
A05	The economic climate in Rumania
A06	The plight of Turks living in Huttenheim, Germany
A07	The hijack of the TWA passengers and the release of the Shi'ites
A08	Security checks at Athens airport
A09	The new government in Namibia
A10	The plight of the Tamil refugees
A11	Report on Gorbachev and his government
A12	The financial state of banks in Hong Kong

Category		No. of texts	Total words	% Total
A	Commentary	12	9066	17
B	News broadcast	4	5235	10
C	Lecture type I	3	4471	8
D	Lecture type II	1	7451	14
E	Religious broadcast	2	1503	3
F	Magazine-style reporting	4	4710	9
G	Fiction	5	7299	14
H	Poetry	5	1292	2
J	Dialogue	6	6826	13
K	Propaganda	2	1432	3
M	Miscellaneous	9	3352	6
	Grand Total:	53	52637	

Figure 1. Composition of the Spoken English Corpus

Category B - News Broadcasts

B01 Radio 4 News

B02 Radio 4 News

B03 Radio 2 News

B04 Radio 3 News

These are news reports of current and recent events in Great Britain and abroad. B04 consists of one speaker, B01-B03 consist of a main newsreader and additional reporters. The style of the main newsreaders is more formal than that of the reporters.

Category C - Lecture type I

C01 The Reith Lectures - III

This is a lecture addressed to the general public on economics entitled 'Needs, Centralism, and Autarchy'.

Category D - Lecture type II

D01	Open University - Modern Art
D02	Open University - Science and Belief
D03	Open University - Development of Fractions

These lectures are designed to be used as part of an Open University course. D01 covers the Berlin Dada movement in Germany, and so contains some German names and words. D02 is a discussion of theology and science in 18th-century France. D03 describes the development in the notation used in the representation of fractions, and contains some simple mathematical formulae.

Category E - Religious Broadcast

E01	Daily Service
E02	Daily Service

These are religious services with the hymns edited out.

Category F - Magazine-style reporting

F01	Money Box
F02	Money Box
F03	Money Box
F04	Review of the Year

These texts contain magazine-style in-depth reporting of financial news. Topics covered are: the perks of owning shares; the upgrading of state benefits; listeners' trusts; and Building Society rates.

Category G - Fiction (general)

G01	Story Time
G02	Listening and Reading
G03	Streamline English course samples
G04	Streamline English course samples
G05	Morning Story

All these texts are general fiction. G01 is a story aimed at an adult audience, *Through the Tunnel*, by Doris Lessing. G02 is aimed at children aged between 5 and 10, *Lion at School*, by Philippa Pearce. G03 and G04 are stories taken from the ELT course book *Streamline English.* G05 is aimed at adults - *What shall we do if it rains?*, by Graham Seal.

Category H - Poetry

H01	John Betjeman
H02	John Betjeman
H03	John Betjeman
H04	Time for Verse
H05	Time for Verse

This section consists of poetry readings of the work of John Betjeman and Sir Henry Newbolt. H01-H03 are John Betjeman's readings of his own poems: *Eunice*, *The Last of Her Order*, and *Harrow-on-the-Hill.* H04 and H05 are actors reading Sir Henry Newbolt's poems: *The Linnet's Nest*, and *The Nightjar*.

Category J - Dialogue

J01	Review of the Year
J02	course sample from *Streamline English*
J03	course sample from *Streamline English*
J04	course sample from *Streamline English*
J05	course sample from *Streamline English*

J06 Kempson and Green dialogue

These are dialogues of varying degrees of informality. J01 consists of a radio discussion of notable sports events of 1986. J02-J05 are dialogues contrived to illustrate a particular facet of English (although this is not immediately noticeable) for the *Streamline English* ELT course. J06 is an informal dialogue between two MA students about working abroad.

Category K - Propaganda

K01	Week's Good Cause
K02	Week's Good Cause

These two texts are charity appeals.

Category M - Miscellaneous

M01	John Betjeman
M02	Motoring News
M03	Weather Forecast
M04	Programme News
M05	Oratory
M06	Oratory
M07	Travel Roundup
M08	Weather Forecast
M09	Programme News

M01 is a sample of John Betjeman reading a section of prose: *An Unpleasant Nursemaid.* M02 and M07 consist of reports on road conditions. M03 and M08 are weather forecasts. M04 and M09 give details of forthcoming programmes on Radio 4. M05 and M06 are speeches delivered at degree ceremonies before the presentation of honorary degrees to Nelson Mandela and Tom Stephenson.

Speakers

As far as possible, the texts selected for the corpus were spoken in received pronunciation (RP). This was relatively easy where material from the BBC programmes *From our own Correspondent* and the *News* was concerned, as the BBC themselves make similar requirements of their presenters of news or news commentary programmes. Most of the speakers in the corpus have accents reasonably close to RP - even if, in some cases, the concept of 'RP' has been interpreted rather widely - and those with particularly strong regional accents were excluded.

A balance was sought wherever possible between male and female speakers. Of the 53 texts in the corpus, 17 were produced wholly or in part by female speakers. This represents 30 per cent of the corpus. In the highly stylised texts - poetry, religious broadcast, propaganda, and dialogue, there is a reasonably good balance. The higher percentage of male speakers in the News and Commentary categories reflects the tendency of the BBC to use mainly male speakers in these types of programme.

The following lists give the speakers in the corpus by category. In some cases it has not been possible to identify speakers by name, and so they are simply listed as 'male speaker' or 'female speaker'.

A01 Rosemary Hartill
A02 Gerald Butt
A03 Jon Silverman
A04 John Carlin
A05 James Morgan
A06 David Smeeton
A07 Laurie Margolis
A08 Keith Graves
A09 Graham Leach
A10 Alan MacDonald
A11 Peter Ruff
A12 Jim Biddulph

B01 Brian Perkins
Mike Wooldridge
Laurie Margolis
Janet Trewin

B02 Brian Perkins
James Cox
Clive Small
Kevin Bocquet
Ann Cadwallader
Peter Burden

B03 David Geary
Peter Smith
Colin Blane
David Davis

B04 Peter Bragg

C01 David Henderson

D01 Dawn Adies
D02 Dr Robert Fox
D03 Graham Flegg

E01 Frances Gumley
E02 Rev Stephen Oliver

F01 Louise Botting
Peter Day

F02 Louise Botting
Vincent Duggleby

F03 Louise Botting
Juliet Johnson
Frances McDonald

F04 Kevin Geary
Chris Florence
Harry Peart
Simon Taylor
Linda Spurr
Chris Poole
Mike Costello

G01 Elizabeth Bell
G02 John Hollis
G03 Male speaker
G04 Female speaker
G05 Martin Jarvis

H01 John Betjeman
H02 John Betjeman
H03 John Betjeman
H04 Isabelle Dean
H05 Martin Jarvis

J01 Kevin Geary
Martin Fookes
Paddy Feeny

J02 Male speakers
J03 Male speakers

J04 Male speaker
Female speaker
J05 Male speaker
Female speaker
J06 Heather Kempson
Rita Green

K01 Brian Redhead
K02 Susan Hampshire

M01 John Betjeman
M02 Male speaker
M03 Male speaker
M04 Male speaker
M05 Colin Lyas
M06 Colin Lyas
M07 Male speaker
M08 Male speaker
M09 Male speaker

Dates of composition and recording

For material obtained from BBC radio programmes the date of broadcast was as follows:

A01	In Perspective	24th November, 1984
A02-A06	From our own Correspondent	24th November, 1984
A07-A12	From our own Correspondent	22nd June, 1985
B01	News (R4)	24th November, 1984
B02	News (R4)	22nd June, 1985
B03	News (R2)	5th December, 1985
B04	News (R3)	14th January, 1986
C01	The Reith Lectures III	20th November, 1985
E01	Daily Service	26th November, 1985
E02	Daily Service	27th November, 1985
F01	Money Box	24th November, 1984
F02-F03	Money Box	22nd June, 1985
F04	Review of the Year	December, 1986
G01	Story Time	25th June, 1985
G02	Listening and Reading	28th January, 1987
G05	Morning Story	26th November, 1986
H04-H05	Time for Verse	26th November, 1986
J01	Review of the Year	December, 1986
K01	Week's Good Cause	18th January, 1987
K02	Week's Good Cause	25th January, 1987
M02	Motoring News	18th January, 1987
M03	Weather Forecast	18th January, 1987
M04	Programme News	18th January, 1987
M07	Travel Roundup	25th January, 1987
M08	Weather Forecast	25th January, 1987
M09	Programme News	25th January, 1987

For material prepared at the Media Services Unit, Lancaster University, the actual dates of recording were:

J06	Kempson and Green dialogue	11th March, 1987

M05	Nelson Mandela speech	29th January, 1987
M06	Tom Stephenson speech	29th January, 1987

The samples from *Betjeman Reads Betjeman* are all dated 'since 1954':

H01 Eunice
H02 The Last of Her Order
H03 Harrow-on-the-Hill

M01 An Unpleasant Nursemaid

The *Streamline English* texts were first published in 1982:

G03 SE Unit 10 - A funny thing happened...
G04 SE Unit 19 - Night flight

J02 SE Unit 16 - Inside Story
J03 SE Unit 25 - Murder at Gurney Manor
J04 SE Unit 72 - Getting things done
J05 SE Unit 75 - Messages

The material obtained from the Open University unfortunately contained no information on date of composition or publication. The texts concerned are:

D01 OU Modern Art
D02 OU Science and Belief in 18th-Century France
D03 OU Development of Fractions

The dates of composition of the Newbolt poems were:

H04	The Linnet's Nest	May, 1924
H05	The Nightjar	May, 1925

The duration of text extracts

The total duration of the corpus is 339 minutes 18 seconds. The average length of sample is 6 minutes, but individual texts vary greatly from this. Texts were not kept to a fixed duration as it was considered important to be able to study complete sections of speech (e.g. to observe the ways in which monologues begin and end). A predetermined cut-off point based on a number of words or minutes would have resulted in an unnatural-sounding endpoint to speech samples. The following table gives details of extract lengths in the corpus.

Cat	m:s	
A01	15:00	
A02	4:28	
A03	4:01	
A04	5:41	
A05	4:48	
A06	4:32	
A07	3:54	
A08	4:08	
A09	5:12	
A10	4:26	
All	4:15	[Tot A]
A12	4:05	[64:30]
B01	9:32	
B02	9:40	
B03	5:00	[Tot B]
B04	5:00	[29:12]
C01	30:00	[30:00]
D01	19:00	
D02	19:00	[Tot D]
D03	19:00	[57:00]
E01	6:48	[Tot E]
E02	4:30	[11:18]
F01	3:48	
F02	3:32	
F03	4:54	[Tot F]
F04	13:16	[25:30]

Cat	m:s	
G01	20:00	
G02	8:56	
G03	2:39	
G04	5:30	[Tot G]
G05	9:20	[46:25]
H01	1:41	
H02	2:03	
H03	1:00	
H04	2:59	[Tot H]
H05	1:17	[9:00]
J01	7:58	
J02	1:31	
J03	2:04	
J04	0:27	
J05	1:28	[Tot J]
J06	24:00	[37:28]
K01	4:32	[Tot K]
K02	4:09	[8:41]
M01	0:41	
M02	1:10	
M03	0:48	
M04	1:40	
M05	4:33	
M06	7:05	
M07	1:06	
M08	0:47	[Tot M]
M09	2:24	[20:14]

SEC text details

The following table gives for each text:

- the category letter and text number in the category (e.g. B02)
- the text number in the corpus as a whole (e.g. 14)
- the programme title
- the name of the speaker(s)
- the number of words

Category A - Commentary: 9066 words

A01	01	In Perspective	Rosemary Hartill	793
A02	02	From our own Correspondent	Gerald Butt	734
A03	03	From our own Correspondent	Jon Silverman	620
A04	04	From our own Correspondent	John Carlin	977
A05	05	From our own Correspondent	James Morgan	804
A06	06	From our own Correspondent	David Smeeton	828
A07	07	From our own Correspondent	Laurie Margolis	716
A08	08	From our own Correspondent	Keith Graves	618
A09	09	From our own Correspondent	Graham Leach	787
A10	10	From our own Correspondent	Alan MacDonald	800
A11	11	From our own Correspondent	Peter Ruff	785
A12	12	From our own Correspondent	Jim Biddulph	604

Category B - News Broadcasts: 5235 words

B01	13	Radio 4 News	Brian Perkins Mike Wooldridge Laurie Margolis Janet Trewin	1722
B02	14	Radio 4 News	Brian Perkins James Cox Clive Small Kevin Bocquet Ann Cadwallader Peter Burden	1720
B03	15	Radio 2 News	David Geary Peter Smith Colin Blane David Davis	940

B04	16	Radio 3 News	Peter Bragg	853

Category C - Lecture Type I: 4471 words

C01	17	The Reith Lectures - III	David Henderson	4471

Category D - Lecture Type II: 7451 words

D01	18	OU Modern Art	Dawn Adies	2410
D02	19	OU Science and Belief	Dr Robert Fox	2434
D03	20	OU Development of Fractions	Graham Flegg	2607

Category E - Religious Broadcast: 1503 words

E01	21	Daily Service	Frances Gumley	915
E02	22	Daily Service	Rev Stephen Oliver	588

Category F - Magazine-style reporting: 4710 words

F01	23	Money Box	Louise Botting Peter Day	671
F02	24	Money Box	Louise Botting Vincent Duggleby	667
F03	25	Money Box	Louise Botting Juliet Johnson Frances MacDonald	850
F03	26	Review of the Year	Kevin Geary Chris Florence Harry Peart Simon Taylor Linda Spurr Chris Poole Mike Costello	2522

Category G - Fiction: 7299 words

G01	27	Story Time	Elizabeth Bell	3163
G02	28	Listening and Reading	John Hollis	1221
G03	29	A funny thing happened...	Male	442
G04	30	Night Flight	Female	810
G05	31	Morning Story	Martin Jarvis	1663

Category H - Poetry: 1292 words

H01	32	Eunice	John Betjeman	248
H02	33	The Last of Her Order	John Betjeman	286
H03	34	Harrow-on-the-Hill	John Betjeman	157
H04	35	The Linnet's Nest	Isabelle Dean	405
H05	36	The Nightjar	Martin Jarvis	196

Category J - Dialogue: 6826 words

J01	37	Review of the Year	Kevin Geary Martin Fookes Paddy Feeny	1674
J02	38	Inside Story	Males	279
J03	39	Murder at Gurney Manor	Males	375
J04	40	Getting things done	Male & Female	74
J05	41	Messages	Male & Female	277
J06	42	Kempson and Green dialogue	Rita Green Heather Kempson	4147

Category K - Propaganda: 1432 words

K01	43	Week's Good Cause	Brian Redhead	798
K02	44	Week's Good Cause	Susan Hampshire	634

Category M - Miscellaneous: 3352 words

M01	45	An Unpleasant Nursemaid	John Betjeman	93
M02	46	Motoring News	Male	200
M03	47	Weather Forecast	Male	140
M04	48	Programme News	Male	298
M05	49	Nelson Mandela speech	Colin Lyas	738
M06	50	Tom Stephenson speech	Colin Lyas	1112

M07	51	Travel Roundup	Male	187
M08	52	Weather Forecast	Male	143
M09	53	Programme News	Male	441

Versions of SEC material

There are five versions of the material in the Corpus:

1. Spoken recording
2. Unpunctuated transcription
3. Orthographic (punctuated) transcription
4. Prosodic transcription
5. Grammatically tagged version

The unpunctuated transcriptions and the prosodic transcriptions were produced using the spoken recordings; the punctuated transcriptions were produced from the unpunctuated transcriptions; and the tagged versions were produced using the punctuated transcriptions. Versions 1, 2, 3, and 4 are produced manually; version 5 is produced semi-automatically. The following sections give details of the different versions.

Spoken recording

The spoken recordings are of three types:

1. those made on high-quality tape facilities at IBM and on cassette at Lancaster University
2. those made on high-quality tape facilities using Media Services at Lancaster University
3. those purchased from the relevant source (on cassette), and later copied on to high-quality tape at IBM.

Type 1 covers all material obtained from the BBC. The relevant programmes are:

In Perspective

From our Own Correspondent

News (R4, R3, R2)

The Reith Lectures

Daily Service

Money Box

Story Time

Listening and Reading

Morning Story

Time for Verse

Week's Good Cause

Motoring News

Weather Forecast

Programme News

In some cases it was necessary to edit out portions of the programmes where there was unintelligible speech, background noise, or some feature that was felt to be unacceptable in the corpus. The resulting clean copies of the recordings are now stored on video tape. The video tapes are used as the master copies, from which cassette copies are made as necessary.

Type 2 recordings are those made using volunteer speakers from Lancaster University. The Media Services Unit at the University provided recording facilities and technical staff to supervise recording sessions. Recordings were made using 10″ reel-to-reel tape, 7.5ips. The relevant samples are:

Colin Lyas: Nelson Mandela speech

Colin Lyas: Tom Stephenson speech

Rita Kempson and Heather Green dialogue

These recordings have now been copied (after appropriate editing) on to video tape as for type 1 recordings.

Type 3 covers the following samples:

Open University tape: Modern Art

Open University tape: Science and Belief in 18th Century France

Open University tape: Development of Fractions

Review of the Year

OUP: Streamline English series

Decca tapes: Betjeman reads Betjeman

The Open University samples were supplied on cassettes in the same format as is used by students or by the BBC for broadcasting, i.e. there is an introductory tone before each text, accompanied by the name of the course, course details, etc. This information was edited out before the master copy was made.

The *Review of the Year* tape is not strictly a type 3 recording as it was supplied on a 10″ reel-to-reel tape, and is therefore of higher quality than the cassettes obtained. It has been edited and copied to video tape.

The Oxford University Press *Streamline English* Series is supplied on cassettes with introductory material before each unit of the course. This material was edited out before copying on to video tape.

The Decca tapes of John Betjeman reading his own poetry are cassettes which were purchased from Virgin Records, Lancaster. The four samples used were copied on to video tape.

The completed video masters include an introduction to each sample, identifying it by category and number. There are pauses between the samples enabling easy cuing to any text on the tape. A full cassette copy of the corpus is held at Lancaster (one category per cassette), and video and reel-to-reel masters are held at IBM UKSC.

Unpunctuated transcriptions

The unpunctuated transcriptions were made using the spoken recordings. The text was typed directly on to computer, and it was at this point that unacceptable text was noted, and replaced by a comment in the transcription, for example [speech extract omitted]. Speaker details were also included in comments, for example [change of speaker: speaker name]. No word-initial capitals are used apart from those in proper names and abbreviations, thus no indication of start of sentence is given in this format of text. Stops are not used in abbreviations, for example, 'PLO' is used rather than 'P.L.O.' and similarly 'Mr' rather than 'Mr.', as this seems to be the more common convention in general use. Numbers are treated in the same way as in a standard text, for example, in addresses they are written as digits: '10 Green Street', and also in telephone numbers, quantities of money, and decimal numbers. They are written as words if they would normally be found so. Each text is preceded by four lines of comments giving details of absolute number (the position of the text in the corpus as a whole), category, number in the category, title, speaker(s), and recording details, e.g.:

[001 SPOKEN ENGLISH CORPUS TEXT A01]
[In Perspective]
[Speaker: Rosemary Hartill]
[Broadcast notes: Radio 4, 7.45 a.m., 24th November, 1984]

The unpunctuated transcription was used in the production of the punctuated transcriptions and the prosodic transcriptions. These versions were made independently, so that neither influenced the other, i.e. the punctuated version was made independently of any prosodic information, and the prosodic version was made without any cues from punctuation. The only way to ensure this was to have the unpunctuated transcription as the starting point for both of these versions.

Orthographic transcriptions

As mentioned above these were produced from the unpunctuated transcriptions. The volunteer punctuator was asked to insert punctuation at appropriate points in the text without access to the spoken recording. As an aid, a handbook on punctuation conventions was provided (based on Appendix lll of the *Comprehensive Grammar of the English Language*); if the punctuator was doubtful about a particular mark, he was to be guided by the handbook. Volunteers at Lancaster University and IBM participated in this exercise. Help was given when the punctuator could not decide on appropriate punctuation, for example, in cases where the sentence was ambiguous, and could be interpreted in two ways, or where the unpunctuated section of text seemed to make nonsense whichever way it was punctuated. There were very few of these cases.

For the following samples a transcript or original text was already available:

Streamline English material (G03, G04, J02, J03, J04,J05)

The Reith Lectures (C01)

John Betjeman's poems (H01, H02, H03)

Sir Henry Newbolt's poems (H04, H05)

The Kempson and Green dialogue (J06)

Colin Lyas speeches (M05, M06)

For the *Streamline English* material the transcriptions were taken from the students' book which accompanied the tapes.

For the Reith Lectures the transcription was taken from *The Listener* magazine (21st November, 1985), but was amended to take account of the speaker's use of enclitics *it's, there's* in the broadcast as opposed to the longer forms *it is, there is* in the written text.

The transcription of John Betjeman's poems was taken from John Betjeman's *Collected Poems*, John Murray Publishers, 1958. The prose sample was treated as an unscripted text (see above).

The transcription of Henry Newbolt's poems was taken from *A Perpetual Memory and Other Poems*, John Murray Publishers.

The Kempson and Green dialogue was partly scripted and transcribed orthographically by the speakers, and this was used to produce the full transcription.

Colin Lyas kindly supplied full orthographic transcriptions for the Nelson Mandela and Tom Stephenson speeches.

Grammatically tagged version

The corpus was grammatically tagged using the LOB suite of tagging programs (otherwise known as CLAWS1) with the orthographic text as input. It has also been tagged using a more recent version of the programs (CLAWS2).

A full description of CLAWS1 can be found in Garside et al. (1987). Briefly, the system works in five stages, all but the last being automatic.

1. The first stage, pre-editing, involves converting the text into a vertical format, with one word per line, in preparation for the next stage of processing. Punctuation marks are treated as words, and are separated off if necessary.

2. The second stage, word-tagging, involves deciding which tags are appropriate for each word. This may be done by either finding the word in the word-list, or its ending in the suffix-list, or stripping the plural *-s* off the word and searching the lists, or in the case of hyphenated words searching for each part of the word separately. If all strategies fail, the word will be assigned a default list of tags.

3. The third stage, idiom-tagging, deals with combinations of words such as *in order to*, assigning them a 'ditto' tag, i.e. overall tag, rather than leaving the structure with each word tagged individually.

4. The fourth stage, disambiguation, chooses the correct tag from the list of tags against the word, basing its decision on the surrounding context.

5. The last stage involves some manual post-editing. The post-editor has to check that the tag chosen against each word is the correct one, and if it is not, to indicate the correct tag, so that the re-formatter will pick it up.

The tagged texts are stored in two forms: a vertical format with one word per line along with line reference number and tag; and a horizontal format with the word linked to its tag by the underline character. The horizontal format requires far less storage space, but is more difficult to process if used as input to other programs. An additional form of the tagged texts has the text in horizontal format with the appropriate tag underneath the word on the next line. This form is a lot easier to read, and a program has been written to produce it using the vertical format as input.

Details of the coding symbols used in the LOB corpus to aid tagging and to preserve the format of the original texts can be found in Johansson et al. (1986). As the material in the Spoken English Corpus was transcribed from tape, there are no special codes in the tagged version to indicate type changes or special characters.

The prosodic version

The prosodic transcriptions were produced using the unpunctuated versions of the text and the audio tapes. Transcribers were Gerry Knowles at Lancaster University and Briony Williams who was at that time research fellow at IBM Scientific Centre. The transcribers were each allocated equal sections of the corpus, and they transcribed these sections independently. In order to compare and check on the consistency of transcription, and on the usefulness of the transcription system, the sections allocated were made to overlap at certain points, so that some passages were transcribed twice. There was at least one overlap passage in each corpus category, and the overlaps formed either part of a long text (usually the middle, when one transcriber did the first half and the other the second half), or the whole of a short text.

The overlap sections are:

Category	No. of Words	Category	No. of Words
A04	168	F04	235
B01	179	G01	291
B02	lS0	G02	211
B03	201	G05	222
B04	141	H03	157
C01	116	H04	148
D01	114	J01	200
D02	165	J02	279
D03	152	J04	74
E01	128	J06	597
E02	134	M01	93
F01	219	M06	306

The 24 overlap passages (a total of 4680 words) constitute 9 percent of the corpus. They have become the focus of much subsequent work on the prosodic transcription of the corpus; on this see (Knowles et al. 1996), especially chapters 4 and 5.

Samples of different versions

Unpunctuated transcription

[001 SPOKEN ENGLISH CORPUS TEXT A01]
[In Perspective]
[Rosemary Hartill]
[Broadcast notes: Radio 4, 07.45 a.m., 24th November, 1984]

good morning more news about the Reverend Sun Myung Moon founder of the Unification church who's currently in jail for tax evasion he was awarded an honorary degree last week by the Roman Catholic University of la Plata in Buenos Aires Argentina in announcing the award in New York the rector of the university Dr Nicholas Argentato described Mr Moon as a prophet of our time next week a delegation of nine Protestant ministers from Argentina visits the Autumn assembly of the British Council of Churches it's meant as a symbol of reconciliation between Christians following the Falklands War Protestants however are a tiny minority in Argentina and the delegation won't be including a Roman Catholic the assembly will also be discussing the UK immigration laws Hong Kong teenagers in the church and of course church unity schemes in the Free Churches there's some renewed grumbling about Anglican ambivalence to the British Council of Churches though the Anglicans still talk about doing as much as possible with other churches some Free Church people feel that in practice the Anglicans go it alone whenever they can an article in this week's Baptist Times asks what Bishop wants to confer when he can have a camera and a microphone all to himself when the Church of England's general synod can now get so much attention from the press the role of the British Council of Churches seems to fade into the background of course what concerns church leaders isn't necessarily what worries ordinary churchgoers even less the general public I can't recall ever having had a single letter on the British Council of Churches and its problems going by my postbag most people are worried about the problem of pain the existence of God and miracles they want to know whether for instance in a scientific age Christians can really believe in the story of the feeding of the five thousand as described or was the miracle that those in the crowd with food shared it with those who had none is the aid beginning to flow into Ethiopia any less a miracle than the five loaves and two fishes well just recently a day conference on miracles was convened by the research scientists' Christian Fellowship it was chaired by Professor Sir Robin Boyd a fellow of the Royal Society and the key question was when is a miracle not a miracle I suppose the popular notion of a miracle is an event unexplained by science or natural laws but the scientists themselves weren't having any of that on this definition they say very few events can confidently be called miracles because we have no idea what natural laws may be discovered in the future more important however is that the biblical writers themselves thought that events that followed natural laws could still be regarded as miraculous take the crossing of the Red sea by the Israelites for instance this was made possible by a strong wind the wind itself follows patterns of natural law the miracle is that it happened just when and where it was needed so it's the timing that can be miraculous but the real problem the scientists say with defining miracles as events unexplained by natural law is that it springs from an understanding of nature as a machine which runs itself it's the notion of an impersonal uncaring universe relentlessly following laws of cause and effect that's a position recently expounded by Don Cupitt in his BBC TV series the sea of faith this understanding say the scientists is in fact unscientific and the reason is they say that natural laws do not cause or dictate events they're merely descriptions of what we expect to happen on the basis of previous experience the research scientists say that to claim that all events follow these patterns is a philosophical position and not a scientific one they call that philosophical position naturalism and they say it is quite contrary to the Christian view of the world the Christian view they argue is to see events that can be covered by natural laws as God's usual activity we get so used to the usual patterns that we forget how amazing they are but at times they say God does unusual things too the usual and the unusual are both God's doing and it's miracles which confront us with God most clearly Don Cupitt was presumably one of the people the conference members had in mind when they emphasised their confidence in the miracles as stated in the Bible and deplored the tendency of some to try to reduce them to merely mechanical events by suggesting scientific explanations it's a useful reminder that some scientists find Don Cupitt unscientific the debate goes on

Orthographic transcription

[001 SPOKEN ENGLISH CORPUS TEXT A01]
[In Perspective]
[Rosemary Hartill]
[Broadcast notes: Radio 4, 07.45 a.m., 24th November, 1984]

Good morning. More news about the Reverend Sun Myung Moon, founder of the Unification church, who's currently in jail for tax evasion: he was awarded an honorary degree last week by the Roman Catholic University of la Plata in Buenos Aires, Argentina. In announcing the award in New York, the rector of the university, Dr Nicholas Argentato, described Mr Moon as a prophet of our time. Next week a delegation of nine Protestant ministers from Argentina visits the Autumn assembly of the British Council of Churches; it's meant as a symbol of reconciliation between Christians, following the Falklands War. Protestants, however, are a tiny minority in Argentina, and the delegation won't be including a Roman Catholic. The assembly will also be discussing the UK immigration laws, Hong Kong, teenagers in the church, and of course, church unity schemes. In the Free Churches there's some renewed grumbling about Anglican ambivalence to the British Council of Churches: though the Anglicans still talk about doing as much as possible with other churches, some Free Church people feel that, in practice, the Anglicans go it alone whenever they can. An article in this week's Baptist Times asks: What Bishop wants to confer, when he can have a camera and a microphone all to himself? When the Church of England's general synod can now get so much attention from the press, the role of the British Council of Churches seems to fade into the background. Of course, what concerns church leaders isn't necessarily what worries ordinary churchgoers, even less the general public: I can't recall ever having had a single letter on the British Council of Churches and its problems. Going by my postbag, most people are worried about the problem of pain, the existence of God, and miracles. They want to know whether, for instance, in a scientific age, Christians can really believe in the story of the feeding of the five thousand as described, or was the miracle that those in the crowd with food shared it with those who had none? Is the aid beginning to flow into Ethiopia any less a miracle than the five loaves and two fishes? Well, just recently, a day conference on miracles was convened by the research scientists, Christian Fellowship. It was chaired by Professor Sir Robin Boyd, a fellow of the Royal Society, and the key question was: When is a miracle not a miracle? I suppose the popular notion of a miracle is an event unexplained by science or natural laws; but the scientists themselves weren't having any of that: on this definition, they say, very few events can confidently be called miracles because we have no idea what natural laws may be discovered in the future. More important, however, is that the biblical writers themselves thought that events that followed natural laws could still be regarded as miraculous. Take the crossing of the Red sea by the Israelites, for instance: this was made possible by a strong wind; the wind itself follows patterns of natural law; the miracle is that it happened just when and where it was needed; so it's the timing that can be miraculous. But the real problem, the scientists say, with defining miracles as events unexplained by natural law is that it springs from an understanding of nature as a machine which runs itself; it's the notion of an impersonal, uncaring universe relentlessly following laws of cause and effect. That's a position recently expounded by Don Cupitt in his BBC TV series, The Sea of Faith. This understanding, say the scientists, is in fact, unscientific, and the reason is, they say, that natural laws do not cause or dictate events: they're merely descriptions of what we expect to happen on the basis of previous experience. The research scientists say that to claim that all events follow these patterns is a philosophical position and not a scientific one. They call that philosophical position 'naturalism', and they say it is quite contrary to the Christian view of the world; the Christian view, they argue, is to see events that can be covered by natural laws as God's usual activity; we get so used to the usual patterns that we forget how amazing they are, but at times, they say, God does unusual things too. The usual and the unusual are both God's doing, and it's miracles which confront us with God most clearly. Don Cupitt was presumably one of the people the conference members had in mind when they emphasised their confidence in the miracles as stated in the Bible, and deplored the tendency of some to try to reduce them to merely mechanical events by suggesting scientific explanations. It's a useful reminder that some scientists find Don Cupitt unscientific. The debate goes on.

Grammatically tagged versions

Horizontal formats

Horizontal format I

```
A01  2 (_( In_IN Perspective_NP )_)
A01  3 (_( Rosemary_NP Hartill_NP )_)
A01  5 ˇ good_JJ morning_NN ._. ˇ more_AP news_NN about_IN the_ATI
A01  5 Reverend_NPT Sun_NP Myung_NP Moon_NP ,_, founder_NN
A01  6 of_IN the_ATI Unification_NNP church_NN ,_, who_WP 's_BEZ
A01  6 currently_RB in_IN jail_NN for_IN tax_NN evasion_NN :_:
A01  7 he_PP3A was_BEDZ awarded_VBN an_AT honorary_JJ degree_NN
A01  7 last_AP week_NN by_IN the_ATI Roman_JNP Catholic_JNP
A01  8 University_NPL of_IN La_NP Plata_NP in_IN Buenos_NP_Aires_NP
A01  8 ,_, Argentina_NP ._. ˇ in_IN announcing_VBG
A01  9 the_ATI award_NN in_IN New_NP York_NP ,_, the_ATI rector_NN
A01  9 of_IN the_ATI University_NPL ,_, Dr_NPT Nicholas_NP
A01 10 Argentato_NP ,_, described_VBD Mr_NPT Moon_NP as_IN a_AT
A01 10 prophet_NN of_IN our_PP$ time_NN ._. ˇ next_AP
A01 11 week_NN a_AT delegation_NN of_IN nine_CD Protestant_NP
A01 11 ministers_NNS from_IN Argentina_NP
A01 12 visits_VBZ the_ATI Autumn_NP assembly_NN of_IN the_ATI
A01 12 British_JNP Council_NP of_IN Churches_NPLS ;_;
A01 13 it_PP3 's_BEZ meant_VBN as_IN a_AT symbol_NN of_IN
A01 13 reconciliation_NN between_IN Christians_NNPS ,_,
A01 14 following_VBG the_ATI Falklands_NPS War_NP ._. ˇ
A01 14 Protestants_NNPS ,_, however_RB ,_, are_BER a_AT tiny_JJ
A01 15 minority_NN in_IN Argentina_NP ,_, and_CC the_ATI delegation_NN
A01 15 will_MD n't_XNOT be_BE including_VBG
A01 16 a_AT Roman_JNP Catholic_NNP ._. ˇ the_ATI assembly_NN
A01 16 will_MD also_RB be_BE discussing_VBG the_ATI UK_NP
A01 17 immigration_NN laws_NNS ,_, Hong_NP Kong_NP ,_, teenagers_NNS
A01 17 in_IN the_ATI church_NN ,_, and_CC ,_, of_IN
A01 18 course_NN ,_, church_NN unity_NN schemes_NNS ._.
```

Horizontal format II

```
A01   2  ( In Perspective )
         ( IN     NP      )

A01   3  ( Rosemary Hartill )
         (    NP      NP    )

A01   5  good morning . more news about the Reverend Sun Myung Moon ,
          JJ     NN    .  AP    NN    IN   ATI     NPT     NP   NP    NP   ,

A01   5  founder
           NN

A01   6  of the Unification church , who 's  currently in jail for tax
         IN ATI      NNP         NN    , WP  BEZ     RB      IN  NN  IN  NN

A01   6  evasion :
           NN    :

A01   7   he  was  awarded an honorary degree last week by the Roman
         PP3A BEDZ   VBN    AT     JJ       NN     AP   NN  IN ATI  JNP

A01   7  Catholic
           JNP

A01   8  University of La Plata in Buenos Aires , Argentina . in announcing
            NPL      IN NP  NP   IN   NP     NP   ,    NP      . IN    VBG

A01   9  the award in New York , the rector of the university , Dr
         ATI  NN   IN NP   NP    ATI   NN   IN ATI    NPL      , NPT

A01   9  Nicholas
            NP

A01  10  Argentato , described Mr  Moon as a  prophet of our time . next
            NP     ,    VBD    NPT  NP  IN AT   NN    IN PPS  NN  .  AP

A01  11  week a  delegation of nine Protestant ministers from Argentina
          NN  AT     NN     IN  CD     NP          NNS      IN     NP

A01  12  visits the Autumn assembly of the British Council of Churches ;
           VBZ  ATI   NP      NN    IN ATI   JNP     NP     IN   NPLS   ;

A01  13  It  's  meant as a  symbol of reconciliation between Christians ,
         PP3 BEZ  VBN  IN AT   NN   IN       NN          IN       NNPS    ,

A01  14  following the Falklands War . Protestants , however , are a  tiny
            VBG    ATI    NPS    NP  .    NNPS          RB     , BER AT  JJ
```

```
A01  15  minority in Argentina , and the delegation will n't be including
            NN     IN     NP     , CC  ATI      NN       MD XNOT BE     VBG

A01  16  a  Roman Catholic . the assembly will also be discussing the UK
         AT  JNP     NNP    . ATI     NN     MD    RB  BE     VBG     ATI NP

A01  17  immigration laws , Hong Kong , teenagers in the church , and , of
             NN       NNS  ,  NP   NP  ,     NNS    IN ATI   NN   , CC  , IN

A01  18  course , church unity schemes .
           NN   ,   NN     NN     NNS   .
```

Vertical format

A01	2	001	(	(
A01	2	010	IN	In
A01	2	020	NP	Perspective
A01	2	021	)	)
A01	3	001	(	)
A01	3	010	NP	Rosemary
A01	3	020	NP	Hartill
A01	3	021	)	)
A01	5	001	--	________________
A01	5	010	JJ	good
A01	5	020	NN	morning
A01	5	021	.	.
A01	5	022	--	________________
A01	5	030	AP	more
A01	5	040	NN	news
A01	5	050	IN	about
A01	5	060	ATI	the
A01	5	070	NPT	Reverend
A01	5	080	NP	Sun
A01	5	090	NP	Myung
A01	5	100	NP	Moon
A01	5	101	,	,
A01	5	110	NN	founder
A01	6	010	IN	of
A01	6	020	ATI	the
A01	6	030	NNP	Unification
A01	6	040	NN	church
A01	6	041	,	,
A01	6	050	WP	who
A01	6	060	BEZ	's
A01	6	070	RB	currently
A01	6	080	IN	in
A01	6	090	NN	jail
A01	6	100	IN	for
A01	6	110	NN	tax
A01	6	120	NN	evasion
A01	6	121	:	:
A01	7	010	PP3A	he
A01	7	020	BEDZ	was
A01	7	030	VBN	awarded
A01	7	040	AT	an
A01	7	050	JJ	honorary

A01	7	060	NN	degree
A01	7	070	AP	last
A01	7	080	NN	week
A01	7	090	IN	by
A01	7	100	ATI	the
A01	7	110	JNP	Roman
A01	7	120	JNP	Catholic
A01	8	010	NPL	University
A01	8	020	IN	of
A01	8	030	NP	La
A01	8	040	NP	Plata
A01	8	050	IN	in
A01	8	060	NP	Buenos
A01	8	070	NP	Aires
A01	8	071	,	,
A01	8	080	NP	Argentina
A01	8	081	.	.
A01	8	082	--	______________________

Texts

001 SPOKEN ENGLISH CORPUS TEXT A01
In Perspective
Broadcast notes: Radio 4, 07.45 a.m., 24th November, 1984
Transcribed by BJW

↓Good ˋmorning || ↑ˋmore ·news about the ¯Reverend _Sun ·Myung ˋMoon | _founder of the Unifiˋcation ·Church | who's ˇcurrently in ·jail | for ˋtax evasion || ↑he was a¯warded an _honorary deˇgree last ·week | by the ¯Roman _Catholic Uni_versity of la ˋPlata | in ·Buenos ¯Aires | Argenˋtina || in anˋnouncing the aˋward in New ˇYork | the ˇrector of the uni·versity | ↓Dr ¯Nicholas Argenˊtato | deˇscribed Mr ·Moon as | a _prophet of our ˋtime || ↑ˇnext week | a ¯delegation of ˋnine Protestant ·ministers | ˇfrom Argentina | ¯visits the _Autumn Asˏsembly | of the _British ·Council of ˋChurches || ↑it's _meant as a ¯symbol of reconciliˋation | between ˏChristians | ˏfollowing the ˏFalklands ˋwar || _Protestants how¯ever ¯are | a _tiny miˋnority in Argen·tina | and the ¯delegation ˇwon't be including | a _Roman ˋCatholic || the assembly will ˇalso be dis·cussing | the _UK immiˇgration ·laws | ·Hong ˏKong | ˋteenagers in the ¯Church | ↑and of _course | ·church ˋunity ·schemes || in the ↑ˇFree Churches | there's some re¯newed ˋgrumbling | ↓about ·Anglican amˋbivalence to the ·British Council of ·Churches || ↓though the ¯Anglicans still ¯talk | ↓about _doing as ·much as ˊpossible with other ·churches | ↑ˋsome Free ˇChurch people | ·feel that in ˇpractice | the _Anglicans go it aˋlone whenever they ·can || an ¯article in this week's ·Baptist ˇTimes | asks ˋwhat ·bishop wants to conˇfer | ↑when _he can have a ˏcamera | and a ˏmicrophone | ˏall to himˋself || ↓when the ¯Church of ·England's General ˇSynod | can ˋnow get so much atˇtention from the ·press | the ¯role of the ˋBritish Council of ˇChurches | ¯seems to _fade into the ˋbackground || ↑of course ˋwhat concerns ·church ˋleaders | ¯isn't necesˏsarily | ¯what ·worries ordinary ˋchurchgoers | even ¯less the _general ˋpublic || ˇI can't recall | ·ever _having ·had a single ˋletter on the ·British Council of ·Churches and its ·problems || ·going by ˇmy postbag | ˋmost people are ·worried about the ·problem of ˊpain | the eˋxistence of ˏGod | and ˋmiracles || ↑they _want to know ˏwhether for ˏinstance | in a scienˇtific ·age | ¯Christians can _really be_lieve | in the ˏstory of the ˏfeeding of the _five ˋthousand | as deˋscribed || or _was the ˏmiracle that those in the crowd ˇwith ·food | _shared it with ·those who had ˋnone || ↓is the ¯aid beginning to ·flow into Ethiˏopia | any ˏless a ·miracle | than the _five loaves and two ˋfishes || ↑well just ˏrecently | a ˇday conference on ·miracles | was conˏvened by the Reˇsearch ·Scientists' | ·Christian ˋFellowship || it was ˋchaired | by Proˏfessor ·Sir _Robin ˋBoyd | a ¯Fellow of the _Royal Soˋciety | and the ˇkey ·question was | ¯when is a _miracle ˋnot a ·miracle || I sup↑ˉpose the ˯popular notion of a ·miracle is | an e_vent | unex_plained by ˉscience or ·natural ˋlaws || but the ˋscientists themˏselves | ˉweren't having ˋany of ·that || on ˇthis defi·nition they say | very ˋfew events | can ˋconfidently be ·called ˇmiracles | because we have ˇno i·dea | ˋwhat natural ·laws | may be dis_covered in the ˋfuture || more imˇportant how·ever | is that the ˉbiblical _writers themˇselves | ˉthought that e_vents that ˇfollowed natural ·laws | could ˉstill be re_garded as miˋraculous || ↑take the _crossing of the ·Red ·Sea by the ˋIsraelites for ·instance || ˋthis was made ˉpossible by a strong ˋwind || the ·wind itˇself | follows _patterns of ·natural ˋlaw || the ˋmiracle | is that it _happened just ˉwhen | and _where it was ˋneeded || so it's the ˋtiming that can be mi·raculous || but the ˋreal ·problem | the ˏscientists ˏsay | with deˉfining ˏmiracles | as e_vents unex·plained by natural ˇlaw | is that it _springs from an ˉunderstanding of ˯nature | as a maˋchine | which _runs itˋself || ↑it's the _notion of an ˇimpersonal | ˇuncaring ·universe | reˋlentlessly ˏfollowing ˏlaws of ˏcause and efˋfect || ˇthat's a po·sition | ˇrecently ex·pounded | by _Don ˋCupitt | in his ·BBˇC ·TV ·series | The _Sea of ˋFaith || ↑ˋthis underˇstanding say the ·scientists | ˇis in ·fact | ·unscienˋtific || ↓and the ·reason ˊis they ·say | that ˇnatural laws | do ˇnot ·cause | or dic_tate eˋvents || they're ·merely deˇscriptions | of _what we exˋpect to ·happen | on the ˏbasis of ˏprevious exˋperience || ↑the re_search ·scientists ˊsay | that to ·claim that ˇall events ·follow these ·patterns | is a philoˇsophical po·sition | and ˋnot | a scienˋtific ·one || they ˋcall that philo·sophical position ˊnaturalism | and ˋthey say it is ˇquite ·contrary | to the _Christian ·view of the ˋworld || the ˇChristian view they ·argue | is to ·see e_vents that can be ˇcovered by natural ·laws | as _God's ˋusual ac·tivity || we get ˋso ·used to the ˇusual ·patterns | that we forˏget how a_mazing they ˋare || but at ˇtimes they ·say | ˉGod _does ˇunusual things ˎtoo || ↓the ˋusual | ˋand the ˇunusual | are ˇboth God's ·doing | and it's ˋmiracles | which conˏfront us with ˏGod most ˋclearly || ↑Don _Cupitt was pre·sumably ˇone of the ·people | the _conference ·members had in ˇmind | when they _emphasised ˇtheir ·confidence in the ·miracles | ·as ˇstated in the ·Bible | and deˋplored the ·tendency of ˇsome | to _try to reˋduce them | to ·merely meˇchanical e·vents | by sug_gesting ·scientific explaˋnations || it's a ˇuseful re·minder | that ˇsome ·scientists | ·find _Don ˊCupitt | ·unscienˎtific || the deˉbate | goes ˎon ||

002 SPOKEN ENGLISH CORPUS TEXT A02
From our own Correspondent
Broadcast notes: Radio 4, 11.30 a.m., 24th November, 1984
Transcribed by GOK

¯correˏspondents | ¯seeking ˎaccess | to the _PNC ˬmeetings | were reˇquired the ·other ·day | to ˋfill in ˬforms | to a¯pply for perˇmission | from the _PLˎO || at ˇone ·point | the ·forms ˆ ¯asked us to ˏstate | our ¯last ˎcontact | with the _organiˎsation || for ˇmany of us | it was a ˋbrilliantly ¯sunny ˏday | in the ˋbattle-·marked | ¯port of ˇTripoli | in ·Northern ˬLebanon | last Deˋcember || ·wrecks of ˊships | ˋhit in the ·inter-Pales·tinian ˇshelling | had been ˎcleared aˇway | to aˎllow ˇferries | ·flying U_nited ·Nations ¯flags | to ·take Mr ¯Arafat and his ˏmen | ·into their ˇsecond | enˋforced | ¯exile from _Lebanon | in _just ·over a ˎyear || the ˇfighters | ·looked a ¯sorry ˎsight | with their ˊsuitcases | and ˏbedding ·rolls | their ˋcarrier-·bags | and kaˎlashnikovs || they de¯parted | wi·thout ¯any preˋtence | that _this was a ˎvictory || on ¯that _day | it ˎdid | ¯finally ˬseem | ¯like the ˎend || it ↑ˇwasn't of ·course | and ˬTripoli | ·seems like a ˋdecade a·go | eˏspecially | seeing Mr ˇArafat | ¯here in Aˋmman | with ¯all the ˊpomp | and the inˋcredibly ·tight seˬcurity | ˋlaid on by the Jorˇdanians | for the _Palestine ·National ˎCouncil || the ↑ˇatmosphere | on ˋthat De·cember ·day in ˬTripoli | was ˎsombre || the ˇfighters | ·may not ·feel much ·different toˋday | as ˇthey wait | in ˬcamps | a_round the ·Middle ˎEast || but for ˋMr ˬArafat | and the poˋlitical ·movement suˬpporting him | the ¯atmo·sphere | is _anything but ˎsombre || there's a ˊsense | of reˎlief | that at ˇlast | ¯something is being ˎdone | to ·reˇbuild | the _PLˏO | after so ¯many | de¯pressing ˏmonths | of in_ternal ˎwrangling || even ˋif it's a _shrunken organiˋsation | with ¯pro-ˇSyrian ·groups | for the ˎtime ·being at ¯least | _staying ˎout || ¯Yasser ˏArafat | the ¯master of ˏcompromise | and of ·keeping ¯all sides ˬhappy | the po¯litical chaˎmeleon | is at ¯last ˏsaying | e_nough is eˎnough || he's ˏseeking | to ·take the ¯boldest ·move of his ˎlife | and his deˇcision | ·seems to be ·going down ˬwell | with his con·stituency at ˋlarge | if ˋnot with ·all the _groups | wi_thin the PLˎO || ¯like at ˇall ·party ·conferences | ·round the ˬworld | there's a par¯ticular _atmosphere | of ·camaˎrade·rie || but it ¯does ˏseem | that ˬthis ·meeting | ˎis | a _little bit ˎspecial || ˊperhaps | with the diˏvisions | that have ·opened ˊup | ˏand | with ¯all the re·crimiˋnation | the ˋPale·stinian ˬmovement | ·thought there was ¯little ˏhope | for a ·PN_C at ˎall || ˇone ·lady | in her ˏseventies | was ¯brought ·here | on a ˋstretcher | from a ˬhospital | in Beiˋrut || she was ˏtold | that the ˏjourney | _might ˎkill her || I'm ·going to ·die ˇanyway she ·said | I'd ¯rather _die | a·mong my _fellow

·PaleˎstiniansⅡ ˬso | ↑ˇsuddenly | ˉhere it ˎis | ˊand | in Aˬmman | of ˎall ·places || ˇno de·cision | could have been ˬcalculated | to a·nnoy the ˇSyrians | ˎmore || and as the ˉred ˏcarpets | are ·laid ˊout | for Mr ˏArafat | and his suˊpporters | it's ˉhard to iˏmagine | ˉBlack Sepˋtember | the ·bloody ˊbattles | in ˉnineteen-ˇseventy | between the Jor·danian ˬarmy | and the ˍPLˎO || a ˉphysical ˍclash | ·leading to ˰ re·grettable eˎvents | as ·King Huˍssein ·put it | in his ˉopening aˏddress | on ˍThursday ˎnight || ·bringing out ˉold ˍghosts | in the ˉhope | that they'd ˎthen be ·laid ˍfinally to ˎrest || ˋthings ·do ˬchange in ·this part of the ·world | in the ·most unbeˇlievable | ˎways || a ·forty-year-old Palesˋtinian | who'd been a ˋfighter ·most of his ˎlife | with a ˇLibyan-·backed ·group | oˋpposing ·Mr ˎArafat | the ˇone in ·fact | that ·helped to ˇforce the ·PLO ·leader | ˋout of ·Tripoli last ˇyear | ˎhe's ·here || he ˊsays | ˋhe and ·many of his ˬcolleagues | ˋleft their ·organiˏsation | just beˋfore the ·Tripoli ˎfighting || he's ˊhappy | to be in Aˏmman | not ˇunhappy with the i·dea | of a ·joint iˋnitiative with ·King Huˎssein || and there's the ˋdoctor I ˍcame a·cross | who I'd ·interviewed in ˍTripoli | ˇduring the ·fighting last De·cember | in a ˍmakeshift ˎhospital | in a ˍschool ˎbasement || ˋhe now ·works in ˎCairo | and ˬsays | only ˇhalf ·jokingly | the ˬnext PN·C | ˍcould be ˎthere || ˋthat's how ·fast things ˎchange || but ˋwhile ˇsome changes o·ccur | a ˬgreat deal | reˍmains the ˎsame || that ˋform I ·mentioned ˎearlier for e·xample || it ˇshould have a·llowed us | ˬall to be ·present | for the hi·storic ·opening ˏsession | on ˍThursday ˎnight | which ˇboth ·sides | ˋdesperately ·wanted reˎported | as ·much in ˊEurope | and the U·nited ˏStates | as ˎanywhere || but the ·fact ˇis | the maˊjority | of reˉporters | and ˉcameramen | ˊspent | that hiˉstoric ˏevening | ˉfreezing ˏcold | with ˉno faˏcilities | in the ˋcar-·park of the ˎconference ·centre || there ·simply was ˉno ˋroom inˎside || not ˋlike those em·battled ·days in ˋTripoli | when ˉany | and ˇevery ·foreign re·porter | was ˍalways ˎwelcome || just ˋone of the ·ups and ˇdowns I su·ppose | of ·covering a ˍrevoˎlution ||

003 SPOKEN ENGLISH CORPUS TEXT A03
From our own Correspondent
Broadcast notes: Radio 4, 11.30 a.m., 24th November, 1984
Transcriber: BJW

↑in a _city where there's •always ˇsomething to •see | _twenty-four •hours a ˇday | the ¯latest at,traction | is the ¯federal `courthouse | in Man`hattan || ,every ,morning ¯long ˇqueues are •forming | _out•side •courts ˇthree one •eight | and _five o `nine || ↓if you •can't get into ˇone •trial | there's ↑`always an outˇside •chance | that a •seat ˇmight be •free | at the `other || ¯as ,ever | the A¯merican ,public | `and the •world's ,press | are _hungry for `drama || and the ¯main pro`tagonists in •both ,trials | `seem to be `going out of their `way to pro↑`vide it || •Ariel Shaˇron | ac¯cuses •Time ˇmagazine | of com¯mitting a _blood `libel || re,calling the ,medieval ˇslander | that ¯Jews ˇmurdered •Christians | to `use their ˇblood | in `Passover •rituals || ¯General Westˇmorland | says ¯CB,S | `rattlesnaked him | ↓in a ¯nineteen _eighty-_two •docu`mentary | on the _Vietnam `war || they ¯robbed my repu`tation he •claims || the ↑`two •cases then have •obvious simi`larities | and in`deed | the same ˇlaw •firm | is de,fending both ,Time and ¯CB`S || •Time's chief ˇcounsel | •Thomas ˇBarr | has ¯no `doubt | that the ¯same _funda•mental `principle | is at `stake | in both `trials | the _freedom of the `press || atˇtacking that •principle | is be¯coming a ¯popular `thing | for •ex-ˇgenerals | to `do | he •comments •wryly || but `some people ,say | the ¯two ˇlibel •actions | ¯go even ˎfurther than •that || that they're an at¯tempt to _rewrite `history || •George ˇCryal | a _CBS pro´ducer | who's a deˇfendant | in the Westˇmorland •case | says ˇboth •generals | pre_sided over di`sasters || ˇnow | _sensing a ¯change in the •public ˇmood | they're _trying to ¯rescue their repu`tations || it's ↑¯certainly ˎclear | from what ˇboth •men | have already `said | on the ˇwitness •stand | that `they feel ↑`their •side of the ˇstory | has _never been `told || Westˇmorland for e•xample | became par`ticularly ˇpassionate | when `talking about the •influence ¯television reˇporting from Viet•nam | had `had on the ˇWhite •House | in the •late `sixties || he said that in the `Oval ˇOffice | `President ˇJohnson | had ¯all _three ,networks | •running simul`taneously || he `even had a ¯TV in the `bathroom || ↓senˇsational ¯coverage | ↓on ¯television | ↓said West¯morland | had a ¯far `greater `impact on the ˇpresident | than my re`ports did || ↑Sha_ron `too | has a ,strong his,torical per`spective || ˇso •strong in •fact | that he acˇcuses •Time | of ¯having been _anti-Seˇmitic | since the ¯state of •Israel was ˇfounded | in ,nineteen ,forty-`eight || to ¯prove his `point | `as he was •giving ˇevidence | he dra`matically ¯flourished a ˇcopy of •Time | from ,nineteen •fifty-`three || ↓with a ,story

| about an Is¯raeli ˇraid | on a ·Jor_danian ˋvillage | ˏled by Sha_ron himˋself || ↑but it's not ˋjust a reˋvising of the ˋpast | which ˋworries many obˋservers of these two ·trials | it's the impliˏcations for the ˋfuture || ¯both ˏplaintiffs have ˏpowerful ˋbackers || Westˇmorland | is supˏported by a ˏnumber of conˏservative founˋdations || be¯hind Shaˇron | is the Is_raeli ˋgovernment || ¯interested ˇbodies | ↓like the ˋLibel Deˋfence Reˇsource ·Centre | say the ¯two ˬactions | are the ˇvanguard | of a new ˋkind of ·libel case || where the ˋplaintiff is con¯cerned | ˋnot so much about his ˋpersonal repuˇtation | but in ˏwinning a poˏlitical or _idealogical ˋbattle || ˋtake for eˏxample | what the _two ex-ˇgenerals | have ˋsaid | about their own ˋcases || Westˇmorland ·says | he's de¯fending the _honour of the ˋmilitary || Shaˇron says | he ¯wants to re·move a ˇslur | on the ¯state of _Israel | and the _Jewish ˋpeople || but many ob_servers ˇfeel | that the ˇreal in·tention | is to in_timidate the ˋmedia | which ˋsince the ·high point of ˇWatergate | in the mid ˇseventies | has ˋlost ·much public eˋsteem || ↓if ·verdicts go against ¯Time and ·CBˇS | ·both pre-ˋeminent in their ˇfields | the ˋimpact on ˇlesser ·news organisations | ˏcan be exˏpected to be _far-ˋreaching || but ˋthese conside·rations ˋaren't ·likely to ¯bother the ˋpublic | who ˇstand on line | ·each ˋday at the Manhattan ˋcourthouse || they're ˏdrawn by the ˏspectacle | of ¯two _silver-haired ex-ˇgenerals | ˋfighting for their repuˋtations || after ˋall | ·who needs teleˇvision ·drama | ¯when you can _see the ·real ˋthing ||

004 SPOKEN ENGLISH CORPUS TEXT A04
From our own Correspondent
Broadcast notes: Radio 4, 11.30 a.m., 24th November, 1984
Transcribed by GOK

the ˋNew ·York ˇTimes corre·spondent | ˋlooked ·out of his ˉcar ˇwindow | and ˉtold me the gueˇrrillas | had ˉtaken ·Suchiˋtoto || ˉdid I ·want a ˎride || I ˉjumped ˋin | and we ˉset ˎoff | at the ˉmanic ˎspeed | which for ˉsome ˍreason | is a ˉcharacteˎristic | of the ˉway ˋall ·journalists ·drive | ˉhere in El ˎSalvador || ˉSuchiˏtoto | is a parˋticularly | ˋbullet-·holed | ˋbombed-·out ˎtown | a ˋtenuous | ˉgovernment ˋstronghold | in the ˋheart of gueˋrrilla-con·trolled ˎterritory || ˉthirty ·miles ˎnorth | of the ˎcapital | ˉSan ˎSalvador || ˋevery ·correˇspondent ·here | aˋgrees | that the ˎfinal | ˋsix-·mile ˎstretch | through ˉSuchiˎtoto | is the most ˋeerie | the ˋscariest ·bit of ˎroad | in El ˎSalvador || the ˋlast re·porter to be ˎkilled ·here | ˉback in ˋMarch | was ˉshot ˋdead | in a ˎcrossfire | ˉon that ˎroad || aˋnother re·porter's ˋcar | ·hit a ˋmine ·there | ·two ˎyears a·go | and he ˋtoo was ˎkilled || ˋeveryone's had ˉnarrow ˎscrapes | on the ˉSuchi·toto ˎroad || there were ˋthree of us in the ˎcar | ˋall ·rather ˎnervous || the ˇthird re·porter | was with the ˉWashington ˎPost | a ˏwar corre·spondent | for ˋtwenty ˇyears | who'd ˋcovered ·Vietˎnam || the ˉWashington ˇPost ·man ·said | he ˇhoped | that ^ at an ˉarmy ˇcheckpoint | just ˋbefore the ·final ˎstretch | to ·Suchiˋtoto | they would ˋstop us from ·going ˎthrough || they ˎdidn't || there had been ˉheavy ˋfighting | between the gueˉrrillas and the ˎarmy | for ˉten ˇhours | but it was ˍnow subˋsiding || we could ·hear ˇairforce ·bombing | conˋtinuing | a ˋfew ·miles ˎnorth | but the ˋsoldiers at the ·checkpoint ˋtold us | the ˋarmy had ·sent reinˎforcements | and was ·now ˉback in conˎtrol | of ˉSuchiˎtoto || a ˋlittle ·reaˎssured | we ·drove ˎon | ·very ˇwarily | and ·very ˎslowly | as you ˉalways ˎmust | on these ˉno-·man's-·land ˎroads || the ˋgrass is ·really overˎgrown | ·all aˎlong | the ˉSuchi·toto ˎroad | a·bout ˉten foot ˎhigh | ˉleaning ˋover | ˋforming a ·sort of ˋcanopy | ˋadding to the disˉquieting senˎsation | that you're ˇentering | into the ˇjaws | of ·something unˋpleasant || the ˋcountryside ·all aˇround | what ·little you can ˇsee of it | is ˉdensely ˋvegetated | ˋperfect gue·rrilla teˎrrain || ·as we drove ˎon | towards ˉSuchiˎtoto | we could ˉsee | ˉover to the ˎleft | the ˋsun | be·ginning to ˎset | ·over the ˋcraggy | ˉalways ˇawe-inspiring | ˋmountain of Juˎcuapa || a gueˉrrilla ˋbastion | for the ˉfive ˋyears | of the ˍcivil ˋwar || unˋdoubtedly | the most ˊbombed | the most ˇrocketed | most ˋmortared ˋland ·mass | in El ˋSalvador || with just ˋtwo ·miles to ˎgo | to ·Suchiˎtoto | we were beˋginning to ˎbreathe a·gain | ·when to our disˋmay | we ·saw a gueˉrrilla ˎcolumn | ·up aˎhead || to our disˋmay | ·not because we ˋfeared the gueˎrrillas | but because ‸ the ¯chances of ·being ˎbombed | or being ¯caught in a ˇcrossfire | had ¯suddenly ·inˎcreased | draˎmatically || the gueˇrrillas | ¯stopped our ˎcar || they were ˋcourteous | as they ˋusually ·are with the ˎpress || ¯what's ˍmore they ·looked | ¯discon·certingly ˎplacid | ˎgentle | and reˎlaxed | as ·if ‸ ˎdrugged on ˎwar || the ˋfighting that had ·just ˎended | had ·been the ˋfiercest | in ¯four ·months of ˎwar || the ˇyoungest gue·rrilla ·looked | ·fourˋteen | the ˇoldest | ˎtwenty || they were ¯well ˎarmed | with ¯heavy maˋchine-·guns | and A¯merican-ˎmade | ¯automatic ˎrifles | they ˋposed for ˎphotographs | ˇsmiling | and ¯oddly ˎsilent || the gueˋrrillas | the ·point was ˋmade | ¯very ˋclearly | con·trolled the ˎroad || ˋsix ·months beˇfore I re·called | ¯sixty ˋsoldiers | were ˎlured | ·down that ˎroad | ¯by the gueˎrrillas | and ·all ˋsixty | were ˋwiped ˎout || ¯much ˇbombing ·here | I ¯asked one gueˎrrilla | a ·young ¯woman ˎfighter || eˎnough ‸ she re·plied || just ˇthen | a ˋplane a·ppeared | ¯right aˎbove us | the gueˇrrillas | ˇliterally | ¯didn't ·raise an ˎeyebrow || for ˇthem | it was ¯all | in a ¯day's ˎwork || ˇwe | ¯jumped into the ˬcar | and ¯drove like ˎmad | for ¯Suchiˎtoto || ˋfive ·minutes ˎlater | we were ˎthere || the ˋtown ·looking | ˋeven ·more ˋderelict | and ˋdevastated than ˎusual | the few inˋhabitants | in their haˋbitual ·state of ˎshell-·shock || ˋsoldiers of the e¯lite ‸ ˇParachute Ba·ttalion | were ˋevery·where || they'd ¯come in by ˋhelicopter | in ·fourˋteen ·helicopters in ˎall | ¯flying in forˎmation | ˋshuttling | ¯back and ˎforth | from their ˋbase | in ·San ˎSalvador || a ˋtactic | ¯recently emˎployed | to ·step ˋup | the ·use of the Aˋmerican-su·pplied ˋhelicopters | had ¯served ˋwell ·this time | to a¯void the ˋambushes | the gue·rrillas ¯always ˋplace | a·round ˍtowns they've ˋpenetrated || a ˋlot of ˎsoldiers | were ˇkilled | in ˋfighting | ·in the ˎtown | but the gueˇrrillas | ·several ˇhundred of them | ˋhad been ·beaten ˎback || a ˋgroup of ·rather ¯smug ˋofficers | in ˋclean ·pressed ˇuniforms | exˇplained to us | the ¯day's ˎaction || ¯as they ˍspoke | we could ˋhear | ¯airforce bomˎbardments | conˋtinuing | to the ˎsouth || the ˍslow-·motion ˇbangs | ˋholding | like ˋrumbles of ˎthunder || it was ¯getting ˏdark | and we ¯had to ·head ˎsouth | ourˎselves | ˋback to the ˎcapital || ¯as we preˎpared | to ·leave ˎtown | an Aˋmerican ¯HˎP re·porter | ¯drove ˎin || he was ¯white | and ˬshaking | ↑but a ˍperson of ˋwry ·dispoˇsition | he was ¯still | ¯self-poˇssessed e·nough | to ˋcrack || you ˋnearly had | a ¯fried ˋjournalist | on your ˎhands ·there || a ˋbomb had just ˎdropped | ¯fifty ˎyards | in ·front of his ˎcar || ˇfaced ·now | with a ˋchoice | of ¯staying the ˋnight | in ·Suchiˎtoto | or ·going ˋback | ¯down the ˎroad | we ˋopted | to ¯head ˎback || a ¯journalist ˇconvoy | of about ˋfifteen ˬcars | was aˎssembled | and ¯lights ˇflashing | it was ˬdusk

| we ¯tore ·down the ˎroad | ·holding ¯white ˇflags | ¯out of our ˎwindows || ¯two or ·three ˋtimes | we ·heard ¯automatic ˎfire | a few ˎyards a·way | we ¯drove ˎon || a ˋjet a·ppeared aˎbove | diˋrectly a·bove | it ·held its tra¯jectory for ·one ˋminute | ¯flashes ˎburst | from its ˎwings | and ¯rockets exˎploded | ¯safely beˎhind us || our ˇdriver | the ˋNew ·York ˇTimes ·man | ¯pressed his acˎcelerator | and ˎducked | his ˇeyes | ˋpeering ·over the ˎdashboard || ¯more ˋrockets | or perˋhaps ·more ˇbombs | ¯landed beˎhind || what ·seemed like ¯hours ˇlater | we ¯reached the ·army ˎcheckpoint | ·six ˋmiles ·down the ˎroad || a ˋlittle ·further ˇon | a ˋtown | where there was a ˎfair | ·going ˎon || a ¯big ˇwheel | was ˎspinning || ˋchildren ·ate ˇpopcorn | and ˋcandyfloss || ˋfairground ·music ¯filled the ˎair || for the ¯millionth ˇtime | you ·thought that ^ ¯foreign ˋjournalists | may ¯never get ˎused to all ·this | but the ˋpeople of ·El ˎSalvador | ·while they may ¯ache for ˋpeace | have be·come aˋnaesthe·tised to ˎwar ||

004 SPOKEN ENGLISH CORPUS TEXT A04

From our own Correspondent
Speaker: John Carlin
Broadcast notes: Radio 4, 11.30 a.m., 24th November, 1984
Overlap passage

Transcribed by BJW

a ˋjournalist ˇconvoy | of about ˋfifteen ˇcars | was asˋsembled || and ¯lights ˇflashing | it was ˇdusk | we ˋtore ·down the ˋroad | ·holding ¯white ˇflags | out of our ˋwindows || ˋtwo or three ˋtimes | we heard ¯automatic ˋfire | a few ˋyards away || we ¯drove ˎon || a ˋjet appeared aˋbove | diˋrectly a·bove || it ¯held its tra·jectory for ·one ˋminute | ˋflashes ¯burst | from its ˋwings | and ˋrockets exˋploded | ˋsafely beˋhind us || our ˋdriver | the ¯New York ˋTimes man | ˋpressed his acˋcelerator | and ˋducked || his ˇeyes | ˋpeering over the ˋdashboard || ·more ˋrockets | or perhaps more ˇbombs | ˋlanded beˋhind || what ·seemed like ¯hours ˇlater | we ˋreached the army ˋcheckpoint | ¯six ˍmiles down the ˋroad || a ·little further ˇon | a ˋtown | where there was a ˋfair | going ˎon || a ¯big ˋwheel was ˋspinning || ¯children ate ˋpopcorn and ˋcandyfloss || ˋfairground ·music ˋfilled the ˋair || for the ˋmillionth ˇtime | you ¯thought that | ¯foreign ˋjournalists | may ·never get ˋused to all ·this || but the ¯people of El ˋSalvador | ˍwhile they may ˋache for ˋpeace | have be·come aˋnaesthetised to ˋwar ||

Transcribed by GOK

a ¯journalist ˇconvoy | of about ˋfifteen ˬcars | was aˎssembled | and ¯lights ˇflashing | it was ˬdusk | we ¯tore ·down the ˎroad | ·holding ¯white ˇflags | ¯out of our ˎwindows || ¯two or ·three ˋtimes | we ·heard ¯automatic ˎfire | a few ˎyards a·way | we ¯drove ˎon || a ˋjet a·ppeared aˎbove | diˋrectly a·bove | it ·held its tra¯jectory for ·one ˋminute | ¯flashes ˎburst | from its ˎwings | and ¯rockets exˎploded | ¯safely beˎhind us || our ˇdriver | the ˋNew ·York ˇTimes ·man | ¯pressed his acˎcelerator | and ˎducked | his ˇeyes | ˋpeering ·over the ˎdashboard || ¯more ˋrockets | or perˋhaps ·more ˬbombs | ¯landed beˎhind || what ·seemed like ¯hours ˇlater | we ¯reached the ·army ˎcheckpoint | ·six ˋmiles ·down the ˎroad || a ˋlittle ·further ˬon | a ˋtown | where there was a ˎfair | ·going ˎon || a ¯big ˇwheel | was ˎspinning || ˋchildren ·ate ˇpopcorn | and ˋcandyfloss || ˋfairground ·music ¯filled the ˎair || for the ¯millionth ˬtime | you ·thought that ‸ ¯foreign ˋjournalists | may ¯never get

ˏused to all ·this | but the ˋpeople of ·El ˏSalvador | ·while they may ¯ache for ˋpeace | have be·come aˋnaesthe·tised to ˏwar ||

005 SPOKEN ENGLISH CORPUS TEXT A05
From our own Correspondent
Broadcast notes: Radio 4, 11.30 a.m., 24th November, 1984
Transcribed by GOK

ˋarriving in ‸ ·Bucha ˏrest | on a ¯grey No·vember after ˏnoon | is ¯pretty ˏmuch | as one _might ex ˎpect || a ·light ˏrain was | ·turning into ˏsnow | the ˏplane | ˎtaxied ·past | ·serried ˏranks | of anti-ˏaircraft ·guns | and the ˋdozen or ·so ˏpassengers | from the _Austrian ˏAirlines ·plane | were ˎbussed ·into a ˋtotally un·heated _airport ˎbuilding || eˇventually | it was ·my ˏturn | to be in_spected by the immi ˎgration o·fficial | who ˎgazed at me | from his _little ˋbooth || but ˇhere | ·things took an unexˋpected ·turn || you are ¯here for the ˏCongress ‸ he ·asked || ˏyes ‸ I ·said || he ¯then went ˏout | to ·call a _large poˋlice-officer ·over || the ·officer ˇbellowed ·at me | ·over _various ˎbarricades || ↑you have ·inviˊtation || I have a ˊˇvisa || ¯no ˏvisa | you have ·inviˊtation || ˏno ‸ I ·said || ¯O ˏK | ¯carry ˏon || ˇall ·communist ·countries | have a ·sort of ‸ ·through the ˇlooking ·glass e·ffect || from ¯Ber ˏlin | to ·Vladi ˏvostok | you can ˏgaze | at a·ppalling ˏstatues | of ˎlantern-·jawed ˏminers | ·clutching _buxom ·female ˏtractor ·drivers | the ·two ·gazing into an ·unseen ˏfuture | with an ˎair of ·vapid ˇconfidence | but a ˏround you | there ·scurry _shabby ·little ˏmen | de·manding ˎdollars | or _ciga ˎrettes || in Ruˇmania | the ˎgulf be·tween ˇrhetoric | and re ˇality | is un_usually ˎwide || but ˋfirst it's worth ·stressing how the _country is ˇdominated | by the ˋpresident | _Nico·lai Ceau ˎse·scu || his ˇpicture a·ppears ˎeverywhere on im·portant o ˏccasions | his ˏwife | is a ˏmember | of the ‸ _top po·litical ˏbody | and ˋone of his ˇsons | is ¯moving up ˎfast || two ˏothers | hold im·portant _government ˎposts || ˋCeau·sescu's ˎspeech | to the ‸ ˋCommunist ·Party ˇCongress | ·lasted ¯four and a ·half ˏhours | and drew ¯forty-ˏthree | _standing o ˎvations || on ·each o ˏccasion | an a¯ppropriate ˋslogan was ˎshouted || ¯each _time | Ceau ˋsescu | was the ˎfirst ·word of the ˎslogan || ˇmuch of the ·speech | con·sisted of a ˇeulogy | of Ru_mania's ˏprogress | of the _Party's con ˏcern | for the ·people's ˏliving ·standards | and the ‸ ¯new ˎheights | of ·civili ˎsation | which Ru_mania had ˎreached || ¯out ˏside | ·people _queued for an ˏhour | in the _slush for ba ˏnanas | ˎfar ·longer for ˇmeat | and had ˎtrudged ·past shop ˇwindows | where ˎsuits ·cost ˎtwo-·thirds of a _month's ˎincome || at ·every ˇroad inter·section | stood ¯two ˋpolicemen | ˎsupple·mented by ci ˇvilians | who ˋhanded out di·rections to ˏthose | who ˎmight be ·thinking of _taking a ·wrong ˎturning || ¯after ˇfood | ˋenergy conser·vation | is the ˎsecond most im·portant _problem | for _ordinary Ru ˎmanians || ˏsometimes | ·homes are un ˏheated | ˏother times | the _gas is ·turned ˎlow || and ·one _lamp

‸ per ˏroom | is ˍall that's perˎmitted || ˋenergy inˎspectors | enˍsure the ·rules are ˎfollowed || ˇrestaurants | are ˎfull how·ever | ·often with ¯people | who ·have to ˍsit in their ˎcoats | be·cause of the ˎcold || in ˇrestaurants | you can be ˎsure of ·getting ˏmeat | and there ˋare ˍpeople with ˎmoney || ˍthey in·clude | ·foreign ˏstudents | ·black markeˏteers | and the ˍoffspring of the eˎlite || ˋhow ‸ Ru·mania ˇgot into this situ·ation | is ˍwell-ˎknown || e·normous inˏvestment ·projects | that ·haven't proved ˏprofitable | neˍglect of ˏagriculture | and ˋso on || and the Ruˇmanians | ·say their ‸ ˎinde·pendent ˇattitude | to·wards the ˍSoviet ˬUnion | has deˍprived them of ·Soviet ˎoil || the reˇdeeming ·features | inˍclude the reˎsilience | of the ˎpeople || the Ruˏmanians | are a ˋLatin ·race | and there's ˬsometimes | a ¯lightness of ˎtouch | ·not seen elseˋwhere | in ·this part of the ˎworld || as ¯I sat ˏwrestling | with a ·piece of ˏmeat | de·scribed as a ˏsteak | in ˊone restaurant | the ˋwaiter came ·over | ¯full of conˎcern | and ·said ‸ ↑ˋhow do you ·like your ↓ˎknife ‸ ·sir || one of my ˋcolleagues ·wanted a reˎceipt ·after a ˏmeal | and his ·waiter ·asked ‸ ¯would you ·like a ˏbig one ·sir || ˋoh ·yes ˬplease || the ·waiter reˋturned with a re·ceipt for the eˋquivalent of a ·thousand ˎpounds | for ˍone ˎlunch || ↑the ¯local ˇcurrency | the ˬLeu | is the ˍsource of ˎmany ·stories || it's reˍjected in any tran·saction in·volving ˏforeigners | exˍcept the most ˎsimple || beˎtween themˇselves | Ruˍmanians ·often ex·change ˬdollars | or ·packets of Aˍmerican cigaˎrettes || ˬthey're ·rarely ˎsmoked || but the ˋunde·sired ˬlocal ·currency | has ·recently ·been ‸ ˍreˎvalued || it ·gained ¯twenty per ˎcent | a·gainst the alˍmighty ˎdollar | on the ˍfirst of Noˎvember || the oˇfficial ·reason ·was | that the ¯move was ˎnecessary | to enˍcourage ˎexports || now ˋevery·where ˇelse in the ·world | ˍgovernments have ˇdevalued their ·currencies | to in·crease ˏexports | it ˍmakes their ·goods ˋcheaper | on ¯world ˎmarkets || the reˏverse process | was aˍdopted in Ruˏmania | beˍcause it was ˏargued | that ˋif ·firms got ˇless money for their ·exports | they would ˍtry all the ˎharder | to inˍcrease their ˎearnings || ˏsimilarly | ·President Ceauˋsescu a·nnounced | that the ˎpenalties imˇposed on ·firms | which ˎfailed to ·meet planned ˇtargets | would be ˎeased || in the next ˏbreath | he ·said the ˍpenalties | would be ·taken from ˍfunds | a·llotted for ˍpaying the ˎworkers || at the ˇend of the ·Party ·Congress | ·President Ceauˇsescu | was ¯re-elected uˎnanimously | as the ˍGeneral ˎSecretary | for aˍnother five ˎyears || in acˇcepting the ·honour | he ˍmade a ˎspeech | which conˇcluded | with a ¯statement | with which ˍnobody | could ˎquarrel || we ¯may have to reˎpeat | many ˎhardships | ˏbut | more ˋcontroˇversially he ·added | we are not aˍfraid of ˎhardship ||

006 SPOKEN ENGLISH CORPUS TEXT A06
From our own Correspondent
Broadcast notes: Radio 4, 11.30 a.m., 24th November, 1984
Transcribed by BJW

on ¯one _side of the ·main road through ˬHutten·heim | ˋsteel ·works ¯stretch away into the ˎdistance || ¯on the ˏother | there's a ¯leafy ˎsuburb | of ¯workers' _houses and ˋflats || ¯homes _built by the ·giant ˇsteel con·cern | ˋMannesmann | in the ¯early _years of the ˋcentury || ↑but there's ¯little _sign of ˇlife | in the ¯seven _blocks of ˋflats || ˇmost of ·them | are ˋempty || for the ¯thousand ·Turkish ·workers and their ˏfamilies | who ˇlived in them | have ˋleft || ¯taking adˏvantage of a ¯double ˎpay offer || a ¯cash ·grant from the ˏgovernment | ↑and ˏmoney from ˬMannesmann | to re_turn ˋhome || the ˇsteel ·firm | that's ¯drastically cut back its ˬwork·force | ¯wants to _pull the ·flats ˋdown || it ¯claims it would be ·too ex_pensive to ˋrenovate them || ↓their soˊlution is to _bring in the _bulldozers | and ¯turn the ˬarea | into a ˋpark || but ¯this i_dea is ¯firmly reˬjected | by the ¯local ·German ˎresidents || ↑though there was a _large concenˇtration of Turkish ·workers | ↑many ˬGerman ·families con_tinued to ˋlive in ·Huttenheim || and ¯like _George Baˇrent | ¯chairman of the local ˇaction ·group | they re¯gard it as their ˎHeimat | their ˋneighbourhood || ˇGeorge | a re¯tired ˇsteel worker | ·sums up their ˋfeelings when he ¯says | I ¯raised my ˬfamily here | _buried my ¯parents here | and I ·want to ˎdie here || ˋhe and others ˇfear | if ¯Mannesmann is al·lowed to pull ˋdown the ·flats | then ˋtheir houses will be the ˇnext to ·go | and ˋHuttenheim will be deˋstroyed || if ˋMannesmann ˇbring in the ·bulldozers | ·George Ba_rent says he'll be the ˋfirst to ˋlie down in ˋfront of them || his ¯action ˏgroup includes ¯not only ˏGermans | but ˋTurks | who've de_cided to stay ˋon in ·Huttenheim || be¯fore the ˬexodus | there was a ¯great deal of ˬenmity | and dis¯crimiˎnation | between the ¯two natioˎnalities || there was an in¯visible _line beˋtween us says ·George || though he ¯adds | that ¯when the ·Turkish families ˎleft | there was ¯suddenly a _different eˋmotion || it re¯minded us he ·said | of the ¯depor_tation of the ˎJews || and ¯now | ·attitudes have ˋchanged || ˇGermans | are ¯going to ˎnight-·school | to ¯learn ˎTurkish || ˋhousewives have ¯got toˇgether | to ¯help draw up the peˋtition | to the _mayor of ˋDuisburg || ·Turks and ˋGermans | have ·formed an aˋlliance | to _save their ˋneighbourhood || ↑but ¯up at the ˬRathaus | the ¯city ˬhall | the ¯mayor and the ˬcouncillors | are in a diˋlemma || they ˋwant to ·save and reˋvive their ¯inner city ˋareas || but they ˋhaven't got e·nough ˋmoney || re¯cession and unemˏployment | now at ¯sixteen per ˬcent in ·Duisburg | has ¯driven people a_way from the ˋcity || ¯ten ˋyears ago it

¯boasted | ˋsix hundred ·thousand ˋpeople | ¯now the ·population's ˍdown to ˋfive hundred and ˋforty-four ·thousand || the reˋsult is ·less ˋincome | from ˋrates and ˋtaxes | and ¯not enough in the ˏtreasury | to ¯take over the ˍHuttenheim ˋflats | and reˋfurbish them || the ¯Huttenheim ˏresidents | have aˋnother i·dea || ↑they've ˏdrawn up a ˍlist of ˋpeople | ˏGermans and ˇTurks | ˏyoung and ˏold and reˇtired | who'd ¯be preˇpared | for a ¯reasonable ˇrent | to ¯move into the ˍflats and ˋrenovate them || it's an ˋidea the ·council's conˋsidering | to¯gether with the possiˇbility | of de¯claring the ˍbuildings | of ˋspecial ¯architectural ˎinterest | and ˆthat ·way | obˋtaining ·special ˋgrants || and ˆso far | the ¯council's reˆfused ·Mannesmann | perˍmission to ¯bring in the ˎbulldozers || ¯Frau ·Barbel ˎZieling | a ¯member of the ˆplanning committee | says the de¯bate over ˇHuttenheim i¯lluminates the ˆstructural ·problems | ·facing inˍdustrial ·cities like ˎDuisburg || ¯when an area like ˇHuttenheim | and there have been ¯others in ˍDuisburg ˆlike it | ¯loses its popuˏlation | ↓it a·ffects the ˋshops | the ˋbanks | the ˋschools | the ·city ˎservices || and wi¯thout reˏnewal | the deˏcline ˋspreads || when ˋasked about the ˆprospects | of ·help from ˆBrussels | ↓and the ¯European Coˆmmunity | ¯Frau Zieling's ·eyes ˎflash | and she ·says that ¯Duisburg can't expect ˍmuch from ˆthat di·rection | ↓when ¯so much is being ¯spent | ↓on ¯Europe's ˍsmall per·centage of ˋfarmers || com¯pared to what's ˎneeded to ¯help the ·large ˍnumbers of ˋpeople in deˋclining in·dustrial ˋcities || ¯Duisburg is making re·newed ˏefforts | throughˆout the ·city | to ¯help the reˆmaining ·Turkish families ˋintegrate || it ¯could be ˆeasier | ·now there are ˍnot so ˋmany of them || the ¯Huttenheim coˆoperative idea ·might ˋwork | and pro¯vide a social ˋfocus for a ˆnew community | no ·longer ˋriven by anˋtagonism || but the ¯financial ˍquestion reˋmains | ↓is it ˏworth ˍrenovating the ˋflats || ¯Mannesmann says ˎno | the ¯locals say ˋyes || but un¯less the city can ˍfind some more ˎmoney | and the ¯steel firm can be diˍssuaded from ˋgrassing over its ¯former responsiˋbilities || the ¯new community ˍspirit that's e·merged in ˆHuttenheim | after ¯years of racial ˎtension | could be ˍshort-ˋlived || the reˊaction of the ˇlocals in ·all ·this | ¯also ·points ˍup the ¯grass roots ˆactivism | that's ˍswept West Germany || ↑George Baˍrent sums it ˍup when he ¯says | ↑in the ˍpast we ·left the deˍcisions to ˍMannesmann and the ˋCouncil || ¯now we want ˎour ·voice | to be ˋheard || and it ˋcomes as no surˋprise | to ˋfind that ˆGeorge | a ¯middle-of-the-road ·Social ˇDemocrat | ↓from the in¯dustrial ·heartland of ·West ˎGermany | has been ¯welcoming the su·pport | of the ˋGreen ·Party | ↓in his camˋpaign ||

007 SPOKEN ENGLISH CORPUS TEXT A07
From our own Correspondent
Broadcast notes: Radio 4, 11.30 a.m., 22nd June, 1985
Transcribed by GOK

the ˋunfolding ·hijack ˏdrama | has been ·only _one of ˋthree major ˏstories | that have been ·running _here all ˎweek || IsˇraeIis | have been ¯just as conˏcerned | with ·what can ¯best be deˏscribed | as the ¯economic _crisis | conˋtinued | which e·merged ˇthis week | in a ·rash of ˊstrikes | a·cross a whole ·range of acˏtivities | and the ˋforecast | of the ˎterrifying inˏflation ·rate | ·getting _even ˎworse || the Isˋraeli ˬmedia | have ˋalso given | ˎacres of ·space and ˏtime | to the _Tabah diˎspute | the ·clash with ˏEgypt | over a ˋtiny ·speck of ˇSinai | which is ˎseen as the ·crystalliˋzation of ˇall the ·problems | of what's ·called the _cold ˎpeace | between _Israel and ˎEgypt || ¯this ˏtopic | ˏTabah ˄ inci·dentally | ·seems to con·cern ˬmost people ·here | ·not in the ˋslightest || ↑¯as for the ˏhijack | ·interest in ˏthat | ·focusses on the ¯military ˏprison | at Atˋlit | which ˋdoesn't ·actually ˇlook much like a ·prison | at ˎall || it's ˇtucked in | at the ·foot of the _Kabul ˋmountain ·range | a ·mile or so ˋin from the ·Mediteˏrranean | ¯near the port ˏcity | of ˎHaifa || there's a ¯grey ˏwall | ·not all that ˏhigh | some ˏwatchtowers | ·manned by _well-armed ˏguards | and a ·lot of ˏmilitary | _comings and ˎgoings | like ·any _army ˎcamp || ˇbut we're a·ssured | the ˬShi'ites | at the ·centre of the ˏcrisis | _are inˎside || ˏcamera ·crews | from the A·merican ˏnetworks | have been ˋshooed a·way from the ˏentrance | but they're ˋstill ·staking the place ˏout | from a ·distance aˎway | ·watching for ·any im·pending deˏpartures | through _powerful ·tele·vision ˎcamera ·lenses || the ˋShi'ites inˬside | are ˎnot the ·hard cases of the _terrorist ˎworld || in·deed ˇmost of them | ·probably did ·little ˏmore | than ·be in the ¯wrong ˏplace | at the _wrong ˎtime | when the Isˏraelis | were ·picking _people ˎup || ↑they were aˋrrested in South ˏLebanon | for any ˇnumber of ·reasons | as the Isˏraelis | _scrambled to ˎleave || and ˋwere at ·first ˏheld | at the ˇAnsar ·prison ·camp | which _Israel ˋused | in _South ˎLebanon || ¯with the ˏpullback | _that was ˎclosed | and more than a ¯thousand ˏShi'ites | were _moved to Atˋlit || ↑¯back in ˬApril | ˎIsrael a·nnounced a _policy of ˇsending these ·prisoners ˋhome | ˊsubject | to the ¯level of ˏviolence | a·gainst ˬIsrael | and her ·allies in _South ˎLebanon || be↑ˋtween ·four and five ˏhundred | have al_ready ˋgone | in·cluding ˇone batch | that was inˬcluded | in a ¯big | and ˋhighly ·controˇversial re·lease | of ·more than a ˇthousand ·terrorists | ˎswapped for just ·three Is_raeli ˎcaptives || ↑it's ˋbeen ·widely suˬggested ·here | that the ·great imˋbalance in ˇthis ex·change | ·might have ˋprompted the ·Beirut ˎhijackers | into ˇthinking | they could ˬforce

·Israel | into reˏleasing | ˍmore ·Arab ˎprisoners || ˇIsrael | was ·making it aˋbundantly ˇclear to·wards the ·end of the ·week | that the reˉmaining ˏShi'ites | ˉwere to be reˏleased | ˋanyway | ·not as ·any ·conse·quence of the ˊhijack | but ˋpurely as a ·function of the ˉlevel of ˏtrouble | in ˍSouth ˎLebanon || so the ˇanswer to the ·question | ·lies ˉjust ˏoff | the ·Haifa ˍTel A·viv ˋmotorway || the ˇtrouble is | that ˬno one | a·part from the ˇhijackers | has been ˍasking the ˎquestion || ˇIsrael | says ˋshe won't con·sider re·leasing the ˏShi'ites | as an ˉanswer to the ˇhijack | un·less aˍpproached by Aˎmerica || ·then the ˍcabinet will diˎscuss it || but Aˇmerica | won't ˋask | beˊcause | as ·seen from ˏhere | ˋthat would ·mean the iˋnitiative to ·buckle ·under to ˏterrorism | had ˍcome from ˋWashington | ·rather than Jeˎrusalem || it's ˋnot so ·much a ·question of ·pass the ˇparcel | as of ‸ I'd ˋrather not ˇhave the ·parcel | ˍthank you ·very ˋmuch || ˋall this has ˋirritated Isˏraelis | as ·shown in specˇtacular ·fashion | when the deˇfence minister | ·Yitzhak Raˬbin | ˋpretty well ·blew his ˎtop | on an A·merican ˇnews ·programme | on ˎThursday || Is↑ˋraeli oˬpinion | has been ·deeply diˇsturbed | by the eˋleven ·hundred for ˍthree ˎswap | which put ·back on the ˍstreets | some ·very tough ˎcustomers | and which pro·voked ˉoutraged ˏcomment | from ˇmany | who'd lost ˏfamily | in ˍterrorist aˎttacks || my ·son is ˊdead | and his ·killer is ·walking ˋfree | was ·one such ·published reˋaction || Is↑ˇraelis | have ·sympathy and ˬliking for A·mericans | which is ·just as ˏwell | since the ·country is ˋswarming | with ˉtransat·lantic ˎvisitors || the ˋlinks with the U·nited ˏStates | are ˍwarm and ˎclose | and ·this inˍcludes | an aˋbiding Is·raeli aˏffection | for the ˋdollar | the ·uno·fficial ˍfirst ˋcurrency ·here || but the ↑ˇhijack | is ·seen as an Aˍmerican ˎproblem | to be ·solved ˇby that ·country | and ˇnot ‸ in a ·way | that will put ˉIsrael and her ˏpeople | at ˉgreater ˏrisk | from ˎterrorism ||

008 SPOKEN ENGLISH CORPUS TEXT A08
From our own Correspondent
Broadcast notes: Radio 4, 11.30 a.m., 22nd June, 1985
Transcribed by BJW

a ˋfew days beˇfore the ·hijacking | of the ˋTWA ˏaircraft | ˎsoon after it ˋtook off from ·Athens ˇairport || I was ˏcatching a ˇsimilar TWA flight | ¯from the ·same ˎairport || ↑when you ˍspend ˋmuch of your ·working ˋlife on ˇaeroplanes | ˋflying around the ˋMiddle East and the Medite¯rranean | you take more than a ˍpassing ˋinterest | in ˍairport seˋcurity || ˋhijacking is a ¯bit of an occupational ˋhazard || and ˋAthens has always had a repuˋtation | for being one of the ˋlaxest in the ˋregion || it's ˇfrequently been used | by ˇArab hijackers || as the ˇstarting point | for their opeˎrations || be·cause it's such an easy ˋtouch | for anyone wanting to smuggle ˋweapons onto an ˋaircraft || TWA have been so ˇworried about it | that ˋthey've installed their own seˇcurity checking equipment | for ˍbaggage ¯going | into the ˍaircraft ˋhold || but ˇhijackers | as opposed to ˇterrorists | ·bent on actually deˋstroying an ·aircraft | in mid ¯air || ¯need their ˏweapons on ˋboard || and ˋgetting them through the Athens airport seˋcurity check is no ˋproblem || there are ¯two ˬscanning machines || which give an ˇX-ray picture | on two teleˇvision ·screens || of the ˍcontents of ˋhand ·baggage || when ˇI've been through ·Athens airport || and ˋthat's about ·two dozen ˋtimes in the past ·two ˇyears || there's ˇnever been more than ¯one seˬcurity man on ·duty || and ¯he's ˎfrequently reading a ˋnewspaper || or ¯chatting with ˍother ˋairport ·staff || he ˋseldom | ·seems to be keeping an ˋeye | on the teleˋvision ·screens || on ˇone occasion | the ˍscreens were unaˋttended || hardly surˋprising | that ¯Athens is a ˍfavourite airport for ˋhijackers || ↑ˋBeirut is aˋnother easy ·touch | but for ˋdifferent ·reasons || ˋgiven the state of ˇlawlessness | that eˋxists in ˆLebanon || the ˋuninformed out¯sider might ˋreasonably ex·pect seˆcurity | at ˍBeirut ˊairport || to be aˍmongst the ˋtightest in the ˋworld || but the ˋopposite is ˋtrue || ·earlier this ˍyear the di¯rector of ·airport seˍcurity reˋsigned || his ¯job | he ¯said | was imˋpossible || ↑the problem ˋis | that | while there ˇis an airport se·curity staff || ↓and the ˋLebanese genˏdarmerie | ¯and ˏarmy | have ˍairport ·staffs as ˇwell || ↑it's ¯really under the conˏtrol | of the ˋgunmen || so ˋnot only has ·Beirut ˋairport this ˏyear | ˍwitnessed a ¯member of its own seˇcurity staff || ˇhijacking an ·aircraft | as a ˋprotest about low ˇpay || it's ˋalso been the ·scene of ˇone ·hijack || ¯where | after ˋposing for ˋphotographs at the ·side of the ˊaircraft || the ˋhijackers ·blew it ¯up || and ·drove ˋoff | into the ˋShi'ite ·Muslim ¯shanty town | that ˍstands at the ·side of the ˋairport || ˋprobably to a ·hero's ˋwelcome || the electronic ˇscanning device | at ¯Beirut airport | ·broke down ˋyears ago || the oˇccasional | ˋcasual ·glance at ˋhand baggage is the order of the ˋday || so as ˋfar as seˇcurity is con·cerned || Beiˋrut is a ·lost ˋcause || ↑a ˋhundred and twenty ·miles to the ·South is Ben-ˋGurion || ˋIsrael's international ·airport | and ˋquite a ˋcontrast || ˋit has probably the ˋtightest security in the ˋworld || before ˏcheck-in | ˋeveryone not only has their ˇbags ·searched || ˋsometimes even ·taken aˉway | and ˉX-ˏrayed | after the ˋcontents have been ·taken ˉout | and per·haps the ˇtoothpaste ·opened and ·squeezed || but ˋeveryone is ˇsearchingly questioned | by a seˋcurity officer || ˍhow long ˋhere || ˋwho did you ˋmeet || ˋwhere did you ˋgo || ˋwhat did you ˋbuy || ˇsometimes it's fruˋstrating || ˏsometimes | the ˏquestioners are ˏless than poˋlite || ˋsometimes the ·questions ˋsound | ˋstupid || but it's ˋworth reˋmembering that ˇhijacking | from Ben-ˇGurion || ↓ˋinternational airport of the ˋcountry that's the ↑ˋtarget of ˇmost hijackings || ↑are unˎknown || ↑airport seˇcurity | ˋcan go a bit ˋfar ·though || at ˉHeath˯row ·once | a ˉlarge and ˍstern seˇcurity lady || ˋrummaging with ˉsome | obvious ˋrelish through my ˉbriefcase || got ˉquite exˍcited by my ˋbeard trimming ·scissors || they were ˋconfiscated || I've ˉoften ˯wondered | how you ˇhijack an ·aircraft | with ˋbeard trimming ·scissors || I've ˋalso often ·wondered what she ˋdid with them ||

009 SPOKEN ENGLISH CORPUS TEXT A09
From our own Correspondent
Broadcast notes: Radio 4, 11.30 a.m., 22nd June, 1985
Transcribed by GOK

on ˉtop of a ˏhill | overˇlooking ·Windhoek | there is ·one of the ˉmany eˏxamples | of ·German ˇarchitecture | ·dotted aˏround | this ·capital ˎcity || ·South West ˏAfrica | ·once having been ˋruled | by ˬGermany | ·until its deˋfeat | in the _first world ˎwar || since ˏwhen | the ˏterritory | has been _run by South ˎAfrica || the ˉbuilding is ˏcalled | the ˋTintenpa·last | or ˄ ˎink ·palace | in its _German transˎlation || ↑it was ˇgiven this ·name | be·cause it was ˉwhere | the ˋGerman im·perial ·government in Berˇlin | deˬcided ˄ ·that | the adˉministrative ˇcentre of its ·colony | should be loˎcated || it was ·where all the ˋbureaucrats | or ˎpen ·pushers | were ˉgathered toˏgether | ·under _one ˎroof | _hence its ˎname || ↑ˇthis week | it ·wasn't the ˇbureaucrats who ·came to·gether | in the ·main ˏhall | of the ˏtintenpa·last | ·but ˄ the adˉministrators and ˎlegislators | ˏthose | who have ·been inˏstalled | by South ˏAfrica | with the _task of ˬrunning | the ˎcountry || although ˇcrucial ·areas | like deˋfence and ·foreign ˬpolicy | will ↑re_main | in the _hands of Preˎtoria || in a ˋbrief | ·twenty ˋminute | aˬppearance | which itˋself ·spoke ˋvolumes | a·bout Preˬtoria's | ·growing imˋpatience | with the Na·mibian ˬproblem | ˉPresident ˏBotha | ·signed the ˉformal ·proclaˏmation | esˋtablishing the ˉnew ·interim ˏgovernment | ·uttered a ˋfew ·words of enˇcouragement | and ·then ˄ ·promptly ˎleft | to ·fly _back to South ˎAfrica | ·leaving ˉthose | ˉinternal ˏleaders | who've ˉcome toˋgether | to ˇform a new ·government | to _get ˋon with it || ·quite ˊclearly | ˋSouth ·Africa's ˇheart | is ·not ˋin | ˉthis new ˎdeal | and they are ·under ˉno iˇllusions | a·bout its _chances of sucˎcess || they are ˋright | to be ˎsceptical || ↑the ˉgovernment is comˏprised | of ˋsix | of the ˇmultitude | of ˊethnic | ˇcross-·ethnic | and poˉlitical ˏparties | who ˉtwo ˏyears a·go | ˉcame toˏgether | to ·form the ˉmulti ·party ˎconference || yet aˉnother aˋttempt | by Na·mibia's inˋternal ˊgroupings | ↑to a·gree on ˉsome ˏform | of _local ˎgovernment || at a ˇnews ·conference | ˋafter their ·instaˬllation | the ˉparty ˇleaders | ˉclearly be_trayed | the ˉdifferences beˎtween them | could ˋnot even aˏgree | on a ˏchairman | or ˇpresident of the new ·government | ·and ˄ enˋgaged in ·petty ˇbickering | a·gainst their oˬpponents | ˋSWAPO | inˬstead per·haps | of ˉlaying ˏout | a ˉprogramme | or ˇpolicy a·genda | which ˉmight have ˏcaptured | the iˉmagiˏnation | of ˇsome at ·least | of the ·dissi·llusioned South ˏWesters | and con·vinced the ˇworld | that the ˉnew _government | was ·anything ˇmore | than ·proxy _ruled from Preˎtoria || howˋever | ·such is the in¯cestuous ˋnature | of Na·mibian ˬpolitics | and ·so aˋpparent | the ¯self-imˋportance | of ·some of its pracˬtitioners | that ¯those inˇvolved in the new ·government | ˋobviously ·find it ˬdifficult | to ·rise aˇbove | the ·level of _small town ˎpolitics || ˏcertainly | the U·nited ˋNations | ˋhas been ˏstaging | a ·major deˋbate this past ˬfortnight | on ·South Africa's ˬpolicies | to_wards NaˎMibia || ·but ‸ it is a deˋlusion to beˬlieve | as ·some Naˋmibian ·poliˋticians ·clearly ˇdo | that the ·issue is ¯near the ˋtop of the po·litical aˬgenda | of the _major ·Western ˎpowers || the ˇsame de·lusion | is ·shared to a ˇcertain ex·tent | by ˋSWAPO | who aˋppear to have ˋtotal ˋconfidence | in the aˋbility of the ·world coˬmmunity | to ˇforce South ·Africa | into reˋlinquishing the ·territory || ˋwestern ·condemˇnation of South ·Africa | at the UˎN | may ˇsound ·fine | but ↑ˋwould the ·western ·powers ·really ˋwant to ·see Pre·toria's ˇhold on the ·mineral-rich ·territory | reˋplaced by a ·possibly ¯marxist ˇSWAPO ·government || ˋSouth ·Africa's ˇpolicy in Na·mibia | a¯ppears ˏaimed | at ¯building ˏup | the ˋnew ·interim ˏgovernment | in the ¯hope | that it could ·put up a sub¯stantial ˋchallenge to ˬSWAPO | in ·any _subsequent ·indeˋpendent eˎlections || ˇcoupled with ·this | is the ˇmilitary ·effort | ·aimed at deˋstroying ·SWAPO's ·armed ˏwing | and ˇforcing the ·organi·sation | to ·come to the neˬgotiating ·table | as ·just aˇnother | Na_mibian ˎparty || at a ˇbriefing this ·week | in ˬWindhoek | an ˊofficer | in the inˬtelligence ·corps | ↑·stated that the ˋwar a·gainst ˏSWAPO | could ˋjust a·bout be ˬwon | wi·thin the next _two to ·three ˎyears || he was conˋvinced | the ˊbattle | for the ¯hearts | and ¯minds of the ˊpeople | was ·being ˎwon | eˇspecially | a·mong the Oˋvambo | who ·form the maˋjority | of _SWAPO's suˎpport || the ˏofficer | who had ˋobviously | been ·brushing ˋup | on his ˎFrantz ˇFanon | ¯pointed to the miˎstakes | which the ˇFrench co·lonial au·thorities | had ·made in their ·handling of the Alˋgerian ·people || it was ˋthen pointed ˇout to the ·officer | by a ˬFrench ·journalist | that the Alˋgerian ˬwar was ·lost in ˋParis | ˋnot in Alˎgiers || ↑¯is there ·going to be a ˇsimilar co·llapse | of South ˬAfrican ·willpower | to con·tinue ˇgoverning the ·territory || ˏweariness | fruˏstration | and a deˋsire to get ˬout | there _certainly ˎis || but ˇnot | at _any ˎprice || and ˇcertainly ·not to ·make way | for an ·unchecked ˋSWAPO ˎgovernment | in ˎWindhoek || with ↑its _recent ·opeˏrations | in An¯gola and Boˬtswana | South ˋAfrica has di·splayed a ¯growing aˎssertiveness || once ˋmore | it is ¯flexing its ˬmuscles | as a ·regional ˋsuper·power | and is in·forming the ˊworld | ·that ‸ deˇspite its ·condem·nation | ¯South ˇAfrica | will suˋrrender ·Africa's ¯last deˇpendency | on its ˇown ·terms | and _nobody ˎelse's ||

010 SPOKEN ENGLISH CORPUS TEXT A10
From our own Correspondent
Broadcast notes: Radio 4, 11.30 a.m., 22nd June, 1985
Transcribed by BJW

the ˋTamils may have e·scaped the ˋphysical ·conflict in their ˋown ·country by coming to ˉBritain || but they ˋnow find themselves ˇcaught | in the ˍmiddle of a propaˋganda war || ↓the ˉhighly e·fficient ˍTamil propaˋganda machine in ˇLondon || ˋseeks to aˋssert that ˇany returning ·Tamil || will be ˍslaughtered on the ˋspot || ↓or at ˋleast aˋrrested and ˋtortured || ↑the ˋless efficient ·Sinhalese ˋgovernment puˉblicity men || ˋpoint out the aˋtrocities of the ·Tamil gueˋrrillas || and ˋcite the number of ˋTamils still in ·government ↑ˋservice || but ˋwhat happens if they ˋare sent back || the ↑ˉfirst ˏhurdle | is the ˋroad from the ˋairport || an ·hour's ˋdrive into Coˋlombo || which ˋno wise ·Tamil would want to ˋrun | at the ˍdead of ˋnight || ·memories of the ˍviolence against ·travelling ·Tamils on ˋthis stretch of ·road | during the ·big ˋriots of nineteen eighty-ˋthree || are ·still ˋfresh | in peoples' ˋminds || ↑but ˉonce in Coˬlombo | they ˍmight join the ˉlarge | and often ˇprosperous ·Tamil community || ˋgoing about their ˋbusiness as ˋusual || ˉthese are the ·so-called Coˎlombo Tamils | the ˋthird largest concenˇtration of Sri ·Lankan Tamils | ˋanywhere in the ˋcountry || and ˇtheir lives | have been hardly ˎtouched | by the ˉviolence in the ·north and ˎeast | ˍalthough they suffered ˋterribly in ·nineteen eighty-ˋthree || ˏcertainly they must carry iˋdentity cards | and adopt a low ˋprofile at times of ˋtension | and ˉwoe betide any ·Tamil from aˋnother area | who ˋcannot satisfactorily explain his ˋpresence in the ˋcapital || but there's been ˋno ·communal violence to ·speak of in Coˋlombo and the ˋsouth for two ˋyears || ˏunlike in the ˍmixed ·Tamil ·Muslim and ˋSinhalese areas | in the ˋeast | where ˍgetting on for ˉone hundred people ˋdied in recent ˋclashes | in which the eˍlite police coˋmmandos | were ˋalso involved || ↑there's ˋalso a danger of ˋcommunal violence in the ˉareas | ˍbordering the Tamil ˋnorth || where ·tensions are ˍstill running ˉhigh || ˉfollowing the ˋmassacre | of nearly ˍone hundred and fifty ciˇvilians || in the ˍmainly Sinhalese ˋtown of Anuradhaˋpura last ·month || in the ˍfar ˇnorth | where virtually ˋno Sinhalese ci·vilians live at ˋall || the ˋmain danger to the ˇTamils | is from the ˍarmed ˋforces || people have been ˏkilled or ˍrounded up | almost ˎdaily | in ˉruthless ·search and deˬstroy operations | aˋgainst the eˋlusive gueˋrrillas || a ˋprominent Tamil ˋlawyer | who ˉpainstakingly coˍllates alleged human ˇrights violations || ˉsays he has ˍfiles on eleven ˋhundred | ci·vilian ˎdeaths | at the ˉhands of the armed ˎforces over the past ˋyear | ˉmost ˍbacked by ˋsworn affiˋdavits || ↑the gueˍrrillas have widespread suˋpport | amongst the ciˋvilians | but ˉnot ˎusually to the eˉxtent | of _willingly giving up their ˉsons | and ˏsometimes their ˬdaughters | to the gue_rrilla ˋcause || ˋhence the ˋdesperate ˋscramble | by ˋmany Tamil ˋparents || to sell ˎall | to •pay for a •one way ˋticket | to any ˋcountry | they _think will ˋhave them || ↑the most ˬpopular | and ˇeasiest destinations are | South ˇIndia || where •one hundred ˇthousand have •gone || and West ˋGermany | where the ˉloophole of East Ber_lin | aˉllows in any ˎperson saying he's a poˋlitical refuˋgee || ↓_no questions ˋasked || ˋthousands poured in ˉthis way | after an ˋarticle appeared in the Colombo ˋpress | exˋplaining | how to ˋdo it || ˇsimilarly ˋBritain became ˏpopular || after a ˋrumour got about | that Mrs ˋThatcher | had de_clared open ˋhouse || a swift deˊnial | by the •British high coˇmmission in Colombo | ˋfailed to •stem the ˋtide || and the _widespread puˋblicity about the aˇppeals employed | to preˉvent | _instant deporˉtation || only ˎserved | to enˋcourage ˋothers || ˉonly when the government inˋsisted | on ˉall Sri Lankans having ˋvisas | beˋfore arriving in ˇBritain | did the ˬmessage | be_gin to sink ˋin || ↑aˉpart from the ˬviolence | and the _fear of ˉyoungsters being _wooed into the guerrilla ˋranks | the ˉTamils comˬplain | of con_tinuing discrimination in ˋjobs || although president Jayeˊwardene has _sought to reˋmove o↑ˇfficial discrimination || ˇunofficially | it a_ppears to conˋtinue || and _some Sinhalese would deˋfend this || on the ˉgrounds | that the •Tamils are ˋstill | a ˉprivileged miˋnority | ˋstemming from the ˋdays of the ˋRaj | when the ˋBritish | gave them ˋmost of the best ˋjobs || in the ˉlower ranks of the civil _service | many _Tamils | conˋtinue to be emˋployed || a _glance down the ˋtelephone directory under •customs and ˋexcise for instance | re_veals that about ˋhalf | the listed oˋfficials have Tamil ˋnames || but the •number in ˋsenior positions | has _dropped draˋmatically || ↑one who ˋstill has his job | is the •chief of poˎlice | in an •almost enˉtirely _Sinhalese ˋarea north of Coˋlombo || he's a •man _tipped for a great ˋfuture | and on _merit | ˋshould be a ˋcandidate | for the most ˉsenior po_sition in the poˋlice force || which aˋnother Tamil | has just vaˉcated | to become amˬbassador | in Indoˋnesia || but ˋhow does he maintain ˋdiscipline | with his ˋlargely | ˋSinhalese ˋconstables || ˋno problem he •says || he speaks •fluent ˉSinhala | and •gets total reˏspect from his •men | and the ˎpublic || and his ˊfamily || ˉwell that was ˎdifferent || perˋhaps he would ˋtry and send his ˋdaughters aˋbroad | as the ˋfuture | was •so unˋcertain ||

011 SPOKEN ENGLISH CORPUS TEXT A11

From our own Correspondent
Broadcast notes: Radio 4, 11.30 a.m., 22nd June, 1985
Transcribed by GOK

↑in the or¯nate ˊoffices | of the ·Kremlin ˏpalace | which ·houses the ·central comˬmittee of the ·Communist ·party | in the ˋministry ˊbuildings | throughout ˊMoscow | and ↑in the ·tiny com_mittee ·rooms | of the _party through·out the ·fifteen reˬpublics | there ˇis we're ·told | a ˋnew ·tempo of ˎwork || the ˊword | is ·coming _down the ˏline | in a ¯number of ˏways | ↑that the ·Soviet _Union | must ˋkick-start it·self into ˎaction || Mr ·Gorbaˊchev | in a ·speech ¯loaded with ˏcriticism | of the ·system he now ¯orchestrates | re¯vealed to ˬall last ·week | that the ·next _five-year ˋplan | the ·eco·nomic ˋbible of the ˬparty | ↑had been sent ˏback | by the ¯central coˏmmittee | for re¯vision ˄ and imˎprovement || we shall ·have to ˏwait | un·til next ˇFebruary | and the ·twenty-·seventh ·party ˬcongress | to ˋsee the ·final ˇshape of it | ↑but the pre·diction ˏis | that it ↑will _break the e·xisting ˎmould || it ˏwon't per·haps | ·challenge the ˄ ·Moscow- ˏbased | ·central ˋplanning ·system itˇself | ↑but _try to ·put it on a more _modern ˎfooting || the ¯blueprint itˏself how·ever | and Mr ˎGorbachev's ·blunt exhorˇtations | do ¯not in them_selves | ˋchange the ·petrifiˬcation that's set ·in | through ¯fifteen ˎyears | of ·President ˊBrezhnev's ·rule | and the ·helter ·skelter ˏmonths | of ¯sickness | and ·indeˬcision | which a·ffected _two of his sucˎcessors || as the ˋnew ·leader has acˋknowledged | the ¯party structure itˬself | ¯must be ˏaltered | and ¯early in Juˏly | when the ˋcentral co·mmittee ˊmeets | and then reˋports to the ·national aˋssembly | the su·preme ˊSoviet | we ˇshould see | ¯how he's ·going about ˎthat || ˏwhat for e·xample | is he ¯doing to en·sure that ˋhis grip on ˎpower | is ˇstrong e·nough | to _make the ·necessary ˎchanges || for ˊthat | we ˇhave un·fortunately | to reˏly | on the ·semi-oˏfficial | _Moscow ˋrumour ma·chine || ˋthis de·livers the ˊgoods | in a va¯riety of ˏways | by ·casual reˏmarks | at ·diplo·matic re¯ceptions | ·nods and ˋwinks from o¯fficials | and ↑a_pocryphal ˎstories || ˋwhat it's ·telling ˋme at the ˇmoment is | that ˬGorbachev | is inˇdeed | ¯slowly but ˏsurely | ˇisolating | ¯those who oˎppose him || ↑let's conˇsider for e·xample | the ˏcase of Griˏgory Roˋmanov | the ˎLeningrad ˇparty ·chief | ↑who was _seen as a ˇrival to Mr Gorba·chev | for the ˎleadership || ↑he's _not been in ˋevidence much ˏrecently | ↑and the ·current reˏport | from the ˇrumour ma·chine | is that he's ˬdrying out | at a _clinic for ·alcoˎholics || ·whether ·this is reˋmotely ·true or ˊnot | we _don't ˋknow | ↑but it ·hardly ˎmatters | be·cause it's a ˊtale | which is being ¯actively enˏcouraged | by ¯men | ¯known to be ˏloyal | to the ˎleadership || who ˇis it ·after ·all |

who's •mounted the ˋtoughest •ever camˍpaign a•gainst ˋalcoholism | •Mr •Gorbaˋchev || the ˏstory •then | is ˋnot only a ˉcute ˏway | of •underˉmining | the eˋsteem of a ˉrival | ↑but ˍserves as a ˇwarning | to the •popuˍlation as a ˋwhole || if a ˋpolit•buro ˊmember | is in ˎtrouble with the ˊbottle | and is being ˉpunished | by •losing his ˇinfluence | ↑what ˍchance is ˏthere | for Iˋvan | or ˋIgor | or Naˎtasha | who've ˇsimilar •problems | and •regularly •fail to •turn up for •work as a reˎsult || it's per•haps worth ˋstaying with •Mr Roˊmanov | for aˇnother •indi•cation | that Mr ˉGorbaˏchev | and his ˊteam | are ˍsettling old ˎscores || a reˊliable | but ˎnot nece•ssarily inˇfallible •source | has ˊwritten | that when ˋPresident •Cherˋnenko was •close to ˇdeath | ˉMr Roˏmanov | •tried to •organise a ˋcoup | to pre•vent the ˇclear •favourite | from ˎwinning || the reˉport ˏsays | he ˉpushed ˏforward | the ˇMoscow •party •leader | ˋGrishin | •now in his ˎseventies || when ˇthat failed | Groˋmyko | the ˇforeign •minister | was put ˎup | but ˉhe | ˇshrewdly | reˍsisted the ˎoffer || Groˊmyko | the ˋmaster•mind of ˇforeign •policy | ˍknew his ˎplace || but ˋwhat have the ˉpeople | who su•pport Roˏmanov and ˋGrishin | to do ˋnow | •faced with a ˋfifty-•four year old ˊleader | at the ˎheight of his ˉpowers | and ˉwith the poˏtential | for ˎtwenty or ˉmore ˏyears | at the ˎtop || the ˋanswer ˇis of •course | that •they caˎpitulate | and their ˉmen | •quietly •fade aˎway || it's •quite ˊlikely | that aˋnother old •timer | the Prime ˊMinister | Mr ˋTikhanov | will reˍtire ˏsoon | and be reˏplaced | by a •young ˊtechnocrat | ↑with the ˍGorbachev ˎstyle || the ˋphrase that ˎstruck •me with ˇmost •force | in his •recent ˊspeech | was ˋwhen he was •talking a•bout the ˉneed | for a •psychoˇlogical •change | from ˍtop to ˎbottom | in ˍSoviet soˎciety || and he ˇpushed this •thought a•gain this •week | when he ˊcalled | the •heads of •all the state ˇmedia •organi•sations | •in for a ˋpep talk || it was ˋtheir ˇjob he •said | to exˋpose inˎadequacies in the ˊsystem | by •changing ˍpeople's perˎceptions || Mr Gorbaˋchev | and his ˎwife | are doing ˍtheir bit as ˋwell || he •waved aˋway | his proˋtection •detail | in ˎLeningrad a •couple of ˏweeks a•go | to ˉplunge into a ˏcrowd | and ˉin e•ffect ˉtell them | that ˇeveryone | must try ˉharder | to make ˍsocialism ˎwork || it's ˇclearly | his ˍtop priˎority | •while at the ˉsame ˏtime | •trying to ˉbuild ˏbridges | ↑and conˏsolidate | ˋold •ties aˎbroad ||

012 SPOKEN ENGLISH CORPUS TEXT A12
From our own Correspondent
Broadcast notes: Radio 4, 11.30 a.m., 22nd June, 1985
Transcribed by BJW

¯there have been ˏtimes | in this ¯past few ˬweeks | when ↑¯what's been _happening in Hong ˇKong has been | like `one of those ¯old _old _western `movies || ˇyou know | the `ones where | ↑the _wagons are •gathered into a `tight circle on the `hostile ˇprairie | `under attack and `down to the last ˇbullet | when ¯lo and be_hold | the `US ˇcavalry | `rides over the •hill to the `rescue || ¯well it's _been | ↑the _government `bankers and `stock exchanges | that have _seemed to be be`leaguered in Hong `Kong | al•though to call them a ˇtight circle | would `probably be over`stating things a •little || ¯but the ˬcavalry | ˏdid come _riding over the `hill | •how_ever to | ˇeveryone's sur•prise | it was the | Chiˇnese cavalry | that _dashed in and | `saved a few `scalps || ˇhurriedly | ˇlet me add | ¯this was _not the People's •Liberation `Army | `swarming across the ↑ˇborder | _twelve years in ad•vance of Britain's ˇhandover | `of Hong Kong to Pe`king || it was _far more `gentlemanly and con↑`structive | ↑`as you would ex`pect financiers to `be || in ¯fact it was the ˎBank of `China || ↑the fi`nancial •cavalry `rescue | ¯had its ˏorigins | ¯back at the be_ginning of the `month | when | `Hong Kong's `fourth biggest `bank | the _Overseas ˇTrust Bank | ↓went `bust || ˏseveral of its ↓o´fficials ↓have been aˇrrested | ¯including ˬone | who was | inter`cepted at the ¯airport | with a _case full of `cash || ¯this was a tre_mendous `shock | for the `government || e_specially as it had | `had to use `tax-payers' ↑`money | to _buy another ˇsmaller | but _still subˇstantial •bank | _less than •two years `previously || ¯well | ↑`this month | de•spite a lot of | ˇgrumbling and ˬmumbling and | `threats of `never aˇgain | from the | `legislative ↑ˇcouncil | the ¯government ˎbought out | `Overseas •Trust ´Bank | at a _cost ˇestimated | a_round | `two hundred and fifty `million US `dollars || ¯so the _lucky Hong Kong ˇtax-payer | ˇnow owns | ↑`two banks || ↑when ˎbig banks go ˇunder | ˇsmall banks | how¯ever ˏsound | and ¯well ˬmanaged | be_gin to ˇtremble | in the ¯gale of ˏrumour and specu`lation || with ¯four _stock exˇchanges | and nearly `fifty daily ˇnewspapers | `Hong Kong is never •short of `either || ¯sure e_nough | within a ¯few _days | there was a ˇrun | on a ¯relatively ˇsmall bank | ¯which is | _where the •Chinese `cavalry | _rode `in || to↑¯gether with the _Hong Kong and ˇShanghai •Bank | the ¯Bank of ˏChina | de¯cided the | ¯troubled ˬsmall bank | was fi`nancially ´sound | and ↑iˬmmediately ¯guaran_teed it | ↑a _massive `credit || •business con_tinued | •uninte`rrupted || ↑the `Bank of China `operation ↑ˇin Hong Kong | is ↑a _very `big one || ↓after ´all | _more than a ˇthird

| of ·all China's foreign ˇearnings | pass ˋthrough Hong ˋKong || but ˋfor it to interˋvene | in _Hong Kong fiˋnancial aˉffairs | like ˋthis | was unˇprecedented | beˋcause of the | poˋlitical and ↑fi_nancial ˋmotives || the _Bank of ˊChina | even went to the uˇnusual extent | ↑of _holding a ·press ˋbriefing || to ˉsay that its ·action | ·showed its deˇtermination | to main·tain | the ↑sta_bility and proˬsperity of ↓Hong ˋKong || _local government oˉfficials here | pooh ˇpooh the i·dea | of ˋany poˋlitical ↑ˋmotive | but ˋfairly ˇobviously | ˉthat _motive | ·was ˋthere || the sta_bility and pro·sperity of Hong ˉKong | ˋhas to be mainˇtained | ↑to _make it worth_while for Peˉking | to _take it ˋback | in _nineteen ninety-ˋseven || ↑ˋthese hiccups aˋpart | ·business is ˋbooming || alˉthough there ˏhave been exˏcitements in the ˋstreets | ↑to ˏparallel ˏthose of the fiˋnanciers || a ˉseries of _armed ˋraids | was ˉmade on | ·some of the ˋcity's ↑ˇmultitude of | _goldsmith's ˋshops || in ˏone of them | poˉlice _lay in ˇambush | ˋone ·hundred and ↑ˋtwenty shots | were exˉchanged | and ↑the _thieves got ˋclean aˋway || but ˋtheir loot | would ·look pretty ˏpaltry | com·pared with the ˋbillions | that have ˇdisappeared | in fiˇnancial circles | ·over the ·past ˋtwo or three ˉyears | with·out a _single ˋshot | ↓being _fired in ˋanger ||

013 SPOKEN ENGLISH CORPUS TEXT B01

BBC News

Broadcast notes: Radio 4, 8.00 a.m., 24th November, 1984

Transcribed by BJW

_BBC ˊNews | at _eight o'clock on ˉSaturday the ·twenty-fourth of Noˎvember || ˉthis is ·Brian ˎPerkins || a ˋthousand ·people were led to ˋsafety after being ˋtrapped by a ˉfire | in the ˉLondon ˎUnderground last ·night | _many had to ·walk along the ˉtrack to the ·nearest ˎstation ||

Mr ˋEnoch ˊPowell | has ˉpraised Mrs ˇThatcher | for ˉstanding _firm at the _Anglo-·Irish ˋsummit ||

the ˉOverseas Deˏvelopment ·Minister | is _visiting Ethiˇopia this week·end | to ·see the ·famine reˋlief ope·ration ||

ˉhigh winds | and ˉheavy ˬseas | have been causing ·further ˉproblems | in the ˇsouthern ·part of ·Britain | leaving ˉhomes ·flooded | and _roads ˎblocked ||

a ˉbig ˎrescue ope·ration was ˉmounted in central _London | ·late last ˉnight | after a ˇfire | at ˉOxford _Circus ˋUnderground ·Station || the eˉmergency _services were ˉhampered by _thick ˎsmoke | which ·spread ˇquickly through the ·station | and into ˇtunnels | where ·five ˋtrains were cut ˋoff || ˋsome ·passengers were ˋstranded for two ˋhours | ↓and ˋthen had to be ˋguided on ↑ˋfoot along the ˋtrack || a ˉsenior ·fire brigade ·officer ˇestimated | that as many as a ˇthousand people | were led to ˇsafety from the ·trains | and from ˋplatforms || there were ·no ˉserious ˏinjuries | but ˉfifteen _people were taken to ˉhospital ·suffering from the e_ffects of ˋsmoke | and ˉseven were ·treated by _ambulancemen | at the ˋscene || ˋtube ·trains were ˋhalted on ˇthree ·lines | the Vicˇtoria | ˬBakerloo | and ˇCentral | when the ˉcurrent was turned ˎoff | ↓and ˉso far this ˉmorning | _services are ˋstill being disˋrupted || our reˉporter ·Janet Treˋwin | _went to the ˉstation | _shortly after the e·mergency beˋgan ||

[change of speaker: Janet Trewin]

the ˋfire ˇstarted | ˋjust after ˉten o'ˋclock | and within ˋminutes | ˋthick ·black ˋsmoke was ˋbillowing out of ˋthree of the ˇfour entrances | to the ˋtube station || it's ˉthought the _blaze beˇgan | in a conˉtractor's ˋhut | on one of the ˋplatforms | where renoˋvation work | ↓was being carried ˋout || more than ·two ˇhundred ·firemen | with ˇbreathing apparatus | ˉworked in ˋrelays | ↓going ˉdown ˇinto the ·tunnels | to ˉreach the ˋhundreds of

ˋpassengers ˋtrapped || visiˇbility | was ¯down to ˋzero | ↓at •Oxford •Circus itˇself | so ¯teams of ˏfiremen | •disˋpersed to suˋrrounding •stations | and •worked their way ˇback down the •line | to the _crowded ˋtrains || Steve ˋAnnett | •talked to ˇsome of the •passengers | as ˇthey arrived | on the ¯platform at Piccaˇdilly •station || ˇthey'd been •stranded | for •two ˋhours | and had ¯walked about •half a ˋmile along the ˋtunnels ||

[interview by Steve Annett is omitted]

the ˇfire caused ˋchaos on the ˋtube system || ˇscores of •trains | on ˋthree lines were ˋhalted | because the ˋpower | ↓had to be turned ˋoff | and for ˋhours ˇroad traffic | had to con¯tend with diˇversions | because of ˋstreet •closures ||

[change of speaker: Brian Perkins]

¯London •Regional ¯Transport | say that ˋso far this ¯morning | only ¯tube trains on the ˇCentral •Line | are ˋstopping at Oxford ˋCircus || ¯Bakerloo Line •trains are •running ¯through the •station without ˎstopping || there's ˋno service on the Vicˇtoria •Line | between Vic_toria and ˋWarren Street || it's •hoped that ˇall services | will be ¯back to _normal ¯later toˎday ||

po¯lice in •West ˎYorkshire | _say they're in¯vestigating a ¯fire | at the _home of a ¯working ˎminer | early toˎday || the ˇbungalow | at ˇUpton | about ˋfive miles ¯south of ˇPontefract | was ˋunoccupied at the ˋtime ||

the ¯General _Secretary of the •TUˊC | ↓Mr Norman ˊWillis | has said the ˋCoal •Board's ˇstrategy | of _trying to ˋlure miners ¯back to _work by ¯offering ˇbonuses | will ˎfail || he ¯told ˏminers | ↓at a •meeting in ˊChatham in ˇKent last •night | that the ¯board should i_nitiate new disˋcussions with the ¯mineworkers' ˬunion | in an ¯effort to ˎend the dis•pute || ↓he said the ¯TU¯C | ↓would be getting an •extra ¯quarter of a •million ˋpounds | to ˋhelp •striking ˋminers || Mr ¯Willis was warmly aˋpplauded | as he aˋrrived at the •meeting || the ˇlast •time | he a_ddressed striking ˊminers | ↓in South ˊWales | _earlier this •month | he was ˋjeered || and a ¯hangman's ˎnoose | was ¯dangled in ˎfront of him ||

Mr •Willis' ˇpredecessor | as ¯General Secretary of the •TU¯C | Mr •Len ˇMurray | is •said to be in a very ˇcomfortable con•dition | at the ¯National ˇHeart Hospital | in _London this ˎmorning || he had a ¯coronary •artery ˇbypass operation •there | on ˎThursday ||

↓the ¯Ulster Unionist MˊP | Mr ˍEnoch ˊPowell | has ¯praised the ˍstand | taken by Mrs ˊThatcher | in her ˍtalks at ¯Chequers | ˍearlier this ¯week | with the ¯Prime Minister of the ˍIrish Re·public Dr ˍGarret FitzˋGerald || Mr ¯Powell | told a ˍmeeting at New¯castle in ·County ˍDown last ¯night | that by a¯sserting herˍself | ¯Mrs ˍThatcher had ˋbroken | ¯what he ·called the | ˍvicious ˇspiral | which ˋwould have led to ˋNorthern ˏIreland being ¯trapped | in an ¯all-Ireland ˎstate || our po¯litical correˏspondent says | Mr ¯Powell's remarks have ¯dashed ˍgovernment ˍhopes | ↓that the ¯Ulster ˇUnionists | would ¯not exˎploit | the ¯sudden ˋstrain in reˋlations | between ¯London | and ¯Dublin | which ˋfollowed the ·summit ||

at ·least ¯three ˏgunmen | opened ¯fire on a poˍlice station in Stra¯bane in County Tyˍrone last ˋnight || they ·held a family ¯captive | at a ·house near¯by | and ˇfired | from an ·upstairs ˎwindow || ¯several ˍbullets | ¯hit the poˬlice ·station | but ˍno one was ˋwounded || the ˍgunmen es·caped in a ¯car | ·thought to have been ˍstolen | ¯earlier in the ˎday ||

the ¯Minister | for ˍOverseas Deˏvelopment | Mr ˍTimothy ˏRaison | and ¯eight Aˍmerican ˏcongressmen | are ¯visiting Ethiˇopia this week·end | to ¯judge for themˍselves | the eˋffectiveness of the ¯famine re¯lief opeˎration || the Ethiˋopians say the ˋflow of emergency su¯pplies | is slowing ˎdown | and that su¯pplies | sent by ˇsea | through the ¯country's two ·main ¯ports | have ˍpractically ˋstopped || ·yesterday | they took ¯diplomats to the ˋports | to ˍunder·line the ˋurgency of the ¯situˋation || from ·Addis ¯Ababa | our ˍEast Africa corre¯spondent | ¯Mike ˋWooldridge re·ports ||

[change of speaker: Mike Wooldridge]

the ˇdiplomats | were ·shown ¯empty ˋwarehouses | at ¯Assab | and Maˇssawa | as ˇevidence | of ¯Ethiopia's conˋcern | that the ¯international reˇlief ope·ration | is ˍlosing moˋmentum || ↓with ¯food aid ˇpledges | still ˋwell short of what's ˇneeded | it's ˋclear that the A¯merican ·congressmen | ¯and Mr ˇRaison | will be ˍpressed for ¯more aˎssistance || the United ˋStates is | ˏnow co·mmitted | to suˍpplying just over ¯two hundred ˍthousand ˋtons of ˋgrain || Aˍmerican oˏfficials are ˏanxious | ↓that the ¯Ethiopian ˏgovernment | for ˇits part | ¯keeps to its aˇssurances | that the ¯food will reach ˍall in ˋneed | inˇcluding those | in the ˍareas of ·civil ˋconflict in ˋnorthern Ethi·opia || the ˏcongressmen | and ˏMr ·Raison | can ˋalso expect to be ¯lobbied for ·help in the ˍsearch for ˋlong-·term soˋlutions to ¯Ethiopia's ˍfood ˋcrisis | and in parˇticular | in reˋsettling | ·two-and-a-half ˇmillion ·people | from the ˇdrought-·prone areas | to more

ˇfertile ·land | ·over the next ten ˋyears || this ¯vast | and ˇcostly ·scheme | is ·currently re·ceiving top priˋority | from the ¯Ethiopian ˋgovernment ||

[change of speaker: Brian Perkins]

at ·least ˋeighteen more ¯Polish ˏtourists | are reˍported to have de¯fected while on a ˍvisit to West ˎGermany | bringing the ¯number ˍfailing to re·turn to their ¯ships | in ˍGerman ¯ports | in the ¯past ˍweek | to ¯well over three ˎhundred || the ˇlatest ·group | had a·rrived on an exˇcursion ·ferry | in the ˋBaltic ·port of ·Traveˋmunde || on ˋTuesday nearly ¯two ·hundred ˍPoles | left the ¯cruise liner | ·Stephan Ba'ˋthory | in ˋHamburg ||

there's been ˋmore ·violence in the ˇBasque country in northern ˎSpain | ·one policeman has been ¯killed | and ¯two have been ˎinjured in a gre¯nade | and maˇchine-gun a·ttack | on their paˋtrol-car || ·masked ˍmen | ·ambushed them on a ˇmotorway | near the ¯border town of IˎRun || ˍtension has been ¯high in the ·region | since the ¯murder ·earlier this ˍweek | of a ·leading ˍBasque ¯Separatist poliˎtician ||

the ¯south and ˍwest ·coasts of ¯England and ˏWales | have ·taken a ˇbattering from ¯strong ˍwinds | ·high ˍseas | and ·heavy ˎrain | overˎnight || in ¯some places ˍsea defences were ¯breached | and ·many ˍroads have been ¯blocked | by ¯flood water | and ˍfallen ˋtrees || ·Laurie Marˋgolis reˎports ||

[change of speaker: Laurie Margolis]

↑North ˎDevon | was the ˇworst-hit ·area over·night | and this ¯morning's ex·ceptionally high ·tide | brought some ˋfurther ·flooding | ·mainly to parts of ˍBarnstaple and ˋLynmouth || in ·all about four ˇhundred homes in ·Barnstaple | were ˍflooded to ·depths of up to ·three ˋfeet | and ˇother North Devon ·towns and ·villages | have been a¯ffected to ˍvarying deˋgrees || a¯cross the Bristol ˍChannel ˋsea de·fences were ¯breached | at ˋAmroth | near ·Tenby in ˏDyfed | with ˋhomes and ˋbusiness ·premises a¯long the ˍfront suffering ˋdamage || some ¯roads in ˍWest and ˋSouth ·Wales re¯mained ˎblocked | by ·trees and ˇflood ·waters | and in the ·south of ˇEngland | ˋSussex police say | ·coastal roads there are ˋlittered | with ·shingle and ˋdebris washed ˋin by high ˋseas || the ¯night's ˬmain ·casualty | ·seems to have ˍbeen a ¯thirty-foot-ˍlong ˋwhale | which is ·lying ¯dead on the ·beach at ˍBexhill-on-ˋSea || the ·local au¯thority | will be ·trying to work out ˋwhat to do with the ¯carcass | ˍlater this ˋmorning ||

[change of speaker: Brian Perkins]

to`rrential ¯rain | and _gale-force ¯winds | have _caused `havoc all a¯cross the _continent of ˏEurope | with ¯power ·lines brought _down | and ¯many _roads `flooded || in ¯West ·Germany | a ¯middle-aged ·woman | was ¯killed by a _falling ¯tree | near ˊMunich | and in ¯Hessen | a ¯young ·fireman was ¯sucked into a _sewer | and ·swept aˎway || a¯long the ·coast of northern ˎFrance | many ·boats were ¯torn from their _moorings | and ¯washed out to ˎsea ||

the ¯BB_C's | ·Children in ˇNeed A·ppeal | ˇclosed last ·night | after ¯viewers and _listeners had ¯pledged a _total of ¯one _million | ·four hundred and ¯eighty-six _thousand ˇpounds | to _help de·prived `youngsters || the a¯mount _fell ·slightly `short of the `target the ·organisers had ¯hoped for | ·one-and-a-_half million ˎpounds ||

¯cricket | on the ·fourth and `final day of their ¯match | a·gainst ¯England at ˏRajkot | ·West Zone de¯clared | at _three hundred and `ninety-three for `seven || ˏEngland | who were ¯four hundred and ˬfifty-eight for ·three | in their _first innings | were `fourteen without ¯loss at ˎlunch || ↓and in the ¯second test in ˇBrisbane | the _West Indies were ¯two hundred and _sixty-three for ¯five at _tea | ↓in re¯ply | to Au¯stralia's _first innings ·total of ¯one hundred and _seventy-ˎfive || ·Richie ¯Richardson | is ¯one hundred and ˎtwelve | ˎnot ·out ||

·finally the ·headlines a¯gain | Mr _Enoch ¯Powell | has _praised Mrs ¯Thatcher | for _standing ˇfirm | at the _Anglo-Irish `summit || the ·Overseas De¯velopment ·Minister | is ·visiting Ethiˇopia this week·end | to ·see the ·famine re`lief ope·ration || ¯high winds | and _heavy ¯seas | ↓have been ·causing further ¯problems | in the _southern part of ¯Britain | ·leaving _homes ¯flooded | and _roads `blocked || and the ¯main news this ˏmorning | a ˇthousand people | were _led to ¯safety after being ·trapped by a _fire | in the ·London `Underground last `night || ·many had to ·walk along the ˇtrack | to the _nearest `station || ¯BB_C Radio ˎnews || it's ·now ¯ten past ˎeight ||

013 SPOKEN ENGLISH CORPUS TEXT B01
BBC News
Broadcast notes: Radio 4, 8.00 a.m., 24th November, 1984
Overlap passage

Transcribed by BJW

¯Cricket | on the ·fourth and ˋfinal day of their ¯match | a·gainst ¯England at ˏRajkot | ·West Zone de¯clared | at ˍthree hundred and ˋninety-three for ˋseven || ˏEngland | who were ¯four hundred and ˬfifty-eight for ·three | in their ˍfirst innings | were ˋfourteen without ¯loss at ˎlunch || ↓and in the ¯second test in ˇBrisbane | the ˍWest Indies were ¯two hundred and ˍsixty-three for ¯five at ˍtea | ↓in re¯ply | to Au¯stralia's ˍfirst innings ·total of ¯one hundred and ˍseventy-ˎfive || ·Richie ¯Richardson | is ¯one hundred and ˎtwelve | ˎnot ·out ||

·Finally the ·headlines a¯gain | Mr ˍEnoch ¯Powell | has ˍpraised Mrs ¯Thatcher | for ˍstanding ˇfirm | at the ˍAnglo-Irish ˋsummit || the ·Overseas De¯velopment ·Minister | is ·visiting Ethiˇopia this week·end | to ·see the ·famine reˋlief ope·ration || ¯high winds | and ˍheavy ¯seas | ↓have been ·causing further ¯problems | in the ˍsouthern part of ¯Britain | ·leaving ˍhomes ¯flooded | and ˍroads ˋblocked || and the ¯main news this ˏmorning | a ˇthousand people | were ˍled to ¯safety after being ·trapped by a ˍfire | in the ·London ˋUnderground last ˋnight || ·many had to ·walk along the ˇtrack | to the ˍnearest ˋstation || ¯BBˍC Radio ˎnews || it's ·now ¯ten past ˎeight ||

Transcribed by GOK

ˊCricket | on the ¯fourth and ˋfinal ·day of their ¯match | against ¯England | at ¯Rajkot | ˋWest ·Zone de¯clared | at ¯three ·hundred and ¯ninety-ˍthree | for ˋseven || ˏEngland | who were ˋfour ·hundred and ˇfifty-·eight | for ¯three | in their ˍfirst ·innings | were ˋfourteen wi·thout ¯loss | at ˎlunch || and ˰ in the ˬsecond ·test | in ˇBrisbane | the ˎWest Indies | were ˋtwo hundred and ˋsixty-·three for ¯five | at ˍtea | in re¯ply | to Auˋstralia's | ˋfirst ·innings ¯total | ↓of ˎone ·hundred | and ˍseventy-ˋfive || ¯Richie ˰ ¯Richardson | is ˋone ·hundred and ˇtwelve | ¯not ˎout ||

ˋFinally | the ˋheadlines a¯gain | Mr ˍEnoch ˊPowell | has ˍpraised ·Mrs ˏThatcher | for ˍstanding ˇfirm | at the ˋAnglo-·Irish ˎsummit || the

ˎoverseas deˇvelopment ·minister | is ˉvisiting Ethiˋopia this weeˏkend | to ˉsee the ˍfamine reˋlief ope·ration || ˉhigh ˍwinds | and ˍheavy ˇseas | have been ˍcausing ·further ˉproblems | in the ˇsouthern ·part of ·Britain | ˍleaving ˉhomes ˍflooded | ↓and ˍroads ˋblocked || and the ˎmain ·news this ˏmorning || a ˋthousand ˏpeople | were ˍled to ˊsafety | ˍafter being ˉtrapped | by a ˉfire | in the ˉLondon ˋUnderground last ·night || ˉmany | had to ˉwalk along the ˉtrack | ↓to the ˋnearest ˎstation || ˉBBˍC | ↓ˉRadio ˎnews || it's now ˉten past ˎeight ||

014 SPOKEN ENGLISH CORPUS TEXT B02
BBC News
Broadcast notes: Radio 4, 8.00 a.m., 22nd June,1985
Transcribed by GOK

_BBC ¯news | at _eight o'¯clock | on _Saturday | the _twenty-·second of ˎJune || ↓¯this is ·Brian ˎPerkins || seˋcurity in ˬWashington | has re¯ceived a se_vere ˎjolt | with a ˋdouble ˬkilling | ¯in_side the ˋstate de·partment || the _Beirut ¯hostage ·deadlock | goes ¯on | _bringing ¯mounting _pressure | on _President ˎReagan || a ¯car | has been ¯hit by a ˊtrain | on a ¯level _crossing in ˎHampshire | ¯one _person is ˎdead || _and | ¯Nemo the ˇwhale | _goes to ˋWindsor ||

↑a ¯major se¯curity reˬview | has been ¯ordered | at the ¯state de_partment in ˬWashington | after a ¯gunman | ¯entered the ˏbuilding | ¯shot _dead his ¯mother | who ¯worked ·there | and _then _killed himˎself || the ¯secretary of ¯state | Mr ˋGeorge ¯Shultz | was a ¯short ·distance a_way at the ˇtime | in ¯his ˏoffice | on the _same ˋfloor || of¯ficials | have deˇscribed the ·shooting | as a doˇmestic a·ffair | but ¯staff | have al¯ready been ˏtold | that some ¯extra se_curity _measures | are being _brought into ˎforce | and a ¯thorough investiˋgation | of the se¯curity ˋsystem | is being ¯carried ˎout || ¯James ˎCox | reˎports ||

[Change of speaker: James Cox]

ˇState de·partment o·fficials | are ˋflabbergasted | to ¯learn | that a ˇgunman | could ¯gain ˏentry | to the de¯partment headˇquarters | eˇspecially in a ·week | in which ˋterrorist aˇttacks | have ˋdominated | ¯Washington's | _waking ˎhours || ˇnormally | ¯visitors to the ˇstate de·partment | reˋquire creˇdentials | and ¯even ˋthen | they ¯have to _pass through ˋmetal de·tectors || but ¯twenty year ·old | ¯Edward ·Steven ˇDoster | _managed to eˇvade the se·curity a·rrangements | and ¯carry | a col¯lapsible ˇrifle | ¯inˏside | and ¯up to the _seventh ˋfloor | ˇwhere | the ¯secretary of ˇstate | has his ˋoffices || ˏthere | in a¯nother ˏoffice | ˋDoster shot his ˇmother | forty-ˇfour year ·old | ˇCarol ·Doster | who _worked as a ˇsecretary | and _then ·turned the _gun on himˎself || ¯both were ˬdead | by the ˬtime | po_lice aˎrrived || Mr ˇShultz | ˋwas in his ·office ·suite at the ˇtime | but the de¯partment ·stated | he was ˇnot in·volved | and the ¯incident had _nothing to ˇdo | with o¯fficial ˇbusiness | or ˇany | de¯partment oˎfficials ||

[Change of speaker: Brian Perkins]

the ˋforty | ˋpassengers and ˊcrew | of the ¯hijacked A·merican ˬairliner | have ¯now be_gun | their ¯second ˬweekend | as the ¯victims of ˎterrorism || the ¯three ·members of the ˇflight crew | are ¯still _thought to be on ˇboard the ·aircraft | at _Beirut ˏairport | while the ˇpassengers | are being ¯guarded | by ¯Shi'ite ˇmilitia ·men | _somewhere in the ˎcity || their ˇplight | has been de¯scribed by ·President ˇReagan | _speaking ˏyesterday | as ¯simply _part | of a ¯wider | ¯criminal ˎthreat | to ¯civiliˎsation || he ˏemphasized | that barˏbarians ˆ as he ·called them | would ¯not _weaken the reˋsolve | of the U¯nited ˏStates | to re¯sist ·terrorism | in _all its ˎforms || the _strong ˏline | from ˏWashington | in¯sisting | that ¯no conˋcessions will be ˇmade | has been ¯welcomed by ˋIsrael | which is ¯holding | more than ¯seven ˋhundred | ¯Shi'ite ˋprisoners | whose reˋlease is being deˋmanded by the ˋgunmen in Beiˎrut || but as ¯Clive ˏSmall | now re¯ports from _Washington | the ˋpressures on ¯President ˏReagan | are inˋtensifying ||

[Change of speaker: Clive Small]

_here in ˊWashington | in Beiˊrut | ¯and in JeˇRusalem | there's ˇno ·hint | that ¯any _diplomatic ˏmove | has ¯broken | the ¯three way ˎdeadlock | and o¯fficials | ¯give the imˇpression | that they ¯may be _in | for a ˇlong | ¯contest of ˎwills || and ¯while there ˋis no | ¯visible ˏprogress | A¯merica | ¯takes _comfort in the ˏfact | that the ˇcaptives | ¯seem to be ¯reasonably _well looked ˋafter || but the ˋnation's ˇdiplomats | ¯can't take ·that for ˋgranted | and ˇtime | ¯may not ·be on their ˋside || in ¯wearing ·down the reˋsolve | of the ¯hostage ˎtakers || if ˇanything | Bei¯rut toˬday | is ˇmore ex·plosive | and ¯unpreˇdictable | than ¯TehˇRan was | ¯five ˋyears ago || so ¯President ˏReagan's | ¯method of | ¯handling the ˇcrisis | _may grow ¯more ·difficult to suˇstain | as the _days go ˋby || ˊsoon | his o_fficials ¯may have to adˏvise | ¯canceˇllation | of his ˇholiday ·break | in ¯Caliˇfornia | in a _week's ˋtime || and ˋthat would ˋdraw him ˇpersonally | ¯closer to the ˎcrisis | a preˇdicament | ˇhe's tried to aˋvoid | _knowing how ¯Jimmy ˋCarter's | _own ¯single-¯minded coˇmmitment | _five ˇyears a·go | _seemed to en¯courage the ˇterrorists | and ¯virtually deˋstroyed | ¯his ˎpresidency || _almost ˇdaily ·now | ¯Mr ˏReagan | and ¯his oˏfficials | reˋpeat their ¯declaˏrations | that they ¯won't ˏyield | and _won't neˋgotiate | while in the ˇbackground | A¯merica's ˇdiplomats | ¯seek ·ways of ¯striking an inˇformal ·deal | that could ˋfree the ˎhostages ||

[Change of speaker: Brian Perkins]

at the U¯nited ˇNations | ˍboth the Uˍnited ¯States | and ˬBritain | have ˊjoined | in the ˇsecurity ·council's | ¯latest condemˋnation | of ˍSouth ˎAfrica | this ˊtime | for its ¯raid ·last ˏweek | in BotˇSwana | aˍgainst what were a¯lleged to be | gue¯rrilla ˎbases || the ¯UN resoˊlution ·said | the aˊttack | in ·which up to ˇfifteen ·people | were ¯shot ˏdead | had been ¯unpro¯voked | and ¯unˎwarranted ||

the ˇjustice ·ministry | in ˇIsrael | has ex¯pressed ·some ˇscepticism | that the ¯body | ex¯humed in Braˏzil | ¯is ˏthat | of the ¯Nazi ˏwar ·criminal | ¯Josef ˎMengele || o¯fficials ·say | they're ¯not conˍvinced | beyond ¯reasonable ˎdoubt | and are ˍwaiting to reˍceive the ˋevidence | from Braˎzil || the ¯scientists themˇselves ·though | have ˋno ·doubts || ˍone of the Aˏmericans on the ·team ·said | there was a ¯very ¯very ·high probaˋbility | that the ¯body | ¯was ·that of ˏMengele | the ˍodds a¯gainst he ·said | were ¯astroˎnomical ||

¯one ·person was ˎkilled | ¯late last ˊnight | and ¯five ·others ˊinjured | when their ¯car was inˍvolved in a co¯llision with a ˏtrain | at an ¯automatic level ˏcrossing | near ¯Romsey in ˎHampshire || ˍKevin Bo¯cquet | of ˍBBC ˍRadio ˬSolent | has ¯been to the ˎscene of the ·crash ||

[Change of speaker: Kevin Bocquet]

the ¯accident ˍhappened | in the ¯village | of ¯East ˬDean | near ˎRomsey || a ˇfreight ·train | which had ¯just left Souˏthampton | on its ˍway to ˇLiverpool | co¯llided with a saˇloon ·car | on an ¯unˎmanned | ¯half ˍbarrier ˋcrossing || the ¯car was ˍshunted | about ¯twenty ˎyards | up the ˎtrack || ˍone of the ˏpassengers | who was ¯less ·seriously ¯injured | than his comˇpanions | ˍraised the aˋlarm | and ¯two ˋdoctors | who ¯happened to be ˍdriving ·through the ˇarea | ¯both ˇstopped | and ¯did what they ˋcould | to ˍhelp the ˇinjured | until ˇambulances aˋrrived || the sur¯vivors from the ˇcar | were ¯all ·taken to ¯Southampton ·General ˋHospital || the ˇtrain ·driver | ¯wasn't ˇinjured | and there were ¯no ˬpassengers | on the ˎtrain || for ¯several ˇhours | ˊfiremen | ¯worked under ˋfloodlights | to ¯clear the ˎwreckage | a¯ssisted ·by the poˎlice || inˍspector ¯Peter ˇDawson ·said | that at ˇthis ·stage | the po¯lice | have ¯no iˋdea | ¯why the ˍaccident ˋhappened || as ˋfar as they ˇknow | the ˋautomatic ˋbarriers on the ˇcrossing | ¯were ˍworking ˋnormally || they're ¯hoping | they'll get a ˇclearer i·dea | ¯later toˇday | when they ¯talk to the ˇtrain ·driver | and the surˍvivors from the ˋcar ||

[Change of speaker: Brian Perkins]

reˉports are ˍcoming ·in from ˇBrussels | of an exˇplosion | aˍpparently ·caused by a ˊbomb | at an ˉoffice | beˍlonging to the ˇWest ·German | ˇchemicals ˆ ·group | ˎBayer || there are ˉno reˍports of ˉany ˎcasualties ||

a ˊbomb ex·ploded last ·night | at ˉBanbridge in ·County ˎDown || ˍtwo poˊlicemen | were ˍhit by ·flying ˏglass | but ˇneither of them | was ˍseriously ˋhurt ||

in the ˉIrish Reˋpublic | ˉcounting has beˊgun | after ˇlocal ·government e·lections | and the reˍsults ˊso far | ˉindicate | that the ˋopposition ˍFianna ˇFail | is ˍgaining ˇground | at the exˉpense | of the ˉtwo coaˋlition ˉgovernment ˬparties | ˉFine ˏGael | and ˋLabour || ˍSinn ˊFein | have imˉproved ˏslightly | on their ˍshowing ˇlast time ·round | and ˋsmaller ·parties ˇgenerally || have ˋstrengthened ˉtheir poˎsition || ˉfrom ˏDublin | ˉhere's | ˉAnn Cadˎwallader ||

[Change of speaker: Ann Cadwallader]

ˉas the reˍsults ·came ˇin | and ˋCharles ˇHaughey's ·party | ˍscented ˬblood | they iˇmmediately ·called | ↓for a ˉgeneral eˎlection || but al↑ˉthough ·Fine ˍGael and ˍLabour | ˇhave lost ·ground to the oppo·sition | it's ↑ˉfar from ˎclear | that ˍFianna ·Fail would ˎsweep the ˬboard | if it were ˍcalled toˋmorrow || ˋon the ˍshowings ˇso ·far | and there's ˉmany ˋhours of ˍcounting | to ˎgo | in ˍIreland's ·system of pro·portional ·represenˇtation | the ˇsmaller ·parties | have ˍdone | ˉunexˍpectedly ˋwell || ˇthey in·clude | ˍSinn ˋFein | who've held ˇon to their ·share of the ·vote | and ˇmay make ·gains | in ˇDublin | and ˍsome ˋborder ·areas || ˉso the preˇdicted ·setback | to ˍDoctor Fitz·gerald's ˏgovernment | ↓ˍseems to have ·taken ˎplace || but ˍFine ˊGael | have alˋready ·said | they're to ˉsoldier ˏon | into ˍnineteen ·eighty-ˋseven | by ↑ˇwhich ·time | they ˉhope | their ecoˇnomic ·policies | will have beˍgun to pay ˋoff || and it ↑ˉwouldn't be ˍfair | to ˍsee this ˏpoll | as a ˏvote | of no ˏconfidence | in ˍDoctor Fitzˏgerald's | ˏhandling | of ˏAnglo-ˏIrish aˋffairs || ↑ˇthese e·lections | were ↓ˍfought on ˎlocal ·issues ||

[Change of speaker: Brian Perkins]

the ˉdeputy ˏleader | of the ˇLabour-con·trolled | ˉLiverpool ˊcouncil | Mr ˉDerek ˇHatton | has ·said ˇany of his | ˉtown ˍhall ˉstaff | who coˇoperate | with the ˋdistrict ˇauditor | ˉfaced the ˍthreat of suˎspension || ↓ˇyesterday | ˍtwo ˉsenior oˏfficials | who'd ˍdone

‸ ˉjust ˏthat | were ˉsent _home | ˉpending an investiˎgation || the ˉauditors | were ˎcalled in | imˉmediately _after the ·council aˉgreed | to a ˉnine per ·cent ˇrates ·increase | to ˋfund ˎspending | beˉyond ·government ˎlimits || Mr ˇHatton ·said last ·night | he ˋdidn't know _whether | ˋofficers were o_bliged by ˇlaw | to coˋoperate with the ·district ·auditor || he ·added ‸ I'm not ˎbothered about ·that ||

the ˉpoet | _Phillip _Larkin | re·mains ˉseriously _ill | in ˉhospital in ˎHull || there are ˉstill no ˎdetails | of his ˎillness ||

ˊNemo | the _killer ˏwhale | who'd _grown | too ˉbig | for his ˏpool | on _Clacton ˏpier | has aˉrrived ˏsafely | at his ˉnew ˏhome | in _Windsor sa·fari ˎpark || but the ˇjourney | was _not wi·thout ˋmishaps || ˇNemo ‸ ·weighs | ˉone and a ·half ˊtons | and he ˉnearly _proved | ˉmore than a ˎmatch | for a ˋcrane | ˉbrought in to ˎlift him | from the ˎpool || ˉour re_porter | ˉPeter _Burden | has been ↓ˉfollowing eˎvents ||

[Change of speaker: Peter Burden]

the ˋnine hour opeˇration | to ˇmove ·Nemo from ·Clacton to ·Windsor | in·volved a poˋlice ˇescort | _medical ˇspecialists | _civil ˇservants | _ten ˇfrogmen | and a _mobile ˋcrane || at ˏClacton | it _took some ·five ˋhours | to get _Nemo out of the ˏwater | and _into the ˋlorry || but _once on ˊboard | he was a _perfect ˋpassenger || as the ·managing diˋrector | of the _Windsor saˇfari ·park | Mr _Andrew ·Heyworth ˇBooth | exˎplained ||

[interview omitted]

on aˇrrival at ·Windsor | ˉNemo was ˋwinched | into his ˎnew | more ˉspacious ˎquarters || after a _day's ˊrest | he'll ˉmove ˋin | with a ˇfemale ·killer ·whale | called ˋWinnie || and it's ˬhoped | they'll be _able to ˋmate || as for ˊWinnie | she's ˉcurrently in the ·next ˋpool | but she ˋsaw ·Nemo aˇrrive | and aˋccording to her ˇtrainer | was ˉvery ˎeager | to ·meet her ˉnew ˎmate || ˉWinnie | exˇpressed her ·feelings | ˉloud and ˎclear ||

[Change of speaker: Brian Perkins]

a ˉwhale's ˏwelcome | from ˎWinnie || ˉfinally | the _headlines aˏgain | in Beiˊrut | the ˉhostage _deadlock | ·drags ˎon || ˉone ·person was ˊkilled | and ˊfive ·injured | when their ˉcar was ·hit by a ˏtrain | at a ˉlevel ·crossing in ˎHampshire || and this ·morning's ˉmain _news | a ·major seˉcurity reˏview | has been ·ordered at the ˇstate de·partment | in

ˊWashington | after a ˊgunman | ¯entered the ˏbuilding | ¯shot ·dead his ˏmother | who ↓ˇworked ·there | and _then ·killed himˎself || ¯BB_C | ¯radio ˎnews || it's ·now ¯ten past ˎeight ||

014 SPOKEN ENGLISH CORPUS TEXT B02
BBC News
Broadcast notes: Radio 4, 8.00 a.m., 22nd June, 1985
Overlap passage

Transcribed by BJW

on aˇrrival at ·Windsor | Nemo was ˋwinched into his ˇnew | more ¯spacious ˎquarters || after a ·day's ¯rest | he'll move _in with a ˇfemale ·killer whale | called ˋWinnie | and it's ¯hoped they'll be able to ˎmate || as for ˏWinnie | she's ·currently in the next ˋpool | but she ˋsaw Nemo aˇrrive | and a·ccording to her ˋtrainer was very ˋeager to meet her new ˋmate || Winnie exˇpressed her ·feelings | ·loud and ˎclear ||

[Change of speaker: Brian Perkins]

a ·whale's ¯welcome | from ˎWinnie || ¯finally the _headlines aˇgain | in Bei¯rut | the ·hostage ˏdeadlock | ·drags ˎon || ·one person was ¯killed | and ·five injured when their ¯car was _hit by a ¯train | at a ·level crossing in ˎHampshire || ↓and this ·morning's main ¯news | a ·major se¯curity re¯view has been _ordered at the ˋstate department in ¯Washington | after a ¯gunman ˬentered the ·building | ˋshot dead his ¯mother | who ˇworked ·there | and ·then killed himˎself || ·BB_C Radio ˎnews || ↓it's now ¯ten past ˎeight ||

Transcribed by GOK

on aˇrrival at ·Windsor | ¯Nemo was ˋwinched | into his ˎnew | more ¯spacious ˎquarters || after a _day's ˊrest | he'll ¯move ˋin | with a ˇfemale ·killer ·whale | called ˋWinnie || and it's ˬhoped | they'll be _able to ˋmate || as for ˊWinnie | she's ¯currently in the ·next ˋpool | but she ˋsaw ·Nemo aˇrrive | and aˋccording to her ˇtrainer | was ¯very ˎeager | to ·meet her ¯new ˎmate || ¯Winnie | exˇpressed her ·feelings | ¯loud and ˎclear ||

[Change of speaker: Brian Perkins]

a ¯whale's ˏwelcome | from ˎWinnie || ¯finally | the _headlines aˏgain | in Beiˊrut | the ¯hostage _deadlock | ·drags ˎon || ¯one ·person was ˊkilled | and ˊfive ·injured | when their ¯car was ·hit by a ˏtrain | at a ¯level ·crossing in ˎHampshire || and this ·morning's ¯main _news | a ·major se¯curity reˏview | has been ·ordered at the ˇstate de·partment | in

ˊWashington | after a ˊgunman | ˉentered the ˏbuilding | ˉshot ·dead his ˏmother | who ↓ˇworked ·there | and _then ·killed himˎself || ˉBB_C | ˉRadio ˎnews || it's ·now ˉten past ˎeight ||

015 SPOKEN ENGLISH CORPUS TEXT B03
BBC News
Broadcast notes: Radio 2, 1.00 p.m., 5th December, 1985
Transcribed by BJW

it's one o'¯clock | here's the _news ·read by David ˋGeary || the ¯latest unem ˎployment figures ¯show | a ·slight ˎfall || nearly a ·million ˋschool children in ˇScotland | have the ·day ˇoff because of a ˋstrike by their ˊteachers | and the ˋnational ·union of ˇmineworkers | con¯cede a _point to the ˎcoal board || there's been a¯nother ·fall | in the _number of people out of ˎwork | and it's a ¯genuine ˏtrend | ˋnot | a re·sult of ˋseasonal disˋtortion || the de¯partment of emˏployment says the ˋnumber of people unemˏployed | and ¯claiming ˏbenefit | last ˏmonth | was ·three ˇmillion | ·two hundred and ¯fifty-eight ˏthousand | ˋeight hundred and ·sixty-ˋeight || ¯that's a reduction of ·just under eighˎteen thousand on the Ocˋtober ·total || our in¯dustrial corres·pondent Peter ˎSmith | reˎports ||

[change of speaker: Peter Smith]

there's ˋusually little ˋchange in unemˏployment | beˋtween October and Noˋvember || with a ¯normal seasonal ˇincrease | in _out-of-work ˇadults | ˋoffset by ˋschool leavers ¯getting _jobs | or _joining ˋtraining ·schemes || but the ˋrise in ˋadults joining the ˏdole ·queues | was _much ˋsmaller than ˋusual || with the re¯sult | that the ˇreal ·trend | after ·taking all these ˋseasonal disˋtortions into aˇccount | was ˎdown || it's the ˋthird month ˇrunning | there's been a ˇgenuine reduction ˋlike this | and ¯that hasn't _happened | since _nineteen seventy-ˋnine || the em·ployment ˇsecretary | _Lord ¯Young | said the ˋfigures | added ˋweight to the ·view | that the ˋunderlying ˇtrend in unem·ployment | was _now ˋflat || ·and | we could ¯all be enˋcouraged by them || there's ˋalso en·couragement for ˋwomen ·workers || in ¯recent _months | it's ˋmen who've ˇbenefited | from the ·slackening ˋpace | of _unemˋployment || but ·now ˋthis seems to be ·helping ˋwomen as ˋwell || al¯though the number of _unemployed ˇwomen | ˋis still on the ˇincrease | there's been a ¯sharp reˋduction | in the ˋsize of that ·increase ||

[change of speaker: David Geary]

¯almost _every ˋschool in ˋScotland | has been ¯closed by a ·one-day ˎstrike | ↓by the ·country's ˋteachers | an ¯estimated ˋforty-nine ˇthousand teachers | have been ˇcalled out | by their ˇthree ·unions | who're ˋholding a ˋseries of ˇrallies around the ·country | in suˋpport of their ·cam·paign for an ˋindependent ˋpay review || aˋccording to the ˇorganisers | the ˋmain one in ˇGlasgow attracted a ¯crowd of about ·ten ˋthousand || ˋthis report from our ˇScottish affairs corre·spondent | ·Colin ˎBlane ||

[change of speaker: Colin Blane]

it's a ˋyear to the ˋday | since the ·main ¯union | the ˍeducational ˋinstitute of ˊScotland | led by ·Mr ·John ˇPollock | ·held their ¯first ˍone-day ·strike of the ¯present camˎpaign || ˏnow they've been ˏjoined by two ˇother teachers' ·unions | including the ˇsecond largest ·one | the ˍScottish ˋsecondary teachers associˋation || ·teachers' ˇleaders main·tain | it'll be the ·most disˋruptive ·single ˋstrike | in the ·history of Scottish eduˋcation || the ˋstrike's been conˋdemned | by the ·secretary of ˇstate for ·Scotland | Mr ˍGeorge ˋYounger | but John ˏPollock | of the ˍmain union EIˊS | says ·teachers only ˇlost ground in the ·past | by ˎnot ·striking ||

[change of speaker: David Geary]

ˋleaders of the ¯teaching ˋunions in ˋEngland and ˋWales | are ·meeting in ˋLondon | to discuss ˇtheir pay dis·pute || as they aˋrrived for the ¯talks | they were ˍmet by more than ·five ˋhundred | ˇstriking ·teachers | ˍchanting | ↓no ˋsellout || ↑¯leaders of the ·national union of ˬmineworkers | meeting in ˇSheffield this ·morning | de¯cided to give the ˬcoal board a co¯mmitment on producˎtivity | so that ¯talks on ˍpay could beˋgin || the ˋmove had been deˇmanded by the ·coal board | and our ˋMidlands inˇdustrial corre·spondent says | the deˋcision by the ˋNUM eˇxecutive | ˍmarks | a ˋturn-round in ·union ˋpolicy || ↑¯staff | on ¯Brent ˎcouncil in ˇLondon | are ˇmeeting to·day | to dis¯cuss the ˋsacking of ·three ˇsocial ·workers | over the ¯death of ·Jasmine ˎBeckford || ↓union ˊleaders | ↓have a¯ccused the ˍcouncil of ·making them ˋscapegoats || ↑the ˋgovernment is ex¯pected to con¯firm this afterˍnoon that ¯Britain | ¯is to withˍdraw from UˋNESCO | ↓the u¯nited ·nations ˍcultural and scienˇtific ·agency | at the ¯end of the ˎyear || ˏministers ˍmet at ·Downing ˇStreet this morning | to take a ˍfinal deˋcision | ↓and a ¯statement | will be ¯made in the ˬCommons | ¯later toˎday || ↑ˋhere's our poˇlitical corres·pondent | David ˎDavis ||

[change of speaker: David Davis]

ˋBritain's de·cision to ˋfollow the Aˋmericans | ˇout of U·NESCO | ˋwon't come as a surˋprise || the ˋnecessary ˋone year's ·notice ˇhas been given by the ·government | and ˋlike President ˇReagan | Mrs ˋThatcher was conˋvinced some time aˋgo | ↓of the ˋneed to pull ˋout || ˋeastern block

ˋinfluence inˇside UNESCO | is now ˉtoo ˋgreat | ↓the ˍgovernment beˉlieves | and reˋform from in·side is imˋpossible || so it ˋseems the ·widespread ˇpressure to stay in | has been reˎsisted || ↓it's ˉcome | ↓from the ˊcommonwealth | ↓from the ·European coˊmmunity | ↓and at ˇhome | from a ˉHouse of Commons seˍlect coˇmmittee | with a Conˋservative maˋjority || ↓the expected ˊstatement | ˊin the ˍCommons this after·noon | will be ˉmade | by the ˉoverseas deˇvelopment ·minister | Mr ·Timothy ˋRaison ||

[change of speaker: David Geary]

the ˋleader of the Aˇlliance party | in ·Northern ˇIreland | Mr John ˇKushnahan | has ·asked the ˋNorthern Ireland ˇsecretary | Mr ·Tom King | to susˉpend the ˬbusiness of the ˉNorthern ˍIreland aˋssembly || Mr ˋKushnahan says the aˇssembly | has been eˋffectively ˇhijacked by the ˋUnionist ·parties || ↑the ˋgovernment has ˋwelcomed a reˉport | by an Auˋstralian ·royal coˋmmission on the eˋffects of ·Britain's aˋtomic ·bomb ˇtesting programme | in the Auˋstralian ˇdesert | in the ·fifties and early ˋsixties || the deˉfence minister | Mr ·Norman Laˉmont | has aˇccepted an offer | to ·hold ˇtalks on the findings | with | Auˍstralian oˋfficials || ↑the ˋnephew of Miss ˋWorld organiser Julia ˇMorley | has aˉppeared in ·court in ˏLondon | accused of ˋblackmailing her ˉhusband ˇEric Morley | for ˉtwenty thousand ˎpounds || ˉEdward ˎCrozier | a former ·personal aˇssistant to the ·Morleys | who comes from ˇSydenham | in South ˍLondon | was reˉmanded on ˬbail | for a ˋmonth || now ˇshare news | the fiˋnancial times ˇindex at noon | was ˍdown ten point ˉnine | ·at one ˋthousand one ·hundred and ˋfour | ·point ˉnine | ·and | the ˊweather | ˇnorthern areas will have ˋbright intervals and ˋshowers | which will be ˇheavy in places | ˋrain in some ˇsouthern areas will clear a·way | ↓but ˉfurther rain is likely toˎmorrow || and that's the ˉnews | at ˍfive minutes past ˎone ||

015 SPOKEN ENGLISH CORPUS TEXT B03
BBC News
Broadcast notes: Radio 2, 1.00 p.m., 5th December, 1985
Overlap passage

Transcribed by GOK

the ↑ˋleader of the Aˇlliance ·party | in ·Northern ˇIreland | Mr ·John ˇKushnahan | has ·asked the ˋNorthern ·Ireland ˎsecretary | Mr ·Tom ˬKing | to su¯spend the ˎbusiness | of the ¯Northern _Ireland aˎssembly || Mr ˇKushnahan ·says the a·ssembly | has been eˋffectively ‸ ˇhijacked | by ‸ the ˎUnionist ·parties || the ↑ˋgovernment | has ˎwelcomed a reˊport | by an Au¯stralian ·royal coˎmmission | on the ·effects of ¯Britain's | aˋtomic _bomb ˇtesting ·programme | in the Auˋstralian ˇdesert | in the _fifties and ·early ˎsixties || the deˊfence ·minister | Mr ·Norman Laˇmont | has ac¯cepted an _offer | to ·hold ˇtalks on the ·findings | with Au_stralian oˎfficials || the ˋnephew of | Miss ˎWorld ·organiser | ¯Julia ˋMorley | has a¯ppeared in ·court in ˏLondon | a·ccused of ˋblackmailing her ·husband ˇEric ·Morley | for ¯twenty ·thousand ˎpounds || ¯Edward ˎCrozier | a ˋformer ·personal aˇssistant to the ·Morleys | who ·comes from ˇSydenham | in ·South ˏLondon | was re¯manded on _bail | for a ˎmonth || ↑now ˇshare ·news | the fiˋnancial ·times ˬindex | at ˏnoon | was ↓ˎdown | ↑¯ten point ˏnine | at one ˋthousand one ·hundred and ˬfour point ·nine || and ‸ the ↑ˊweather | ˇnorthern ·areas | will have ˋbright ·intervals and ˬshowers | which will be ˇheavy in ·places | ˋrain in some ˬsouthern ·areas will ·clear ˏaway | but ¯further ·rain is _likely toˎmorrow || and ·that's the ˊnews | at ↓¯five ·minutes past ˎone ||

Transcribed by BJW

the ˋleader of the Aˇlliance party | in ·Northern ˇIreland | Mr John ˇKushnahan | has ·asked the ˋNorthern Ireland ˇsecretary | Mr ·Tom King | to sus¯pend the ˬbusiness of the ¯Northern _Ireland aˋssembly || Mr ˋKushnahan says the aˇssembly | has been eˋffectively ˇhijacked by the ˋUnionist ·parties || ↑the ˋgovernment has ˋwelcomed a re¯port | by an Auˋstralian ·royal coˋmmission on the eˋffects of ·Britain's aˋtomic ·bomb ˇtesting programme | in the Auˋstralian ˇdesert | in the ·fifties and early ˋsixties || the de¯fence minister | Mr ·Norman La¯mont | has aˇccepted an offer | to ·hold ˇtalks on the findings | with | Au_stralian oˋfficials || ↑the ˋnephew of Miss ˋWorld organiser Julia ˇMorley | has a¯ppeared in ·court in ˏLondon | accused of ˋblackmailing her ¯husband ˇEric Morley | for

¯twenty thousand ˎpounds || ¯Edward ˎCrozier | a former •personal aˇssistant to the •Morleys | who comes from ˇSydenham | in South _London | was re¯manded on ˬbail | for a ˋmonth || now ˇshare news | the fiˋnancial times ˇindex at noon | was _down ten point ¯nine | •at one ˋthousand one •hundred and ˋfour | •point ¯nine | •and | the ˊweather | ˇnorthern areas will have ˋbright intervals and ˋshowers | which will be ˇheavy in places | ˋrain in some ˇsouthern areas will clear a•way | ↓but ¯further rain is likely toˎmorrow || and that's the ¯news | at _five minutes past ˎone ||

016 SPOKEN ENGLISH CORPUS TEXT B04
BBC News
Broadcast notes: Radio 3, 1.00 pm, 14th January, 1986
Transcribed by GOK

ˋnow it's ·one o'ˎclock | and ·this is ˉPeter ·Bragg in ˉLondon | ↑with the ˍRadio ·3 ˋnews ·summary || the ˉboard of ·Westland ˎhelicopters | have ˉmade ˍclear | that ·they ˋwon't ·put the ‸ ˋAnglo-·Euro·pean ˋrescue ·bid for the ˏcompany | to their ˎshareholders | ˋeven if the ‸ ˋrival Aˇmerican ·bid | ˎfails || the ˇshareholders ·meeting | ˉcalled to ˇvote on the A·merican ·offer | was adˋjourned this ˏmorning | until ˋFriday as ˎplanned || the ˋWestland ˊchairman | Sir ˍJohn ˇCuckney | ·said ‸ the ˋworkforce was ˎsuffering | be·cause of the unˋcertainty | over the ˏcompany's ˎfuture || ˊWestland | had ·gone through an ˉeight ·month ˏperiod | of ˎturbulence | which had been ·thoroughly ˋbad for the ˎstaff || Sir ˇJohn said | the ˉboard | would have a ˉnumber of conˇtingency ·plans | ˋready | in ·case they ˉdidn't sucˍceed | in ·winning eˉnough suˍpport | for the Aˎmerican ·offer || it be·came ˉclear ˍafterwards | that the Euroˇpean ·bid | was ˋnot aˎmong those ·options || and the ˉPrime ˍMinister | is exˉpected to ˍface | ˉfurther ˍcriticisms | of the ˉgovernment's ˍhandling | of the ˊWestland a·ffair | during ˋquestion ·time | in the ˎCommons | this afterˎnoon || the ˊtrade | and ˏindustry ·secretary | Mr ˋLeon ˇBrittan | ·said ‸ he's ˋnot ·planning to reˎsign | over his ·Commons ˍstatement | ˎyesterday || the con↑ˉfedeˍration | of ˉBritish ˎindustry | has ˉsaid | the ˋChancellor should ·use the ˇbudget | to ˉtry | to ˉbring ˍdown | unemˋployment | ·rather than ‸ to ·make ·widespread ˎtax ·cuts || ↑in its recommenˋdations to the ˉChancellor | the ˋCBˉI ·says | a ˉthousand ·million ˎpounds | should be ·spent on ˉjob creˎation ·measures || it ·says ‸ unemˉployment | could be ˉcut | by a ˉthird of a ˎmillion | over ˉtwo ˎyears in this ·way || the ˉCBˍI ·says ‸ if there ˇis money a·vailable for ·tax cuts | it should ˉgo on ˍraising aˎllowances | ·rather than reˉducing the ˍbasic ·rate of ˎincome ·tax || the ↑ˇbuilding so·cieties | have reˉported | a ˉgood ˎmonth | in Deˎcember || alˋthough in·vestors withˉdrew | more than ˋfour thousand ·million ˎpounds | ˉeven ˍmore | ˇnew ·money | was inˎvested || to ·give the so·cieties a ˉnet ·income | of ˋeight ·hundred and ˎsixty-·five | ˍmillion ˎpounds || ·that's the ˇhighest ·figure | for ˋany ·month | in ˉnineteen ·eighty-ˎfive || the ·secretary ˊgeneral | of the ˇbuilding so·cieties a·ssoci·ation | Mr ·Richard ˇWeir | ·said the ˉoutlook for ˬJanuary | was ˍless enˎcouraging | but there was ·no imˇmediate ·need | for an ˋincrease | in ˎinterest ·rates || and the ˉBank of ˎEngland | has ˇindicated that it ·wants | ˇbank ·interest ·rates | to ˋstay at their ·present ·level | for the

ˍtime ˎbeing || there were ˋfears ˬearlier | that ˎinterest ·rates | might ·have to ˋrise | and ˎthis ·brought a ˉfall | of ·more than ˉeighteen ˎpoints | in the Fiˍnancial ·Times ˎshare ·index || but ·prices reˉcovered ·somewhat | ·after the ˍBank of ·England's ˎsignal || at ˊnoon | the ˉFT ˏindex | was ˊdown | eˉleven point ˏeight | at ˉone ˏthousand | and ·ninety ˍseven | eˎxactly || the ↑ˉunions | at ˉFord ˎmotors | ·say ‸ the ˉcompany's ˇhourly ·paid ·workers | aˉppear to have reˎjected | a ˉtwo year ˎpay ·offer || the ˋchief ·union neˇgotiator | Mr ·Mick ˬMurphy | ·said ‸ the ˇfirst indi·cations were | that a ˉclear maˍjority | had ˍvoted aˎgainst || the oˬfficial re·sult of the ·ballot | will ˉnot be aˍnnounced | until ˋFriday | when ˉunion ˍleaders | will deˋcide ·whether to ·call for ‸ for ˋstrike ·action || the ˊoffer | de·scribed by ˬFord | as ˇfinal | would ˉgive ˋpay ·rises of be·tween | ˋthir·teen and a ˇhalf | and ˉfif·teen point ˋseven per ·cent | ·over ˍtwo ˎyears || ˉworkers from the Gartˇcosh | ˋsteel works | near ˬGlasgow | who've ˉmarched to ˊLondon | as ·part of a camˏpaign | to ·save the ·plant from ˇclosure | have ˉheld a ·meeting with the ˇLabour ·party ·leader | ·Mr ˋKinnock || but their reˋquest for a ·meeting with ·Mrs ˉThatcher | has been ˍturned ˎdown || the ˇLiberal ·leader | Mr ·David ˬSteel | deˉscribed | the ˎPrime ·Ministers deˍcision | ˇnot to ·see the ·marchers | as ‸ a ˉslap in the ·face for ˎScotland || during ˉmeetings this ˏmorning | with a ˉnumber of MˏPs | the ˋmen ·said they beˉlieved | the ˉwhole of ·Scottish ˎsteel ·industry | would be at ˏrisk | if ˍGartcosh ˎclosed || the ↑ˋPrime ·Minister of ·South ˎYemen | who's in ˬIndia | has postˋponed a ·trip to ˎChina | ·after the aˍttempted ˋcoup ‸ in his ·country || a ˉspokesman for the ·Prime ·Minister ·said | ˋno infor·mation had been re·ceived from ˬAden | for the ˍpast two ˎdays || he deˉscribed the situ·ation ˍthere as ‸ ˍabˎnormal || ·Aden ˊRadio | ·said ˏyesterday | that the ˋleaders of a ˬplot | to aˋssassinate the ˬPresident | had been ˎexecuted || there's ˇsince been | ˋuncon·firmed reˍports of ˎfighting || the ˉNorthern ˇIreland ·secretary | Mr ˉTom ˬKing | has ˉsaid | that the ˋforth·coming ˇbyelections | ·caused by the ·resig·nation of ˎfifteen ˇunionist M·Ps | will ˋnot ·change | the ·government's suˉpport | for the ˍAnglo-·Irish aˎgreement || at a ˋnews ·conference in ·Belˉfast | Mr ˇKing ‸ ·said | there was ˋno way that the ˉbyelections | could ˍoverturn a ·vote in ˎparliament || the aˉgreement | was eˉstablished || and ˍwould go ˎforward || he ·said he was aˉvailable for ˋtalks with poˎlitical ·leaders | in the ˎprovince || the Con↑ˇservative ·party ·chairman | Mr ·Norman ˬTebbit | has ·had an opeˊration | at ·Stoke ˇMandeville ·hospital | in ˎBuckinghamshire | for ˋinjuries he ·received in the ˉBrighton ˎbomb a·ttack | ·fifteen ˎmonths a·go || a ˉspokesman ˍsaid | ˋeverything had ˍgone ˎwell | and Mr ˉTebbit | ˍspent a ·comfortable ˎnight || he's ex·pected to ¯stay in ˏhospital | for _up to ·two ˎweeks || and ˏfinally the ˎweather ·forecast || it will be ¯very ˎwindy | with ¯showers | in ˊmany _areas | and ¯snow ^ on the ˎhills || the ·wind and ¯showers | will ·die ˎdown ·somewhat | toˎnight || and that's the ·end of the ·news and ˊweather | with ↑the _time | ˎjust ·after _five past ˎone ||

016 SPOKEN ENGLISH CORPUS TEXT B04
BBC News
Broadcast notes: Radio 3, 1.00 pm, 14th January, 1986
Overlap passage

Transcribed by BJW

↓at a ˋnews ·conference in ·Bel¯fast | Mr ¯King | said there was ˋno way that the ¯byelections could ˇoverturn | a _vote in ˋparliament || the aˋgreement was e¯stablished | and _would go ˋforward || he ˋsaid he was a¯vailable for ˋtalks with poˋlitical ·leaders | ↓in the ˋprovince || the Conˋservative ·party ¯chairman | Mr ¯Norman ˎTebbit | has ˋhad an opeˊration | at _Stoke ˇMandeville hospital | in ˋBuckinghamshire || for ˋinjuries he re¯ceived | in the ·Brighton ˇbomb a·ttack | ·fifteen ˋmonths ago || a ¯spokesman _said ˋeverything had gone ˋwell | ↓and Mr ¯Tebbit | _spent a _comfortable ˋnight || he's ex·pected to ¯stay in _hospital | for _up to two ˋweeks || and _finally the ˋweather forecast || it will be ·very ˎwindy with ¯showers | in ¯many _areas | and ¯snow | on the ˎhills || the ·wind and ¯showers | will die ˎdown somewhat | toˎnight || ↓and _that's the ¯end of the ·news and ·weather | with the _time just after ·five past ˋone ||

Transcribed by GOK

at a ˋnews ·conference in ·Bel¯fast | Mr ˇKing ‸ ·said | there was ˋno way that the ¯byelections | could _overturn a ·vote in ˎparliament || the a¯greement | was e¯stablished || and _would go ˎforward || he ·said he was a¯vailable for ˋtalks with poˎlitical ·leaders | in the ˎprovince || the Con↑ˇservative ·party ·chairman | Mr ·Norman ˬTebbit | has ·had an opeˊration | at ·Stoke ˇMandeville ·hospital | in ˎBuckinghamshire | for ˋinjuries he ·received in the ¯Brighton ˎbomb a·ttack | ·fifteen ˎmonths a·go || a ¯spokesman _said | ˋeverything had _gone ˎwell | and Mr ¯Tebbit | _spent a ·comfortable ˎnight || he's ex·pected to ¯stay in ˏhospital | for _up to ·two ˎweeks || and ˏfinally the ˎweather ·forecast || it will be ¯very ˎwindy | with ¯showers | in ˊmany _areas | and ¯snow ‸ on the ˎhills || the ·wind and ¯showers | will ·die ˎdown ·somewhat | toˎnight || and that's the ·end of the ·news and ˊweather | with ↑the _time | ˎjust ·after _five past ˎone ||

017 SPOKEN ENGLISH CORPUS TEXT C01
The Reith Lectures 1985 - III
(First part)
Broadcast notes: Radio 4, 7.45 pm, 20th November, 1985
Transcribed by BJW

ˇlast week | I ¯showed my ˏhand | as the ˇprice mechanist | that I ˋam | ↓and I ˊargued | ↓with the ˋhelp of my ˋfictional ·colleague Mr MacˇQuedy | that ˋindividual ¯willingness to ˏpay | should be the ˇmain test | of ˋhow resources are ˋused || you may reˏcall | that we made ˏfun | of a ˋnumber of ·soap-ˋopera ˇnotions | of ·do-it-yourˇself eco·nomics | ˍDIY¯E || in ˇthis lecture | I want to enˋlarge | on the ˋcontrast | ↓between ˋDIY¯E | and ˋeconomic ˋorthodoxy ||

I ¯want to consider ˬfirst | an ˇaspect of DIY·E | which ˇI call | ˋunreflecting ˋcentralism || it has ˏtwo | ¯mutually suˍpporting ˋelements || ˏone | is the ¯disposition to aˏssume | that ·outcomes ˇhave to be ·planned | and de·cided by ˋgovernments || the ˇsecond | is the ¯tendency to ˇthink | of ¯governments | ˇand states | as the ¯principal | or ·even the ˋonly actors | ↓on the ·economic ˏscene | and to aˋttribute to them ¯roles | and ˇfunctions | which ˍaren't neceˍssarily ˋtheirs ||

a good eˋxample of this tendency | aˏppeared | ↓in a ¯speech which I had the pleasure of ˏhearing | in ˇBrussels | ·last ˏyear | by the ˍIrish Prime ˋMinister | Dr ˍGarret FitzˋGerald || ˇinterestingly | Dr FitzˇGerald | is one of ˇtwo Prime Ministers | within the ·European Coˇmmunity | ↑who ˏcount as proˍfessional eˋconomists || the ˇother | ↓being the ·Prime Minister of ˊGreece | Dr Anˍdreas Papanˋdreou || ˇin his speech | he deˎscribed himself | enˇgagingly | as an eˇconomist on ˎleave || ·nevertheˋless | in reˋviewing the ·problems of the Coˇmmunity | he adˍvanced a ·prize ˇspecimen | of ·unreflecting ˋcentralism ||

↑for ˍDoctor FitzˏGerald | there are ˇtwo | ˋeconomic ˋsuperpowers | the Uˇnited ·States | and Jaˎpan || ˇand he ·argued | a¯ttempts to comˏpete on an ¯equal ˏbasis | in the ¯economic ˏsphere | ˋwith these ˇsuperpowers | by ·indeˇpendent indiˋvidual ˇaction | are ¯quite ˏsimply | ¯bound to ˎfail ||

the ·moral ˇdrawn by Dr Fitz·Gerald | in ·common with many ˇother influential ·people | ˋis that the ¯governments of the ˍEuropean Coˏmmunity | must take con¯certed ˏaction | to ˋstrengthen the comˋpetitive poˇsition | of the Coˋmmunity as a ˇwhole | ˋvis-a-vis the Uˇnited ·States | ↓and Jaˋpan ||

ˋthis argument aˏssumes | that ·compeˋtition in the markets of the ˏworld | is between ˋstates || and that only ˇlarge states | can suˏccessfully enˍgage ˋin it || ˉboth propoˍsitions | ↓are ˋfalse || ˏcompetition | is ˏlargely between a ˏmultitude of ·business ˋenterprises | of ˉall ˎkinds | over a ˉwide ·range of ˍproducts and ˎmarkets || ↑it's ˎtrue | that ·governments can ˋinfluence the ˇoutcome | of the com·petitive ˏprocess | in ·various ˏways | ˏand | that parˍticular business ˇenterprises | can be ˍowned | or ˏbacked by ˋgovernments || but ˋeven when this is aˋllowed for | it's not ˋstates | ↓that are ˉgenerally the ˏsole | or the ˋprincipal ·parties | to the ˉvast aˍrray of indiˇvidual tran·sactions | aˋround the ˏworld | ↑in ˏwhich the comˏpetitive ˍprocess | ↓takes ˋshape ||

as to ˇlarge states | being ˉnecessarily more suˋccessful on the con·temporary economic ˏscene || ˋthis notion is hard to ˋreconcile with the ˊfact | that in ˇEurope | it's two ˇsmall countries | ˍSweden and ˇSwitzerland | ˋwhich by conˇventional tests | are ˏpossibly the ˏmost ecoˏnomically adˋvanced || the ˏproducts of ˏSwedish | and ·Swiss ˇenterprises | have for ˋdecades | comˉpeted suˍccessfully on world ˏmarkets | without ˋbenefit of conˉcerted | ˍtransnational | inˋdustrial ˇstrategies | ↑of the ˏkind that are ˏnow so ˏfavoured in oˍfficial and ·business ˉcircles | wiˍthin the European Coˋmmunity || if we look outˇside Europe | and at the ˉgrowth of income per ˏhead | and of ˏexports to ·world ˏmarkets | the outˉstanding suˏccess stories | of the ˉpast two ˏdecades | are to be ˍfound among the deˇveloping countries | ↓of ˉEast and ˍSouth-East ˋAsia || ·three of the ˇmost successful | Hong ˉKong | ↓Singaˍpore and Taiˊwan | ↓are ˊsmall | while ˋnone of the group is very ˇlarge || in ˋany case | it's ˋnot the ˇgovernments of these ·countries | through conˋcerted action among themˇselves | that have a·chieved rapidly increasing ˏshares | in ex·panding world ˏmarkets || ˋthis has been the ˇwork | of ˏindividual ˋenterprises | ˇhelped | it should be ˋsaid | by government ˇpolicies | which have proˋvided an enˇvironment | in which ·enterprises could ·grow and ˇflourish || but which have ˇnot been based | on the misˉtaken aˏssumption | that ·competition on world ˉmarkets | is ˏlargely | between ˎstates ||

ˉlet me ˍquote aˋnother | oˉfficial ˏinstance | of ˏunreflecting ˏcentralism | which will ·take us ˏback | into ˋenergy policy || a ˉfew ˏyears ago | in an ˋinteresting ·letter to The ˏTimes | about the Uˋnited Kingdom nuclear ˇpower programme | ↑a ˍformer ˍsenior British government oˏfficial | ↓Peter ˊVinter | ob·served that ˇas a nation | we have ˉnot yet suˏcceeded in ¯setting ˏup | an eˏffective | ¯nuclear re_actor conˋstruction company || I _think his ·point is a ˇfair one | and perˏhaps he'd say the same toˋday || but ·why ˋshould it | be the co¯llective responsiˏbility | ↓of ¯we as a ˇnation | to eˋstablish a ·nuclear reactor con·struction company || ˇwhy should such a ·company | if inˋdeed there's a ˇplace for it | not eˏmerge | from the ˇimpersonal | com_petitive seˇlection process | of ˇmarkets | without ˇbenefit | of ˇhigh-level | o_fficial coˋmmittees ||

the ˇhistory | of ¯British nuclear ˏpower programmes | ¯over the past thirty ˏyears | ↑pro_vides a de¯pressing eˎxample | of ¯unreflecting _centralism in ˋaction || ˋstoutly reinˋforced | _I may ˊadd | by ˇother forms | of _DIYˋE || ˋone aspect of this ˏcentralism | is the iˇdea | which has been em¯braced by su·ccessive British _governments of ˇboth parties | that a ˏchoice | ˋhas to be made | at ˇCabinet level | of ¯one parˏticular reˇactor system | for _future nuclear ˋpower stations | in ˎBritain || _here for ˊinstance | is Mr ·David ˋHowell | giving ·evidence to a House of _Commons Select Coˊmmittee | in _nineteen-ˊeighty | ˋwhen he was ·Secretary of State for ˊEnergy | ·under Mrs ˎThatcher || ¯we must deˏvelop | a ¯sound | ·thermal reactor ˎstrategy he ·said || ↑we're _virtually the ¯only major in·dustrialised ˏcountry | wiˋthout | a ·chosen reˇactor system | a_vailable for ˇserious ˋordering || we can ¯not conˏtinue | to ˏrun | ˇtwo systems | inˎdefinitely ||

here aˊgain | ↓it's ¯we as a ˇnation | with Her ·Majesty's Government as ˇagent | that ˏhas to deˎcide these things || in Mr ¯Howell's _world | in the ¯world of his ⌄predecessors | ¯and his su⌄ccessors | and their o¯fficial adˏvisers | ˋno other ˋpractical ˋpossibility | eˎxists || it's been _taken for ˋgranted | whatˋever the ↑ˋparty in ¯office | ↓that the ¯Secretary of State for ˊEnergy | ˋor inˋdeed the ¯Cabinet itˋself | must de¯termine the _size | of the ¯nuclear power ˊprogramme | the _choice of reˊactor | ¯and the appropriate ˎstructure | for the ¯nuclear ˎindustry ||

↑but in _fact | there ˋare other ·ways of handling these ·issues || a few ˏyears ago | an interesting ˏarticle | made me aˏware of how nuclear ˏpower had de·veloped in ˎSwitzerland || the ˇtitle of the article | sigˇnificantly was | ↑how _Switzerland has ˇbenefited | from the ¯market aˎpproach || ↑at the ˏtime | when it aˏppeared | there were ˋfour ¯nuclear re_actors in ope·ration wiˇthin ·Switzerland | at _three different ˋpower stations || ↓the ·choice of reˊactors | as of ˋother systems | and e·quipment ˇin the stations | was ˏmade | ˋnot by the ·federal ˇgovernment | but _by the indi_vidual uˋtilities con·cerned || which are ˋsmall | by ˇBritish standards | since the _Swiss electricity suˇpply industry | is _much more deˋcentralised || ˇtwo |

ˋdifferent re•actor systems | have been ˉchosen | and ˍare in opeˎration || a•ccording to the ˇarticle | the ˍfour operating ˇnuclear units | were ˍbuilt in reˋmarkably good ˊtime | ˋand within their o•riginal •cost ˋbudget || an aˋchievement I might ˋadd | which is in ˉmarked ˋcontrast | with ˇBritish results | over the ˍpast two ˋdecades || as to ˇoperating per•formance | ↑a •recent comˍparative ˏtable | ↓shows the •load factors a•chieved ˉround the ˏworld | by ˉtwo hundred and thirty-ˏtwo | •nuclear reˋactors || taking ˇcumulative performance | over the •whole operating ˇlives of these re•actors | ↓the ˊbest | of the •Swiss quarˊtet | was •ranked ˇthird | out of the ˋtwo hundred and thirty-ˊtwo | while the ˇworst was •placed | at ˍtwenty-ˋninth ||

one ˇreason for •centralism | which a•pplies in ˉenergy ˏpolicy | and a ˋnumber of ˇother fields | is the unˉcritical aˏcceptance | of •what I called ˇlast week | eˇssentialist | iˎdeas || in the ˇcase of energy | ˉeach ˏcountry is perˏceived as having ˉneeds which ˍmust be ˎmet || and ˉeach national ˇgovernment | as having an ineˋscapable responsiˇbility | to anˏticipate | and proˇvide for these ˎneeds || in the more ˇrustic treatments of these •questions | ↓ˏreference is ˏmade to a •possible •energy ˋgap | which the •government has to enˏsure | ↓is ˎbridged || •even in more soˋphisticated oˇfficial presentations | ˉgovernments usually aˏppear | as indiˉspensable proˎviders || here aˇgain is David •Howell | from his ˏperiod as ˏSecretary of ˏState for ˋEnergy ||

↑the ˏGovernment | ↓in Mr ˇHowell's view | ˉmust enˏsure | that we have eˋnough energy in the ˏfuture | to ˉheat our ˍhomes | and to ˉpower our ˎindustries || ˍfailure to aˊchieve this | could mean ˉlower living standards for us ˍall | and a ˉvery severe conˏstraint | on our soˎciety ||

so eˇssentialism | leads ˉnaturally | to ˍunreflecting ˋcentralism || also ˏhere in its ˏplace | on the ˉDIYE ˏstage | is ˏMr Micawber's diˋchotomy || •either | •we-as-a-ˏnation | have eˇnough energy | or we ˎdon't || ↑but ˍwho's to ˋsay | how •much ˋis enough || you'll •search in ˋvain | in oˋfficial White ˇPapers | and staˋtistical publiˇcations | for ˋfigures | showing •national energy ˇneeds || for the ˍsimple ˏreason that the ˏconcept | can be •neither deˏfined | ↑nor ˎmeasured || ↓if you ˏask someone who ˍuses the ˇterm | what ˋare the ˇcurrent | or proˇspective | ˍenergy ˊneeds | of the United ˏKingdom || the ˉonly answer you'll ˏget | is a ˏfigure which reˏlates to deˋmand || in ˉother ˏwords | to ˏactual or proˏspective ˋpurchases | of ˉenergy ˎproducts || deˇmand | is iˉdentified with ˏneeds | for ˉno better ˏreason | than that ˇenergy | ˉlike ˏfood | is ˋcast in the ˋsoap-opera ˉscript | as eˎssential ||

ˋthis takes ˉno aˇccount of the ·fact | that not ˇall purchases of a ·product | or ˏservice | are of ·equal ˋvalue | to ·those who ˋmake them || to ·class ˇall energy purchases | indiˇscriminately as eˏssential | is to ˏmiss the ˏpoint | that ˏmost tranˏsactions take ˏplace at | the ˋmargin || and at the ˇmargin | ˉenergy ˏproducts | ↓like ˉother ·products | are ˏgenerally ˏvalued | by ˉpeople and by ˏbusinesses | ˉat the ˍprices | which they ˇshow themselves | as ˍwilling to ˋpay for them ||

↑and ˍthere's a simple ˋproof | to ˋhand || ˍpurchases of ·energy reˊspond | to ˋchanges in relative ˇprices | which they ˋwouldn't | if they were ˇliterally | reˇquirements | that ˋhad to be ˋmet || beˉtween nineteen seventy-ˏthree | and nineteen ˏeighty-three | the ˉreal national ˏproduct | of the United ˏKingdom | in ·other ˉwords | the ·total ˏoutput of ˍgoods and ˏservices || ˋrose | by ˏsomething like ˏten per ˎcent || if there were inˋdeed national reˋquirements for ˇenergy | in any ˋliteral ˋsense | ˇthese | would no ˏdoubt have ˏrisen ˏsomewhat in reˋsponse || but ·over these ten ˉyears | ˍestimated inland ·energy conˏsumption | ·actually ˋfell | by ˍmore than ·ten per ˎcent || ↑ˋthis of ·course was ˋnot because the ˋgovernment ˋfailed in its su·pposed ˋduty as proˇvider | ↑but ˏlargely | because ˍenergy prices rose conˇsiderably | in reˏlation to ˋother prices || the ˍpattern of expenditure ·changed aˏccordingly | ↑reˍflecting indiˉvidual deˏcisions | ˏbased on | ˏwillingness to ˎpay ||

now at ˇthis point | I ·fancy I hear the ˉgroans | from ˍsome of my pro·fessional ˎcolleagues || ˉHenderson they're ˍsaying | is ˉwasting the Reith ˏLectures | labouring ˉpoints | ↓which are faˉmiliar | to ˉevery first-year ecoˉnomics student | and ˍaren't imˏportant ˋanyway || ˉwell | as to imˇportance | ˉI shall let the ˍevidence that I've preˏsented | and ˇwill present | ˍspeak for itˎself || ˋas to familiˇarity | I'd make ˋtwo responses to the ˋcritics || ˏfirst | they're ˋbadly ˋout of ˋtouch | with ·first-year ecoˇnomics ·students | ↑and ˏsecond | they should ˏnote | that inˉtuitive economic iˏdeas | have ·cast their ˇspell | not ˋonly on our ˋeminent pro·fessional ˇcolleague | Dr FitzˇGerald | ↑but ˏalso | on Mr ˋHowell || who himˋself | has a ˉfirst class deˏgree | in ecoˋnomics ||

↑both in the ˇenergy ·field | ˇand else·where | eˇssentialist i·deas | ˉlend suˏpport | to aˇnother aspect of DIY·E || the beˍlief that ˇautarchy | or ˉnational self-suˏfficiency | is an imˏportant ˎgoal || ↑here's a ˇrecent illu·stration | from the ˏEuropean Coˏmmission | in ˋBrussels || ↓the Commissioner for ˊIndustry | ˏKarl Heinz ˏNarjes | was ·quoted as ˏsaying | that ˉcurrent Commission ˏpolicy | seeks to en·courage ˉfood self-su˅fficiency | in de¯veloping ˏcountries | as the ¯only re_liable ¯long-term soˏlution to ·their ˎneeds ||

the iˋdea that it's imˋportant | for de¯veloping _countries to become ·self-suˋfficient | ↑in ˏfood | is ˏwidely | and unˋcritically aˏccepted | ˋnot just in ˋBrussels || ·but from the ˋorthodox ˋeconomic ¯standpoint | it's wi_thout founˋdation || ↑there's ˋno ¯magic a_ccession of ˏstrength | that a ¯country deˏrives | from re¯ducing imports of _food to ˅zero | ·whether for individual co¯mmodities | ·or across the whole ˎrange || ↑Hong ˏKong | ↑has de_veloped over the past three ˏdecades | ↑as _rapidly per_haps as ¯any _country in ˎhistory || it's at _present de·pendent on ˏimports | for a˅pproximately ¯seven-_eighths of its ·food conˎsumption || there's ¯no reason to suˏppose | that it would have ·gained in the ˏpast | ˋor would ¯gain in the ˎfuture | from de¯liberate o¯fficial aˎttempts | to bring ˋdown this ·ratio || while a ˅hundred per cent ·self-sufficiency | would be ab˅surdly ˋcostly || ·neither in Hong ˏKong | nor ·anywhere ˋelse | does it ¯make _sense to ˅specify | as an ¯aim of ˏpolicy || ¯on the ˏbasis of ¯soap-opeˏratic ¯intuˏition aˏlone | a par·ticular ˏratio of do¯mestic pro·duction | to ¯total conˎsumption || this generaliˏsation aˏpplies to ¯all ˏproducts | in¯cluding ˏfood | ˋand to all ˋcountries | ↓whether ¯rich | or ˎpoor ||

for ↑˅some ·people | this ˋstatement of ˋorthodox ˋeconomic ˅doctrine | ¯may a_ppear too unˋqualified || since it ¯fails to _mention ex˅plicitly | se_curity of suˋpply || ˏoften | though not ˅always | the ˋcase for self-su·fficiency is ˅argued | with ¯reference to a ·country's ·need to en_sure se˅curity | by ¯minimising deˏpendence on ˏforeign ˎsources || the ¯outside world is ˏseen | ↓at ˊbest | as unre˅liable | and ·subject to insta˅bility | ↑at ˏworst | as _actively ˋhostile || from this ˋfortress-men˅tality ˅standpoint | ˅autarchy aˏppears to be _common ˎprudence || _two sets of ¯measures | then suˏggest them·selves | ↓ˏone | is to ˏbuild up do¯mestic production of eˊssentials | _so as to reduce ¯imports | to a ˊminimum || ↑the ˏother | is to restrict ˋexports | so as to en˅sure | that do·mestic su˅pplies | are a_vailable for do·mestic ˎuse ||

017 SPOKEN ENGLISH CORPUS TEXT C01
The Reith Lectures 1985 - III
(Second part)
Broadcast notes: Radio 4, 7.45 pm, 20th November, 1985
Transcribed by GOK

for ↑ˇsome ·people | this ¯statement of ˋorthodox eco·nomic ˬdoctrine | ¯may aˏppear | _too unˋqualified || since it ˎfails to ·mention exˇplicitly | se_curity of suˎpply || ˏoften | ·though not ˇalways | the ˋcase for ·self-su_fficiency is ˇargued | with ˎreference to a ·country's ·need to en·sure seˇcurity | by ¯minimising de_pendence | on _foreign ˎsources || the ˋoutside ·world is ˏseen | at ˊbest | as unreˇliable | and ·subject to instaˬbility | at ˏworst | as _actively ˎhostile || ¯from this ˎfortress-·menˇtality | ˏstandpoint | ˇautarchy | aˏppears | to be ·common ˎprudence || ·two sets of ˏmeasures | then suˏggest them·selves | ˏone is to ·build up | do_mestic pro·duction of eˏssentials | ·so as to re·duce ˏimports | to a ˏminimum | ↑the ˏother | is to re·strict ˋexports | ·so as to enˬsure | that do¯mestic suˇpplies | ↑are a_vailable | for do_mestic ˎuse ||

↑¯not surˏprisingly | the ˎtendency to ˇthink in these ·terms | has been ˋstrengthened in ˬrecent ·years | ↑by de_velopments | on ·inter_national ˎenergy ·markets || and in parˇticular | by the two ˬoil ·crises | of _nineteen ·seventy-·three to ˏfour | ↑and _nineteen ·seventy- ˏnine to ˋeighty || ¯here for eˏxample | is the ˋthen ·President of the U_nited ˏStates | ˊRichard ˏNixon | in an A¯ddress to the ˏNation | in Noˋvember ·nineteen ·seventy- ˇthree | ¯launching the ˏprogramme | ˏknown | as _Project Indeˋpendence ||

¯let us ˏset | as our ¯national ˏgoal | that by the ¯end of this ˇdecade | we will have de¯veloped the po_tential | to ·meet our ˋown ·energy ^ ˏneeds | wi¯thout deˏpending | on ˇany | ¯foreign ˎsources ||

aˏgain | the A·merican ·Energy Seˇcurity ·Act | of ·nineteen ˏeighty | ·laid down a spe¯cific ˏprogramme | for re·ducing deˏpendence | on im·ported ˏoil | ¯through the proˏduction | of at ¯least | ¯five hundred _thousand ˏbarrels | of ¯crude ·oil per ˏday | of ¯synthetic ˎfuel | by ¯nineteen ·eighty- ˎseven || ˏalso in ·nineteen ·eighty | ·following the ·second ˬoil ·crisis | the ˇthen | ˋLiberal ·government of ˇCanada | a_dopted | a _compre·hensive | _National ˎEnergy ·Programme || ·one of the ¯three ˇprecepts | for ·federal ˏaction | underˏlying it | was ·stated as being to e¯stablish the ·basis for Ca·nadians | to ˋseize con·trol of their

ˉown ·energy ˊfuture | through seˉcurity of suˍpply | and ˉultimate indeˇpendence | of the ˍworld ˎmarket ||

ˊwell | ˉwhat's the ·orthodox e·conomist's reˎsponse | to these ˎarguments | and to the ˎpolicies | ˎbased on them || Mr MacˇQuedy | would aˋgree | that the ˎquestion of se·curity of suˬpply | has to be ˇfaced | by ˬgovernments | as ˋwell as by ·other ˬagents | wiˍthin an eˎconomy || ˏand | that it may ˉwell be ·worth ˍwhile | to inˋcur some ·extra ˋcost | ·at the ˏmargin | to aˇchieve | a ˍhigher deˋgree of se·curity || but ·Mr Mac·Quedy does ˇnot ·share | the ˍfortress menˇtality | ˉnor | does he ˉthink ˏmuch | of the ˬkinds | of auˉtarchic ˏmeasures | that are ˍprompted ˎby it ||

ˉone ˇreason | for ˬscepticism | is the eˍventual ˋfate | of the ˬenergy ·policies | that were ˋlaunched | in reˎsponse | to the ˉoil ·crises | of the ˍnineteen ˎseventies || ˉwho now re↑ˋmembers | ↓ˉProject Indeˎpendence || in ·nineteen seventy- ˏthree | the ·year in ·which it was ˏlaunched | with such ˏfanfare | the ·estimated ˏshare | of Uˍnited ·States ˏenergy con·sumption | suˬpplied | ˇby do·mestic ·sources | was ·eighty- ˍfive per ˋcent || in ·nineteen ˊeighty | when the ˇauthors of ·Project Inde·pendence | had enˏvisaged | that it would ·be a·pproaching a ˇhundred per cent | it ˉwas in ˍfact | ·eighty- ˋsix per ·cent || ·as for the ·nineteen ˇeighty | ·US syn·thetic ˊfuel ·target | of ·five hundred ·thousand ˍbarrels | of ˏoil e·quivalent | per ˏday | by ·nineteen eighty- ˏseven | the ˉlikely ˋoutcome | in ˉthat ˍyear | is ˋsomething | ˋvery ·much ˇlower | ·possibly ˉten | or fifˋteen ·thousand ·barrels per ·day || and ˉthis is ˋfortunate | because if the ˋtarget had been ˬreached | the ˉcosts in·volved | would have been iˇnordinately | ˎhigh || the Caˏnadian | ·National ˏEnergy ·Programme | of ·nineteen ˏeighty | no ˇlonger | eˋxists as ·such || the ˏaim | of ˉisolating ˏCanada | from ·world ˉenergy ˇmarkets | has been ↑aˎbandoned ||

↑it's ˎtrue | that ˉsuch ˏfailures | and reˉversals of ˏpolicy | are ˍpartly ·due | to the ˏfact | that ˏgovernments | like indiˋviduals | can ˬeasily | ˉmisˋjudge the ·future ·course of e·vents || but ˉeven if eco·nomic ·change were more preˇdictable | ↑there would reˎmain | ˉbasic obˎjections | from the ˇorthodox ·point of ·view | to the ˇkinds | of auˉtarchic ˏpolicies | ˉwhich are aˏssociated | with eˇssentialism | and the ˍfortress menˋtality ||

↑in parˇticular | it's ˬwrong | to ·think of se·curity of suˏpply | in eˇssentialist | ˎterms || se·curity of suˏpply | is ↑ˉnot | a ·separate di·mension of ˎchoice || it's ˍone of the ecoˋnomic | ˎaspects | like ˉother

·features | of the ˏquality | of a ˏpurchase | such as reliaˇbility | in ˏservice | it _has a ˋvalue | and the ¯best indiˇcation of this ·value | is ·willingness to ·pay at the ˎmargin || this can _easily be ˋseen | in ·those ·markets where _buyers | are ·offered a free ˇchoice | between inte¯rruptible | and ˎnon-inte·rruptible | suˇpply ·contracts | ↑and more ˎgenerally | con·side_rations | of seˏcurity | ˋdo a·ffect deˏcisions | about ¯how far a·head to ·make coˏmmitments | ↑and _what sort of _contracts | to ˎsign || ˋjust as there are ˋno pre·cisely de·fined _national ˬneeds | that ·have to be ˏmet | re¯gardless of ˬcost | ˇso | there are ·no ove¯rriding reˏquirements | for ¯uninte·rrupted suˏpply | which can be i¯dentified | in ¯central buˏreaucracies | ↑and _used | as a _basis for ˎpolicies ||

to ˇsee | where ¯this argument ˏleads | ¯let's con·sider _export prohiˎbitions || aˏccording | to ¯do-it-your·self ecoˏnomics | these are ˇcalled for | ↑in the _case of ˏproducts | that are both e¯ssential | and ˎscarce || ·British ˏpolicies | towards ¯North ·Sea | ˏoil | and ˏgas | pro¯vide an illuˎstration || ¯governments have con_sistently | ¯ruled ˎout | ¯exports of ˏgas | ↑on the ˏgrounds | that ¯estimated reˏserves | are too ˋlimited || in ˇthis ·case | ¯scarcity's ˏviewed | as ˎchronic || ↑by ˏcontrast | ·exports of ˇcrude ·oil | are ·generally unreˬstricted | though ·subject to ˋlicence || it's ˇclear how·ever | that ¯freedom to ˏexport | is ·liable to be curˬtailed | in _periods of ˎshortage || ·just be_fore the ·general e·lection of ·nineteen seventy- ˇnine | the ˋthen ·Secretary of ·State for ˇEnergy | ·Tony ˬBenn | ↑was re_ported | as ·having re_acted to ˏnews | that an ˬoil ·company | ˎoperating in the ·North ˏSea | had ¯seriously conˏsidered | cutting ˋback on su·pplies in ˏBritain | and _selling the ˏsurplus | at ˇhigher ·prices | in ˎEurope || his reˇaction was | to ·ask the ˇchairmen | of ˋall the ·major oil ˏcompanies | ˇoperating ·here | to ·give him their ¯personal aˏssurances | that they were ¯not taking adˏvantage | of the ¯general oil ˏshortage | in ·this ˎway ||

shortly ˇafterwards | it was reˏported | of Mr ·Benn's Con¯servative sucˏcessor | David ˏHowell | that he'd ¯started | a di¯screet | but ¯forceful ˏsqueeze | on ¯North Sea ˏoil companies | to keep ˇmore | of their pro¯duction at ˎhome || the ˬsqueeze | ¯had to be diˋscreet | since ˇformal re·strictions | might ˎwell have been ·hard to ˬreconcile | with obliˋgations | which ·Britain has aˏssumed | as a ·member ˋboth of the Euro·pean Coˆmmunity | ˎand of the ·Inter_national ˋEnergy ·Agency || but it ˎcould neverthe↑ˋless | be ˇforceful | ·since an _oil company that ·failed to reˏspond | ·might ·prejudice its _chances of sucˏcess | ↑in the _next ·round of appliˏcations | for _North Sea ˋlicences || the ¯situation ·hasn't ˎchanged | since those ¯early ˏdays | of Mrs _Thatcher's ·prime

ˎministership || if a¯nother oil ·crisis aˏrose | ↑¯ways would ·probably be ˎfound | whaˋtever ·government was in ˏpower | to ¯safeguard the ˇprinciple | laid ˋdown by ·Mr ˏHowell | in a ¯speech | of June ·nineteen seventy- ˊnine | that the ¯interests | of ¯British conˏsumers | must ·come ˎfirst ||

↑in ˏcases | ˇlike ·oil and ·gas | it's con_sidered iˋrrelevant | that ˎexports ·might co_mmand | a _higher ˋprice | than doˎmestic ·sales || ¯prohi_bitions | should ¯still aˎpply || inˋdeed | ˎHamish ˇGray | who at the ¯time | was Con¯servative ·Minister of ˊState | at the ·Department of ˇEnergy | ↑was re_ported a ·few years aˏgo | as _having coˇmmitted him·self | while ·speaking of a parˇticular | ˎNorth ·Sea ˇgasfield | to the re↑ˋmarkable ˇstatement | that ·Britain ¯wouldn't con·sider ˏselling | ¯its ˏshare | of the ¯Statfjord ˏgas | whaˇtever ·price | a ¯foreign ˏbuyer | _might ˎoffer ||

¯this conˇception | of ¯national ˏinterest | is ¯not ˏshared | by ·Mr MacˎQuedy || for ˏhim | the ¯test | of ¯willingness to ·pay at the ˏmargin | ˋdoesn't ·cease to hold ˏgood | ¯just beˏcause | _national ˋfrontiers are in·volved || ·how much par_ticular ˏexports | are ¯worth to the eˏconomy | deˋpends on the ·value of the ˇimports | for _which they can ·be exˋchanged | which in ˏturn de·pends | on ˏhow much | ˏforeigners | are preˏpared | to ˋpay for them || ˋwhy should do·mestic con_sumers | of the ¯product conˏcerned | be ·given un¯limited ˋpreference | ·or inˋdeed | _any ·preference at ˋall || suc_cessive ·British ˇgovernments | have reˎjected | ¯any suˋggestion | that in ˎnormal ˇcircumstances | do¯mestic conˏsumers | should pay ˋless | than the ·world ˎprice | for ¯North Sea ˎoil || and the eˎxistence of a ˇshortage | ¯doesn't a·ffect the ˏlogic | that ¯underˏlies | this ¯non-di·scriminatory ˎpolicy || suˇppose for e·xample | that ¯oil will _fetch | a ˋhundred ·dollars a ˊbarrel | on the ·inter_national ˎmarket || ˏthen | the ¯value to the eˏconomy | of a ¯barrel of ˏoil | ·sold ˇon that ·market | is a _hundred ˋdollars | since ˏthis is | ·what do_mestic con·sumers in ˏgeneral | would be ¯willing to ˏpay | for the ˋimports | that it _makes ˎpossible || ˋif this a·mount is ˇmore | than ·anyone at ˋhome | is ·willing to ˏpay for the ·oil | ˏthen | ¯prima ˏfacie | the ¯balance of adˏvantage | ˏlies | in exˋporting it || in ˏgeneral | ¯export ·prohiˏbitions | ¯only ·serve to enˏsure | that ˏoil | ˏgas | ˏscrap ·metal | ˏsoya ·beans | or whaˋtever | the co¯mmodity may ˏbe | is put to ¯lower-·value | ·rather than ˇhigher-·value | ˎuse || ¯freedom to ˏexport | should ·be the ˎrule ||

`this ·argument ¯still aˇpplies more·over | ↑to the ˏcase | where there ˎare _limited do·mestic reˏserves | of ·some _non-re·newable reˏsource | ¯as with ˏgas | ˎfrom the ·UK _Conti·nental ˎShelf || in ˏBritain | the ˎoil ·companies `rightly ˇargue | that ·freedom to ·export _gas from the ·North ˏSea | would in¯crease the inˏcentive | to ·find ¯new deˏposits | of ˎgas ·there || ¯this ˇisn't how·ever | the ·fundaˎmental ·point | which ˏis | that ¯even ˇin a situ·ation | where re·serves were ´known | ¯and ˏlimited | the ·orthodox _argument | would _still aˎpply || if ˎforeigners are ·willing to _pay ´more | at the ´margin | ↑then _exports ·repreˏsent | a _higher-·value ˎuse || the ˏpresent | and `long-e·stablished reˇstrictions | on the ¯export of ˏgas | from the U¯nited ˏKingdom | ↑are _therefore ·not ˎjustified ||

¯arguing in this ·way | is `not myˎopic || `longer-·term ·national ˏgains | `wouldn't be ·sacrificed ^ to i·mmediate ·profit || ↑it may _well `be | that ¯oil and ˏgas | will be `so ·much `more ·valuable in the ˏfuture | even aˇllowing | for the ˎinterest ·factor | that ·has to be ˏtaken into aˏccount | ˎin such ·calcuˏlations | ↑that _governments | should `limit pro·duction ˇnow | and ·possibly ˇalso en·courage `imports | in _order to conˇserve | doˇmestic re·sources | _for the ˎfuture | ·this is _quite con`sistent | with the `orthodox ^ e·conomists' aˏpproach | because if the a¯ssumption's coˏrrect | the e`ffect of ·such ¯conservation ˏmeasures | would ·be to ˏsubstitute | a ˏfuture | ˏhigher-·value ·use | ↑for a _present | `lower-·value ·one || but the `case for ·giving ˎmore ·weight to the ˇfuture | and ¯less to the ˇpresent | ·doesn't in `any ·way e·stablish a ˏcase | for di`scriminating in ·favour of doˇmestic con·sumers | as a_gainst ˎforeigners ||

¯let me ˏadd | that ¯as in ˇother appli·cations | of the `willingness-to-·pay criˏterion | ¯freedom to ˏexport | is a ¯general | pre¯sumptive ˇrule | ˇnot | a ·categorical imˇperative | which ad_mits of ·no exˎceptions || ↑reˏstrictions | on par·ticular straˇtegic ·exports | may `well be ·justified | on ¯grounds | of _national deˎfence || `taxes on co·mmodity ˎexports | which ·have the e_ffect of re·ducing their ˇflow | ¯can in ˇsome ·circumstances | be a _useful ·instrument of ˎpolicy | in deˎveloping ·countries || aˏgain | re_strictions on ˏfood ·exports | are ˇjustified | in ˏgenuine | _national eˎmergencies | as in some ˎAfrican ·countries | at ˎpresent || `even ˇthough | in themˇselves | such reˏstrictions | `won't give ·those in ˇneed | the ¯wherewiˏthal | to ob_tain ˎfood || ↑¯all ˏthese how·ever | are exˇceptional | or ˇfringe | ˎcases | in the ·modern ˎworld || they ˇdon't | ¯underˏmine | the ¯general ·orthodox ˏargument | that

¯export reˏstrictions | based on eˋssentialist iˬdeas | are ˬcontrary | to the ¯interests | of a _country | that imˎposes them ||

¯what about the ˎsecond ·type ^ of ·autarchic ·policy | ·that of ¯minimising deˏpendence | on ˋimports || ˇhere | the ¯orthodox ˏview | is _more sympaˇthetic | since it's ˋobvious | that ¯serious _consequences | ¯can reˏsult | if a ·major inter_national ·source of suˏpply | for ¯key coˏmmodities | ¯like oil or ˏgas | is _suddenly withˏdrawn | or disˎrupted || but ˋdo-it-your·self ecoˏnomics | ¯here as _elsewhere | is ¯no ˎhelp || it leads ¯people | ¯and ˏgovernments | both to e¯xaggerate the ˏrisk | ˋand to ·use ¯inappropriate ˏways | of ˎdealing ·with it ||

↑on the ˇfirst ·point | there's a ˬchronic | ˋDIY·E ˬtendency | to ¯overˏstate | the ¯dangers | of ˬusing | overˇseas | ·sources of suˎpply || in ˏpart | this is be·cause of the mi¯staken | eˬssentialist | beˏlief | aˏbout | _national ˎneeds || aˇnother ·reason | is that ˎunre·flecting ˇcentralism | ¯conjures ·up a ˏpicture | in which ˇimports | are ¯always ˏbought | diˇrectly | from ·chronically ¯unreˏliable | _foreign ˎgovernments || more ˇtypically how·ever | it's ¯not ˏgovernments | but ·business ˋenterprises ^ which ·ship the ·imports || and whether ¯publicly | or ˇprivately ·owned | ¯these ˏenterprises | ·have an ˏinterest | ˋboth in re·taining ¯profitable ˏmarkets | ˇand | in ¯keeping their ·repuˏtation | for _honouring ˎcontracts || of ↑ˋcourse | ·inte_rruptions to im·ported suˏpplies | ˋmay ·none the _less take ˎplace | but as ˎBritish ·energy conˬsumers | need ·hardly be reˇminded | ·after the _recent ˇcoal ·strike | doˎmestic su·pplies | may ˋalso be ·subject | to inteˏrruption | and ˎthreats || ˋwhether ·foreign ·sources are ˇless re·liable | than doˏmestic ·sources | will de_pend on the ˎcircumstances || ↑it ˎcan't | ¯just be preˎsumed ||

↑on this ˇquestion of se·curity | ¯orthodox ecoˏnomics | has a ¯strong | ˎpositive ·message | which ·comes in ¯two ˎparts || ↑in the ˏfirst ·place | it ¯points to the ˏrole | of ¯broad | ¯well-ˎfunctioning | ¯inter·national ˎmarkets | as a ·means to re¯ducing unˏcertainty | and pro¯viding for eˎmergencies || the eˇxistence of such ·markets | with ¯free ˏaccess | for ·buyers ¯and ˏsellers | pro·vides the ¯best aˏssurance | that ·purchases ^ can ¯always be ˎmade | an aˎssurance which is reˋduced | if ·countries re_sort | to _export ·prohiˎbitions || the ˇsecond ·part of the ·message | is that ˎin the ·case of ˇstorable co·mmodities | like ˏoil | se¯curity can be imˏproved | ·often at ˋmuch ·lower ˎcost | than by ·substituting ˋhome pro·duction for ˬimports | ↑by the ˏholding | of ˏample | re_serve ˎstocks || ·these stocks can be ˏprivate | ·or they can ·be oˋfficial | ·as in the ˏcase | of the ˏpresent | ¯US | Stra_tegic Peˎtroleum Re·serve || ·Mr

Mac¯Quedy | has ¯no ˋprejudice | a·gainst ¯government ˏaction | on _these ˎlines ||

¯these two _parts | of the ˬmessage | are ¯not diˎstinct | for unˋless ·markets are ¯allowed | to ¯function ˏproperly | the ¯level of _stocks | will be ˏlower | than it ˎshould be || ¯holding ˏstocks | _costs ˎmoney || ¯why | should ¯any ·private ˏagency | ·go to the exˏpense | of ·keeping _special | e¯mergency ˏstocks | ex·cept per·haps for its ·own ex¯clusive ˏuse | ↑if it beˏlieves | that in the e¯vent of a ˇshortage | the ·government will at ¯once | im·pose ˬprice con·trols | to pre·vent so-ˇcalled | profiˬteering | ↑and _possibly ·also make su·pplies a·vailable from its ˇown ·stocks | at con_trolled ˎprices || ↑if ˋstocks are to ·play their ¯full po·tential ˏrole | in pro¯viding inˎsurance | a¯gainst eˏmergencies | ˎmarkets have to be a·llowed to set _prices ˊfreely | and ¯sales | from ˎgovernment stra¯tegic ˏstocks | ↑should be _made | by ˎauction ||

ˋthis ·orthodox ˏmessage | ↑is a ˎgeneral ·one || but it's eˇspecially ·relevant | in the ˬenergy ·field | be_cause | it's ˇhere | in parˬticular | that ¯risks | are in¯evitable | and the ·possible ¯consequences of diˇsturbance | are _still ˎserious || ¯over the ·past ˬdecade or ·more | ·Western ˏgovernments | have ·taken ˏaction | ¯individually ˇand co·llectively | _both to re·duce deˏpendence | on im·ported ˏoil | ˏand | to pro·vide for an eˇmergency | ·should it aˎrise || ↑in parˏticular | they have ·made con¯siderable ˇprogress | _some of it ·quite ˬrecent | in ˬfreeing | inˇternal ·markets | for ¯energy ˎproducts || ¯where they've ˬfailed to ·act | ˎlargely be·cause of the ˇdominance | of miˋstaken eco·nomic ˇnotions | is in eˏstablishing | and ·making acˬceptable | the ¯principle | that ¯even in _times of per·ceived ˬscarcity | ·energy ·markets should be a·llowed to _function ˏfreely | and ·prices should re_flect | ·willingness to ˎpay || beˇcause of this ·failure | the ·risk of a·nother ·energy ˇcrisis | is ˋgreater than it ¯need be | and the _possible ˇconsequences | _more aˎlarming || the ¯contriˎbution | of ˇmarkets | to ↑seˏcurity | is ˬstill | ¯unˎrecognised ||

017 SPOKEN ENGLISH CORPUS TEXT C01
The Reith Lectures 1985 - III
Broadcast notes: Radio 4, 7.45 pm, 20th November, 1985
Overlap passage

Transcribed by GOK

for ↑ˇsome •people | this ¯statement of ˋorthodox eco•nomic ˬdoctrine | ¯may aˏppear | ˍtoo unˋqualified || since it ˎfails to •mention exˇplicitly | seˍcurity of suˎpply || ˏoften | •though not ˇalways | the ˋcase for •self-suˍfficiency is ˇargued | with ˎreference to a •country's •need to en•sure seˇcurity | by ¯minimising deˍpendence | on ˍforeign ˎsources || the ˋoutside •world is ˏseen | at ˊbest | as unreˇliable | and •subject to instaˬbility | at ˏworst | as ˍactively ˎhostile || ¯from this ˎfortress-•menˇtality | ˏstandpoint | ˇautarchy | aˏppears | to be •common ˎprudence || •two sets of ˏmeasures | then suˏggest them•selves | ˏone is to •build up | doˍmestic pro•duction of eˏssentials | •so as to re•duce ˏimports | to a ˏminimum | ↑the ˏother | is to re•strict ˋexports | •so as to enˬsure | that do¯mestic suˇpplies | ↑are aˍvailable | for doˍmestic ˎuse ||

Transcribed by BJW

for ↑ˇsome •people | this ˋstatement of ˋorthodox ˋeconomic ˇdoctrine | ¯may aˍppear too unˋqualified || since it ¯fails to ˍmention exˇplicitly | seˍcurity of suˋpply || ˏoften | though not ˇalways | the ˋcase for self-su•fficiency is ˇargued | with ¯reference to a •country's •need to enˍsure seˇcurity | by ¯minimising deˏpendence on ˏforeign ˎsources || the ¯outside world is ˏseen | ↓at ˊbest | as unreˇliable | and •subject to instaˇbility | ↑at ˏworst | as ˍactively ˋhostile || from this ˋfortress-menˇtality ˇstandpoint | ˇautarchy aˏppears to be ˍcommon ˎprudence || ˍtwo sets of ¯measures | then suˏggest them•selves | ↓ˏone | is to ˏbuild up do¯mestic production of eˊssentials | ˍso as to reduce ¯imports | to a ˊminimum || ↑the ˏother | is to restrict ˋexports | so as to enˇsure | that do•mestic suˇpplies | are aˍvailable for do•mestic ˎuse ||

018 SPOKEN ENGLISH CORPUS TEXT D01
Open University - Modern Art: Berlin Dada
(First part)
Broadcast notes: Radio 4, 11.30 p.m., 26th June, 1985
Transcribed by BJW

¯Berlin ⌄Dada | is ¯often de_scribed as ¯more | poˋlitical | than _Dada ˋelse•where || I ¯want to _look at this ˋstatement | in the ¯light of •Dada's ˇown •claims | ˋand those of contemporary ˋcritics | in ¯order to con⌄sider | ˋwhat in •these ˇterms | is ¯meant ˋby political || and ¯whether it is in the _end an a¯ppropriate _term to ˋuse || I'll ˇfocus the •argument | on •one of the ¯major e_vents from •Dada's life in Berˋlin || the ¯exhibition of nineteen _twenty •called | the ¯First Inter•national _Dada ˋFair || ↑¯Berlin was the only ˏcity | where •Dada coinˋcided with an ˇactual | though ¯short-ˎlived | po•litical revoˋlution || the con¯ditions were •very ˎdifferent | from ˋthose in •neutral ˋZurich | where ¯Dada beˎgan || ↑Richard ˎHuelsen•beck | a ˋfounder of ¯Dada in Berˏlin | com¯pared the _smug •fat ˋidyll | of ˋZurich | in _nineteen sevenˋteen || where the ¯international _profiteers | sat in ˋrestaurants | and ¯smacked their _lips in a ¯merry huˎrrah | for the ¯countries that were _bashing each others' ˇskulls in | ↑to Berˎlin | on the ¯verge of deˎfeat | ↓and starˋvation || a ¯city where _men's •minds were ¯concentrating ¯more and _more | on ¯questions of naked eˎxistence || ↑what ˋis the evidence ˋused | to su¯pport _Dada's own ˋclaim | that it was poˋlitical | ↓in Ber_lin || indiˇvidual members of ¯Berlin ˏDada | ¯were _genuinely inˋvolved in ˋpolitics || ˋone at ˋleast | •Wieland ˇHerzfelde | was a ¯member of the _newly-formed •German ˋcommunist •party | and his ¯brother John _Heartfield was in •close ˋsympathy | as was •George ˋGrosz || ↑this _certainly ˋcoloured the political ˋspectrum of •Dada | but ¯has I _think to be •kept to some extent ˋseparate | from the _movement itˋself || what I ˇam suggesting there•fore | is that ¯Berlin _Dada con•sisted of a ¯hetero_genous •group of ¯writers and ˎartists | whose ˋcoming together ¯constituted | a ¯brief a_lliance between ¯radical ˎpolitics | and _radical aesˋthetics || ↑Dada's per_vasively reˋbellious state of ¯mind | u¯nited | _and for a •time ¯blurred the _differences beˋtween | the ¯anarchist ˏprotests of ¯Dadaists | like ¯Huelsenbeck | ¯Hausmann | or ↑Hoch | the ¯anti-•bourgeois _anti-•art ˋhatreds of •George ¯Grosz | and the ¯more politically-ˎfocussed | aniˋmosities | of the ˋHerzfelde •brothers || the ¯Dada state of ˏmind | ¯disillusioned by the _war | ¯turned in this ˎcontext | to the ¯Berlin tradition of ˎsatire | ¯rather than _systematic political coˋmmitment || ↑¯turn ˏnow | to the •first ˋplate || the ˇphotograph | is a ¯partial ⌄view | of the ¯First Inter_national •Dada ˋFair || ↑it's the ˎnearest | ˋvisually | to a co•llective ˋstatement || the ¯fair a_roused a

ˋgood deal of contemporary ˋinterest | and critical ˋcoverage || in ˋfact | it provoked a ˋlaw suit for defaˋmation | whose po¯litical impliˎcations | have ¯subsequently been e_xaggerated by ·certain hiˋstorians || ↑a¯mong the _hundred and ·seventy-four exˋhibits | ˋlisted in the ˇcatalogue | ¯were | ·photomonˊtage | ˏphoto·graphs | reˊliefs | ˊcollage | ˊpaintings | conˊstructions | ˊdolls and ˎdummies || on the ¯walls were inter_spersed ·large ˋplacards | ·bearing ˋslogans || ↑in ¯plate ˇone | you can see ¯two ·large ˎpaintings on the ·walls | ˋboth now ˋlost || a¯bove the _slogan | ¯Dada ist _politisch | was ¯George ·Grosz' | _Germany | a ·winter's ˋtale || ↑¯Grosz had ˇfinished this | in ·nineteen nineˎteen || and ˇlater | ¯wrote in his autobiˎography |

↑my _mood was ·turned into a ¯large po·litical ˎpicture | ↑in the ˏcentre _sat the e¯ternal _German ˋbourgeois || ˋfat and ˋfearful | at his ¯slightly ·wobbly ˎtable || beˊlow | I _painted the ¯three pillars of soˋciety | ˋarmy | ¯church and ˎschool ||

¯Harry ˎKessler | a ¯left wing ˎaristocrat | and ˎart co·llector || ˋsaw this ·painting in ¯Grosz' ˋstudio | in ¯February nineteen nineˎteen || ¯Grosz _told him that he ¯wanted to be_come the ¯German ˎHogarth || to ˋpreach | imˋprove | and reˋform || ˋhe's ·really a ˋBolshevist | _Kessler wrote in his ·diary | in the ˋguise of a ˋpainter || ↑this _painting | ·marks the ¯start of _Grosz' satirical aˋttacks | ↓on ·German soˋciety || ↑on the _left | _you can ·see ¯Otto _Dix's ¯huge _painting | ˋwar ·cripples | ↓of nineteen ˋtwenty || two ˋother ·works | have been ˋhung on ˋtop of it || ¯covering the _head of the ˇleft-hand ·war cripple | is a ˋcollage ·painting by ¯Grosz | ¯called re¯member ·uncle ˎAugust | the un¯happy inˎventor || in the ˇcentre of this ·painting | is a ¯montage of ˇphotographs | ˇalso by ·Grosz | ¯called | ¯who is the ˎfairest || ˋthis is shown in ·plate ˋtwo || it ¯shows | un¯flattering _photographs | of the ˋnew republican ¯government ˎleaders | and was ¯later _used by ˋHerzfelde | for the ˋfront ·cover of his ˋnon-Dada | but sa¯tirical periˎodical | ·called | _everyone has | ↓his ·own ˋfootball || ↑this _overˋhanging | of ¯Dix's ˎpainting | was deˋliberate || ·being ·both | a ˋpointed piece of ˇmontage | ˋand an oˋffensive icono¯clastic ˎgesture || ˋnot aimed at ˋDix's ˇpainting | but at the ˋpublic || ↑the whole a_rrangement of the exhiˋbition in ·fact | was de¯signed to _break ·down the myˋstique of the art exhiˋbition | ↓and the ·art ˋwork || the ˋwhole of ·Dada | was enˋgaged in a ¯constant ˇstruggle | to ˋredefine ˋart || to ¯reˎthink | its ˋsources | its ˋpurposes | and its ˋmodes || in ¯Ber_lin | ¯this took a _characteristically aˋggressive ˋform || as ¯Huelsenbeck ˎwrote | in the ¯first ·German _Dada maniˋfesto | ↓of ·nineteen eighˋteen ||

the ˋhighest ·art will be ¯that | which in its ¯conscious ˬcontent | pre_sents the ¯thousandfold _problems of the ˋday || the ¯art which is ·being ¯visibly _shattered | by the ex¯plosions of ·last ˎweek ||

↑¯this inˎsistence | on ˋlife | ↓and ¯active inˋvolvement with the ¯vital and _violent everyˬday | ¯led the _Berlin _Dadaists | aˋway from the ·philosophical abˋstractions | ↓which had ·characterised ˋZurich ·Dada | and ˋinto di¯rect ·confronˎtation | with the exˋpressionists || a ˋconfrontation which had poˋlitical | as ˋwell as aesˋthetic | ˋcauses || for ˋinstance | to the ˇDadaists' disˋgust | the ex¯pressionists had _backed the ·social ˋdemocrats | who'd oˋpposed the ·Berlin revoˋlution || the ˊDadaists | ·singled out the ex¯pressionist ·writers and ˏartists | ¯like _Oscar Kaˇkoshka | for ˋspecial aˋbuse || aˋccusing them of being ·ineˋffectual | and ˋhypocritical uˋtopians | ¯interested _only in ˋsaving their own ˋsouls || the ˇDadaist | _Huelsenbeck ¯wrote | con¯siders it _necessary to ·come ¯out aˎgainst ·art | be·cause he has ¯seen through its ˎvalue | ↓as a ˋmoral ˋsafety-·valve || ↑the i¯dea that _art was ·not to be set aˇpart from the ·world | ˋnor im·bued with a purely ˋspiritual ˇmeaning | took ˋtwo ex·treme ˋforms || ¯one ·held that ˎall ·art | that was _not diˋdactic | or propaˋganda | was ˋuseless || the ˇother | more ˋsubtle and paraˋdoxical | ¯held that ¯art | as it was conˋventionally underˋstood | was ˋfinished || if it ˇwas to sur·vive | it would ˋno ·longer be in a ¯recognisably aes_thetic ˋform || as ¯one of the ˎslogans in the ·exhibition ˋhad it | ¯art is ˎdead | ·long live the ma_chine art of ˋTatlin || ¯art in its eˇxisting manifes·tations | ·was | ¯hopelessly enˬtangled by | and ¯compromised _with | the ·social ˋsystem || as ·Tzara ˋput it | in his ·nineteen eighteen ¯Dada maniˬfesto ||

↑is the _aim of ˬart | to ·make ˇmoney | and caˋjole | the ·nice ·nice ˇbourgeois || ¯rhymes _ring | with the ¯assonance of ˎcurrencies | and the inˋflection ¯slips along the _line of the ˋbelly | in ˋprofile ||

↑¯Dada did not _really aˋttempt | itˋself | to ¯offer a con_sistent soˋlution || it was eˋnough | to ex¯pose the ˎcrisis | in the ˋrelevance of ˋart || ↓howˊever | ·Dada ¯did put _forward _some | ·positive proˋposals || the ¯new principles of _Dada conˋstruction | as ˋHuelsenbeck ˋlists them | in his ¯nineteen ·twenty ˋhistory of ˇDadaism | ·En avant Daˊda | ˇwere | ˏbrutism | ↓or ˇnoise-·music | ·simultaˋneity | ¯and the ¯new ˬmedium | of ˋcollage || the ¯first _two were a·dapted from ˋfuturism || the ˇlast | ˇcollage | ˋcame from ˇcubism | but it was ¯this which _Berlin ·Dada transˋformed | into the ¯new ˏmedium | of ·photomonˋtage || as ˋHuelsenbeck ˋwrote ||

↓with the ¯new ˎmedium | the ˋpicture has ˋliterally ·taken a de¯cisive ˍstep from the ho¯rizon across the ˎforeground || ˍit par¯ticipates | ↓in ¯life itˎself ||

018 SPOKEN ENGLISH CORPUS TEXT D01
Open University - Modern Art: Berlin Dada
(Second part)
Broadcast notes: Radio 4, 11.30 p.m., 26th June, 1985
Transcribed by GOK

↑¯Dada did not ·really at`tempt it ˎself | to ¯offer a con_sistent soˎlution || it was e`nough | to ex¯pose the ˎcrisis | in the `relevance of ˎart || howˏever | ↑·Dada ¯did put _forward ˏsome | ¯positive pro`posals || the ¯new principles of ·Dada conˎstruction | as `Huelsenbeck ˎlists them | in his ¯nineteen-·twenty ˎhistory of `Dadaism | En a¯vant Daˏda | ˏwere | ˏbrutism | or ˅noise-·music | ¯simultaˎneity | ¯and | the ¯new ˏmedium | of `collage || the ↑¯first _two were a¯dapted from `futurism || the ˇlast | ˅collage | ¯came from ˇcubism | ↑but it was ¯this | which ¯Berlin _Dada trans`formed | into the ¯new _medium of ·photomon`tage || as ¯Huelsenbeck ˎwrote | with the ¯new ˎmedium | the ¯picture | has ¯literally _taken a de¯cisive ·step from the ho¯rizon a·cross the ˎforeground || ↑it par¯ticipates | in ¯life itˎself ||

↑¯turn to ↓_plate ˎthree || ¯this _shows the ˇcover of the ˅catalogue | of the ¯First | Inter_national ¯Dada ˎFair || the ↑ˇcredits | are ¯printed | ·over a ↑¯nineteen-·nineteen ¯photoˇmontage | which had a ¯joint | ¯rubber-·stamped `signature | by ¯Grosz and ˎHeartfield || the ¯photomon·tage is a ˇmixture | of ty¯pography and ˎimages || ↑in·cluding ¯two _symbols | which ¯strive to sug·gest ef¯fects be¯yond the limita·tions of the ¯static ˎimage || a `claxon | to in·voke a `blaring `noisy enˎvironment | and a ↓_scrap of `film || the ↑¯scrap of ↓_film | ¯also re·fers to the ·technique of monˏtage | in the ¯still undeˎveloped ·medium of ·film || ¯Alder ˎBenjamin | in his ¯essay | the ¯work of _art | in the ¯age of me·chanical repro_duction | pro↑¯posed | that ¯Dada's hi·storical sigˎnificance | ¯was an es¯sential ˎimpetus | to the ¯new _art ˎform | of ¯film itˎself || al¯though he de¯nied indi·vidual `meaning | to ·Dada `works || ↑¯look ˏnow | at the ¯next _three ˎplates || ↑they're ¯all eˏxamples | of the _new ˏmedium | and were ex¯hibited at the ¯Berlin ·Dada `fair || ↑they're ¯not oˇvertly po·litical in ·content | but ¯all _bear | on the ↓¯Dadaist ˏconcept | of the ¯new ˎartist || ↑¯plate ˏfour | is a ¯portrait of _Heartfield ^ the meˎchanic || a ˇwater ·colour | with ¯photograph and ˇpostcard | ·pasted `on || ↑¯Heartfield is _shown with ¯shaven ˎhead | ·wearing ¯workers' ˎoveralls | `bearing ·out his ¯Dada _title mon`teur | ·meaning me`chanic | or ˎfitter || a ↑¯title he `chose | in `preference to ˎartist || the ¯piece of ma_chinery on his ¯chest | `substitutes for a ˎheart | but `also ˅mockingly re·fers to `war ·medals || ·John

ˇHeartfield | had deˇliberately ·anglicised his ·name | from ˎHelmut
ˇHerzfelde | as a ¯gesture a¯gainst ˏwar | and ˎnationalism || in the ¯same
ˎspirit | ¯Grosz had ˍadded a ^ an ˋE | to ˎGeorg || ↑in ˍplate ˏfive |
¯Hausmann's | ¯Tatlin at ˎhome || the ¯pieces of ·pasted ˍphotographs |
and ˎpaper | ¯set in a de¯cilico- ·like inˬterior | re¯late theˋmatically | to
·one aˎnother || the ↑¯head in the ˬforeground | ¯cut | from an Aˋmerican
ˇpicture maga·zine | is in¯tended to ·represent ˋTatlin | al·though
ˇHausmann | ¯didn't at the ·time ˇknow | ¯what ·Tatlin ˇlooked like |
↑¯nor very ˍmuch about the ¯new ¯post-revo·lutionary ·Russian ˋart ||
ˋheralded as the ˎnew maˇchine ·art | by ˎplacards at the exhiˋbition ||
↑ˇTatlin | ¯symbolised the ¯new | ˍrevolutionary ˎartist || and ¯here has an
¯engine and ˎsteering ·wheel | in ·place of a ˋbrain || ↑in ¯plate ˇsix |
¯Hannah ·Hoch's | ¯large photomonˍtage | ·cut with a ˋcake ·knife |
ˋspatial ·reading is deˎstroyed | in a ¯comic amalgaˍmation | of
ˋphotographs | and ˎslogans || the ↑ˇfollowing ·plate | ·number ˬseven |
is a ¯photograph | of ˇHausmann's | ¯Dada ˍhead | ¯spirit of our ˎtime ||
↑¯made ˇafter the exhi·bition | it is a ¯hatmaker's | ¯wooden ˍhead | with
¯various ˎobjects | atˋtached || by ˇcontrast | ¯this | is an i¯ronic
ˋcomment | on ¯modern ma·chine ˎman || ↑¯stuck onto the ˍhead is a
ˋtape-·measure | sug·gesting that ¯man | the ¯measure of ¯all ˏthings | is
¯now him¯self reˎduced | to a ˎcypher || ↑¯turn ˏnow | to ·plate ˋeight |
which ·shows ¯part of Jo¯hannes ˏBaader's | instalˋlation || ¯Baader
ˇcalled him·self | the ˋOberdada | or suˎpreme ·Dada | and pro¯claimed
himself ˇpresident | of a ¯world ^ reˋpublic || ¯he was an ¯ex-ˎarchitect |
who had ¯once been ¯certified as inˎsane || his ↑¯instalˍlation | ¯called the
^ ¯great ˍPlasto-·Dio-ˎDada-·Drama | was de¯scribed in the ˏcatalogue |
as ^ ¯Dada ·monumental ˋarchitecture || the ↑ˋpyramid ^ in the
conˍstruction | is fe¯stooned with ·pages from ¯Dada periˋodicals ||
ˍHausmann's pho·netic ˏpoems | ¯posters ¯torn from street ˎcorners | and
ˋother ¯heteroˬgeneous | ˋobjects || ↑¯turn ˏnow | to the ˎninth ·plate ||
ˋthis mon·tage | of ¯nineteen-ˋtwenty | was in¯tended for an anˋthology
·called | ˋDadaco || ˋunlike the ˋother works you've been ˇlooking at | it is
ˋpointedly saˎtirical | an un¯flattering ˎportrait | of what ¯Grosz ˏsaw | as
the ¯typical ¯German bourˎgeois || his ˇimage | is a ¯negative ˏform |
¯created out of ¯scraps of ¯newspaper and ˎphotographs | with ¯patches of
ˋhair | ¯pasted ˎon || ↑¯framed in his ˏheart | is a ¯picture of ¯marching
ˍPrussian ˎsoldiers | while ¯radiating from his ˎhead | are ˋnews re·ports |
from the ˋmoney ·markets || ↑¯turn ˏnow | to ·plate ˋten || ↑¯this
ˏlithograph | is from ¯Grosz' portˏfolio | ¯God ˎwith us | which was
↓ˋshown at the exhiˎbition || its ↑ˇtitle is | the ¯communists are ˎdying | and
the ¯foreign exˎchange rate | goes ˎup || ¯this ˍimage is ·linked speˋcifically

| to eˎvents | from the ˋBerlin revoˎlution || the ˉanti-·militarist _theme | was the ˉmost perˋsistent | in the saˉtirical ˎworks | in the exhiˎbition || ˉturn ˎback | to the _first ˋplate || ˉin ˏthis | you can ˯see | suˉspended from the ˏceiling | a ˎdummy | by ˉRudolf ˋSchlichter | with the ˉepaulettes | of a ·German ˉofficer | and the ˉhead of a ˎpig | _called | ˉPrussian ˎarchangel || aˇnother ·dummy | which you can ˉsee to the ˇright of the ·plate | was ˉpeg-ˎlegged | like _Dix's ˋwar cripples || it had an eˉlectric ˏlight ·bulb | in _place of a ˏhead | and the ˉmilitary ˯order | of the ˉiron ˎcross | on its ˎback || ↑ˉthese ˏworks | toˉgether with ·Grosz' ˯lithographs | proˉvoked the most ˉoutraged reˎactions | from the ˎpublic | ˋculminating in a ˎlibel ·action || the reˉactions of the ˇart ·critics how·ever | pre_sent ·rather a ˋdifferent ·picture || ˉKurt Duˎkosky | a ˎmarxist ·critic | in the ˉBerliner ˋTageblatt | conˉsidered ·Grosz the ˉonly ·serious ˎartist | whose ˉsatire bit ˏdeep | but ˇcommented | if ˉdrawings could ˯kill | the ˉPrussian _army ˎwould | ˉcertainly be ˎdead || ↑aˉnother ·critic | ˉfound the exhi·bition as a ˉwhole | a ˉmild if ·tasteless ˎspoof | with ˉonly _one ·good ˎjoke || a ↑ˉphotomon_tage by ˏGrosz | ˉsuperim·posing the ˉheads | of the ˉnew _social demo·cratic ˎgovernment | on an ˉold _print of the im·perial ˋfamily || ↑ˇothers | took ·Dada's ·claims more ˇseriously | but ˉtended to disˉmiss ·Dada's po·litical preˋtensions || Aˉdolph ˏBainer | in the ˉBerlin ·newspaper Die ˇFreiheit | ˉwrote that | ˉDada | was the diˉrect exˋpression of the ˎtimes || ↑ˉif ·people reˇsponded | by ˋclaiming the ·times were ˋnot as ·bad as ˇthat | they were ˋwrong || ˋany ·art ˰ he went ·on | that ˋspoke about a ˉlovely ˎworld | was a ˋswindle || ↑but the ˉmain _bearing of ˇhis ·argument | was that in ˉspite of the _posters in the ·exhi·bition | proˉclaiming that _Dada | was on the ˉside of the revoˉlutionary proleˉtariat | ˉDada was in ·fact ˎart || its poˉlitical _claims | were a deˋvice | to add ˉspice | to what ·was esˇsentially | an ↓ˉart exhiˎbition || ↑to reˉturn to the ˎlibel ·case || ˊGrosz | ˏHerzfelde | ˏSchlichter | ˉBurchard ˰ the ˯gallery di·rector | and ˇBaader | were ˉcharged with deˉfaming the ˋReichswehr | the ˉGerman | _national ˎarmy || the ↑ˉreason ˇBaader was in·cluded | was beˉcause he'd ˉgiven him·self the _title ˇOberdada | which ˉled the prose·cution to be_lieve | that ˉhe was inˎdeed | the ˋleader | of the enˉtire ·Dada ˎmovement | and in a poˉsition of ˉoverall responsiˋbility || ↑the deˇfence ·argued | that it was a ˉmatter of ˉart | ·rather than ˎsatire | and that the ˉlithographs and ˯dummies | were atˉtacks | on ˉmilitarism in ˏgeneral | ˏrather than the ˉGerman _army in parˋticular || in the ˊend | the ˉcourt ·found that ·Dada was ˇnot ·frightening | because it was ˉnot deˏfinable | and ˉlet most of the de·fenders ˋoff || ˇGrosz ˰ how·ever | was ˉfined ˉthree ·hundred ˏmarks | and ˎHerzfelde ˋsix ·hundred || ↑the ˉquestion

ˏis | ˉwhat ·was ˉDada's ˎrole | in ·this ˋtrial || ˎcertainly | it was suf·ficiently ˋdistanced | from i·dentifiable po·litical acˎtivity | to eˉnable ·Herzfelde and ˍGrosz | to ·present it as an ˋalibi | a ·kind of arˉtistic ˋcover || ↑yet ·this is ·not an ˎadequate expla·nation | for it would sugˉgest | the ˉwhole alˎliance | as ˉI de·scribed it ˎearlier | be·tween ·radical ˎpolitics | and ·radical aesˋthetics | which ˉconstituted | the ˉbrief | but ˉvigorous ˎlife | of ˉBerlin ˍDada | was ˉmerely a ·matter of exˋpedience | for the ˎformer || ↑in their ˇlater ·text | ˉart is in ⌄danger | of ˉnineteen ·twenty-⌄five | ˉGrosz and ·Herzfelde ˋrecognise | the esˉsential ·qualities of ˉwit and ˎirony | which inˉformed | ↓ˍDada's oppo·sitional ˋtactics || they ·wrote ˄ ˇDadaism | was the ˉonly esˇsential ar·tistic ·movement | in ˏGermany | for ˋdecades || ˉdo not ˎsmile || ˉthis ˎmovement ·made | ˉall the ˇother ·isms in ·art | into ˉlittle ˍstudio pheˎnomena | from the ↓ˉday before ˎyesterday ||

018 SPOKEN ENGLISH CORPUS TEXT D01
Open University - Modern Art: Berlin Dada
Broadcast notes: Radio 4, 11.30 p.m., 26th June, 1985
Overlap passage

Transcribed by BJW

↑¯Dada did not _really a`ttempt | it`self | to ¯offer a con_sistent so`lution || it was e`nough | to ex¯pose the ˎcrisis | in the `relevance of `art || ↓how´ever | · Dada ¯did put _forward _some | · positive pro`posals || the ¯new principles of _Dada con`struction | as `Huelsenbeck `lists them | in his ¯nineteen- · twenty `history of ˇDadaism | · En avant Da´da | ˇwere | ˏbrutism | ↓or ˇnoise- · music | · simulta`neity | ¯and the ¯new ˬmedium | of `collage || the ¯first _two were a · dapted from `futurism || the ˇlast | ˇcollage | `came from ˇcubism | but it was ¯this which _Berlin · Dada trans`formed | into the ¯new ˏmedium | of · photomon`tage || as `Huelsenbeck `wrote ||

↓with the ¯new ˎmedium | the `picture has `literally · taken a de¯cisive _step from the ho¯rizon across the ˎforeground || _it par¯ticipates | ↓in ¯life itˎself ||

Transcribed by GOK

↑¯Dada did not · really at`tempt itˎself | to ¯offer a con_sistent soˎlution || it was e`nough | to ex¯pose the ˎcrisis | in the `relevance of ˎart || howˏever | ↑ · Dada ¯did put _forward ˏsome | ¯positive pro`posals || the ¯new principles of · Dada conˎstruction | as `Huelsenbeck ˎlists them | in his ¯nineteen- · twenty ˎhistory of `Dadaism | En a¯vant Daˏda | ˏwere | ´brutism | or ˬnoise- · music | ¯simultaˎneity | ¯and | the ¯new ˏmedium | of `collage || the ↑¯first _two were a¯dapted from `futurism || the ˇlast | ˬcollage | ¯came from ˇcubism | ↑but it was ¯this | which ¯Berlin _Dada trans`formed | into the ¯new _medium of · photomon`tage || as ¯Huelsenbeck ˎwrote |

with the ¯new ˎmedium | the ¯picture | has ¯literally _taken a de¯cisive · step from the ho¯rizon a · cross the ˎforeground || ↑it par¯ticipates | in ¯life itˎself ||

019 SPOKEN ENGLISH CORPUS TEXT D02
Open University - Science and Belief
(First part)
Open University tape: AMST283/5
Transcribed by BJW

↑the ¯eighteenth ˏcentury in _France | was an ¯age of ˎreason || it was an ˏage | in which ¯certain ·French phiˏlosophers | ¯sought to ex_tend to ˇall areas of ·human ac·tivity | the i_deal which had ˊbeen so suˬccessful | ↑in the ˏscientific ˏmovement of the _seventeenth ˋcentury || ↓ratioˊnality | ¯tempered _by emˇpiricism || the ¯philoˏsophes | ↓as _these French phi·losophers were ˏcalled | ˋset out to ˊfree | the ¯minds of _men | from ¯cant | superˬstition | and the ¯shackles of tra·dition and auˎthority || ˋwhether the au¯thority | was in ¯science | ˇmetaphysics | ¯politics | or reˎligion || the ˇmovement they cre·ated | has become ¯famous | as the Enˎlightenment ||

↑ˇbriefly | their ¯idea _was that ¯men should be ˎfree || both inte¯llectually | ¯and in the _daily _conduct of their ˋlives || ↑and the ¯works of ˎall of them | ¯Montesquieu | ¯Voltaire | ¯Diderot | ¯d'Alembert | ˇHolbach | ¯have the air of a cru_sade against ¯ignorance | ¯in_justice | and inˎtolerance || ↑this is ˬnowhere more ·evident | than in the ¯great encyclo_pedia | ˋpublished in ˇtwenty-·eight | ¯huge _folio _volumes | between ¯seventeen fifty-·one | ↑and _seventeen seventy-ˋtwo || the en·cyclo_pedia | eˋpitomised | the ·thought of the philoˎsophes || inˋdeed it was conˋceived | ↓by ˊtwo of them | ˏDiderot | ↓and ˊd'Alembert | and ˋseveral ˋothers were among the conˋtributors || ↑like ˬmost encyclo·pedias | it was ˏwritten to con_vey ˋtruths || but ¯truths a_rrived at in the ¯only _way that the ¯philo_sophes thought it ˇpossible to ac·quire certain ·knowledge | by ¯reason | and exˎperience || ↑as you might exˏpect | ˏscience and techˏnology were ˎprominent || but ˋif the encycloˇpedia had been ˋno more than a comˋpendium of scienˋtific and technoˋlogical inforˇmation | it ˋwouldn't have ·caused the ˇstir | that it ˋdid ·cause || the ˋarticles that ·made it a senˏsation | in ¯every Parisian _salon | were ˋnot those on ˋscience || but ¯those that _touched on auˋthority || par¯ticularly | in po¯litical | and reˎligious ·matters || ˏpleas | ↓for ˊequity | and ¯tole_ration aˋbounded in the encyclo·pedia || ↑and it's no ˋwonder that there were ¯numerous a_ttempts | to suˇppress it in ·France | eˋspecially on the ¯part of _those authoriˋtarian ˋelements wi¯thin the _church | whose a_buses it so ˋtellingly aˋttacked || ↑it's imˋportant to be¯gin ˇany dis·cussion of the philo·sophes | by ˏstressing the _common ˏground which they ˋshared || ¯most ˬobviously | in their ˋscepticism about the ¯forms | and

ˇrituals | of tra_ditional Christiˋanity || ˏyet | there ¯were im_portant ·differences beˋtween them | and in the ˇrest of this ·talk | I shall be ˇchiefly con·cerned | with the diˋversity | ¯rather than the ˎunity | of ˏFrench | En_lightenment ˋthought ||

↑during the ·first _quarter of the eighteenth ˏcentury | ¯French _natural phi_losophy | was ·almost _totally Carˎtesian || ↓by ˊthen | the phi¯losophy of Des¯cartes | had acˋquired a ˇstanding in ·France | ˇcomparable with that of Aristoˋtelianism | a ¯hundred ·years beˋfore || and its poˋsition was made ˋall the ˇmore se·cure | by the _large _measure of aˇpproval | that it had _won with·in the Catholic ˋchurch || ˏtrue || it was ·still oˇpposed | by ˋDescartes' most imˇplacable ·enemies | the ˋJesuits || ↑but ˇmost Catholic ·scholars | aˋccepted a ¯system of ·Christian apolo_getics | ↑which inˇcorporated such Car·tesian ·notions | as i·nnate i_deas | and the ˎdualism | of _mind | and ˎbody || ↑¯quite ˇsuddenly | in the ¯late seventeen ˏtwenties | Car¯tesian phiˏlosophy in ˏFrance | be¯gan to be ˇchallenged || ↓alˋthough the ·challenge ·came from withˇin ·France | its ˋinspiˇration | was ·unˋquestionably ˋEnglish || ↑¯since the sixteen ˇeighties in ·England | ¯Descartes' ˏphysics | and his psyˏchology | had been ¯so seˇverely a·ttacked | ↓by ¯Newton | and ¯Locke | that ¯by the _early ˇeighteenth ·century | Carˇtesianism ·there | was _almost | ˋtotally | aˋbandoned || ↑Volˏtaire | who was in ˇexile in ·England | from ·seventeen twenty-¯six | to ·seventeen twenty-¯eight | ↓ob¯served the _changes in English phiˎlosophy || and was _duly im_pressed | by ·Newton's ¯splendid ˇfuneral | in ¯Westminster _Abbey | in _seventeen twenty-ˋseven || a ·man whose ˇpall | was ·borne by ˇdukes | and ˇearls | was _clearly of exˋceptional imˋportance || and alˋthough he was no mathemaˇtician | ¯Voltaire ·quickly con_vinced him·self | that ¯Newton's repu_tation | was ˋjustified ||

↑¯English phi_losophy and ˏcustoms | ¯couldn't have _had a ¯better _champion than ·Volˎtaire || he was ¯capable of ·writing with au·thority and ¯wit | on ¯subjects as _varied as the ¯English ·parliament | ˏvacci_nation | the ¯Quakers and the psy_chology of ˎLocke || but his ˇgreatest a·chievement in the seventeen ·thirties | was to con¯vince the _French | of the im¯portance of the _work | of ˎNewton || ↓it's ¯true | that the ¯ninety-_five-year-old ·Fonte¯nelle | ·published an ˋessay deˇfending Car·tesian ·vortices | as ¯late as ·seventeen fifty-ˋtwo || but at ˋleast a ˋdecade before ˇthen | ˋmost ·French philosophers had alˋready aˇbandoned | the ˋspeculative ·physics of Des¯cartes | in _favour of the ·more | experiˋmentally based ·physics | of ˋNewton ||

↑for ˇthis | ˋVoltaire ˇmust take | ↓much ˋcredit || though he was ˋgreatly ˋhelped | by the ˇFrench New·tonians | ↓like ˊMaupertuis | and ˇd'Alembert | who ¯treated the _more matheˇmatical aspects of New·tonian phi·losophy | ↑which Volˬtaire | _tended to igˋnore || his ˋtask was ˇalso made ·easier | by an ·admiˇration for ·England | that was _then widely ˋfelt | in ˋFrance || ↓we should reˆmember that it was a¯bout ˇthis time | that ˇMontesquieu | con¯ceived his reˏspect for ˏEnglish ˏparliamentary deˋmocracy || and it's ˋno coˋincidence | that from the ¯seventeen ˏtwenties | ¯French _views on the reˋlationship be·tween ¯science | and reˬligion | ↑ˋalso be¯gan to re_flect | ¯English ˋinfluence ||

↑¯as you ˏknow | ˇDescartes | had de¯nied the possi_bility | that we could ¯ever ascer_tain ·God's ¯purposes for his creˬation | ¯through the _study of ˎnature || ˏfinal causes for ˬDescartes | could be ·known ˋonly through reveˋlation || ˋNewton | ↓on the other ˊhand | had main¯tained | that ˋnature gave ˇample ·evidence | ↓of God's ˊwisdom | and ˊprovidence || and he was suˇpported in this ·view | by the ¯first repre_sentatives of a ¯school of ˇBritish theo·logians | who re¯lied on the _use of ¯natural ˎreason | ˇrather than reve·lation | for their _knowledge | of ˋGod || ˏthese | were the ¯natural theoˋlogians || who ˏflourished in ˏBritain | until ¯well into the _nineteenth ˋcentury ||

↑I ¯see the _growth of | ˇinterest | in ¯natural the_ology in ˏFrance | as an ˇobvious ·sign | that ¯French re¯ligious _thought | was ˋcoming under ¯English ˬinfluence | in the _seventeen ˋtwenties || ↑for ˇpreviously in ·France | ¯natural theˏology | had been _little ˋpractised || ↓at ˏfirst | the ¯French re_lied on transˋlations || ↑of ˏworks by ˋRay | and ˇDerham for e·xample | but ¯soon a _truly ¯French tra·dition of ·natural the_ology was eˋstablished || and it re¯mained ˏstrong | until the ¯end of the ˏcentury | when its ˇleading ex·ponent was the ˇRousseauite | _Bernardin de Saint-Piˋerre || one can ·see the exˋtravagance to which ˋnatural the·ology was ˇprone | from the ˇmemorable ·statement by Bernar·din | that ¯God _made _fleas ˋblack || so that they ·could be _seen ˇeasily | on our ¯skins | and ˋkilled || which was _all very ˋwell | pro¯vided you _had a white ˋskin ||

↑ˋFrench natural theology in the ¯eighteenth ˏcentury | ¯closely reˏsembled | the ˇEnglish tradition | from _which it ˋgrew || ¯in parˏticular the tra_dition of ¯Boyle | and ¯Ray | who deˏlighted in the ˏevidence of adapˏtation in the ˋliving ˋworld || so ˋI'll say ·no more aˋbout it in this ˋtalk || but ˋdon't overlook the ¯fact | that it eˎxisted || ˏnatural theˏology

ˇmay have been | preˋdominantly a ˇProtestant ac·tivity | but there ˉwere natural theoˬlogians in ˉCatholic _countries ˎtoo ||

↑let's reˏturn to our ·philo_sophes | in par_ticular to ·Volˋtaire || now ˇVoltaire | was ˉnot a ˏChristian | in ˉany _orthodox ˋsense || in ˇhis ·view | ↓the ˊrituals | ˏpriests | and ˇdoctrines of Christi·anity | ↑had _fostered ˏhatred | and exˋtremism | ˋrather than comˇpassion | and toleˇration || ˏyet | un·til his _death in ˉseventeen seventy-_eight || ↑he re_tained | a be_lief in ˎGod || though Volˋtaire's ·God | the ˉGod of a ˬdeist | was ˋone that ˇmost ·Christians | would _scarcely have ˋrecognised ||

ˋdeists | were ˉpeople who be_lieved in ˉGod | as a creˎator || but ˉunlike the ˎtheists | a ˇsimilar ·name | but a ˋvery ˇdifferent ·school | ˉdeists re_jected | reveˋlation || ˇNewton for e·xample was a ˋtheist || Volˇtaire | was a ˋdeist || it was a conˉtinuing be_lief in ˋprovidence | which susˉtained | ·Voltaire's ˎdeism || ↓how^ever we ˉknow | that the ˉsuffering | and ˇevil in the world | ˉmade it inˋcreasingly ˇdifficult for him to mainˋtain this be·lief || ˉquite ˬlate in life | he ·wrote his ˉfamous _novel | ·Canˎdide || _here | he reˋjected the ·Leibˇnizian ·view | that ˉthis | is the ˉbest | of ˉall ·possible _worlds | ˉeven _though in his ˇearlier ·writings | he'd suˋpported it ||

019 SPOKEN ENGLISH CORPUS TEXT D02
Open University - Science and Belief
(Second part)
Open University tape: AMST283/5
Transcribed by GOK

↑let's reˏturn | to our ·philoˍsophes | ↑in parˍticular to Volˎtaire || now ˉVolˏtaire | was ˉnot a ˏChristian | in ·any ˍorthodox ˋsense || in ˇhis view | the ˊrituals | ˏpriests | and ˇdoctrines of ·Christi·anity | ↑had ˍfostered ˏhatred | and exˆtremism | ˋrather than com⌄passion | and ·toleˇration | ˏyet | unˋtil his ·death in ·seventeen ·seventy-ˏeight | ↑he reˏtained | a beˍlief in ˎGod || ·though Volˋtaire's ·God | the ˋGod of a ⌄deist | ↑was ·one that ˋmost Christians ‸ would ·scarcely have ˎrecognised || ˇdeists | were ·people who beˏlieved | in ·God as a creˎator || but ˉunlike the ˇtheists | a ⌄similar ·name | but a ˋvery ˋdifferent ˏschool | ˏdeists | reˍjected ‸ reveˎlation || ↑ˇNewton for e·xample | was a ˎtheist || ·Volˇtaire | was a ˎdeist || it was conˋtinuing be·lief in ˎprovidence | ·which suˍstained | ·Voltaire's ˎdeism || howˏever | we ˊknow | that the ˉsuffering | and ˇevil in the ·world | ·made it inˋcreasingly ⌄difficult ·for him | to mainˆtain this be·lief || ˉquite ˇlate in ·life | he ·wrote his ·famous ˍnovel ‸ Canˎdide || ˊhere | he reˋjected the Leib·nizian ˏview | that ·this is the ·best of ˉall ·possible ˏworlds | ˋeven ·though in his ˇearlier ·writings | ·he'd suˋpported ·it || ˋwhy Vol·taire's i·deas underˇwent this ·change | is ˍnot ˎclear || ˏpossibly | his ·new ˊpessimism was a re·sult of the great ˋearthquake | of ·seventeen ·fifty-ˎfive | which on ˋAll ·Saints ·Day of ˆall ·days | had ˉleft | the ˉgreat | ˉCatholic ·city of ˍLisbon | a ˎruin || but ˋwhether or ·not the ˏearthquake | was ⌄solely re·sponsible | for ·Voltaire's ·change of ˏheart | and ↑I ˍthink that un⌄likely | the ˉfact reˍmains | that from aˋbout seventeen ·fifty-ˍfive | ˉVolˏtaire | oˎpposed the ·optimists' ac·ceptance of ˍevil | as a ˉnecessary ˍelement | in ˉany ˍworld | creˍated by ˎGod || for Volˉtaire | ·evil ˉhad to be ˍseen | as a ˋblemish | that deˋtracted from the per·fection of ˍGod's creˎation || of ˎcourse | ·why ·God should have ·chosen to creˇate such an im·perfect ·world | was a ˋmystery | ↑but Volˍtaire ˏargued | that ˉman's ina·bility to ·fathom the ·ways of his ˍmaker | was ˋno ·reason for a ˍloss of ˎfaith || ↑howˏever | there ˇwere ·some | for ·whom the ˋevil in ·nature | was ˉmore conˍsistent | with ·atheism and ·blind ˋchance | than with ˍdeism and ˎprovidence || ↑and from the ˏmiddle | of the ·eighteenth-ˏcentury | ˉthose who still beˇlieved in ·providence | ˉcame inˋcreasingly ·under aˏttack | from a ˊsmall | but influˋential ·group of ·athe·istic philoˍsophes | who ˊfound | the ˉGod of the ⌄Christians | ˉand the ·God of the ˋdeists | ˇequally | ·unacˎceptable || ˉthis ·new ˍatheism

| e·merged ˇmainly | in the ·writings of the maˍterialists | Laˊmetsuit | ˇDiderot | Helˇvetius | and ˎHolbach || the traˊditional | ·proviˊdentialist | in·terpre·tation of ˍnature | was be·ginning to aˍppear | ·less conˎvincing || this is ˋevidence that we can ˏadd | to ·what we ·know of Volˋtaire's ·change of ·heart || I'm ˋsure we ·can't aˎccount | for the ˋchanging ·attitudes to ·providence | by ˉreference | to ˉany ˍsingle ˎcause | ˉsuch as the ˍLisbon ˎearthquake | ·which I've just ˎmentioned || the ˏgeneral con·dition of ˋEurope | the perˍsistence of ˋwar | ˋfamine | and ˍunfair ·autocratic ˎgovernment | ˋwere I'm ˎcertain | ˋfar more co·rrosive in their e·ffect | than the diˍsaster of ˎLisbon || and ˎwhat's even ˋmore relevant to this ·talk | deˉvelopments in ·science ˋtoo | were ·proving ·most diˎsturbing || of ↑ˋall the ·eighteenth ·century ·French ˏscientists | ˉnone | was more ˉwidely ˍknown | and ˉinfluˍential | than the ˉnatural hiˍstorian | Buˎffon || his vo·luminous ·writings were ˉspecial ˎfavourites | with the ˉreading ·public of ˏFrance | ·until ˋwell into the ˍnineteenth ˋcentury || they were ˏprized | not ˎonly for their illuˊstrations | and their ˉcharming | ↑yet preˋcise aˏccounts | of the ˉanimal ˏworld | and geˏology | but ˇalso | for the ˍfascinating ·specuˎlations | which they conˎtained || ↑in diˍscussing the ·age of the ˋearth for e·xample | Bu·ffon suˏggested | that ˋeach of the ·days of cre·ation in ˍGenesis | ˋrepre·sented an ˋepoch | of ˍseveral ·thousands of ˋyears | ˋrather than ˬliterally | ˍtwenty-four ˋhours || he ˬalso ·castigated ·those | who sought ˋpurpose | and deˋsign ·every·where || ˍafter ˎall said ·Buffon | ˉaren't there ˏmany things in ·nature | ·like ·male ˊnipples | which ·seemingly have ·no ˏpurpose || and ˇseveral ·times | he ˉraised the ·possiˏbility | of ˉsomething reˍsembling | an evoˋlutionary ·history | for ↑the ˍearth | and its inˎhabitants || though ↑Buˍffon | was ˍnot an ·evoˎlutionist | in ˍany ·modern ˎsense || ↑Volˏtaire | ˋjoined ·orthodox ˏChristians | in disˍliking | ˉanything aˍpproaching | ˉevo·lutionary specuˎlation || ↑and there was aˎnother | very ˎdifferent tra·dition of ·scientific reˏsearch | in ·eighteenth ·century ˍFrance | ↑which ·came to be ˍviewed | with ˋequal suˍspicion | by both ˉChristians | and ˎdeists || ˇthis tra·dition | was matheˋmatical | and was conˏcerned | with ˉtying ˏup | the ˉloose ˎends | ·left by ˎNewton || ˏhence | it ·was at least in ˇorigin | a ˉwholly Newˎtonian tra·dition | ↑and it was purˍsued | as ˏsuch | by ˊMaupertuis | ˉd'Alemˏbert | ↑Laˍgrange | and Laˎplace || but ˉthis | did ˉnot | preˋvent it from ˋyielding conˇclusions | eˋspecially in the ·writings of Laˉplace | which ˉNewton himˍself | ↑would have ˍfound ˎhorrifying || in parˎticular | it ˉfostered | a maˋterialist ·view of ·nature | con·sistent ˉonly | with ˉthorough-going ˎatheism || ↑reˬcall for a ·moment | ·Newton's ˎuniverse | reˏmember | ·how he ˊsought | to ·leave ˏroom | for ·immaˋterial

·agents in ˏnature | ¯which would be ·manifesˍtations | of ·God's conˊtinuing | and uniˬversal | acˎtivity || for ˏNewton | ˏgravity | was ˋnot | an ¯iˏnnate | ·property of ˎmatter || ¯rather | it was ˏcaused | by an ˋagent | who ˍwas of ·course ˋGod || ↑now it was ˇpossible | to in·terpret ˏNewton | ·very ˎdifferently | and the ˋeighteenth-·century ·French mathemaˇticians | ↑who ˎmanaged to do wiˇthout ·Newton's ·active ·principles | and ·shared ˋnone of his co·mmitment to ˇtheism | could ¯argue conˍvincingly | that the con·tinued ac·tivity of ˍGod ˋin ·nature | was an unˍnecessary ‸ aˎssumption || ↑there's a ˏstory | that the ·emperor Na·poleon ¯once asked Laˍplace | to exˋplain the ·place of ˎGod in his ·system || ˎsire ‸ La·place re·plied | I have ¯no ˎneed ‸ of ·that hy·pothesis || La·place's ˊuniverse | ·worked ˋperfectly ·well wi·thout a ·God | ·and as a ma¯terialist | he ˋtherefore ·saw ¯no ˎreason | for ˋpostu·lating di·vine acˎtivity || it's ˋin the ·writings of Laˏplace | at the ˬend of the ·century | that we ˋsee the ·culmi¯nation | of the tra¯dition | of ·atheistic ma¯terialist ˍthought | ·which had been de·veloping ˇin France | ˋsince a·bout ¯seventeen ˎfifty || it was a traˏdition | that deˏnied | ¯all ·signs of ˎprovidence in ·nature || it was a traˊdition | in ·which the ‸ ·immaˋterial | had ·no eˎxistence | ·hence a ˊsoul | di·stinct from our ·physical ˏbody | was ·inconˆceivable | ↑and ˍman | was ¯no ˍmore | than an a¯ssemblage | of ¯brute ˍmatter | ˇorganised | in a ˍcertain ˎway || ↑and it was a traˍdition | that ·taught ¯rigorous deˎterminism | a deˋterminism ·given its most ˋcelebrated exˬpression | in ↑Laˍplace's | ¯essay on ·probaˋbilities | of ˍeighteen ·fourˎteen || ˏhere | La¯place ˏargued | that an ˇinfinite ·mind | would be ¯capable | in ˇprinciple | of pre¯dicting | the ¯whole ·future ·course of ˍnature | and ¯human ˍhistory | from ↑a ˍknowledge | of the ˋpresent ·motions of the ˍparticles of ˎmatter || our ˇfate in ·other ·words | is ˏwritten | ·in the ˎatoms | and for ˇsome | ¯this ˬseemed to en·tail | that ¯free ˍwill is an iˆllusion | though ¯most loˬgicians | would ·now ˎquestion this con·clusion || for La¯place's conˍtemporaries | it was ↑a ˎdaunting ·prospect | but ¯one to ·which ˋmid eighteenth ·century en¯lightenmentˍthought | ·led ¯almost inˎexorably || ¯no ˎwonder ·critics of the enˏlightenment | like ¯Rousseau and ˍGoethe | were so ˎhorrified by the de·terminism in the ·teaching of the ma·terialists | and ˋthey ·weren't aˎlone || ˏd'Alembert | ˏVoltaire | and the ˍdeists were ˋalso ·hostile | ¯so ˋmuch ·so | that from aˋbout ·seventeen ˇseventy | the ·year of the publi·cation of ·Holbach's ·atheˇistic ·book | the ·system of ˏnature | it's ¯no ˎlonger ·possible to see the ·philoˍsophes | as in ˋany ·sense | a coˍherent ˎgroup || by ˇthen | the a·lignments were ˎcomplex || a·mong the ˏfriends of the en·lightenment | there was an ˍever-·widening ˎgulf | be·tween the maˎterialists | and the ˎdeists || ·then in the ·writings of the ˎcritics | there was ˋmounting aˎlarm | at the pre¯sumptuousness | of those ¯dangerous ˎreasoners | the ·phrase is ˋRousseau's | who ¯told them | that ·man is no ·more than a maˎchine || ↑and ˍfinally | we ·have the ˍchurchmen | who ^ a·long with the great maˋjority of ·French ·citizens | re¯jected or igˋnored | the ·wranglings of the phiˎlosophers | and ↑reˍmained ˍloyal | to tra¯ditional | ˅orthodox | ·Christiˎanity || ↑I've ¯tried to convey ˏsomething | of the ¯complex | and ˇshifting ·character | of ¯attitudes to re˅ligion | in ·eighteenth-ˍcentury ˎFrance || ·what I've ˇsaid | should be a ¯warning | against ¯simple ·generaliˋsations | a·bout ˋeighteenth-·century ·French ˏthought | ˍas a ˋwhole || and I've ˋno need to reˇmind you | that by the ˋearly ·years of the ˇnineteenth ·century | the ¯situˍation | had been ˋfurther ·compli·cated | by the ¯French revoˏlution | the ¯reign of ˏterror | the ¯rise of Naˍpoleon | and the eˍmergence of roˎmanticism | ˋall of ·which | had im¯portant ˍconsequences | for phi¯losophy | and re¯ligious beˍlief | in ˎFrance ||

019 SPOKEN ENGLISH CORPUS TEXT D02
Open University - Science and Belief
Open University tape: AMST283/5
Overlap passage

Transcribed by BJW

↑let's reˏturn to our ·philo_sophes | in par_ticular to ·Volˋtaire || now ˇVoltaire | was ¯not a ˏChristian | in ¯any _orthodox ˋsense || in ˇhis ·view | ↓the ˊrituals | ˏpriests | and ˇdoctrines of Christi·anity | ↑had _fostered ˏhatred | and exˋtremism | ˋrather than comˇpassion | and toleˇration || ˏyet | un·til his _death in ¯seventeen seventy-_eight || ↑he re_tained | a be_lief in ˎGod || though Volˋtaire's ·God | the ¯God of a ˬdeist | was ˋone that ˇmost ·Christians | would _scarcely have ˋrecognised ||

ˋdeists | were ¯people who be_lieved in ¯God | as a creˎator || but ¯unlike the ˎtheists | a ˇsimilar ·name | but a ˋvery ˇdifferent ·school | ¯deists re_jected | reveˋlation || ˇNewton for e·xample was a ˋtheist || Volˇtaire | was a ˋdeist || it was a con¯tinuing be_lief in ˋprovidence | which sus¯tained | ·Voltaire's ˎdeism || ↓howˆever we ¯know | that the ¯suffering | and ˇevil in the world | ¯made it inˋcreasingly ˇdifficult for him to mainˋtain this be·lief || ¯quite ˬlate in life | he ·wrote his ¯famous _novel | ·Canˎdide || _here | he reˋjected the ·Leibˇnizian ·view | that ¯this | is the ¯best | of ¯all ·possible _worlds | ¯even _though in his ˇearlier ·writings |

Transcribed by GOK

↑let's reˏturn | to our ·philo_sophes | ↑in par_ticular to Volˎtaire || now ¯Volˏtaire | was ¯not a ˏChristian | in ·any _orthodox ˋsense || in ˇhis view | the ˊrituals | ˏpriests | and ˇdoctrines of ·Christi·anity | ↑had _fostered ˏhatred | and exˆtremism | ˋrather than comˬpassion | and ·toleˇration | ˏyet | unˋtil his ·death in ·seventeen ·seventy-ˏeight | ↑he reˏtained | a be_lief in ˎGod || ·though Volˋtaire's ·God | the ˋGod of a ˬdeist | ↑was ·one that ˋmost Christians ‸ would ·scarcely have ˎrecognised ||

ˇdeists | were ·people who beˏlieved | in ·God as a creˎator || but ¯unlike the ˇtheists | a ˬsimilar ·name | but a ˋvery ˋdifferent ˏschool | ˏdeists | re_jected ‸ reveˎlation || ↑ˇNewton for e·xample | was a ˎtheist || ·Volˇtaire | was a ˎdeist || it was a conˋtinuing be·lief in ˎprovidence | ·which su_stained | ·Voltaire's ˎdeism || howˏever | we ˊknow | that the

ˉsuffering | and ˇevil in the ·world | ·made it inˋcreasingly ⌄difficult ·for him | to main^tain this be·lief || ˉquite ˇlate in ·life | he ·wrote his ·famous ˍnovel ‸ Canˎdide || ˊhere | he reˋjected the Leib·nizian ˏview | that ·this is the ·best of ˉall ·possible ˏworlds | ˋeven ·though in his ˇearlier ·writings |

020 SPOKEN ENGLISH CORPUS TEXT D03
Open University - Development of Fractions
(First part)
Open University tape: AM289/08
Transcribed by BJW

the ¯last two ˬunits of the ˬnumbers ·option | units Nˇfour | and Nˇfive | are ¯called | ·written ˬfractions | and ¯methods of calcuˎlation || ¯unit Nˬfour | is con¯cerned with _fractions | ·other than ˋdecimal ·fractions || and ¯unit Nˬfive | ¯deals with the ·history of the ˇcounting ·board | or ˋabacus || ˇand with | ·decimal ˋfractions || ↑in ˏpractice | we can't ˋseparate the two ˋtopics of ¯fractions | and calcuˎlation || ¯so you'll _find in unit Nˏfour | that there's a ¯good deal of ma_terial | de¯scribing how calcu_lations with ˏfractions | were carried ˋout | in ·ancient ˋtimes ||

↑now ¯fractions a·rise _naturally | in _day-to-day ˎlife || as ¯soon as we _want to diˋvide up ¯some whole ˬobject | or ˬquantity into ˋparts || ¯in ·this _way ˋfractions ˋmust have ·entered into ·everyday ˏlife | in ˎancient ·times || diˏviding up an inˋheritance | or a ·piece of ˋland for e·xample || or ¯sharing out _sacks of ˇcorn | or _loaves of ˋbread || inˋdeed | our own ˋword | _fraction | comes from a ˋLatin root | ¯meaning | to _break ˋup || ↑from the ˬspoken ex·pressions for ·fractions | ¯we can inˏfer | that ˋtwo parˋticular ˇkinds of ·fractions ¯played a ·special ˎrole || ↑these were ¯fractions which _have the number ˇone | as the ˇnumerator || we ˏcall ·these | ˋunit ·fractions || one ˋhalf | one ˋthird | one ˋquarter | and ˋso on || ¯and ˏfractions | which ˇadded to ·unit fractions ¯make up the ˎwhole again || ˋtwo thirds | ˋthree quarters | and ˎso on || ↑¯some of _these a·rose ¯very ˬoften | in ˏeveryˏday coˋmmercial ·dealings || and beˇcause of this | we ˏcall them | ˎnatural ·fractions || aˇmongst the ·natural fractions | it's ¯usual to in·clude | ˏone ·half | ˏone ·third | ˏone ·quarter | ¯and their ˎcomplements | ˋtwo thirds | and ˋthree quarters || ↑and ˬsometimes | one ¯sixth | and one _eighth | ↓as ˋwell || we aˋssume | that the ˇnatural ·fractions | ¯came into _general use | ˋfirst || and that as ˋtech·niques of ·calculation deˇveloped | so ˋthese were exˋtended | to inˏclude the ˏuse of ¯unit _fractions ˋgenerally in ·calcuˋlations ||

the ˇancient Eˇgyptians | made exˋtensive ·use of ·unit fractions || they ¯wrote them | by ·placing a ¯special ˬsymbol | which ¯looks like a ˎmouth | ¯over the _number ·representing the deˋnominator || thus one ˊthird for e·xample | was ˇwritten as | ¯three _vertical ˋstrokes | ↓with the ˇmouth symbol placed aˋbove them || the exˇceptions to this were the ˏsymbols for ·one ˏhalf | and one ˋquarter || ¯there were ˬspecial symbols for ˇthese ||

you'll _find them in the ˋradio notes in the ˋunit || and the ˋmouth with ˇtwo ·strokes under·neath it | ↑was _used to de·note | ·two ˋthirds || and was _called | the ·two ˋparts || the ˇthird ·part being of ·course | ↑the _complementary ·unit fraction | ↓one ˋthird || ↑there's a _modern conˇvention | for repreˋsenting these Eˋgyptian ˋfractions || this is _due to ·Otto ˋNeugebauer | and con¯sists of _writing a ˇbar | over the _numeral repre·senting the deˋnominator || or ·in the ˋcase of ·two ˋthirds | ¯writing | ˎtwo bars | a·bove the numeral ˎthree || ¯so for e_xample | the exˇpression | ¯one _sixth | plus ¯one _sixth | ·equals one ˇthird || is _written as | ¯six with a ·bar over it | _plus | a¯nother six with a ·bar over it | ¯equals | ˎthree with a ·bar over it || you'll ˏsee this | in the ˋradio notes | in the ˋunit || ↑this ex⌄pression | is actually ˇfound | in ·hieratic ˇscript | ¯in the leather _roll in the British Muˋseum ||

¯our ·knowledge of E_gyptian matheˏmatics ¯comes _mainly ˋfrom | ·two ⌄hieratic ˋtexts || the ¯Rhind paˏpyrus | and the ˏleather _roll I've just ˋmentioned || and ˇboth | are in the ¯British Muˏseum in ˎLondon ||

¯every multipliˏcation and diˎvision | ¯involving ˎfractions | ˊled to the ˏproblem of ·how to ˋdouble ˋunit fractions || you'll reˏmember that the E_gyptians ˇcalculated by | su_ccessive ˋdoubling || a¯part from the ⌄special case of two ˋthirds | the re¯sult of _doubling ˋany ·unit fraction with an ˇodd denominator | ¯had to be ex_pressed as a ˋsum of ·unit ·fractions || the ¯rules for ⌄doing this | are ˏgiven in the ˏRhind paˋpyrus || in the _form of a ¯special ˎtable | ·which we _call | the ¯two-to-ˎn ·table || because it gives ↑ˋall the ratios | ¯two-to-ˏn | for ˋn equal to ¯three _five _seven _nine and ˋso on | ˋright up to ˋone hundred and ˋone ||

we ¯show the _first ˇfew entries in the ˇradio notes in the ˋunit || for e_xample | ·twice one ¯fifth | is one _third | plus one fifˋteenth || ↓twice one ˊninth | is one _sixth | plus one ˎeighteenth | ↓and ˋso on || the ˋtable wasn't conˋstructed ·all at one ˇtime || ¯different _parts | were com_puted by ·different ˋmethods || the ˇoldest ·section for e·xample | in¯cludes | ˇall the ·cases | where _n is divisible by ˋthree ||

↑now the ¯question aˏrises as to just ˇwhy the E·gyptians | ·chose the par·ticular combiˇnations of ·unit ·fractions | ˏfound in the _two-to-ˋn table || we can su_ggest an ˋanswer to this | ¯if we re_member the _principle of ˇdoubling | ·used in calcu_lation with ˇwhole ·numbers || and i·magine the ˇcomplementary ope·ration | ˇhalving | ¯being a_pplied to the ˋnatural ·fractions ¯one _half and ·two ˋthirds || ↑this _gives us two ˋsequences || ↓one ˊhalf | ↓one ˊquarter | ↓one ¯eighth | ↓one sixˊteenth et ·cetera ||

↓and | ¯two _thirds | ˋone ·third | ¯one _sixth | one ˋtwelfth et ·cetera || and ¯these ˬsequences | play an im¯portant ˏrole in E¯gyptian matheˎmatics || ˇsometimes | they're ¯used in what would to¯day seem | an abˋsurd way | for eˇxample | ˋone ·third of ˇthree | is obˋtained by ˇfirst ·stating that ˋtwo thirds of ˋthree is ˇtwo || and ˇthen calculating by ˇhalving | ·so as to obtain ˇone third of ·three | is ˋone ||

↑we ˋdon't know when it was ·first aˇppreciated that the ¯unit ˏfraction | ¯one upon ˏn | could be _doubled | by di_viding ·two by ˋn || but we ˋmust ·recognise that for the Eˇgyptians | the ˇdoubling ·problem | was ¯different in ˋprinciple | from diˎvision || in the _Rhind paˏpyrus | we have eˏxamples such as the ˋfollowing || ¯what _part of ˋtwo | is ˋfive || _one ˇthird | is _one plus ˋtwo thirds || one fifˋteenth | is ·one ˋthird || that is to _say | a ¯third of _five | is ·one and two ¯thirds || a fifˇteenth of ·five | is ˎone third || and _these | add up to ˋtwo || so the reˋsult of the diˋvision of ˇtwo by ·five | is ¯one _third | plus _one fifˋteenth || ˇthis compu·tation | is _all set ·out ˏfor you | in the ˋradio notes ||

↑pro¯fessor ˬNeugebauer has suˏggested a ˋgeneral method | for _doubling unit ˋfractions | which may ˇwell have been ¯used | for com_puting ˇsome of the ·entries | in the _two-to-ˋn table || as an eˬxample of the ·method | we'll suˎppose | that we ¯want to ˬuse it | to com_pute ·twice one ˋfifth || we ¯try to repreˏsent the reˏsult as the ¯sum of a ˇnatural ·fraction of one ·fifth | and _some other ˋunit fraction || after exˋperimenting with one ˇhalf | of ¯one fifth ˇfails to provide an ·answer | we ˏtry one ˋthird || and ˋthis ·gives ·one fifˋteenth | plus a reˇmainder | which ¯has to _make the reˇmaining one and two ·thirds of one ·fifth | ·that is | ˋtwo fifths in ˋall || we ˇdo this | by _counting the ˋthirds || ˇone | con_sists of ˋthree thirds || and ˇtwo thirds of ˎtwo || ˇthree and ·two | are _written in ˋred | ˏunder the ˏsymbols for ˏone and two ˋthirds | as we've ˏshown in the ˋradio ·notes || now ¯these ·red ˏentries | are ¯called au_xiliary ˋnumbers || and you'll ¯find them dis_cussed in ˇgreater ·detail | in the ˋunit || so the reˇmainder we ·want | is ¯one _fifth | of ¯five ˎthirds || that is _just ˋone third || giving ˇtwice one ·fifth | ·equal to ˋone third | plus ¯one fifˎteenth | as we ¯had beˎfore || and ˏas we _have it | in the _two-to-ˋn ·table || ↑other ˏentries in the _table | can be aˏrrived at | by ˏusing the _various | ↓_natural ˋfractions ||

now the Eˋgyptian ·method of | ·calcuˏlation using ˏfractions was ˋvery ˋclumsy | and ·made a ˇdifficult ·problem out of diˋvision | and _out of a·ddition and subˋtraction of ·fractions || and as a reˏsult | their ˏalgebra was ¯very ˏprimitive | ¯being ˏlimited to the so_lution of ¯simple ·linear eˏquations | in _one un`known ||

we ˇfind unit ·fractions ˇalso | in Su`merian ·texts | from the _diggings in U`roc || ¯dating from the _end of the ¯fourth mi_llenium before `Christ || ¯these ˎtexts | re¯veal the eˇxistence of a ˇsystem of ·fractions | obˏtained by reˏpeated `halving || and there are `special ·cuneiform `signs | for ˇone ·half | ·one ¯third | ˇtwo thirds | and ·five `sixths || ¯these ˏfractions | are di¯rectly re_lated to the ¯choice of _units for _weights and `measures ||

020 SPOKEN ENGLISH CORPUS TEXT D03
Open University - Development of Fractions
(Second part)
Open University tape: AM289/08
Transcribed by GOK

↑¯these ˏfractions | are di¯rectly reˏlated | to the ·choice of _units | for _weights and ˎmeasures | and ¯lead ˋnaturally | to ˬgroupings | in ¯twelve | _thirty and ˋsixty | ˇall of ·which are to be ·found | in ·systems of _units | in ¯Mesopo_tamian meˎtrology || ¯as we _saw | in ·unit Nˎthree | the _Ba↑byˏlonians | had a ·sexaˇgesimal | ·place value ˬsystem | for _writing ˎnumbers | which was exˋtended | to in·clude sexa_gesimal ˎfractions || ˋthis meant | that ˋcalcu·lating the ˇfractions | was as ˏeasy | as ·calcuˏlating the ·whole ˋnumbers | and it ¯made ˏpossible | a ¯much more de·veloped ˎalgebra | than _that found in ˎEgypt || the Babyˇlonians ^ were for e·xample | ¯able to ·solve _systems of ¯linear and quaˋdratic eˏquations | in ˏtwo | or ·even ¯more unˎknowns || ↑an im·portant re_lated ·unit of ˎweight | was the ˎshekel | which was a ¯sixtieth ˎpart | of the ˋmanah || a ˇspecial ·symbol | a ¯small ˋcircle was ˏused | oˬriginally | to ↑de_note one ¯sixth of a ˎmanah | that _is | ten ˋshekels | and ˇthis ·later be·came | the ¯L-·shaped ˎwedge | in ·cuneiform ˎscript || we can ¯thus _see | an e¯xact ˬpara·llel | between ˋwriting ˬfractions | and _writing ·down ˎweights || ¯two _manah | ˋtwenty-·three ˊshekels ^ for e·xample | is ·written ·just as ^ ¯two ˏunits | and _twenty-·three ˎsixtieths | ¯two ˇvertical ·wedges | ·followed by ·two ˋL-shaped ·wedges | and _three ˎvertical ·wedges || ¯forming ˬordinary ·fractions | of the ·form ˋm over ˬn ^ in ·sexa·gesimal no·tation | ↑was con_sidered as a ·multipliˋcation of ˏm | by the ˇunit ·fraction | _one over ˋn || ex¯tensive ˎtables | of ¯one over ˎn | ·that is ^ ·sexa·gesimal reˇciprocal ·tables | ·have been ˎfound || ¯these are Suˎmerian | and ¯date from a_bout ¯two ˏthousand | ¯BˎC || ¯in the ˬearlier ·tables | ˋonly ·values of _n | which are ¯multiples of | ·two _three or ˋfive are in·cluded || ˇthese of ·course | ˋall ·give eˋxact | ·sexa·gesimal ˎfractions || ˇsometimes we find ·tables | with the re¯marks | ¯seven ·doesn't diˋvide | eˋleven ^ ·doesn't di·vide | but in ˇlater ·tables | ↑a·pproxi·mations ¯are ˎgiven | for re·ciprocals of ˏnumbers | such as _seven and eˎleven || ¯tables of ·multipli_cation comˋbined with ·tables of re·ciprocals | pro·vide a com¯plete | ·compu¯tational _system | for ¯all | ·sexa¯gesimal di_visions | ¯m upon ˎn | wi¯thin the _range of the ˎtables || as ¯Neuge·bauer reˎmarks | ¯this _system of ¯tables aˋlone | would ·put the ˋBaby·lonians a¯head | of ¯all nu·merical com_puters | in anˎtiquity || now ˋBaby·lonian aˬstronomy | be·gan ¯much _later | than ·Baby·lonian ·matheˋmatics || the aˋstronomers di·vided the ˎzodiac | that ·is ˆ the ¯sun's ·yearly ˎpath | into ¯twelve ˏsigns | of ¯thirty deˎgrees || ˋfollowing the ·sexaˇgesimal ·system | ¯each deˏgree was di·vided into ¯sixty ˏminutes | and ¯each ˏminute | into ˏsixty ˋseconds || ˋthis Baby·lonian di·vision of the ˏzodiac | was ↑a_dopted | by the ˆ ˋGreek a·stronomers | ↑and ˏlater | by the Hin·dus and the ˋArabs | and as we ·all ˏknow | it ↑con_tinues | ˋright ·up to the ·present ˎday || we ¯don't ˋknow | ·which Greek a·stronomer was the ˋfirst to | a·dopt the ·sexa·gesimal diˎvisions | be¯cause ¯Ptolemy's ·great ˆ ·Syntaxis Matheˋmatica | ·usually re·ferred to as the ˆ ˋAlma·gest | a coˋrruption of the ˆ ˋArabic | ·meaning the ˎgreatest | ↑has e_clipsed the ·work of ·all his ˎpredecessors | ↑but we can be ·pretty ˏcertain that | Hiˋpparchus | who ·lived a·bout ˆ one ·fifty BˇC | some ·three ˇcenturies before ·Ptolemy | ¯used sexa·gesimal _fractions | in his ·calcuˎlations | since we ˇknow | he was con¯versant with ·Baby·lonian aˎstronomy || ˇPtolemy | was a ·virtuˋoso with these ·fractions | diˊviding | and ˏmultiplying them | ex¯tracting ·square _roots | and _so on | wiˋthout ·feeling ˋany need to ex·plain in ˇdetail | the techˋniques that he was ·using || ¯our thanks are ·due to his ˇcommen·tator | ·Theon of AlexˇAndria | ↑for pro_viding us | with the ˇdetails | of ·actual eˎxamples || for ¯purposes ˇother than a·stronomy | the ¯Greeks | made _use of ·natural ˇand unit ·fractions | ¯just as the E_gyptians and ·Babyˋlonians ·did || we ˇknow a·bout their no·tation | for ˊfractions | from the ¯works of ˆ for e·xample _Archiˋmedes | ˎHeron | and _DioˎPhantus | ↑and from a _number | of o·riginal sur·viving paˎpyri || ¯they gave _names | to the ·unit _fractions | from the _ordinal ˎnumbers || one ˇthird for e·xample | could be ¯written out in ˏwords | as ¯to ˆ ˎtriton | or it ¯might be aˋbbreviated to ˎto | just ¯T ˎO | ¯followed by the ·letter ˏgamma | ·repre·senting ˏthree | with ˇon | ¯O ˏN | as a ˋsuper·script || ˇlater | ¯unit ˏfractions were ·repre·sented | ¯simply by the ˋletter | or ˏletters | of the deˏnominator | _followed by an ˋaccent || ¯one ˏthird | ·would ˆ ·thus ·just be ·written as ˆ ·gamma ˋdash || the ˋGreeks were faˇmiliar | with ·more ˋgeneral ·fractions | as ˋwell || _sometimes | the ˊnumerator | would be ¯given a ˋstroke | and the de¯nominator an ˋaccent | but ¯this could _lead | to mis_underˋstandings | and ↑from the ·time of Archiˇmedes | that ·is ˆ the ˋthird ·century ·B_C | we ¯find the de_nominator | ·written aˋbove the ·numerator | ↑for e_xample | ¯epsilon a·bove ˋgamma | _five a·bove ˋthree | to ↑de_note ·three ˎfifths || a paˋpyrus from the ·first ˋcentury AˇD | ¯has the ˏfraction | in our ¯more faˋmiliar ·form | the _three a·bove the ˎfive | _gamma a·bove ˎepsilon | though wi¯thout the ·fractional ˇbar | which is a comˏparatively | _late inˎvention || ↑we _find | the _same noˏtation | for ·general ˏfractions | in ·Hinˋdu works | ↑from a_bout | the ˆ ˋeighth

·century | AˎD || ↑we find aˇnother e·xample of ·fractions | a·ssociated with ·units of ⌄measurement | with ↑the ˏRoman | ˍduoˋdecimal ·fractions || we ˉdon't ˋknow for ˏcertain | the ⌄time | or the ˉplace | or the ˋorigin of ·these || ↑howˍever | we ˇdo ·know | that the ˉRoman ˎAs | ˉA ˎS | which was a ˉcopper ˏcoin | oˋriginally ·weighing a ⌄pound | but reˉduced | un·til by a·bout one ˇninety B·C | it ·weighed only ·half an ⌄ounce | ↑was diˍvided | into ˍtwelve ^ ˎunciae || ˉeach | duoˉdecimal | ·subdi·vision of the ˍAs | had its ˉspecial ˏname | and ˎsymbol || for eˎxample | ˋsix ^ ·unciae | that ·is ^ ˇhalf an ·As | was ·called ^ ˋSemis | and ·given the ·symbol ^ ˎS || eˇleven ^ ·unciae | that ·is ^ the ˉfraction | e·leven ˇtwelfths of an ·As | was ·called ^ ˋDeunx | from ^ ˉDe ˎUncia | ·that is the ˇwhole | ·less ·one ˋuncia || ˇthis was ·written | as an ˎS | ˋfollowed by ˉfive ˏlines | or ↑ˇsometimes | ·five ˎdots | as we ˍshow in the ˎradio ·notes || the ˉuncia it⌄self | was ·subdiˏvided for e·xample | into the siˊcilicus | one ⌄quarter of an ·uncia | the ˊscripulus | one ·twenty-ˎfourth | ↑and ˎso on || we can ˉsee | that ·these ˏfractions | ˇdon't ·follow | the ⌄decimal pro·gression | that we ˍhave with the ^ ˏone | ˏten | ˏhundred | a ˏthousand | in ˉRoman noˏtation | for ˋwhole ·numbers || ↑ˋcalcu·lation ˇusing these ·fractions | was ·clumsy and ·inconˎvenient | parˇticularly | as ˋonly a ·limited ˇnumber of them | was aˍvailable for ˎuse || for eˋxample | ˇVarro | ˉfirst century BˏC | ·mentions ·only ˋtwelve such ·fractions ↑though ˍlater ˏwriters | deˍscribe ˎmore || ·Victor of ˊAquitaine | ·fifth century AˉD for e·xample | ·lists ˍsevenˋteen | and ˋAdelard of ˊBath | ⌄twelfth ·century | ·mentions ˍtwenty-ˋfour || ↑ˉRoman ˏfractions | can be deˍscribed | as ·something of a ˎcul-de-·sac | in the ·history of the ·evo·lution of ·fractional noˎtation || the ˇmainstream of de·velopment | can ↑be ˍseen | as ·coming from the ˎGreeks | to the ·HinˎDus | and ˉthen to the ˏWest | ·via the ˎArabs | who ·introˍduced our fa·miliar ˋbar | with the ˉnumerator aˍbove | and the deˍnominator beˎlow || ˉnot ˇall Arab ·writers used the ·bar how·ever | and it was ˉfrequently oˎmitted | in ·Latin ·medi·eval ˎmanuscripts || it ·came into ˇgeneral ·use | in the sixˇteenth ·century | though ˋinstances of ·fractions ·written wiˇthout any ·bar | oˉccur as ·late as for e·xample | the a·rithmetic of ·Paulo Caˎssate | ·published in Boˍlogna | in ˍsixteen ·eighty-ˎfive || ⌄lastly | ↑a ˍword a·bout the ^ ˎsolidus | or ˎstroke | which eˋnables the ·numerator and deˍnominator | to be ˋprinted on ·one ·line of ˎtype | inˇstead of ·having | to ·use up ˋthree ·lines | ·one for the ˊnumerator | ·one for the ⌄bar | and ˍone for the deˋnominator || ˉthis ·seems to have oˏriginated | aˉround the ·end of the ˇeighteenth ·century | in ˉLatin Aˋmerica | oˋriginally as a ˉcurved ⌄line | ˉrather ˍlike | our ˍmodern ˎintegral ·sign || the ˋuse of the ˇordinary ·stroke | was

¯reco_mmended by De ˇMorgan | in ↑his _paper | of ·eighteen ·forty-ˏfive | en·titled ˄ the _calculus of ˎfunctions | al·though ¯he himˬself | ·used a ˋcolon | which had ·been the ·customary ·sign for a ˬratio | since the _mid ·seventeenth ˎcentury || the ¯stroke was a_dopted by ˋStokes | in his mathe¯matics and ˎphysics ·papers | ¯published in _eighteen ˎeighty | and yet aˋnother ·English ·mathema·tician | ˋCayley | when he ¯first _saw the ¯stroke | in ¯Stokes' ˎpapers | ˋwrote to ·him and ·said | I ˋthink the ·solidus looks ¯very well inˎdeed || it would ¯give you | a ¯strong ˎclaim | to be ¯president | of the soˋciety for the pre·vention of ·cruelty to ˎprinters ||

020 SPOKEN ENGLISH CORPUS TEXT D03
Open University - Development of Fractions
Open University tape: AM289/08
Overlap passage

Transcribed by BJW

↑pro¯fessor ⌄Neugebauer has suˏggested a `general method | for _doubling unit `fractions | which may ˇwell have been ¯used | for com_puting ˇsome of the ·entries | in the _two-to-`n table || as an e⌄xample of the ·method | we'll suˎppose | that we ¯want to ⌄use it | to com_pute ·twice one `fifth || we ¯try to repreˏsent the reˏsult as the ¯sum of a ˇnatural ·fraction of one ·fifth | and _some other `unit fraction || after ex`perimenting with one ˇhalf | of ¯one fifth ˇfails to provide an ·answer | we ˏtry one `third || and `this ·gives ·one fif`teenth | plus a reˇmainder | which ¯has to _make the reˇmaining one and two ·thirds of one ·fifth | ·that is | `two fifths in `all || we ˇdo this | by _counting the `thirds || ˇone | con_sists of `three thirds || and ˇtwo thirds of ˎtwo || ˇthree and ·two | are _written in `red | ˏunder the ˏsymbols for ˏone and two `thirds | as we've ˏshown in the `radio ·notes ||

Transcribed by GOK

Pro¯fessor ˇNeugebauer | has su_ggested a `general ·method for _doubling ·unit ˎfractions | which may ˇwell have been ·used | for com·puting ⌄some of the ·entries | in the ¯two-to-ˎn ·table || ¯as an exˏample of the ·method | ¯we'll su⌄ppose | that we ·want to _use it | to com·pute _twice one ˎfifth || we ¯try to ·repre·sent the re_sult | as the ¯sum of a ˇnatural ·fraction of one ·fifth | and ·some other `unit ·fraction || after ex`perimenting with one ˇhalf ^ of one·fifth | ⌄fails to pro·vide an ·answer | we ˏtry one `third | and ¯this _gives ¯one fifˎteenth | ·plus a re⌄mainder | which ¯has to _make the reˇmaining ·one and two ·thirds of one ·fifth | that ·is ^ ¯two _fifths in ˎall || ↑we ⌄do this | by ˏcounting the ˎthirds || ˏone | con_sists of `three ·thirds | and ˇtwo thirds | of ˎtwo || ¯three and ˏtwo | are ·written in `red | ·under the ˏsymbols | for _one and two ˇthirds | as we've _shown in the ˎradio ·notes ||

021 SPOKEN ENGLISH CORPUS TEXT E01
Daily Service
Broadcast notes: Radio 4, 10.45 a.m., 26th November, 1985
Transcribed by BJW

[speech extract omitted]

ˇFather | we ˋthank •you | for the ˋwonder of your ˋdealings with manˋkind || from the beˉginning until ˎnow || for ˉyour creative ˎword || by •which the ˉheavens and the ˍearth were ˋmade || for ˋmaking us | in your •own ˋimage | ˍable to ˉhear | and ˍanswer your ˋcall || for the ˋwritten •word | which ˉhas been a ˍlamp to our ˋfeet | and still ˋshines upon our ˋway || for the ˋmystery of the •word | made ˉflesh in the •coming of our ˍLord •Jesus ˎChrist || for the preserˋvation | of your ˉtrue and ˬliving •word | in the ˋChurch || and ˉfor your •word to ˎus | ˋeven in ˋthese •violent •days | ˉspeaking | through the ˍvoices of ˉthose who ˍneed our ˎcare || we ˋthank you ˏFather | and ˋpraise your ˋname || and ˉnow | in the ˉwords your •son ˍtaught us | ˉlet us ˎpray | ˉour ˎFather ||

[speech extract omitted]

ˉmany of the reˬligions | of the ˋancient ˇworld | ˉpromised salˬvation | to an eˋlite || who knew ˋsecrets | ˋhidden from the ˋmasses || but ˉnothing could be •more ˍopen than the ˉkingdom ˋJesus •promised || it can be ˉfound in ˋeveryone | who ˋreaches •out to us in ˋneed || as we ˉfind in toˇday's •reading | from St ˉMatthews ˍgospel | ˍchapter •twenty ˋfive || ˉJesus ˍsaid | ˉwhen the •son of ˏman | comes in ˬglory | and ˉall his •angels ˍwith him | ˉthen he will ˍsit on his ˉglorious ˎthrone || ↑beˇfore him | will be ˍgathered ˉall the ˎnations | and he will ˋseparate them | •one from aˋnother | as a ˬshepherd | ˇseparates | a ˋsheep from the ˋgoats || ↓and he will •place the ˋsheep | at his •right ˋhand | but the ˋgoats | at the ˋleft || then the ˋKing | will ˉsay to ˍthose at his •right ˍhand | ˋcome | oh ˍblessed of my ˏFather | inˉherit the ˍkingdom preˋpared for •you | from the founˋdation of the ˋworld || for I was ˋhungry | and you ˉgave me ˎfood || I was ˋthirsty | and you ˉgave me ˎdrink || ˉI was a ˏstranger | and you ˋwelcomed me | I was ˉnaked | and you ˎclothed me || ˉI was ˎsick | and you ˋvisited me || ˉI was in ˎprison | and you ˋcame to me || then the ˋrighteous will ˉanswer him || ˋLord || ˏwhen did we see ˋthee •hungry | and ˎfeed thee || or ˋthirsty | and •give thee ˋdrink || and ˋwhen did we •see thee a ˋstranger and ˋwelcome thee | or ˋnaked and ˋclothe thee | ↑and ˍwhen did we see thee ˇsick | or in ˍprison and ˋvisit thee || and the ˉKing will ˍanswer •them || ˋtruly I ˋsay to you | ˉas you ˎdid it | to the ˉleast of _these my `brethren | you `did it to `me || `then he will ·say to ·those at his `left ·hand || de`part from `me you `cursed | into the e`ternal ·fire | pre¯pared | for the `devil and his `angels || for ·I was `hungry | and you ˏgave me no _food || ·I was `thirsty | and you ˏgave me no _drink || ˏI was a ˬstranger | and you did ¯not ˬwelcome me || ˇnaked | and you _did not `clothe ·me || ¯sick and in _prison | and you _did not ˇvisit me || then ·they will `also ·answer | ↑`Lord | _when did we ¯see thee `hungry | ↑or ˬthirsty | ↑or a ˬstranger | or ˬnaked | or in ˬprison | and ·did not ˬminister to thee || ¯then he will _answer to ·them || ˎtruly I `say to you | `as you did it `not | to ·one of the `least of `these | you `did it `not | to `me || ˇFather | `help us to `walk | in your _son's ·footsteps | re¯membering | ·his self-for_getting hu`mility | his `love for all `people | his com`passion for the `fallen | his forˎbearance with the mis`taken | and his ˎpatience with the `slow | and his for¯giveness of ·all ˎthose | who `hurt him || ¯Lord | I be`lieve in you || in`crease my `faith || I `trust in you | `strengthen that ·trust || I ˎlove you | ¯let me _love you ¯more and ˎmore || I'm `sorry for my `sins || `deepen my ·sorrow || I ˇworship you || as my ¯first beˎginning || I `long for you || as my ¯last ˎend || I ¯praise you | as my ¯constant ˎhelper || and `call on ·you | as my `loving pro`tector || ¯guide me | by your ˎwisdom || co¯rrect me | with your ˎjustice || `comfort me | with your `mercy || pro`tect me | with your `power || ↑I ˎoffer you ·Lord | my `thoughts || to be ˎfixed on you || my ¯words to have _you for their `theme || my `actions | to re¯flect my _love for `you || my ´sufferings | to be en`dured | for your ¯greater ˎglory || I ¯want to _do | what you ˇask of me | ˇin the ·way you ·ask | for as ˇlong as you ·ask | because ¯you ˎask it || ¯Lord | en`lighten my underˇstanding | `strengthen my `will | ¯purify my ˎheart | and `make me `holy || ¯help me to reˎpent | of my ·past ˬsins || ¯help me to re_sist temp`tation | in the `future || ¯help me to ·rise a_bove my `weaknesses | and to ·grow `stronger | as a `Christian || `let me ˇlove you | my ¯Lord and my ˬGod | and ¯see myˏself | as I ¯really ˎam || a `pilgrim | in this ˬworld || a ¯Christian | ·called to re¯spect and _love | ¯all _those whose ¯lives I ˬtouch || ¯those in authority ¯over me | or ·those under ˎmy authority || my ¯friends | and my ˎenemies || `help me to ·conquer `anger | with ˎgentleness || ¯greed | by geneˎrosity || ˬapathy | by `fervour || ¯help me to for_get my`self | and ·reach ¯out towards ˎothers || make me `prudent in `planning || and cou`rageous in ·taking `risks || make me `patient | in `suffering | and unaˇssuming | in pro`sperity || `put me on ¯guard | a`gainst my ¯weaknesses || ·let me ˬcherish | ·your ˏlove for me | and ˇkeep your ·law | and ¯come at _last | to `your sal`vation || ¯teach me to _realise | that `this world is ˇpassing |

and that my ˇtrue ·future | is in the ¯happiness of ˎheaven || that _life on ·earth is ¯short | and the _life to ˇcome | eˋternal ||

021 SPOKEN ENGLISH CORPUS TEXT E01
Daily Service
Broadcast notes: Radio 4, 10.45 a.m., 26th November, 1985
Transcribed by GOK

[speech extract omitted]

ˇFather | we ˇthank you | for the ˋwonder | of your ˎdealings | with manˎkind || from the beˊginning | until ˎnow || for ˉyour cre•ative ˎword | by •which the ˉheavens | and the ˍearth were ˎmade || for ˋmaking us | in your ˉown ˎimage | •able to ˉhear | and ˍanswer your ˎcall || ↑for the ˋwritten •word | which ˉhas been a ˋlamp | to our ˎfeet | and still ˋshines | u•pon our ˎway || for the ˋmystery of the ˏword | •made ˉflesh | in the ˍcoming | of our ˉLord •Jesus ˎChrist || for the •preserˋvation | of your ˊtrue | and ˉliving ˏword | in the ˋChurch || and ˉfor your •word to ˎus || ˉeven in ˋthese •violent ˎdays || ˉspeaking | through the ˍvoices | of ˉthose who •need our ˎcare || we ˋthank you ˏFather | and ˋpraise your ˎname || and ˊnow | in the ˊwords | your ˉson ˎtaught us | ˉlet us ˎpray || ↓ˉour ˎFather ||

[speech extract omitted]

↑ˉmany of the reˬligions | of the ˉancient ˬworld | ˉpromised salˬvation | to an eˋlite | who •knew ˇsecrets | ˋhidden from the ˎmasses || but ˉnothing could be •more ˎopen | than the •kingdom ˋJesus •promised || it can be ˊfound | in ˋeveryone | who ˉreaches •out to us in ˎneed | as we ˊfind | in toˉday's ˏreading | from St ˉMatthews ˏgospel | •chapter ˉtwenty- ˎfive || ↑ˉJesus ˍsaid | •when ↑the ˉson of ˏman | ˉcomes in ˏglory | a nd ˉall his •angels ˏwith him | ↑ˉthen he will ˍsit on his •glorious ˎthrone || beˇfore him | will be ˏgathered | ˉall the ˎnations | and ↑he will ˋseparate them | ˉone from aˋnother | as ↑a ˬshepherd | ˉseparates | a ˋsheep | from the ˎgoats || and he will •place the ˋsheep | at his •right ˬhand | but the ˇgoats | at the ˎleft || ↑•then the ˋKing | will •say to •those at his •right ˍhand | ˋcome | oh •blessed of my ˍFather | inˉherit the ˍkingdom preˋpared for you | from the founˉdation of the ˎworld || for •I was ˎhungry | and you ˉgave me ˎfood | I was ˋthirsty | and you •gave me ˎdrink | ˉI was a ˎstranger | and ˉyou ˎwelcomed me | I was ˉnaked and you ˎclothed me | ↑ˉI was ˎsick | and you ˎvisited me | I was imˎprisoned | and you ˎcame to me || then the ˉrighteous will ˍanswer him | ˋLord | ˏwhen did we see ˋthee •hungry | and ˎfeed thee | or ˋthirsty | and •give thee ˋdrink | and ↑ˋwhen did we ˏsee thee a ˋstranger | and ˋwelcome thee | or ↑ˋnaked and ˎclothe thee | and ↓ˍwhen did we •see thee

ˏsick | or in ˍprison and ˬvisit thee || and the ¯King will ˍanswer them | ˬtruly | I ˋsay to ·you | ↑¯as you ˬdid it | to the ¯least of ·these my ˎbrethren | you ¯did it to ˋme || ·then he will ·say to ·those at his ˋleft ·hand | deˋpart from ·me you ·cursed | ·into the e¯ternal ˎfire | pre¯pared | for the ˇdevil | and his ˎangels || for ·I was ˎhungry | and ↑you ˍgave me no ˏfood | I was ˋthirsty | and you ¯gave me no ˏdrink | ·I was a ˎstranger | and you did ¯not ˇwelcome ·me | ˋnaked | and you ˋdid ·not ˇclothe ·me | ¯sick and in ˏprison | and ↑you ˍdid not ˬvisit me || then ¯they will ˋalso ·answer | ↑ˋLord | ˏwhen did we ·see thee ˋhungry | ˋor ·thirsty | ˋor a ·stranger ˆ or ·naked ˆ or in ·prison | and ↓¯did not ˎminister to ·thee || ↑¯then he will ˎanswer to ·them | ↓ˎtruly I ·say to ·you | ¯as you ·did it ˎnot | to ·one of the ¯least of ˎthese | you ¯did it ˍnot | to ˋme || ˇFather | ¯help us to ˎwalk | in your ↓ˍson's ˍfootsteps | re¯membering | ¯his ˍself-forˍgetting | huˎmility || his ˋlove for ·all ˎpeople || his comˋpassion for the ˎfallen || his for↓ˋbearance with the misˎtaken || and his ↓ˋpatience with the ˎslow || and his for¯giveness | of ¯all ˋthose | who ˋhurt him || ˊLord | I beˋlieve in ˏyou | inˋcrease my ˎfaith || I ˋtrust in ˏyou | ˋstrengthen that ˎtrust || I ˋlove ˏyou | ¯let me ˍlove you | ¯more and ˎmore || I'm ˋsorry for my ˎsins || ˋdeepen my ˍsorrow || I ¯worship ˏyou | as my ¯first beˎginning | I ˎlong for ˏyou | as my ¯last ˎend || I ˏpraise you | as my ¯constant ˎhelper | and ˋcall on ·you | as my ˋloving proˎtector || ¯guide me | by your ˎwisdom | co¯rrect me | with your ˎjustice | ˋcomfort me | with your ˎmercy | proˋtect me with your ˎpower || I ˋoffer you ˏLord | my ˋthoughts | to be ˋfixed on ·you | my ˊwords | to ·have ˋyou for their ˎtheme | my ˋactions | to re¯flect my ·love for ˎyou | my ˊsufferings | to be enˋdured | for your ¯greater ˎglory || I ¯want to ˏdo | ·what you ˎask of ˏme | ˋin the ·way you ˏask | for as ˋlong as you ˏask | because ¯you ˎask it || ˏLord | enˋlighten my ·underˇstanding | ˋstrengthen my ˏwill | ¯purify my ˬheart | and ¯make me ˇholy | ¯help me to reˎpent | of my ¯past ˏsins | ¯help me to reˋsist ·tempˇtation | in the ˬfuture | ¯help me to ¯rise aˎbove my ˎweaknesses | and to ·grow ˇstronger | as a ˎChristian || ¯let me ˎlove you | my ¯Lord and my ˎGod | and ¯see myˏself | as I ¯really ˋam | a ˋpilgrim in this ˎworld | a ˊChristian | ·called to re¯spect and ˎlove | ¯all ˏthose | whose ¯lives I ˎtouch | ·those in au·thority ˊover me | or ¯those ·under ˎmy au·thority | my ˊfriends | and my ˎenemies || ¯help me to ¯conquer ˇanger | with ˎgentleness | ˊgreed | by ¯geneˎrosity | ˇapathy | by ˇfervour || ↑¯help me to for·get myˎself | and ·reach ¯out towards ˋothers || ·make me ¯prudent in ˎplanning | and cou¯rageous in ·taking ˎrisks || ·make me ˋpatient in ˎsuffering | and ¯unaˋssuming in proˎsperity || ¯put me on ˏguard | aˎgainst my ·weaknesses | ·let me ˇcherish | ˎyour ·love for ˬme

| and ¯keep your ˏlaw | and ¯come at ˎlast | to ¯your salˏvation || ·teach me to ˇrealise | that ˋthis ·world is ˏpassing | and that my ¯true ˍfuture | is in the ¯happiness of ˎheaven || that ·life on ·earth is ˊshort | and the ·life to ˇcome | ˎeternal ||

021 SPOKEN ENGLISH CORPUS TEXT E01

Daily Service

Broadcast notes: Radio 4, 10.45 a.m., 26th November, 1985

Overlap passage

Transcribed by GOK

ˇFather | we ˇthank you | for the ˋwonder | of your ˎdealings | with manˎkind || from the beˊginning | until ˎnow || for ˉyour cre·ative ˎword | by ·which the ˉheavens | and the ˍearth were ˎmade || for ˋmaking us | in your ˉown ˎimage | ·able to ˉhear | and ˍanswer your ˎcall || ↑for the ˋwritten ·word | which ˉhas been a ˋlamp | to our ˎfeet | and still ˋshines | u·pon our ˎway || for the ˋmystery of the ˏword | ·made ˉflesh | in the ˍcoming | of our ˉLord ·Jesus ˎChrist || for the ·preserˋvation | of your ˊtrue | and ˉliving ˏword | in the ˋChurch || and ˉfor your ·word to ˎus || ˉeven in ˋthese ·violent ˎdays || ˉspeaking | through the ˍvoices | of ˉthose who ·need our ˎcare || we ˋthank you ˏfather | and ˋpraise your ˎname || and ˊnow | in the ˊwords | your ˉson ˎtaught us | ˉlet us ˎpray || ↓ˉour ˎFather ||

Transcribed by BJW

ˇFather | we ˋthank ·you | for the ˋwonder of your ˋdealings with manˋkind || from the beˉginning until ˎnow || for ˉyour creative ˎword || by ·which the ˉheavens and the ˍearth were ˋmade || for ˋmaking us | in your ·own ˋimage | ˍable to ˉhear | and ˍanswer your ˋcall || for the ˋwritten ·word | which ˉhas been a ˍlamp to our ˋfeet | and still ˋshines upon our ˋway || for the ˋmystery of the ·word | made ˉflesh in the ·coming of our ˍLord ·Jesus ˎChrist || for the preserˋvation | of your ˉtrue and ˇliving ·word | in the ˋChurch || and ˉfor your ·word to ˎus | ˋeven in ˋthese ·violent ·days | ˉspeaking | through the ˍvoices of ˉthose who ˍneed our ˎcare || we ˋthank you ˏFather | and ˋpraise your ˋname || and ˉnow | in the ˉwords your ·son ˍtaught us | ˉlet us ˎpray | ˉour ˎFather ||

022 SPOKEN ENGLISH CORPUS TEXT E02
Daily Service
Broadcast notes: Radio 4, 10.45 a.m., 27th November, 1985
Transcribed by BJW

[speech extract omitted]

in ¯this _prayer we ¯ask God to ˏcome to us | ¯His ·Spirit to ˎour ·spirit || ·heavenly Father | whose ˋwill is ˋgood and _perfect || we beˏlieve and _trust | that ¯you _will | ¯only what is for the ¯true _happiness | of ¯your ˎpeople || you have ˎshown us your ¯love | and ¯purpose || in the ·life and ¯teaching of _Jesus your ˎson || have ¯mercy u_pon us | when ¯we have _gone our ¯own ˬway || ˋturn us ↑to yourˏself | and ¯grant us the _light of your _spirit | that ¯we may _live | as ˋpeople of ¯light | ¯people of the _new ˎday || ↓and ·grant that we may be ¯so re¯newed and reˬstored | that we may ¯live | in ¯truth with each ˬother | and at ¯peace with ˎyou || ·these our ·prayers we ˇoffer | in the ¯spirit of Jesus ˎChrist | as we ˏpray toˎgether || ¯Our ˎFather ||

[speech extract omitted]

the ˇreading | is from the ˋsecond letter to ˋTimothy | ¯chapter ˎsix | be_ginning at verse ˋten || ˇTimothy | the ˋfaithful ˋfollower | is re¯minded that the ˋcraving for ¯money and | maˋterial ↑ˋwealth | can ¯so ˎeasily dis¯place ˋspiritual ˋdepth | in the ˋhuman ˋheart || ˏriches and ˏwealth | ↓are ·not so much ·wrong in themˇselves | but ˋwhat is done ˋwith them || it is ˋthat | that reˋveals the ˋtrue ·nature | of _what we ˋare || the ˋlove of ˇmoney | is the ˎroot of ˋall ·evils || it is ¯through this ↑ˋcraving | that ˋsome have ˋwandered aˋway from the ↑ˋfaith | and ˋpierced their ˋhearts with ˋmany ˋpangs || but ·as for ¯you | ·man of ˏGod | ˇshun | ·all ˎthis || ˋaim at ˋrighteousness | ˋgodliness | ˋfaith | ˋlove | ˋsteadfastness | ↑ˋgentleness || ˋfight the good ˋfight of the ¯faith | ·take ˋhold of the eˋternal ˋlife | to ˋwhich you were ˇcalled | when you ˋmade the ·good conˋfession || ↓in the ¯presence of ¯God | who ·gives ¯life to all _things | ˋand of ·Christ _Jesus | I ˋcharge you to ˋkeep the coˋmmandment unˋstained | and ˋfree from reˋproach | un¯til the a_ppearing of our ¯Lord ·Jesus ˎChrist || and ¯this will be made ˏmanifest | at the ¯proper ˬtime | by the ˋblessed and ˋonly ˋsovereign | the ˋKing of ˋkings | and ˋLord of ˋlords | who aˋlone | has immorˋtality | and ¯dwells in | una¯pproachable ˬlight || whom ˋno man has ¯ever _seen | or ˎcan ·see | to ¯him be ˬhonour | and eˋternal doˋminion || ˋas for the ˋrich | in ¯this ˬworld | ˋcharge them ˋnot to be ˋhaughty | or ¯high ˎminded || ˋnor to set their

¯hopes on unˇcertain ·riches | but on ˋGod || who ˋrichly ˇfurnishes us | with ˋeverything to enˋjoy || they are to ·do ˋgood | to be ˍrich in good ˎdeeds | ˋliberal | and ˋgenerous || thus ˋlaying up for themˇselves | a ¯good founˍdation for the ˋfuture || so that they ¯may take ¯hold | of the ˎlife | which is ˎlife | inˎdeed || and ˍso to our ˎprayers || we re·member eˏspecially to·day | those who have ˬlost ·hope | ¯those who have ˏnothing to look ˏforward to | the oˍppressed | and the ˏhurt | the conˏfused | and the ·unˏsure || we ·pray eˋspecially | for ˋthose in northern ˍIreland | and the deˋbate | that will take ˍplace in ˋparliament | ¯this afterˎnoon || ˏFather | the ¯happiness of ˏpeople is ˏyour conˏcern | you have ˎmade us | for yourˍself | ¯and for each ˍother || it is ˍyour conˍcern | that ¯we should ˍlive | in ¯happiness | and in ˎpeace || ¯give us the ˍgift we ˍlong for | the ˋwisdom and ˋstrength | to give ¯life | and ˎhope | to ˋthose in deˋspair || so ¯Father | in the ¯mystery of your ˇprovidence | we ¯trust that in ˎthis | we shall ¯find our ˇown ·peace | and ¯life eˍternal || through ¯Jesus ˬChrist | ¯our ˎLord || aˎmen || and ˍso to our ¯last ˍhymn | number ¯twenty-ˎsix | in the ¯BBC ˍhymn book | the ¯Lord is ˍKing | lift ¯up thy ˍvoice || oh ¯earth | and ¯all ye ˬheavens | reˎjoice ||

022 SPOKEN ENGLISH CORPUS TEXT E02
Daily Service
Broadcast notes: Radio 4, 10.45 a.m., 27th November, 1985
Transcribed by GOK

[speech extract omitted]

•in ¯this ˏprayer | we ¯ask _God to ˏcome to us | ¯His •Spirit to ˎour •spirit || •heavenly •Father ˄ whose ¯will | is ¯good and _perfect | ¯we beˏlieve | and ¯trust | that ¯you ˏwill | ˋonly •what is for the ¯true _happiness | of ¯your ˎpeople || ↑you have _shown us | your ¯love | and ¯purpose | in the ¯life | and ˋteaching of •Jesus your ˎson || have ¯mercy uˏpon us | when ¯we | have ¯gone | our ¯own _way || ˇturn us | to yourˏself | and ˋgrant us the •light of your _spirit | that ¯we may ˏlive | as ˬpeople of •light | ¯people | of the ¯new ˎday || and •grant that •we may •be ¯so | re¯newed and reˎstored | that •we may ¯live | in ¯truth with each _other | and at ↓¯peace with ˎyou || •these ↑our _prayers | we _offer | ↑in the ¯spirit of •Jesus ˎChrist | as •we ¯pray toˎgether || ¯Our ˎFather

[speech extract omitted]

the ˇreading | is •from the ˋsecond •letter to ˎTimothy | ¯chapter ˏsix | be•ginning at _verse ˎten || ˇTimothy | the •faithful ˬfollower | is reˋminded that the ˋcraving for ¯money | and ma•terial ˇwealth | can ¯so ˎeasily | di•splace ¯spiritual ˎdepth | in the _human ˎheart || •riches and ˊwealth | are •not so •much ¯wrong in themˇselves | but •what is done ˋwith them | it is ˎthat | that re•veals the ˇtrue nature | of _what we ˎare || the ¯love of ˬmoney | is the ˋroot of ˎall •evils || it is ¯through this ˋcraving | that •some have •wandered a¯way from the ˋfaith | and •pierced their _hearts | with ˋmany ˎpangs || but •as for ¯you | ¯man of ˏGod | ˇshun | ¯all ˎthis || ˋaim at ˎrighteousness | ˋgodliness | ˎfaith | ˋlove | ˋstead•fastness | ˆgentleness || ˋfight the good •fight of the •faith | ¯take ˋhold of the e•ternal •life | to ¯which you were ˬcalled | when you •made the •good conˎfession || in the •presence of ¯God | who •gives ¯life to •all _things | ↑and of •Christ ˎJesus | I ˋcharge you | to ˋkeep the co•mmandment ¯unˎstained | and ˋfree from reˎproach | un•til the aˬppearing | of our ˋLord •Jesus _Christ || and ¯this will be •made _manifest | at the ¯proper ˏtime | by the ˋblessed and ˋonly ˬsovereign | the ˋKing of ˎkings | and ˋLord of ˎlords | who aˋlone has •immorˋtality | and ¯dwells | in •una¯pproachable _light | whom ˋno •man has ¯ever _seen | ¯or ˎcan •see | to ˎhim be ˋhonour | and e•ternal doˋminion || ˋas for the ˋrich in ¯this ˇworld | ˋcharge them •not to be ˇhaughty | or •high

ˇminded | ˋnor to ·set their ˍhopes | on un·certain ˍriches | ↑but on
ˋGod | who ˋrichly ˇfurnishes us | with ˉeverything to enˎjoy || ·they are to
·do ˋgood | ↑to be ˍrich in ·good ˎdeeds | ˋliberal | and ˎgenerous |
·thus ˋlaying ·up for themˇselves | a ˋgood foun·dation for the ˎfuture | so
that ·they ˉmay take ˉhold of the ˎlife | which is ˎlife | in↓ˋdeed || and
ˍso to our ˎprayers || we re·member eˇspecially to·day | ˉthose who have
ˎlost ˏhope | ˉthose who have ˎnothing | to ˋlook ·forward ·to | the
o·ppressed and the ˍhurt | the conˏfused | and the unˏsure || we ·pray
eˎspecially | for ˉthose in ·northern ˍIreland | and the deˎbate | that will
take ·place in ˍparliament | this ·afterˎnoon || ˏFather | the ·happiness of
ˍpeople | is ·your conˏcern | ·you have ˍmade us | for yourˍself | ·and for
each ˍother | ↑it is ·your conˍcern | that ˉwe should ˍlive | in ·happiness
and in ˍpeace || ˉgive us the ˍgift | ↑we ˍlong ·for | the ˉwisdom and
ˇstrength | to give ˉlife and ˍhope | to ·those in deˍspair || so ·Father ˆ in
the ˉmystery of your ˋprovidence | we ˉtrust that in ˎthis
| we shall ·find our ˉown ˍpeace | and ˉlife eˍternal | ˉthrough ·Jesus
ˍChrist | ˉour ˍLord | ↑aˎmen || and ·so to our ˉlast ˎhymn | ↑·number
ˉtwenty- ˍsix | in the ˉBBC ˍhymn book | the ↑ˉLord is ˍKing | lift ˉup
thy ·voice | oh ↑ˉearth | and ˉall ye ˎheavens | reˎjoice ||

022 SPOKEN ENGLISH CORPUS TEXT E02
Daily Service
Broadcast notes: Radio 4, 10.45 a.m., 27th November, 1985
Overlap passage

Transcribed by BJW

[speech extract omitted]

the ˅reading | is from the ˋsecond letter to ˋTimothy | ¯chapter ˎsix | be_ginning at verse ˋten || ˅Timothy | the ˋfaithful ˋfollower | is re¯minded that the ˋcraving for ¯money and | maˋterial ↑ˋwealth | can ¯so ˎeasily dis¯place ˋspiritual ˋdepth | in the ˋhuman ˋheart || ˏriches and ˏwealth | ↓are ·not so much ·wrong in them˅selves | but ˋwhat is done ˋwith them || it is ˋthat | that reˋveals the ˋtrue ·nature | of _what we ˋare || the ˋlove of ˅money | is the ˎroot of ˋall ·evils || it is ¯through this ↑ˋcraving | that ˋsome have ˋwandered aˋway from the ↑ˋfaith | and ˋpierced their ˋhearts with ˋmany ˋpangs || but ·as for ¯you | ·man of ˏGod | ˅shun | ·all ˎthis || ˋaim at ˋrighteousness | ˋgodliness | ˋfaith | ˋlove | ˋsteadfastness | ↑ˋgentleness || ˋfight the good ˋfight of the ¯faith | ·take ˋhold of the eˋternal ˋlife | to ˋwhich you were ˅called | when you ˋmade the ·good conˋfession ||

Transcribed by GOK

[speech extract omitted]

the ˅reading | is ·from the ˋsecond ·letter to ˎTimothy | ¯chapter ˏsix | be·ginning at _verse ˎten || ˅Timothy | the ·faithful ˬfollower | is reˋminded that the ˋcraving for ¯money | and ma·terial ˅wealth | can ¯so ˎeasily | di·splace ¯spiritual ˎdepth | in the _human ˎheart || ·riches and ˊwealth | are ·not so ·much ¯wrong in them˅selves | but ·what is done ˋwith them | it is ˎthat | that re·veals the ˅true nature | of _what we ˎare || the ¯love of ˬmoney | is the ˋroot of ˎall ·evils || it is ¯through this ˋcraving | that ·some have ·wandered a¯way from the ˋfaith | and ·pierced their _hearts | with ˋmany ˎpangs || but ·as for ¯you | ¯man of ˏGod | ˅shun | ¯all ˎthis || ˋaim at ˎrighteousness | ˋgodliness | ˎfaith | ˋlove | ˋstead·fastness | ^gentleness || ˋfight the good ·fight of the ·faith | ¯take ˋhold of the e·ternal ·life | to ¯which you were ˬcalled | when you ·made the ·good conˎfession ||

023 SPOKEN ENGLISH CORPUS TEXT F01
Money Box extract
(First part)
Broadcast notes: Radio 4, 12.00 noon, 24th November, 1984
Transcribed by BJW

↑¯National ˎSavings ˋfollowed the ·building so·cieties ˋthis past ˏweek | by a¯nnouncing ¯cuts of three-ˋquarters of one per ˇcent | in ¯three of their _main ˎproducts | the in¯vestment a·ccount | the de_posit ·bond | and the ˋincome ·bond || it ¯leaves _these _National ·Savings rates ˋbroadly in ˇline | with _comparable ˋbuilding society ·products for ˋbasic rate ˇtaxpayers | and ˋstill ·means ·National ˇSavings offer | ¯far and aˋway the best ·outlets for ¯most _non-ˏtaxpayers | who ˋcannot reclaim ·tax | deˏducted at ·source by the ˏbuilding so·ciety | or _after next ˇApril | by the ˎbanks || the inˇvestment a·ccount will pay e¯leven and a _quarter per _cent from the ¯first of Deˋcember | and the de·posit and ˇincome bond | ˇtwelve per cent | from the _second of ˎJanuary | and the ·common exˇtension ·terms | for old ˋsavings certificates come ˏdown | to ¯eight _point ˋtwo ·eight per ˎcent || the more adˇventurous of you | will ¯now be putting your ¯British ˋTelecom appli·cations in the post | if you've ˋnot done so alˋready || ↑it ·may be your first ˇtaste of shares | and it'll certainly be ˇmany investors' first go | at a ˏshare with a ˋperk || ↑ˋstockbrokers ·Seymour ˇPierce | have made a speciˋality of this field ˏthough | and have just upˋdated their ˋcomprehensive ˋlist | of the ˇgoodies | that are aˎvailable || ↑Peter ˏDay's been ¯taking a ˎlook at it ||

[change of speaker: Peter Day]

the ˋdays when it ·might have been ·thought that ˋshareholder ·perks ¯were | ·well ¯not _quite the sort of thing a ˋblue-chip ·company ·needs to inˇdulge in | are ˋcertainly ˋover || ˏwhat has the ˏgovernment a_ttached to the ˋbiggest ·share ·sale ever ˊseen | ↓that of ·British ˊTelecom | but a ˎperk | a ˋdiscount off your ˋtelephone ·bill || ˇactually ¯Seymour _Pierce ¯say they're not too ˋkeen on the ˋTelecom ·perk || it ˏoffers ˏso-called ˇsmaller in·vestors ¯little in_centive to ˋstay with the ˋshares | but the ·brokers ¯say they're ¯now ·looking ˋforward to ¯something ·really iˋmaginative | from ¯British ˋAirways || ↑meanˇwhile | a ¯browse through the ˇcurrent ·perks ·list | ↓is a re·minder that there ˋare ˇone or ·two | uˇnusual con·cessions | that ˇdon't hit the ·headlines | like re_duced ·cross-·channel ˋferry ·fares || one of the ¯few ways of ·getting ˋbooks at a ·discount | they're still ¯retail ·price mainˇtained of ·course | ˋis to buy _shares in ˋPentos | ↓which carry ¯ten per cent ˊoff | at _shops such as

¯Dillons and ˋHudsons || the ˏshareholder and a ˏfriend | can ˍgo to the ˋdogs ·free | as a ˍperk from ·GRˋA | ·Greyhound ˋRacing A·ssociation || ·perks ˇcan ·come exˋpensive | to ·get a free ˋpass on the Soutˋhampton to ·Cowes ˇferry | an in^vestor in the ˏSouthampton ˏIsle of ·Wight and ˋSouth of ·England ˇPacket ·Company | ˋneeds to buy ·shares worth more than ¯seven ˍthousand ˋfive hundred ˋpounds || ˋsome ·perks are eˋxotic ||

023 SPOKEN ENGLISH CORPUS TEXT F01
Money Box extract
(Second part)
Broadcast notes: Radio 4, 12.00 noon, 24th November, 1984
Transcribed by GOK

[Change of speaker: Peter Day]

the ¯days when it ·might have been _thought that ˇshareholder ·perks were | well ¯not quite the ·sort of _thing a ˇblue-chip ·company | _needs to inˇdulge in | are ˇcertainly ˋover || ¯what has the ¯government at·tached to the ¯biggest _share sale ever ¯seen that of ·British ¯Telecom | but a ˋperk | a ˋdiscount ·off your ˋtelephone bill || ˇactually | ¯Seymour ˏPierce ·say | they're _not too ˋkeen | on the ˎTelecom perk || it ˏoffers | _so-called ˏsmaller in·vestors | ¯little in_centive to ˋstay | with the ˎshares || but the ˏbrokers ·say | they're ˬnow ·looking ˋforward | to ¯something ^ _really iˋmaginative | from _British ˋAirways || ˇmeanwhile | a ¯browse through the ˇcurrent ·perks list | is a re_minder that there ˋare | ¯one or ˏtwo | uˇnusual con·cessions | that ˋdon't ·hit the ·headlines | like re_duced ·cross-channel ˋferry ·fares || one of the _few ways of ·getting ˋbooks at a ·discount | they're _still ·retail ·price mainˇtained of ·course | is to _buy ˏshares | in ˋPentos | which _carry ·ten per ·cent ¯off | at _shops such as ˏDillons and ˋHudsons || the ˏshareholder | and a ˏfriend | can _go to the ˋdogs ·free | as a _perk from ˏGRˋA | ˏGreyhound ˋRacing Associ·ation || ↑perks ˇcan ·come exˋpensive || to _get a ·free ¯pass | on the _Southampton to ·Cowes ˇferry | an in¯vestor | in the ¯SoutˏHampton | ¯Isle of _Wight | and ¯South of _England | ˇPacket ·Company | ¯needs to ·buy ˏshares | ¯worth more than | ¯seven ˏthousand | ¯five ˏhundred | ˎpounds || ˇsome ·perks ^ are eˎxotic || you can ˇstill | be ˇburied ·free | as a ˬshareholder | in Do_minion Interˋnational | _formerly Dunˋdonian | but you'll ¯have to have been a ˬshareholder | ˋsince | _June ·nineteen ·eighty-¯two | and ¯this perk | ¯must _end | in _three years' ˋtime || ¯two little ˇluxuries || the ¯brewers _Greene ˇKing have been ·offering | _shareholders | a _bottle of ^ St ˏEdmund ·Ale | _specially ¯mashed | ↑by the ˏnovelist | ˏGraham ˋGreene | to ¯celebrate his _eightieth ˎbirthday || ˇthat ·perk | ˋlapses | about ˎnow || ¯and | ↑¯just ˇone ·share | in ¯Barker and ˏDobson | _price about ¯eight pence | if you can _actually ˇbuy just ·one | ¯qualifies a ˏshareholder | for a ¯discount of _twenty per ˋcent | ¯on up to _ten pounds of _chocolates | from ¯Charbon_nel et ˋWalker || ↓ˇsome ·chocolate ·buffs think | _they're the _nicest ^ in the ˋworld || and ¯if even ˇthat isn't ·tempting | a _compeˋtition | from ˏWilliam ˏSinclair ˋholdings || ˇthey'll send | a ¯free ˏpacket | of their

ˇKelsai | ˬonion ·seeds | to ¯all ˏshareholders | so they can com_pete in | ¯growing the _largest ˎonion || ↑an ap¯propriate ˬprize will be a·warded | at _Harrogate Exhi¯bition ·Centre | _next Sepˋtember | and you'll ¯have to ˏbeat | the e¯xisting ˏrecord | of ¯seven ˏpounds | e¯leven and three-·quarter ˎounces ||

[change of speaker: Louise Botting]

¯Peter ˎDay || and ¯that ↑¯interesting ·little ˏbooklet | Con¯cessionary ˋDiscounts for ˇShareholders | ↑is a_vailable from the _brokers | ˋSeymour ˏPierce | ¯10 | ↑¯Old _Jewry | ¯London _ECˎ2 || that's ¯Seymour ˇPierce | ¯10 | _Old _Jewry _London ¯EC¯2 | and it _costs | ¯one pound ˎfifty || ↑and ¯that's ˎit from ˏMoney ·Box | so from ˋproducer Tom ˏMaddocks | re¯porter | _Juliet ˏJohnson | and ¯me | Lou_ise ¯Botting | ↑goodˏbye ||

023 SPOKEN ENGLISH CORPUS TEXT F01

Money Box extract

Broadcast notes: Radio 4, 12.00 noon, 24th November, 1984

Overlap passage

Transcribed by GOK

[Change of speaker: Peter Day]

the ¯days when it ·might have been _thought that ˇshareholder ·perks were ˄ | well ¯not quite the ·sort of _thing a ˇblue-chip ·company | _needs to inˇdulge in | are ˇcertainly ˋover || ¯what has the ¯government at·tached to the ¯biggest _share sale ever ¯seen that of ·British ¯Telecom | but a ˋperk | a ˋdiscount ·off your ˋtelephone bill || ˇactually | ¯Seymour ˏPierce ·say | they're _not too ˋkeen | on the ˎTelecom perk || it ˏoffers | _so-called ˏsmaller in·vestors | ¯little in_centive to ˋstay | with the ˎshares || but the ˏbrokers ·say | they're ˬnow ·looking ˋforward | to ¯something ˄ _really iˋmaginative | from _British ˋAirways || ˇmeanwhile | a ¯browse through the ˇcurrent ·perks list | is a re_minder that there ˋare | ¯one or ˏtwo | uˇnusual con·cessions | that ˋdon't ·hit the ·headlines | like re_duced ·cross-channel ˋferry ·fares || one of the _few ways of ·getting ˋbooks at a ·discount | they're _still ·retail ·price mainˇtained of ·course | is to _buy ˏshares | in ˋPentos | which _carry ·ten per ·cent ¯off | at _shops such as ˏDillons and ˋHudsons || the ˏshareholder | and a ˏfriend | can _go to the ˋdogs ·free | as a _perk from ˏGRˋA | ˏGreyhound ˋRacing Associ·ation || ↑perks ˇcan ·come exˋpensive || to _get a ·free ¯pass | on the _Southampton to ·Cowes ˇferry | an in¯vestor | in the ¯Soutˏhampton | ¯Isle of _Wight | and ¯South of _England | ˇPacket ·Company | ¯needs to ·buy ˏshares | ¯worth more than | ¯seven ˏthousand | ¯five ˏhundred | ˎpounds || ˇsome ·perks ˄ are eˎxotic ||

Transcribed by BJW

the ˋdays when it ·might have been ·thought that ˋshareholder ·perks ¯were | ·well ¯not _quite the sort of thing a ˋblue-chip ·company ·needs to inˇdulge in | are ˋcertainly ˋover || ˏwhat has the ˏgovernment a_ttached to the ˋbiggest ·share ·sale ever ˊseen | ↓that of ·British ˊTelecom | but a ˎperk | a ˋdiscount off your ˋtelephone ·bill || ˇactually ¯Seymour _Pierce ¯say they're not too ˋkeen on the ˋTelecom ·perk || it ˏoffers ˏso-called ˇsmaller in·vestors ¯little in_centive to ˋstay with the ˋshares | but the ·brokers ¯say they're ¯now ·looking ˋforward to ¯something ·really i`maginative | from ¯British `Airways || ↑mean˅while | a ¯browse through the ˅current ·perks ·list | ↓is a re·minder that there `are ˅one or ·two | u˅nusual con·cessions | that ˅don't hit the ·headlines | like re_duced ·cross-·channel `ferry ·fares || one of the ¯few ways of ·getting `books at a ·discount | they're still ¯retail ·price main˅tained of ·course | `is to buy _shares in `Pentos | ↓which carry ¯ten per cent ´off | at _shops such as ¯Dillons and `Hudsons || the ˏshareholder and a ˏfriend | can _go to the `dogs ·free | as a _perk from ·GR`A | ·Greyhound `Racing A·ssociation || ·perks ˅can ·come ex`pensive | to ·get a free `pass on the Sout`hampton to ·Cowes ˅ferry | an in^vestor in the ˏSouthampton ˏIsle of ·Wight and `South of ·England ˅Packet ·Company | `needs to buy ·shares worth more than ¯seven _thousand `five hundred `pounds || `some ·perks are e`xotic ||

024 SPOKEN ENGLISH CORPUS TEXT F02
Money Box
Broadcast notes: Radio 4, 12.00 noon, 22nd June, 1985
Transcribed by BJW

in the ˋprogramme ˇthis week | the ˋuprating of ·state ˋbenefits | ↓so who will ˇgain | and who will ˋlose || ·unit ˋtrusts || ˋhow our proˇfessionals | ˋand our ˇlisteners are ·doing | in their aˉttempt to find _winners for ·this year's compeˎtition || _more ·special offers from ˊbuilding societies | ↓for ˉany of you with a ·few hundred ·pounds to inˊvest | ˉso _where should you ˋgo | to get the ·best reˎturn || ˉand ˇfifty ·years | of the Fi_nancial ˉTimes | ·ordinary share ˎindex || ↑but we _start with | ·state ˎbenefits || ˋas you probably _know the Noˇvember ·increase | is to be ˏbased on the ˏMay retail ˋprices index | ↑and the _benchmark is ·therefore | ˋseven per ˋcent || but ↑ˋnot everyone ˋgets that ·seven per ·cent || ↓and beˋcause of the way ˉbenefits interreˊlate | an ˋincrease in ˇone ·place | may be re↑ˋflected by a ˇdecrease | elseˋwhere || ˉhere's _Vincent ˎDuggleby ||

[Change of speaker: Vincent Duggleby]

the deˋcision that's pro·duced the biggest poˇlitical row | is ˋchild ·benefit || ˉup | by only ˇtwo per ·cent | to _seven _pounds a ˋweek || but of ·course it ˋis paid to ˇeveryone | ·rich ˋand poor aˋlike | and the ˇpoorest ·families | ↓on ˉsupplementary ˊbenefit | are ˇinsulated | be·cause their ˋoverall ˇweekly ·payment | takes ˋeverything into a·ccount || ↓although ˉsupplementary benefit itˇself | ˋonly goes up by ˋfive point ·one per ˋcent || ˉthose in ˏwork | but on ˉlow ˏpay | get ˉfamily _income ˋsupplement || ↑ˋthis is a parˇticularly _complicated _benefit to ˎcalculate || but ˉas an eˏxample | ˉlet's ·look at a ˏfamily | with ˉtwo ˏchildren | ˉearning _ninety-·five _pounds a ˋweek || a↑ˋssume a ˇpay increase this ·year | in _line with inˋflation || and ˋthey'll ·find their ˇbenefit | ·going up from ˇtwo pounds ·fifty | to _three ·pounds sixty-ˋeight || on the ˉface of it | they're ˋone pound ·eighteen a ˉweek | _better ˋoff || but ˉas the _benefits for the ·two ˇchildren | were not fully upˇrated | you ˉhave to _knock off | ·seventy ˋpence ||

[Change of speaker: Louise Botting]

and ·then there's ˋhousing ·benefit || the ˉneeds a_llowance to ·work it ˋout | goes up by ·five point eight per ˇcent | ˉbut it's been ˎtapered more ˋquickly | which ˉcosts that _family on ˇFIS | aˋnother ˉseventy ·pence a ˎweek || and ˋthus their nett ˇloss | is _twenty-two ˋpence || though if ˋone of the ·children is over the ·age of eˇleven | they will in _future get a·nother

·fifty pence a ˋweek ‖ ↑ˇhousing ·benefit | is ˍalso | of ˋcritical im·portance to many ˋpensioners ‖ ˋif you take a ˇcouple | with about ˋninety ·pounds a ˇweek | ˋpart from the ˉstate | and ˋpart from an occuˇpational ·pension | and paying ˋfive pounds a week in ˉrates | they'll ˎlose | about a ˇpound a ·week | in ˎbenefit ‖ a ˇsingle ·pensioner | ↓also on ˇninety pounds a ·week | in a ↑ˇhigher rated ·area | might at ˋpresent be ·getting as ˉmuch as | ·two pound ˋtwenty reˋlief | but ˋall ·that | will ˍdisaˋppear ‖ ↓and as a ˋseven per cent ·increase in the basic ˋpension for a ˋsingle person is ·two pounds ˇfifty | they'd see ˋvirtually ↑ˋno rise at ˋall | in their ˍincome | in Noˎvember ‖

[Change of speaker: Vincent Duggleby]

the ˋincrease in the | ˋearnings ·limit | ↓for ˉpensioners | is ˋalso worth a ˋcomment ‖ it ˋgoes up by ˉfive ˇpounds | so proˋvided a ·pensioner earns ˋless than ˇseventy-five ·pounds | the ˍpension isn't reˋduced ‖ how↑ˋever ‖ if a ˉpensioner's ˇwife | is ˋunder ˇsixty | and is ·still ˇworking | the ˉbenefit ˍpaid for ˉher | ↓will ˋstart to be ˇlost | if her ˋincome exˉceeds | ˇthirty ·pounds | inˉstead of the ˍpresent forty-ˋfive ‖ ↓and ˇthat ·income | will inˉclude | ˉany ˬpension she re·ceives | from an emˋployer ‖ ˋso | ˋone way and aˇnother | you'll need to do ˋquite a lot of calcuˋlations | to disˉcover | ˋwhether you'll get as ˉmuch ˬextra | as you ˍfirst ˋthought ‖ ˉone figure inci·dentally | you ˋmay find ˋuseful for | ˇtax ·purposes | the ˉbasic | ˍpension ˇincome | for a ˉsingle ˏperson | in the ˉnineteen ˍeighty-five eighty-ˍsix ˇtax ·year | will be ˇjust over | ˉnineteen ˍhundred ˋpounds ‖ and for a ˋmarried ˇcouple | ˉthree ˍthousand | and ˉfifty-ˎfive ‖

[Change of speaker: Louise Botting]

ˉeven | as the ˍincreases were being aˇnnounced | there were ˉaccuˬsations | that the ˉgovernment was ˍjumping the ˇgun | on ˋsome of the pro·posals put ˉforward in the ·green ˋpaper | on ·social seˋcurity ‖ the ˋinstitute for ·fiscal ˇstudies | have been ˉlooking at it in greater ˉdepth ‖ and so I ↑ˉasked ˎtheir director | ·John ˋKaye | ˋhow ·people due to re·tire in years to ˋcome | are aˎffected ‖

025 SPOKEN ENGLISH CORPUS TEXT F03
Money Box
Broadcast notes: Radio 4, 12.00 noon, 22nd June, 1985
Transcribed by GOK

↑ ˋso much for the ˍunit trust ˎmanagers | but in ↑ˇparallel | we ˋalso give our ˎlisteners | their ˇown compe·tition | with a ˏchance | to ·beat the ·experts at their ˍown ˎgame || to ˋfind out how ↑ˇthey're ·doing | ¯here's ˏJuliet ˋJohnson

[change of speaker: Juliet Johnson]

ˋeight ·months ˇinto the ·compe·tition | the ˇaverage port·folio | ·showed a ˏgain | of ·some ˍseven per ˋcent | but ·that's beˍfore exˋpenses || on ˋMay the ·thirty-ˇfirst | the ·day we ·did the ˇfigures | a ¯listener in ˎDerbyshire was ·in the ˏlead | with a ¯portˏfolio | which ·beats the ˇbest of the ·fund ·managers | by ¯showing a ˏgain | of ·over ˍtwenty per ˋcent || but it ˋis ˇvulnerable | be·cause of ˍHong ·Kong exˎposure || ↑in ˇfact | ˇeight out of the ·top ·ten ·listeners' port·folios | ·have ˋmoney in Hong ˏKong | and ˋas it's a ˇvolatile ·market | which has ·taken a ˇtumble ·recently | the ·field's ·still ¯wide ˏopen | as the ·compe·tition enters its ·last ·few ˎmonths || and ¯by the ˇway | ˇmany listeners ·backed | Jaˇpan | which has been ˋweak this ·year || ·those who chose ˊproperty | fiˏnancial | and ˇincome ·funds | have done ˇbetter on the ·whole | ↑though ˇsome of our ·leaders | have ˇalso made ·gains | by ·picking the ·odd ˇstrong ·fund | in an ˋotherwise ·drab ˎsector ||

[change of speaker: Louise Botting]

↑the ˋbuilding so·cieties | con·tinue to ˍvie with ·one a·nother | to ·top the ˏleague ·tables | ˇthis time | in ¯special ˏproducts | for ·savers with a ·few hundred ˍpounds to inˎvest || ↑¯Frances MacˎDonald | ˋregularly ·monitors the ˇmarket | ↑so ˍwhat's on ·offer at the ˎmoment ||

[change of speaker: Frances MacDonald]

it's ¯almost imˎpossible to ·keep up to ˏdate | with ·what's on ˏoffer | and it's ˋquite ˇlikely | that if you ˋchase the ·highest ·rates by conˇtinually ·switching so·cieties | you'll ¯lose ˎout | in the ˎlong ·run | as the de·spised a·ccount you've just ˇclosed | will ¯probably ˇbetter its ·rates | ·after ˍyou've deˎfected || but if you ˇdo have ·spare ·money | to inˏvest | ¯here's some iˏdea | of ˍwhat you can exˎpect || for ˋinstant ˇaccess | ˇten per ·cent is ·offered | by the Aˏlliance | ˏAnglia | ˏLeeds | and the

_National and Proˋvincial || if you're pre • pared to give ˇone month's • notice | • ten and a ˋquarter per • cent | is _quite ˎcommon | on • offer from the ˏBolton | ˊHampshire | and ˏSwindon ˋPermanent || but ¯leading the ˇfield | are the ˎregulars | the ˏMetrogas | ˏPaddington | and the _Essex ˎEquitable || the ˇbig so • cieties | are _concentrating on ˎthree months' • notice a • ccounts | with the ˊAbbey | ˏHalifax | and ˇWoolwich | • offering _ten and three ˎquarters | ↑though the ˋChelsea and the • Bradford and ˇBingley | _offer ˎmore || ˇsix months' • notice • shares | ˋaren't all • that com • petitive | but ¯top of the _list | are the ˏGuardian | and the • Sussex _Mutual | with _ten point • eight ˎfive || when it ¯comes to ˇterm • shares | eˋleven per • cent is the • top • rate | • whether it's for ˏone • year | with the Aˏlliance | or the • Leamington • Spa's • fixed rate ˊbond | or for ˇtwo • years | with the ˊStroud | or ˇthree | with the _Leeds and ˎHolbeck || ˋtwo a • ccounts that ↑ˇtop that e • leven per • cent • mark | at the ˏmoment | are the ˋYorkshire's ˇtwo month • notice a • ccount | at e • leven point o ˏfive | and the ˋChelsea's ˬthree month a • ccount | at e_leven point ˎone || but • whether that's the • top rate a • vailable • this time ˇnext week | it's _hard to ˎsay || if you ˇare • totally be • mused | by the • rates on ˏoffer | there's a ˇnew i • dea | from • two _Nottingham ˎbusinessmen | who've • just set _up | the ˋbuilding so • ciety • shop || ˏthey'll • tell you • where the ˏbest rates are a • vailable | ˋbased on your • personal ˎneeds | • whether you want iˏmmediate • access to your • money | ↑or are pre_pared to • tie | • some of it _up for ˎlonger || ¯they'll give ˎtwo • quotes | • one from a ˏsmall so • ciety | and ↑the _other | from • one of the top ˎtwenty || the • service is ˊfree | and ↑their a_ddress • is | the ˇbuilding so • ciety • shop | ¯city ˏhouse | ˋmaid • marion ˏway | ˎNottingham | that's the ˇbuilding so • ciety • shop | ¯city _house | ˋmaid • marion ˊway | ˎNottingham ||

[change of speaker: Louise Botting]

as ˋwell as • monitoring what the • building so • cieties and the • unit ˇtrust people are • up to | we ˇalso keep a • check | on • all the new _books | on ˋmoney || ˏmost | as you can iˏmagine | are ˇuseful | • and rather ˋserious | but we ˋhave in • cluded in ˋour up • dated ˇbooklist | the ¯book of ˋmoney • lists | deˎscribed by the ˇpublishers | as • one of the most biˎzarre | and ˋtotally ˋuseless | ˎreference • books | ↓¯ever ˎpublished || ↑¯did you ˏknow for e • xample | that the • most ex • pensive ˬpigeon | was • bought by a Japaˇnese • fancier | for • twenty-five • thousand ˇpounds || did you • know that the • most ex • pensive hoˇtel in the • world | the • Nova • Park Eˋlysee in ˇParis | • costs ¯three ˏthousand | • nine hundred _pounds | a ˎday | ˋwhereas it ˇonly • costs | • six hundred and • fifteen ↑ˋdollars a • day | to • stay in the ˋworld's most ex • pensive ˇhospital | • needless to • say in

·Cali`fornia || `what a·bout ¯testing your·self on ˇholiday to ·find | the `top ·hundred ˇbanks in the ·world | `or the ·dollar ·sterling ex`change ·rate | ·back to ·seventeen ·seventy-`six | the ·war of ·inde`pendence || ·did you _know | that the ˎLatin ·word for `money | peˎcunia | ·as in ·impeˇcunious | `actually ·means ^ a ·herd of ˎsheep || ·that ^ `book of ·money ´lists | by ·Phillip ´Dunn | is ·published by ˎArrow | at ˏtwo pounds ˎfifty | ˏand | ¯is in ˏour | ¯updated ˎbooklist | ˇfree | with a ·stamped addressed ˏenvelope | ·sent ↓to ^ `Money ·Box | ¯BBˏC | ·broadcasting ´house | ¯London | ↑`W1ˏA | _4·WˎW || ·that's ^ ¯Money Box | `BBC `Broadcasting ¯House | ¯London | `W1¯A | ✓4 | ·WˎW || and ˇthis time | we ˇhave to ·say | `no ·stamped a·ddressed ¯envelope | ↓¯no ˎlist ||

026 SPOKEN ENGLISH CORPUS TEXT F04
Review of the Year
(First part)
BBC World Service
Transcribed by BJW

[Speaker: Kevin Geary]

yes Seb ¯Coe at ·last | striking ¯gold at _eight hundred ˏmetres || well ˋlet's now ·turn our aˋttention to ↑ˇcricket | and once ˋmore it's been a ¯year when ·test ^matches | and the uˋbiquitous ¯one day inter¯nationals | proˋliferated around the ¯world || and that's ¯why it was ˇalso a year | when our ·cricket re¯porter | Chris ¯Florence | had to _buy a ¯jumbo-sized ˇrecord book | to keep ˋtrack of it ·all ||

[change of speaker: Chris Florence]

well you're ˋright Kevin | not only a ˇjumbo-sized | ˇrecord book | but ¯also a couple of ˋcalculators as ˋwell 'cause you ·really needed _those rather than just a ¯straightforward ˋscore book | there've been ¯so ˏmany test ·matches in the last twelve ·months || obviously a ˋrecord ˇnumber | that eh | it's been ˋvery difficult to keep ¯track of it ˏall || iˋronically it ˋstarted of course | with that | ¯England _series | in the ·Cariˇbbean in what | be¯fore a ·ball was _bowled was ↑¯really billed as the | ¯unofficial | world ˋchampionship || because | ·England had just ˇbeaten | Au¯stralia to | re·tain the ¯Ashes | West ·Indies ¯naturally going ·well at that _time | and ˋeverybody thought that | ↑given a ˇlittle bit of ·luck | England ˇmight well have | not necessarily ˇwon the series | _that would have been pushing it ˋtoo far | but at ˋleast put up a ˋvery good perˋformance || but | ¯things ˋstarted to go ·wrong ¯right from ˇvery early days | they ¯lost the ·first test _heavily | then ¯straight into the _second test | at ˇTrinidad | and by ¯then | the ˋpattern had been ˋset ||

[live commentary omitted]

[change of speaker: Kevin Geary]

so ¯West Indies ·then | on their ˊway | two nil ¯up | ↓as history will ¯tell us | went ˋon to win | ¯five nil | their ˋsecond successive ˋfive nil ˇvictory | ˇover England | and ¯really | for ·England ¯things didn't get much ˏbetter did they ·Chris | eh when they ˇcame home | they faced ˋIndia | ↓and New ˊZealand | and ·lost ˋboth ||

[change of speaker: Chris Florence]

they started ˇoff with | David ¯Gower still as ˬcaptain | who ˋled the side in the Cari¯bbean || he headed ˋpersonally a diˋsastrous match in the ˋvery first test at ˇHeadingly | a ¯game which was · lost in ˋjust over · three days against ¯India | then they ˇcame to | to ˇLord's | which ˋreally should have been the ˇshowpiece | as far as ˇEngland · cricket was con · cerned | but it ¯went wrong from there as ˎwell ||

[live commentary omitted]

well ˇafter Kapil · Dev | ¯England then came · on to meet yet aˋnother one of the | ˍgreat world all · rounders of the ¯moment | when Richard ˋHadlee in the New ˋZealand side · came | but | by ¯then the | the ˋpattern of the ˋseason had been ˇset for · England | and they ¯lost that ˍseries ¯one ˍnil with | Richard ¯Hadlee playing a · very | ˋprominent ˋpart ||

[change of speaker: Kevin Geary]

¯while all · this had been going ˬon | Ian ˋBotham England's ˋstar allˋrounder had been ˋout of the ˇside | un¯til the · last ˍtest of the ˋseason aˋgainst New · Zealand at the ˋOval | and that ¯really proˍvided | ¯England with their only · bright ˍspot of the ˋseason ||

[live commentary omitted]

[change of speaker: Chris Florence]

and then of ¯course it was only a · matter of a ˇfew minutes before | ¯Botham went on to ˋbreak that record of | eh · Denis ˏLillee | and · now with ¯England | ˋin Australia for the ˇAshes series | · Botham ˇlooks like being | at least a ˋbatsman in the England side | if not a ¯bowler for years to ˎcome ||

[change of speaker: Kevin Geary]

going · back to the West ˋIndies | where we ˋstarted || they didn't have it ˇall their own · way | ↓the · last twelve ˊmonths || ¯who can for · get being · bowled out for · fifty-ˋthree by Pakiˋstan || I mean it's ˋjust been quite an incredible ˋyear ||

[change of speaker: Chris Florence]

we ˋmustn't forˋget New ¯Zealand | beat Auˋstralia at ¯home | having ˋbeaten them aˇway from home || and eh | alˋthough it may not have been a disˋtinguished ˇyear for Australian ·cricket | the ˋAussies' ˋlist of a¯chievements | in ˇother fields | was in_deed ¯long and imˋpressive || and nowhere ˇmore so | than on the ·world's ˇgolf courses | where a ¯man they _call | the ¯great _white ˋshark | was ¯on the ˏprowl | and ¯very hungry inˋdeed || Harry ˋPeart was at ˇTurnberry | at the ¯moment when the _jaws ˋsnapped | a¯round the ·main ˎcourse ||

[live commentary omitted]

[change of speaker: Harry Peart]

that ¯one little ˋtap in at ˊTurnberry | put ·paid ¯once and for ˎall | to the ¯cruel _jibe that ·Greg ˋNorman was ·just a ¯great white fishˎfinger || his ¯transformation | to a ·genuine ˇkiller shark | beˋgan on that ˋwindswept ˋcourse | on the ·east coast of ¯Scotland | and ·ended in a ˋriot of ¯dollars | ¯titles | ↑and ·worldwide aˋcclaim as the ·game's most ˋfeared comˋpetitor || after ¯netting _more than ¯six hundred and ·fifty-three _thousand ¯dollars | he be_came only the ¯second overseas ˎplayer | to ˋtop the United States ˋmoney earnings ·list || only ·Gary ˋPlayer has ·beaten the Aˋmericans | in their _own back ˋyard || his ¯list of _titles ¯grew almost ˎweekly || inˋcluding a run of ¯six _tournaments in a ˋrow || ˏthat was ·followed | by the ¯huge toothsome ˎgrin | of a man ˋrevelling in his ·own ˋtalent || ↑but it was a ·wry _smile from the Au¯stralian at the ˋMasters at Auˋgusta | ˏleading into the ¯final round | ˋhe fell ˋvictim to ¯one of the _golden ˋbear's famous ˋcharges || Jack ˋNicklaus | in his ¯forty-sixth ˎyear | ˏfashioned | an e¯motional _round of ¯sixty-ˎfive | to ¯snatch the ·green _jacket | ↑for the _sixth ˎtime || ¯off the ·circus ˏwent to _Shinacock ˋhills | for the United ˋStates Open || aˋgain ·Norman was in con·tention || but ¯this time | it was aˎnother | _what shall we say | more maˋture player | that ˋtook the ˋtitle || ·Ray ˋFloyd | at ¯forty-_four ¯took the _crown | in ¯fine ˎstyle || ↑then to ˎTurnberry | a ˋwet and ˋwindy ˇvenue | for the ˋoldest of the ·majors || ¯many thought ·Norman's ˋcourse-equalling ¯second round _sixty-ˋthree was the turning ·point || ˇmy lasting im·pression | was of ˋhis mighty ˋframe | ¯battling to stay ˎupright | in the ˋworst of the ˇgale | for ˋhis seventy-ˎfour || it ¯could so _easily | have ·been an ˎeighty || ↑on to _Inverness Oˎhio | and the U¯nited States PGˎA | when it was the ¯young A_merican ·Bob ˋTway who took the ·title | and re·vealed a ˋhuman side | as ¯tears _trickled down his ˋcheeks | with his _first major ˋvictory || there were ˋno such moments of ˏglory | for _Severiano Balleˋsteros || by his ¯own awesome ·standards | ↑it was a mediˋocre

·season | but he ˍstill topped the ˍorder of ˋmerit || ˇsecond | was a ˉtalent of ˋboundless ·prospect | from the ˋBasque country || ˉJose Maˍria Oˋlazabal | the ˉwinner of the ˇEuropean Masters | and the ˍSanyo ˋOpen || it was a ˍgood year for the ˋwomen's ·game || as ˆprize money inˊcreased | Laura ˋDavis took the ·Euroˇpean rankings | while in the ˇStates | Pat ˍBradley reigns suˋpreme | with ˉearnings of almost ˍhalf a million ˋdollars || ↑and a ·final note of ˍpraise for the ·Curtis ˋcup team | who ˉbeat the Aˎmericans | on their ˉhome ˬsoil | for the ˍfirst ˎtime || ˉis that a ·pointer | to ˍnext year's ˉRyder ˋcup | at ˉMuirfield ˉvillage Oˉhio || it's just a ˋpity | ·Greg ˇNorman | doesn't ˎqualify ||

[change of speaker: Kevin Geary]

and ·as I mentioned ˋearlier | Greg ˎNorman's outˋstanding a↑ˋchievements | were just ˋpart of a magˋnificent ˋyear for Auˉstralian ˋsport || ˬfollowing in the ˊfootsteps | of their ·rugby ˋunion grand ˇslam ·side | we've ˉjust ˍseen their ˉrugby league ˇcounterparts | the Kangaˇroos | ˋcome here and ˉteach us a·nother ˍpainful ˋlesson || they gave some suˋperlative exhiˋbitions of fluent ˉrunning | and ·magical ˋhandling | on their ˋway to comˋpleting their ˉtour of England and ˇFrance | with a one ˋhundred percent ˋrecord || and ˋlet's not forˋget that ˉfascinating ˍfortnight in Ocˇtober | when the ˋdowdy London ˋsuburb of ˇWillesden | was the unˇlikely ·venue for a compeˉtition | which has perˋhaps seen the ·birth of ˋhockey | as a ·major specˇtator ·sport | aˋway from its ˇspiritual ·home | on the subˎcontinent || it was ˋthere that the Auˉstralians ˍcarried off the ˉWorld ˍCup | for the ˍfirst ˋtime | and in ˍsplendid ·style ˋtoo || while ˉIndia and Pakiˇstan | aˇstoundingly | finished ˍup playing ˍoff for ·last ˋplace || and ˋstill we're not ·finished with Auˋstralia || because it's ·now a couple of ˋmonths | since the most ·highly ˋpublicized ˋpuncture in ˋhistory | took ˉplace on the ˇmotor racing circuit | in ˋAdelaide || ↓sending Nigel ˉMansell | and his ·championship ˋhopes | caˇreering into a ˋwall || after the reˉgrets | and postˉmortems | the history ˉbooks | will ˉsimply ˍtell us | that ˋnineteen eighty-ˉsix | was the ˉyear when ˍMansell came ˋsecond || ·two points beˇhind | Alain ˋProst || but deˇspite ·that | it was ·still a good ˋyear for the British ˉdriver | as ·Simon ˇTaylor reˋcalls ||

026 SPOKEN ENGLISH CORPUS TEXT F04
Review of the Year
(Second part)
BBC World Service
Transcribed by GOK

[change of speaker: Kevin Geary]

and ˍas I ·mentioned ˋearlier | ·Greg ·Norman's outˉstanding aˋchievements | were ·just ˋpart of a mag·nificent ˋyear | for Au·stralian ˋsport || ˏfollowing | in the ˏfootsteps | of their ˋrugby ·union grand ˇslam ·side | we've ˋjust ·seen their ˋrugby ·league ˇcounterparts | the ·Kangaˬroos | ˇcome ·here | and ˉteach us | a·nother ˍpainful ˎlesson || they ˉgave | some suˋperlative exhiˋbitions | of ·fluent ˊrunning | and ˋmagical ˇhandling | on their ˉway | to comˉpleting | their ˋtour of ·England and ˇFrance | with a one ˋhundred per·cent ˋrecord || and ↑ˋlet's not for·get that ˋfascinating ·fortnight in Ocˇtober | when the ˋdowdy ·London ˊsuburb | of ˇWillesden | was the unˇlikely ·venue | for a ·compeˊtition | which has perˇhaps ·seen the ·birth | of ˋhockey | as a ˋmajor specˇtator ·sport | aˋway from its ˇspiritual ·home | on the ˍsubˋcontinent || it was ˊthere | that the Auˊstralians | ˋcarried ·off the ˉworld ˍcup | for the ˍfirst ˋtime | ↑and in ·splendid ˍstyle ˎtoo || while ˋIndia and ·Pakiˇstan | a↑ˇstoundingly | ˉfinished ˏup | ·playing ˏoff | for ˍlast ˋplace || and ˇstill we're ·not ·finished | with Auˋstralia | be·cause it's ˉnow a ·couple of ˋmonths | since the ˉmost | ˋhighly ˋpublicized ˋpuncture in ˇhistory | ·took ˊplace | on the ˇmotor ·racing ·circuit | in ˋAdelaide | ·sending ˋNigel ˊMansell | and his ˉchampionship ˎhopes | caˋreering ·into a ˎwall || ˏafter | the reˉgrets | and postˊmortems | the ˇhistory ·books | will ˉsimply ˏtell us | that ˉnineteen ·eighty ˏsix | was the ˉyear | when ˍMansell came ˋsecond | ·two points beˇhind | ·Alain ˋProst || but deˇspite ·that | it was ·still a good ˋyear for the ·British ˏdriver | as ·Simon ˋTaylor reˎcalls ||

[change of speaker: Simon Taylor]

↑for ˋNigel himˬself | ˋthis was the ˬseason | that ˊfinally | and wi·thout ˇargument | ˊput him | ·where he ·has for ˉso ˇlong | ˍstriven to ˎbe | a·mong the ˉthree or ˍfour | ˉtop ˎdrivers | in the ˋworld || ˋactually to ˇwin the ·championship | ·takes a ˉcombiˋnation of ·attributes | ˬskill | ˊstamina | ˊracecraft | the ˉright eˍquipment | and ˎluck || in ·nineteen ·eighty-ˉsix | ·Nigel had ˇall ·those | exˎcept the ˋlast || ↑ˋpatriotism aˬpart | there ˇare those in ·Britain | who ·say that the ˋnineteen ·eighty-·six ·title ˉdid ˎgo | to the ·right ˎman || for ˇmuch of the ·year |

the Mc·Laren ˋwasn't ·quite the ˍmatch for the ˋWilliams | ↑and ·yet ˉAlain ˎProst | ˉalways ·seemed to be ·able to ˎuse | his ˎtalent | to ·get the ˎbest | out of ˉany situˎation || but ↑ˇMansell ·showed him·self | ˇmore than ·able to ·cope | with ˍeveryone ˎelse || on ˇmost o·ccasions | he was ˋclearly ˏquicker | and ˉmore comˏpetitive | than his ˉown ˋteammate | ·twice ˍchampion ·Nelson ˋPiquet || ·Nigel ˍdid have his ˋproblems || the ˋspin | that ·could have ·cost him the ˋBelgian ·race || ·that ˉmuffed ˋstart | in ˎMexico || but ˉon his ˎday | when ˉeverything was ˍright for ·him | ↑he was ·simply unˎbeatable || in the ˋultra-com·petitive ˬworld | of ˏGrand Prix ·racing | you're ˉnot ˋmeant to be ·able to ˋdominate a ·race | the way ˉNigel did in ˋCanada | or in ˎPortugal || ↑ˉbut | as ˉNigel him·self ˎsaid | ˋgritting his ˎteeth | after the ˉAdelaide ·disa·ppointment | ↑there's ˍalways ·next ˋyear ||

[change of speaker: Kevin Geary]

ˉand | from ˋblowouts on the ˊtrack | we ˉmove | to the exˉplosive ˏtalent | that is ˉBoris ˋBecker | the reˋmarkable ·young West ˊGerman | who ·took his ˋsecond ·Wimbledon ·title in sucˋcession | this ˋyear || but deˇspite ·that | ˋoveˇrall | the ˋyear was ·dominated by ˉtwo ˋCzech ·born ˋplayers | as ˉLinda ˋSpurr | can ˎtell us ||

[change of speaker: Linda Spurr]

·well there's ˉno ·doubting at ˋall | that Marˉtina Nav·ratiˍlova | was ˉonce aˍgain | the outˉstanding ˍplayer | on the ↓ˉwomen's ˎcircuit || ˇalmost | in comˉplete coˎmmand | ↑I ·say ˇalmost | be·cause she ˋdid ˬlose | ˉthree ˋtimes in ·nineteen ·eighty-ˏsix | but aˉgainst ˍthat | she ·won ˉeighty ˍnine | ˎmatches | inˋcluding ·two grand ˋslam ·titles || she ˊfinished | ˊtop | of ·both the ·grand prix ˊpoints ·list | ˋand the comˇputer ·rankings | and ˋfinished ˇoff the ·year | by ·winning the ˋbest of ˉfive ˎsets | Vir·ginia ˍSlims ˎchampionship || ˋone of her ˇfinest ·triumphs | was unˇdoubtedly | ˉwinning ˍWimbledon | for the ˉfifth ˍyear | in sucˎcession ||

[live commentary omitted]

a ˋtricky o·pponent inˋdeed | in ·Hana ·Mandliˋkova | but Marˉtina | was in ·sparkling ˎform | ·winning ˉseven ˍsix | ·six ˎthree || ↑on the ˇmen's ·circuit | ˋtwo ·names | ·stand ˎout | ˉIvan ˍLendl | and ˍBoris ˎBecker || ˋmy ˇpersonal ·highlight | of ·nineteen ·eighty-ˉsix | is ˉBecker |

¯winning ˍWimbledon | ↑for the ˋsecond ·year | in a ˎrow || ˇthis ·year | ¯victory | over ¯Lendl | was ¯harder | but ¯more ˋsatisfying ||

[interview omitted]

¯Lendl ·though | was ¯number ·one through·out the ˎrest of the ·year || he ·won the ¯French | and U·nited ·States ¯Open ·championships | ·and ^ the ˎMasters || ·some of the ˇold ·names were ·still a·round | ˍJimmy ˋConnors | fo¯rever ˍbattling | but ˋno ·tournament ˋtitles || John ˇMcEnroe is ·back in ·action | ·after a ˊrest | but alˋthough ·temperaˋmentally it ·seems to ·be the ˇold ·McEnroe | his ˇtennis | hasn't ˇquite ·reached | the ·same ˎheights || per¯haps he'll ·come back a·gain | ↓I ·just ˎwonder || ˏbut | there ·seem to be ·plenty of ˋothers | ·coming ˇup the ·ladder | ·Czechoslo¯vakia's | ·Milosiav ˇMecir had a good ·year | and ˋso ˇtoo | did the ¯never ˋending su·pply of ˏplayers | from ˋSweden | Wiˋlander | ˋEdberg | ·Jarryd ˊPernfors | and ˎNystrom ||

[change of speaker: Kevin Geary]

ˏwell | ·even in the ˋworld of ˇhorse ·racing | where ·class and ·breeding are ˇeverything | ¯nineteen ·eighty-ˍsix | will be ¯ranked | in ·years to ˏcome | as a ·classic ˎvintage | par¯ticularly | on the ˋflat || and as ˋChris ·Poole reˋminds us | ¯one ˊhorse | ·played a sig¯nificant ˎpart | in ·making the ¯year | ¯so ˎmemorable ||

[change of speaker: Chris Poole]

his ·name of ˇcourse | ·Dancing ˎBrave || his ˋgreatest ·moment ˊcame | on a ¯balmy | Oc¯tober afterˍnoon | at ¯Longˍchamps | in ˋParis | ·where he ˇbroke | the ˍcourse ˋrecord ||

[live commentary omitted]

·Dancing ˊBrave | ˊwinning | the ˋTrust House ¯Forte | ˋPrix de ·L'Arc de ˎTriomphe | ·and as ↑I ˎsay | ¯smashing the ·Longchamps ·course ˎrecord || by the ˇgreatest mis·fortune | ˋDancing ·Brave did ˋnot | ·win the ·Ever·ready ˎDerby | but ¯even in deˋfeat | he pro¯vided the ˬthrills | as he a¯ttempted | to ¯make up ˍground | on ¯Shahraˍstani | at ¯Epsom in ˎJune || ˋultimately ·Dancing ·Brave | ¯proved him·self | ¯far and aˎway | the ¯pick of his ·geneˎration | by a¯venging | that ˊEpsom ·failure | in ·both the ·King ¯George | ¯and | in the ˎArc || he ˋcouldn't ·catch Maˎnila | in ˋSanta A·nita's | ¯breeder's ·cup ˎturf | on his ¯last aˎppearance in Noˇvember | but ˋthat race | ·came at the ¯end | of a

ˉlong | and ˋgruelling ˬseason | and it ˉdidn't deˎtract | from his ˉoveˍrall magˋnificence || ˋNational ˇHunt ·racing | ·lost a ·great ˋstar | when ˋDawn ˇRun | a ˇrecord ·setter | as ˊwinner | of ·both the ˏchampion ·hurdle | ˋand the ·Cheltenham Gold ˏcup | was ˋkilled in ˬaction | ·racing at Auˋtois | but the ˋGrand ˇNational dis·covered | a ˇnew ·hero | in ˉWest ˋTip | who ˉmade ˏup | for his ˋnineteen ·eighty-·five ·Aintree ˇfall | with a ˉwinning ·clear ˎround | ·last ˎspring || Pat ˊEddery | took ˇfull ad·vantage | of ·Lester ·Piggott's re·tirement from the ˏsaddle | to be·come ˋchampion ·British ·jockey aˏgain | ·after a ˋnine ·year ˇpause || ·Peter ˊScudemore | ·won the ˉjump ·jockey's ·title | and ˉNick ˎHenderson was ·leading ·National ˋHunt ·trainer || but ˉnineteen ·eighty-ˍsix | ·was unˇquestionably | the ˉyear | of ˉDancing ˎBrave || and it'll be a ˉlong ˇtime | be·fore we ·see aˉnother ˇrace ·horse | as ˉgood as ˎhim ||

[change of speaker: Kevin Geary]

ˊwell | our reˊview | is ˉalmost comˎplete ˏnow | but it's ˉreally | only ·right and ˎproper | that the ˉold ·year | should go ˍout with a ˋbang || and ·heavyweight ˊboxing | in these ˆ ·dying ˇweeks of the ·year | has proˇvided us | with a ·couple of ˉreal ˎfirecrackers | that will unˋdoubtedly ˋresonate | ˉlong into the ˍnew ˎyear || ↑ˉhere's Mike Coˎstello ||

[change of speaker: Mike Costello]

at the ˇturn of the ·year | ˋMike ˇTyson | was con·sidered by ˇmany | to be a treˋmendous ˎprospect || but ˇnobody could have con·ceived | the ˉmanner in which he was to ·take | the ˇheavyweight di·vision | by ˋstorm || ˏwhen | in Noˇvember | he ·took just ˉfive ˎminutes | to re·lieve ˋTrevor ˇBerbick | of the ·WBˇC ·crown | he be·came the ˉyoungest | ˋworld ·heavyweight ˇchampion | in ˋhistory | at the ˍage of ˋtwenty || ˇnext ·up | the ˋawesome New ˊYorker | ·meets ˉJames | ·Bonecrusher ˎSmith | the ˏman | who ·caused a ˋmighty ˎupset | by ·knocking ·out ˋTim ˇWitherspoon | in ˉone ˎround | ˋearlier this ˎmonth || but for the ·year's ˇbiggest ·shock | we go ˉback to Sepˎtember | and a ˉfight | for the ˋundisputed ˬwelterweight ·championship | in Atˍlantic ˎCity || the ˊholder | Don ˇCurry | was ·thought to be unˎbeatable | in the ˋten ·stone ˬseven | diˋvision || the ˇchallenger | ˉBritain's | ·Lloyd ˎHoneyghan | ˏor | as the Aˇmericans pre·ferred | ˉLloyd ˊwho || ·but ˆ by ˉround ˎsix of | a reˇmarkable ·contest | they knew ˋall aˎbout him || ˉDes ˎLynan | was ˎringside ||

[live commentary omitted]

and a ˇBritish ·fighter | was in·volved in a`nother | of the ·year's ¯major ˎupsets || ¯Barry Mc`Guigan | as `WBA ˇfeatherweight ·king | ·chose ¯Las ˎVegas | as the ´venue | for his `long a·waited `debut | in the U_nited ˎStates || but the ˏIrishman ·reckoned wi`thout | the ¯crippling _heat | of the Ne`vada ˇdesert | and the de¯fensive ˎcraft | of _Steve ˎCruz || the twenty- `two year ·old ˇTexan | ·made ¯waste ˎpaper | of the ˇform ·book | to ¯win on ˎpoints | ·after ¯fif_teen | ˇgruelling | ˎrounds || else´where | ˎMarvin ˇHagler | ·main·tained his _grip | on the ·undi_sputed `middleweight ·crown | whilst ˇSouth Ko·rea's | `Chang ·Jun ˇCoo | ·kept up his reˇmarkable ·run | as the ¯WB_C | ·light ˎflyweight ·champ || ˎthose who ·bowed ˇout | inˏclude | _Larry `Holmes | to be re´placed | by the ¯sport's | ¯newest amˎbassador | in _Mike ˎTyson | who ·seems ¯destined | to be ¯mentioned | in ¯this ˎspace | for _some ˎyears ||

[change of speaker: Kevin Geary]

so ¯that ·then | the ¯sporting _year | ·nineteen ·eighty-ˎsix || let's ¯all ˏhope | that ·come ·this time `next ·year | we'll be ·looking ¯back | at an ·equally `fruitful | and ↑enˎjoyable | ¯twelve ˎmonths ||

026 SPOKEN ENGLISH CORPUS TEXT F04

Review of the Year
BBC World Service
Overlap passage

Transcribed by BJW

[change of speaker: Kevin Geary]

and •as I mentioned ˋearlier | Greg ˎNorman's outˋstanding a↑ˋchievements | were just ˋpart of a magˋnificent ˋyear for Auˉstralian ˋsport || ˆfollowing in the ˊfootsteps | of their •rugby ˋunion grand ˇslam •side | we've ˉjust _seen their ˉrugby league ˇcounterparts | the Kangaˇroos | ˋcome here and ˉteach us a•nother _painful ˋlesson || they gave some suˋperlative exhiˋbitions of fluent ˉrunning | and •magical ˋhandling | on their ˋway to comˋpleting their ˉtour of England and ˇFrance | with a one ˋhundred percent ˋrecord || and ˋlet's not forˋget that ˉfascinating _fortnight in Ocˇtober | when the ˋdowdy London ˋsuburb of ˇWillesden | was the unˇlikely •venue for a compeˉtition | which has perˋhaps seen the •birth of ˋhockey | as a •major specˇtator •sport | aˋway from its ˇspiritual •home | on the subˎcontinent || it was ˋthere that the Auˉstralians _carried off the ˉWorld _Cup | for the _first ˋtime | and in _splendid •style ˋtoo || while ˉIndia and Pakiˇstan | aˇstoundingly | finished _up playing _off for •last ˋplace || and ˋstill we're not •finished with Auˋstralia || because it's •now a couple of ˋmonths | since the most •highly ˋpublicized ˋpuncture in ˋhistory | took ˉplace on the ˇmotor racing circuit | in ˋAdelaide || ↓sending Nigel ˉMansell | and his •championship ˋhopes | caˇreering into a ˋwall || after the reˉgrets | and postˉmortems | the history ˉbooks | will ˉsimply _tell us | that ˋnineteen eighty-ˉsix | was the ˉyear when _Mansell came ˋsecond || •two points beˇhind | Alain ˋProst || but deˇspite •that | it was •still a good ˋyear for the British ˉdriver | as •Simon ˇTaylor reˋcalls ||

Transcribed by GOK

[change of speaker: Kevin Geary]

and _as I •mentioned ˋearlier | •Greg •Norman's outˉstanding aˋchievements | were •just ˋpart of a mag•nificent ˋyear | for Au•stralian ˋsport || ˏfollowing | in the ˏfootsteps | of their ˋrugby •union grand ˇslam •side | we've ˋjust •seen their ˋrugby •league ˇcounterparts | the •Kangaˬroos | ˇcome •here | and ˉteach us | a•nother _painful ˎlesson ||

they ¯gave | some su`perlative exhi`bitions | of ·fluent ´running | and `magical ˇhandling | on their ¯way | to com¯pleting | their `tour of ·England and ˇFrance | with a one `hundred per·cent `record || and ↑`let's not for·get that `fascinating ·fortnight in Ocˇtober | when the `dowdy ·London ´suburb | of ˇWillesden | was the unˇlikely ·venue | for a ·compe´tition | which has perˇhaps ·seen the ·birth | of `hockey | as a `major specˇtator ·sport | a`way from its ˇspiritual ·home | on the ˍsub`continent || it was ´there | that the Au´stralians | `carried ·off the ¯world ˍcup | for the ˍfirst `time | ↑and in ·splendid ˍstyle ˎtoo || while `India and ·Pakiˇstan | a↑ˇstoundingly | ¯finished ˏup | ·playing ˏoff | for ˍlast `place || and ˇstill we're ·not ·finished | with Au`stralia | be·cause it's ¯now a ·couple of `months | since the ¯most | `highly `publicized `puncture in ˇhistory | ·took ´place | on the ˇmotor ·racing ·circuit | in `Adelaide | ·sending `Nigel ´Mansell | and his ¯championship ˎhopes | ca`reering ·into a ˎwall || ˏafter | the re¯grets | and post´mortems | the ˇhistory ·books | will ¯simply ˏtell us | that ¯nineteen ·eighty-ˏsix | was the ¯year | when ˍMansell came `second | ·two points beˇhind | ·Alain `Prost || but deˇspite ·that | it was ·still a good `year for the ·British ˏdriver | as ·Simon `Taylor reˎcalls ||

027 SPOKEN ENGLISH CORPUS TEXT G01

Story Time: 'Through the Tunnel'
(First part)
Broadcast notes: Radio 4, 4.40 p.m., 25th June, 1985
Transcribed by BJW

ˆgoing to the ˬshore | on the ˋfirst ·morning of the ˇholiday || the ˉyoung ˬEnglish boy | ˉstopped at a ˍturning of the ˬpath | and ˉlooked ˍdown at a ˉwild and ˍrocky ˎbay || and ˇthen | ·over to the ˎcrowded ˋbeach | he ˉknew so ˎwell | from ˋother ·years || his ˋmother ·walked on in ˋfront of him | ·carrying a ˍbright ·striped ˋbag | in one ˋhand || her ˇother ·arm | ·swinging ˎloose | was very ˋwhite | in the ˎsun || the ˉboy ˎwatched that ˉwhite ˍnaked ˬarm || and ˋturned his ˇeyes | which had a ˋfrown be·hind them | toˉwards the ˎbay | and ˋback a·gain to his ˋmother || ˋwhen she ·felt he was not ˇwith her | she ˉswung aˋround || oh ↑ˋthere you are ·Gerry she ·said || ↓she ·looked imˋpatient | ↓then ˋsmiled || why ˋdarling | would you ˍrather not come ˏwith me | would you ˍrather || she ˋfrowned || ·consciˍentiously ˋworrying | over ˉwhat aˎmusements he might ˉsecretly be ˋlonging for | which ˋshe had been too ˋbusy or too ˋcareless to iˋmagine || he was ˋvery faˋmiliar with that ˋanxious aˋpologetic ˇsmile || conˋtrition | ↓sent him ˉrunning ˋafter her || and ˉyet | as he ˋran || he looked ˋback over his ˋshoulder at the ˉwild ˎbay || and ˉall ˎmorning as he ˋplayed on the ·safe ˎbeach | he was ˋthinking of it || ·next ˎmorning | when it was ˋtime for the rouˋtine of ˊswimming and ˏsunbathing | his ˉmother said || ↑are you ˬtired of the ·usual beach ·Gerry || would you ˍlike to go ˍsomewhere ˬelse || ↑oh ˎno | he said ·quickly | ˋsmiling at her | out of that unˋfailing ·impulse of conˋtrition | a ˉsort of ˋchivalry || yet ˉwalking ˍdown the ˬpath with her | he ˉblurted ·out || ˋI′d like to go and have a ˉlook at those ˋrocks | down ˋthere || she ˍgave the idea her aˋttention || it was a ˋwild ·looking ˇplace | and there was ˉno one ˋthere || but she ˍsaid | of ↑ˋcourse ·Gerry || ↓·when you′ve had eˇnough | ·come to the ˋbig ·beach | ˇor | ˉjust go ˉstraight ·back to the ˋvilla | if you ˋlike | she ˉwalked aˋway || that ˉbare ˇarm | ˉnow ·slightly ˋreddened | from ˋyesterday′s ˋsun | ˋswinging || he was an ˉonly ˋchild | eˉleven years ˋold | ˉshe was a ˋwidow || she was deˋtermined to be ˋneither poˇssessive | nor ˋlacking in deˋvotion || she went ˬworrying | ·off to her ˎbeach || ˋas for ˇGerry || ˋonce he ·saw that his ˋmother had ˋgained her ˇbeach || he beˉgan the ˍsteep deˍscent to the ˎbay || ↓as he went ˇlower | he ˉsaw that it ˉspread among ˉsmall ˋpromontories | and ˋinlets | of ˉrough ˉsharp ˎrock || ˇfinally | as he ˉran ˋsliding and ˋscraping down the ˉlast ·few ˬyards | he saw an ˉedge of ·white ˎsand | and beˇyond ·that | a ˊsolid ˏheavy ˎblue || he ˉran ˋstraight into the ˇwater | and beˉgan ˋswimming | he was a

ˇgood •swimmer || he ¯went out ˋfast •over the ˋgleaming ˋsand | •over a ˋmiddle •region | where ˋrocks •lay like dis¯coloured ˋmonsters under the ˋsurface || and ˋthen he was in the ˋreal •sea || a ˋwarm •sea | where i¯rregular _cold _currents from the ˎdeep | ¯shocked his ˎlimbs || ¯when he was _so far _out that he could ˋlook •back ¯not •only on the ¯little ˇbay | but ¯past the ˋpromontory | that was be•tween ¯it and the ¯big ˇbeach || he ¯floated on the _buoyant ˏsurface | and ¯looked for his ˋmother || ⌄there she •was || a ¯speck of ˋyellow | ¯under an um•brella that •looked like a •slice of ˋorange •peel || he ¯swam ˎback | reˋlieved | ↓at being ˋsure she was ˋthere || but ¯all at ˏonce | ¯very ˇlonely || ↑on the _edge of a _small _cape that •marked the •side of the _bay aˋway from the ˇpromontory | was a ˋloose _scatter of ˋrocks || aˇbove them | some ˋboys | were ¯stripping off their ˋclothes || they came ˋrunning ˋnaked ˋdown to the ˋrocks || the ˇEnglish •boy | ¯swam toˋwards them | but ¯kept his ˋdistance | at a ¯stone's ˋthrow || they were ¯of that ˎcoast | ˋall of them were ¯burned •smooth •dark ˋbrown | and ¯speaking a ˋlanguage he did not underˋstand || ↓to be ˇwith them || ˇof them || was a ˋcraving | that ¯filled his ¯whole ˋbody || he ¯swam a •little ˋcloser || they ¯turned and ˋwatched him | with ˋnarrowed aˋlert •dark ˋeyes | then ¯one ˋsmiled | and ˋwaved || ↓it was eˋnough || in a ¯minute he had ˇswum in | and was ¯on the •rocks beˋside them | ˋsmiling with a ˋdesperate ˋnervous suppliˋcation || they _shouted •cheerful ˋgreetings at him | and ˋthen as he preˋserved his ˋnervous ¯uncomprehending ˇsmile | they ˋunderstood that he was a ˋforeigner | ¯strayed from his _own ˎbeach | ↑and they pro_ceeded to forˋget him || ↓but ˋhe was ˋhappy | ˋhe was ˋwith them || ↑they be¯gan ⌄diving | a¯gain and a_gain from a ¯high _point into a ¯well of ˎblue •sea | between ¯rough •pointed ˋrocks || ˋafter they had ˏdived | and ¯come ˏup | they ¯swam a⌄round | ˇhauled themselves •up | and ¯waited their _turn to _dive aˋgain || they were ˇbig •boys | ˋmen | to ˏGerry || ˋhe •dived || and ¯they ˋwatched him || and ¯when he _swam a•round to •take his ˏplace | they •made ˋway for him || ↓he _felt he was aˋccepted || and he _dived aˋgain | ˋcarefully | ˋproud of him•self || ˇsoon | the ˋbiggest of the ˏboys | ˇpoised him•self | ˋshot down into the ˏwater | and did _not come ˋup || the ˋothers | stood aˋbout | ˋwatching || ˇGerry | after ¯waiting for the _sleek •brown •head to aˇppear | ¯let out a •yell of ˋwarning || they _looked at him ˊidly | and ¯turned their •eyes •back towards the ˋwater || after a ¯long ˎtime || the ¯boy •came ˇup | on the ¯other ˎside of a ¯big •dark ˎrock | •letting the ¯air out of his ˎlungs in a ¯sputtering ˎgasp and a ¯shout of ˎtriumph || iˇmmediately | the ˋrest of them •dived in || ¯one •moment the _morning •seemed ˇfull of •chattering •boys | the ¯next the ˋair and the ˋsurface of the ˋwater were ˋempty || ˋGerry •dived | ¯shot

·past the _school of ·underwater ˏswimmers | saw a ¯black ˎwall of ˋrock | ˇlooming at him | ˇtouched it | and ¯bobbed up at _once to the ˋsurface | where the ˋwall was a ˋlow ˇbarrier | he could ˋsee a·cross || there was _no one ˋvisible | ˇunder him | in the ˏwater | the ¯dim ·shapes of the ˏswimmers | had disaˋppeared || then ˏone | and then aˇnother of the ·boys | ˋcame up on the ¯far _side of the _barrier of ˋrock | and he ¯under_stood that they had ¯swum _through some _gap or ˋhole in it || he _plunged ˋdown a·gain || he ·could see ˋnothing | through the ¯stinging _salt _water but the ·blank ˋrock || ˋwhen he came ˇup | the ˋboys were ·all on the ˋdiving ·rock | pre¯paring to a_ttempt the _feat aˋgain | and ˋnow in a ˋpanic of ˇfailure | he ¯yelled up in _English | ¯look at _me ˋlook || and he began ˋsplashing and ˋkicking in the ˋwater like a ¯foolish ˋdog || ↓they ¯looked ˎdown | ˋgravely | ˋfrowning || ¯he _knew the ˎfrown || at ¯moments of ✓failure | when he ¯clowned to ·claim his ˋmother's a·ttention || it was with ˋjust this ·grave emˋbarassed in·spection that ˋshe re·warded him || the ˋrock | ˋlately ˋweighted with ˋboys | ·seemed to ¯rear up _out of the ˋwater as their ¯weight was reˋmoved || they were ¯flying ·down ˇpast him now | ¯into the ˎwater || ↓the ˇair | was ˋfull of _falling ˋbodies || ¯then the ·rock was ˋempty | in the _hot ˋsun·light || he ˎcounted | ˇone | ˇtwo | ˇthree || at ˇfifty | he was ˋterrified || ↑they must _all be ˋdrowning | beˋneath him | in the ¯watery ˋcaves | of the ˋrock || at a ˇhundred | he ¯stared aˋround him | at the ¯empty ˋhillside | ˋwondering if he should ˋyell for ˋhelp || ↑he _counted ˋfaster | ˋfaster | to ¯hurry them ˋup | to ¯bring them to the ˋsurface ˋquickly | to ˋdrown them ·quickly | ˋanything | ·rather than the ¯terror of ·counting ¯on and _on into the ¯blue ·emptiness of the ˇmorning || ↓and _then || ↓at a ¯hundred and ✓sixty || ↓the ¯water beyond the _rock was ¯full of ·boys ·blowing like _brown ˎwhales || they ¯swam back to the ˇshore | without a ˋlook at him || he ·swam ˇback to the big ·rock | ˇclimbed up | and ˋdived into the ·blue ˎpool | ↓a·mong the ¯fanged and ·angry ˋboulders || ¯down he ·went until he ·touched the wall of ˋrock a·gain || but the ˋsalt was so ˋpainful in his ˋeyes | that he ˎcould not ˋsee || he ¯came to the ˏsurface | ¯swam to the _shore | and ¯went back to the _villa to ¯wait for his ˎmother || ¯soon | she _walked ·slowly up the ˏpath | ¯swinging her _striped ˎbag | the ¯flushed _naked _arm ·dangling beˎside her || I ¯want some ˋswimming ·goggles | he ·panted | deˋfiant and beˋseeching || ˋshe ·gave him a ˇpatient | inˇquisitive ·look | as she ·said ˏcasually | ↑well of ˋcourse ·darling || but ˋnow | ¯now ˋnow | he ˋmust have them this ˋminute | and ¯no ˋother ·time || he ˋnagged and ˋpestered until she ˋwent with him to a ˋshop || as ˋsoon as she had ˇbought the ·goggles | he ˋgrabbed them from her ˇhand | as ¯if she were ·going to ¯claim them for herˋself | and was ˋoff | ¯running down the ·steep ˋpath to the ˋbay || he ˉfixed the ˍgoggles ˉtight and ˎfirm || ˉfilled his ˍlungs | and ˉfloated face ˍdown on the ˎwater || ˋnow | ↓he could ˎsee || ↑ˇunder him | ˉsix or ˍseven feet ˏdown | was a ˉfloor of ˉperfectly ˍclean ˍshining ˍwhite ˎsand | ·rippled ˋfirm and ˋhard by the ˋtides || the ˉgreat ˋrock | the ˉbig ·boys had ˇswum ·through | ˉrose ˋsheer out of the ·white ˋsand | ˋblack | ˉtufted ˋlightly with ˉgreenish ˎweed || he could ˉsee no ˋgap in it || he ˉswam ˍdown to its ˋbase || aˋgain and aˋgain he ˋrose | took a ˉbig ˍchestful of ˏair | and ˉwent down aˋgain || aˋgain and aˋgain he ˋgroped over the ·surface of the ˋrock | ˋfeeling it | ˉalmost ˋhugging it | in the ˉdesperate ˋneed to ·find the ˋentrance || and ·then ˋonce | while he was ˉclinging to the ˍblack ˍwall | his ˉknees came ˍup | and he ˉshot his ˋfeet out ˏforward | and they ˉmet no ˋobstacle || ↓he had ˋfound the ˋhole || he ˉgained the ˏsurface | ˉclambered about the ˍstones that ˉlittered the ·barrier ·rock until he ·found a ˋbig one | and with ˉthis in his ˏarms | ˉlet himself ˍdown over the ˍside of the ˋrock || he ˋdropped | with the ˍweight ˉstraight to the ˍsandy ˎfloor || ˉclinging ˋtight | to the ˉanchor of ˏstone | he ˋlay on his ˏside | and ˉlooked in under the ˍdark ˎshelf | at the ˉplace where his ˋfeet had ·gone || it was an iˇrregular | ˉdark ˋgap | but he ˉcould not ·see ˉdeep ˋinto it || he let ˇgo of his ·anchor | ˉclung with his ˍhands to the ˉedges of the ˬhole | and ˉtried to ˋpush himself ˋin || he ˉgot his ˇhead in | ·found his ˋshoulders ˇjammed | ˋmoved them in ˇside·ways | and was ˉinˏside as ˏfar as his ˋwaist || ↓he could see ˋnothing aˋhead || ·something ˋsoft and ˋclammy | ˉtouched his ˇmouth | and ˋpanic ·filled him || he ˉthought of ˋoctopuses | of ˋclinging ˋweed | he ˉpushed himself ·out ˇbackwards | and ·caught a ˉglimpse as he reˎtreated | of a ˉharmless ˍtentacle of ˇseaweed | ˉdrifting in the ˍmouth of the ˇtunnel || but it ˋwas eˋnough || ↓he ˉreached the ˎsun·light | ˉswam to the ˍshore | and ˋlay on the ˋdiving ·rock ||

027 SPOKEN ENGLISH CORPUS TEXT G01
Story Time: 'Through the Tunnel'
(Second part)
Broadcast notes: Radio 4, 4.40 p.m., 25th June, 1985
Transcribed by GOK

the ¯great ˋrock | the ¯big ·boys had ˇswum ·through | ¯rose ↑¯sheer ·out of the ¯white ˎsand | ˋblack | ¯tufted _lightly | with ¯greenish ˎweed || he could ·see no ↑ˋgap in it || he ¯swam _down to its ˋbase || aˋgain and aˋgain | he ˋrose | took a ¯big _chestful of ˏair | and went ↓_down aˋgain || aˋgain and aˎgain | he ¯groped over the ·surface of the ˋrock | ˋfeeling it | ¯almost ˋhugging it | in the ¯desperate _need | to ·find the ˋentrance || and ·then ˋonce | while he was ¯clinging to the ·black _wall | his ¯knees came _up | and he ¯shot his ¯feet out ˏforward | and they ¯met no ˎobstacle || he had ˋfound the ˎhole || he ¯gained the ˏsurface | ¯clambered about the _stones | that ¯littered the _barrier rock | until he ·found a ˇbig one | and with ¯this in his ˏarms | ¯let himself ˏdown | over the _side of the ˋrock || he ¯dropped with the _weight | ¯straight to the _sandy ˎfloor || ¯clinging ˋtight | to the ¯anchor of ˏstone | he ¯lay on his _side | and ¯looked ·in under the _dark ˎshelf | at the ¯place where his ˎfeet had ·gone | it was an irˇregular | ¯dark ˋgap | but he ¯could not _see | ¯deep ˋinto it | he let ¯go of his ˏanchor | ¯clung with his _hands | to the ¯edges of the ˇhole | and ·tried to ·push himself ˋin || he ¯got his ˇhead in | found his ¯shoulders ˇjammed | ¯moved them in _sideways | and was ¯in_side | as _far as his ˋwaist || he could ·see ˋnothing aˎhead || ¯something ˎsoft | and ˋclammy | ¯touched his ˎmouth | and ˋpanic ·filled him || ↑he ·thought of ˋoctopuses | of ¯clinging ˋweed | he ¯pushed himself ·out ˎbackwards | and ·caught a ↑¯glimpse as he reˎtreated | of a ¯harmless _tentacle of ˎseaweed | ↓·drifting in the ·mouth of the ˎtunnel || but it ¯was eˎnough || he ¯reached the _sunlight | ¯swam to the _shore | and ·lay on the ˎdiving rock || he ·looked ˋdown | into the ¯blue _well of ˋwater || ↑he ·knew he ·must find his _way | ¯through that ˏcave | or ˏhole | or ˏtunnel || and ↓·out the ·other ˎside || ˇfirst ˆ he ·thought || he must _learn to con·trol his ˋbreathing || he ¯let himself _down into the _water | with a¯nother big ˇstone in his ·arms | ↑so that he could ·lie ˎeffortlessly | ↓on the ·bottom of the ˎsea || he ˋcounted || ˋone | ˎtwo | ˎthree || he ˋcounted ˎsteadily || he could ˋhear | the ¯movement of ˎblood | in his ˎchest || ˋfifty-·one | ˋfifty-·two || his ¯chest was ˎhurting || he let ¯go of the _rock | and went ¯up into the ˎair || he ·saw the ↑ˋsun was ·low || he ¯rushed to the ˇvilla | and ·found his ˇmother | at her ˋsupper || she said ¯only | ↑did you enˊjoy yourself || and ˇhe said | ˋyes || ↓·that _night | his ˎnose | ˋbled ˎbadly || for ˇhours | he had been ·under ˎwater | ¯learning to ·hold his ˎbreath ||

and ¯now he ·felt ˋweak | and ˎdizzy || ↑his ¯mother ·said | ↑I ¯shouldn't overˇdo things ·darling | if ˇI were ·you || ¯that day and the ˏnext | ·Gerry ¯exercised his _lungs | as if ˋeverything | the ¯whole of his ˎlife | ¯all that he would beˎcome | deˎpended u·pon it || the ˇbig ·boys | had ¯made the ˏpassage | while ¯he ·counted a ·hundred and ˋsixty || he had been ¯counting ˋfast | in his ˎfright || ·probably ↑ˋnow | if he ˋtried | he could get ˋthrough that ·long ·tunnel || but he was ¯not going to ·try ˎyet || a ¯curious | most ¯childlike perˎsistence | a con¯trolled imˎpatience | ¯made him ˋwait || he ˋsat by the ˎclock | in the ˎvilla | when his ˋmother was not ˎnear | and _checked his ˋtime || he was inˋcredulous | and then ↑ˋproud | to ¯find out he could ¯hold his _breath | wi¯thout _strain | for ¯two ˎminutes || the ˎwords | ¯two ˎminutes | ¯authorised by the ˎclock | ·brought ˋclose | the adˎventure | that was ¯so ˋnecessary ·to him || ¯two ·days be·fore they were to _leave | a ¯day of ˋtriumph | when he in¯creased his _count by ¯fifˋteen || his ¯nose ·bled ¯so ⌄badly | that he ·turned ˋdizzy | and ¯had to ·lie ˋlimply | over the ¯big ˋrock | like a ¯bit of ˎseaweed | ·watching the ¯thick red ˎblood | ¯flow onto the ˎrock | and ¯trickle ·slowly _down to the ˎsea || he was ˋfrightened || supˇposing | he ¯turned ˋdizzy | in the ˎtunnel || sup¯posing he ˋdied ·there || ˋtrapped || supˋposing || his ˋhead went aˎround | in the ¯hot ˋsun | and he ˇal↓most ·gave ˎup || he ·thought he would re¯turn to the _house | and ¯lie ˎdown || and ˋnext ·summer per·haps | when he had a¯nother ·year's ˎgrowth in him | ↑ˋthen he would ·go through the ·hole || but ¯even after he had ·made the deˎcision | or ˎthought he ·had || he ·found himself ¯sitting up on the ˏrock | and ¯looking _down into the ˎwater || and he ¯knew that ˋnow | ¯this ˎmoment || when his ¯nose had ·only just ·stopped ˎbleeding | when his ¯head was still ¯sore and ˋthrobbing | ˋthis | was the ¯moment when he would ˎtry || if he did ¯not do it ⌄now | he ¯never ˎwould || he was ˋtrembling with ˎfear | that he would ¯not ˋgo || and he was ˋtrembling with ˎhorror | at that ˋlong ˋlong ˎtunnel | ¯under the ˎrock | ¯under the ˎsea || ˋtons of ·rock | ¯pressed _down on ¯where he would ˎgo || if ↑he ˇdied ·there | he would ˋlie | until ¯one ˎday | per·haps ¯not before ¯next ˋyear | those ¯big ˋboys | would ¯swim ˋinto it | and ·find it ˋblocked || he put ·on his ⌄goggles | ·fitted them _tight | ¯tested the ⌄vacuum || his ˇhands | were ˋshaking || ↑¯then he ·chose the ↑¯biggest ·stone he could ⌄carry | and ¯slipped over the ·edge of the _rock | until ˇhalf of ·him | was in the ¯cool en¯closing ˇwater | and ¯half in the ¯hot ˎsun || he ¯looked ·up ˋonce | at the ¯empty ⌄sky | ¯filled his _lungs | ¯once ˆ ˏtwice || and ·then sank ˎfast | to the ˎbottom | with the ˎstone || he ·let it ˎgo | and be¯gan to ˎcount || he ·took the ¯edges of the _hole in his ˏhands | and ¯drew himself ˋinto it | ¯wriggling his ·shoulders in ˇsideways | as he re¯membered he

ˍmust || ˉkicking himself aˍlong with his ˋfeet || ˉsoon he was ˉclear inˋside || the ˇwater | was ˉpushing him ˍup against the ˋroof || the ˉroof was ˋsharp | and ˉpained his ˎback || he ˉpulled himself aˏlong | with his ˋhands | ˋfast | ˋfast || and ·used his ˋlegs as ˎlevers || his ˋhead | ˉknocked aˋgainst ·something | a ˉsharp ˋpain | ˋdizzied him || ˉfifty | fifty-ˊone | fifty-ˊtwo || there was ˋno strain on his ˇlungs || he ˉfelt like an inˉflated balˋloon | his ˉlungs were so ˍlight and ˬeasy || but his ˋhead was ˎpulsing || ↑he was being conˉtinually ˋpressed | a·gainst the ˍsharp ˋroof | which felt ˋslimy | as ˉwell as ˎsharp || aˋgain | he ˉthought of ˋoctopuses || and ˉwondered if the ˍtunnel might be ˉfilled with ˋweed | that could ˋtangle him || he ˋgave himself | a ˋpanicky | conˉvulsive ·kick ˎforward | ˉducked his ˍhead | and ˋswam || his ˉfeet and ˬhands | ˉmoved ↑ˋfreely | as ˉif in ·open ˋwater || a ˎhundred | a ·hundred and ˋone || the ˉwater ˋpaled || ˇvictory | ˎfilled him || his ˋlungs | were beˉginning to ˎhurt | a ˉfew more ˏstrokes | and he would be ˋout || he was ˋcounting ˎwildly || ↑he said a ˉhundred and fifˎteen | and then a ˋlong time ·later | a ·hundred and fif·teen aˋgain || the ˉwater | was a ˉclear ˍjewel ˎgreen | all aˋround him || ˉthen ↑he ˍsaw | aˉbove ↑his ˍhead | a ˬcrack | running ˉup through the ˎrock || ˉsunlight was ·falling ˎthrough it | ·showing the ˉclean dark ˍrock of the ˍtunnel | a ˉsingle ˍmussel shell | and ˋdarkness | aˎhead || ↑he was at the ˋend | of ·what he could ˋdo || he ·looked ˉup at the ˍcrack | as ·if it were ˉfilled with ˋair | and ˉnot ˏwater || as ·if he could ·put his ˋmouth to it | and ˉdraw ˍin ˋair || a ·hundred and fifˋteen he ·heard himself ·say in·side his ·head || but he'd ˋsaid ˏthat | ˋlong a·go || his ˋhead was ˎswelling | his ˇlungs | ˋcracking || ˉhundred and fifˋteen | a ˉhundred and fifˋteen | ˉpounded ·through his ˎhead || and he ˋfeebly | ˉclutched at ˎrocks | in the ˎdark | ˉpulling him·self ˎforward || he ˍfelt he was ˆdying || he was ·no longer ˋconscious || he ˉstruggled ˋon | in the ˎdarkness | between ·lapses into unˎconsciousness || an imˉmense ˍswelling ˎpain | ˉfilled his ˎhead | and ˉthen the ˍdarkness ˋcracked | with an exˉplosion of ˉgreen ˎlight || his ˉhands ·groping ˍforward met ˎnothing | and his ˋfeet | ˉkicking ˍback | proˉpelled him ˍout | into the ˉopen ˎsea || ↓he ˎdrifted | to the ˎsurface || his ˉface ·turned to the ˎair || he was ˋgasping | like a ˎfish || he ˉfelt he would ˋsink now | and ˎdrown || he could ˋnot ·swim the ˉfew feet ˍback to the ˋrock || ˉthen he was ˎclutching it || and ˉpulling himself ˎup on it || he ˉlay ·face ˎdown | ˎgasping || he could ˉsee ˎnothing | but a ˉred ·veined ˍclotted ˎdark || his ˆeyes must have ·burst he ·thought || they were ·full of ˋblood || he ˉtore off his ˍgoggles | and a ˉgout of ˎblood | went ·into the ˎsea || his ˆnose was ·bleeding | and the ˋblood | had ·filled the ˎgoggles || he ˉscooped up ˍhandfuls of ˎwater | from the ˉcool ˍsalty ˎsea | to

·splash on his ˎface | and did not ˉknow whether it was ˊblood | or ˉsalt ˎwater he ·tasted || he ˉwanted ˎnothing | but to ˉget back ˋhome | and ˉlie ˎdown || in a ˉshort ˍwhile | ˍGerry ˉswam to ˬshore | and ˉclimbed ·slowly up the ˏpath | to the ˎvilla || he ˉflung himself on his ˍbed and ˎslept || ˇwaking | at the ·sound of ˋfeet | on the ˉpath outˋside || his ˋmother was ·coming ·back || he ˋrushed to the ˎbathroom | ·thinking she must ˉnot see his ˍface with ˇbloodstains | or ˬtear stains | ˍon it || he came ˉout of the ˏbathroom | and ˋmet her | as she ˉwalked ·into the ˎvilla || ˉhave a ·nice ˊmorning she ·asked | ˍlaying her ·hand on his ·warm ·brown ·shoulder a ·moment || oh ˎyes ^ ·thank you ^ he ·said || you ˉlook a bit ˇpale || and ˎthen | ˉsharp and ˎanxious | ˉhow did you ˍbang your ↑ˋhead || ˋoh | just ˋbanged it ^ he ·told her || she ˇlooked at him | ˎclosely || he was ˋstrained | his ˋeyes were ˋglazed ·looking || she was ˎworried || and ˇthen she ·said to her·self | ↑oh ·don't ˎfuss | ˉnothing can ˏhappen | he can ˍswim like a ˋfish || ↓they ·sat down to ˋlunch to·gether || ˋmummy ^ he ·said | ˇI can ·stay under ·water | for ˉtwo ˋminutes | ˋthree minutes | at ˋleast || it came ˋbursting ˎout of him || ˊcan you ·darling she ·said || well I ˉshouldn't overˇdo it || ↑ˉI don't ·think you ought to ˍswim any ˋmore to·day || she was ˋready | for a ˉbattle of ˎwills | but he ˉgave ˋin | at ˎonce || it was no ˇlonger | of the ˉleast imˎportance ^ to ·go to the ·bay ||

027 SPOKEN ENGLISH CORPUS TEXT G01
Story Time: 'Through the Tunnel'
Broadcast notes: Radio 4, 4.40 p.m., 25th June, 1985
Overlap passage

Transcribed by BJW

the ˉgreat ˋrock | the ˉbig ·boys had ˇswum ·through | ˉrose ˋsheer out of the ·white ˋsand | ˋblack | ˉtufted ˋlightly with ˉgreenish ˎweed || he could ˉsee no ˋgap in it || he ˉswam _down to its ˋbase || aˋgain and aˋgain he ˋrose | took a ˉbig _chestful of ˏair | and ˉwent down aˋgain || aˋgain and aˋgain he ˋgroped over the ·surface of the ˋrock | ˋfeeling it | ˉalmost ˋhugging it | in the ˉdesperate ˋneed to ·find the ˋentrance || and ·then ˋonce | while he was ˉclinging to the _black _wall | his ˉknees came _up | and he ˉshot his ˋfeet out ˏforward | and they ˉmet no ˋobstacle || ↓he had ˋfound the ˋhole || he ˉgained the ˏsurface | ˉclambered about the _stones that ˉlittered the ·barrier ·rock until he ·found a ˋbig one | and with ˉthis in his ˏarms | ˉlet himself _down over the _side of the ˋrock || he ˋdropped | with the _weight ˉstraight to the _sandy ˎfloor || ˉclinging ˋtight | to the ˉanchor of ˏstone | he ˋlay on his ˏside | and ˉlooked in under the _dark ˎshelf | at the ˉplace where his ˋfeet had ·gone || it was an iˇrregular | ˉdark ˋgap | but he ˉcould not ·see ˉdeep ˋinto it || he let ˇgo of his ·anchor | ˉclung with his _hands to the ˉedges of the ˬhole | and ˉtried to ˋpush himself ˋin || he ˉgot his ˇhead in | ·found his ˋshoulders ˇjammed | ˋmoved them in ˇside·ways | and was ˉinˏside as ˏfar as his ˋwaist || ↓he could see ˋnothing aˋhead || ·something ˋsoft and ˋclammy | ˉtouched his ˇmouth | and ˋpanic ·filled him || he ˉthought of ˋoctopuses | of ˋclinging ˋweed | he ˉpushed himself ·out ˇbackwards | and ·caught a ˉglimpse as he reˎtreated | of a ˉharmless _tentacle of ˇseaweed | ˉdrifting in the _mouth of the ˇtunnel || but it ˋwas eˋnough || ↓he ˉreached the ˎsun·light | ˉswam to the _shore | and ˋlay on the ˋdiving ·rock ||

Transcribed by GOK

ˉgreat ˋrock | the ˉbig ·boys had ˇswum ·through | ˉrose ↑ˉsheer ·out of the ˉwhite ˎsand | ˋblack | ˉtufted _lightly | with ˉgreenish ˎweed || he could ·see no ↑ˋgap in it || he ˉswam _down to its ˋbase || aˋgain and aˋgain | he ˋrose | took a ˉbig _chestful of ˏair | and went ↓_down aˋgain || aˋgain and aˎgain | he ˉgroped over the ·surface of the ˋrock | ˋfeeling it | ˉalmost ˋhugging it | in the ˉdesperate _need | to ·find the ˋentrance || and ·then ˋonce | while he was ˉclinging to the ·black _wall | his ˉknees came ˍup | and he ¯shot his ¯feet out ˏforward | and they ¯met no ˎobstacle || he had ˋfound the ˎhole || he ¯gained the ˏsurface | ¯clambered about the ˍstones | that ¯littered the ˍbarrier rock | until he ·found a ˇbig one | and with ¯this in his ˏarms | ¯let himself ˏdown | over the ˍside of the ˋrock || he ¯dropped with the ˍweight | ¯straight to the ˍsandy ˎfloor || ¯clinging ˋtight | to the ¯anchor of ˏstone | he ¯lay on his ˍside | and ¯looked ·in under the ˍdark ˎshelf | at the ¯place where his ˎfeet had ·gone | it was an irˇregular | ¯dark ˋgap | but he ¯could not ˍsee | ¯deep ˋinto it | he let ¯go of his ˏanchor | ¯clung with his ˍhands | to the ¯edges of the ˬhole | and ·tried to ·push himself ˋin || he ¯got his ˇhead in | found his ¯shoulders ˇjammed | ¯moved them in ˍsideways | and was ¯inˍside | as ˍfar as his ˋwaist || he could ·see ˋnothing aˎhead || ¯something ˎsoft | and ˋclammy | ¯touched his ˎmouth | and ˋpanic ·filled him || ↑he ·thought of ˋoctopuses | of ¯clinging ˋweed | he ¯pushed himself ·out ˎbackwards | and ·caught a ↑¯glimpse as he reˎtreated | of a ¯harmless ˍtentacle of ˎseaweed | ↓·drifting in the ·mouth of the ˎtunnel || but it ¯was eˎnough || he ¯reached the ˍsunlight | ¯swam to the ˍshore | and ·lay on the ˎdiving rock ||

028 SPOKEN ENGLISH CORPUS TEXT G02
Listening and Reading: 'Lion at School'
(First part)
Broadcast notes: Radio 4, 2.20 p.m., 28th January, 1987
Transcribed by BJW

ˉonce u·pon a ˏtime | there was a ˉlittle ˎgirl | who didn't ˇlike going to ·school || she ˉalways ˍset off ˎlate || ˋthen she had to ˋhurry || but she ˋnever hurried ˋfast enough || ˉone ˏmorning | she was ˉhurrying a·long as ˏusual | when she ˉturned a ˏcorner | and ˉthere ˍstood | a ˋlion | ˉblocking her ˎway || he ˋstood ˋwaiting for her || he ˋstared at her with his ˉyellow ˎeyes || he ˋgrowled || and ˉwhen he ˏgrowled | the ˉlittle ˏgirl could ·see that his ˋteeth were as ˉsharp as ˎskewers | and ˋknives || he ˉgrowled | ˉI'm going to ·eat you ˎup || ↑oh ˎdear | said the little ˍgirl | and she beˉgan to ˎcry || ˋwait || said the ˍlion || I ˉhaven't ˍfinished | I'm ˉgoing to eat you ˍup | unˉless | you ˉtake me to ˎschool with you || ↑oh ˍdear | said the little ˍgirl | I ˉcouldn't do ˍthat || my ˍteacher says we mustn't ˉbring ˏpets to ·school || ˋI'm not a ˊpet | said the ˏlion || he ˋgrowled aˋgain | and she ˋsaw that his ˋtail ˉswished from ˍside to ˋside in ˋanger || ˋswish | ˋswosh | ˋyou can ·tell your ˋteacher | that I'm a ˋfriend | who is ·coming to school ˋwith you | he ·said || ˋnow | ˉshall we ˍgo || the ˉlittle ˍgirl had ˉstopped ˏcrying || she ˍsaid | ˉall ˏright | but you ˋmust ·promise ˉtwo ˎthings || ˉfirst of ˏall | you mustn't ˋeat anyone | it's not aˋllowed || I suˋppose I can ˋgrowl | said the ·lion || I suˉppose you ˋcan | said the little ·girl || and I suˋppose I can ˇroar || ˊmust you | ˏsaid the little ·girl || ˋyes | said the ·lion || then I suˉppose you ˍcan | said the little ·girl || and what's the ˋsecond ·thing | asked the ·lion || you must ˉlet me ˍride ˉon your ˍback | to ˎschool || ˉvery ˎwell | said the ·lion || he ˉcrouched ˍdown ˉon the ˏpavement | and the ˉlittle ˏgirl | ˉclimbed onto his ˎback || she ˋheld on by his ˋmane || then they ˋwent on to·gether toˉwards the ˎschool || the ˉlittle ˏgirl | ˉriding the ˎlion || the ˉlion ˍran with the ˉlittle ˍgirl on his ˉback to ˎschool || ˋeven ˋso they were ˋlate | the ˉlittle ˏgirl | and the ˏlion | went ˉinto the ˏclassroom | ˉjust as the ˍteacher was ˍcalling the ˋregister || the ˋteacher ˋstopped ·calling the ˋregister when she ˋsaw the little ˋgirl and the ˋlion || she ˋstared at the ·lion || and ˉall the other ˋchildren | ˎstared at the ·lion | ˋwondering what the ˋteacher was ˋgoing to ˋsay || the ˋteacher said to the little ˋgirl | you ˋknow you're not a·llowed to bring ˇpets to ·school || the ˏlion | beˋgan to ˋswish his ˋtail | ˍswish | ˉswosh || the ˋlittle girl ˍsaid | this is ˉnot a ˍpet | ˋthis is my ˋfriend | who is ˋcoming to ·school ˋwith me || the ˋteacher still ˇstared at the ·lion | but she ˋsaid to the little ˇgirl | ˉwhat is his ˎname ·then || ˋNoil | said the little ·girl | his ˉname is ˬNoil | ˉjust ˎNoil || she ˋknew it would be ˋno ·good to ·tell the ˋteacher that her ˋfriend was a ˋlion | so she had ¯turned his ˍname ˋbackwards || ¯L | ¯I | ˍO | ¯N | ˏlion || ¯N | ˍO | ¯I | ˇL | ˋNoil || the ¯teacher ˍwrote the name ˍdown | in the ˋregister || ˋNoil || and then she ˋfinished ˋcalling the ˋregister || ¯Betty ˏSmall | she ·said || ¯yes | said the little ·girl || ˇNoil | said the ˏteacher || ˋyes | said the ·lion || he ˋmumbled | ˋopening his ˋmouth as ˋlittle as ˋpossible | so that the ˋteacher should ↑¯not ˍsee his ˋteeth as ˋsharp as ˋskewers and ˋknives || ¯all that ˏmorning | the ¯lion sat up on his ˍchair ¯next to the little ˍgirl | like a ¯big ˎcat || with his ¯tail ·curled ˍround his front ˎpaws | as ↑¯good as ˎgold || he didn't ˋspeak unˋless the ˋteacher ˋspoke to ˋhim || he didn't ˏgrowl | he didn't ˋroar || at ˇplaytime | the ¯little ˍgirl and the ˏlion | went into the ˋplayground || ¯all the ˍchildren ·stopped ˋplaying | to ˋstare at the ˋlion || ˋthen they went on ˋplaying a·gain || the ¯little ˏgirl | stood in a ˇcorner of the ·playground | with the ˋlion beˋside her || ˋwhy don't we ¯play | like the ˋothers | the lion ·asked || the ¯little girl ˍsaid | I don't ˇlike ·playing | because ˋsome of the ˋbig ·boys are so ˋbig and ˋrough || they ˋknock you ˋover without ˋmeaning to || the ˋlion ˋgrowled || they ˋwouldn't knock ˋme ·over | he ·said || there's ¯one ˏbig ·boy | the ˋvery ˇbiggest | said the little ˏgirl || his ˋname is ·Jack ˇTall ||

028 SPOKEN ENGLISH CORPUS TEXT G02
Listening and Reading: 'Lion at School'
(Second part)
Broadcast notes: Radio 4, 2.20 p.m., 28th January, 1987
Transcribed by GOK

ˉN ˍO ˋI ˇL | ˋNoil || the ˋteacher ·wrote the name ˏdown | in the ˎregister || ˎNoil || and ·then she ˋfinished | ˎcalling the ˋregister || ˉBetty ˊSmall ^ she said || ↑ˉyes | said the ·little ˏgirl || ˬNoil ^ said the ·teacher || ˍyes | said the ˏlion || he ˋmumbled | ·opening his ˬmouth | as ˋlittle as ˎpossible | so that the ˉteacher | should ˉnot ˎsee | his ˎteeth | as ˋsharp | as ˎskewers | and ˎknives || ˉall that ˏmorning | the ˉlion sat up on his ˏchair | ˋnext to the ·little ˏgirl | like a ˉbig ˎcat | with his ˉtail | ˋcurled ·round his ˉfront ˎpaws | as ↑ˉgood as ˎgold || he ˉdidn't ˎspeak | un·less the ˋteacher ˋspoke to ˬhim | he ˉdidn't ˏgrowl | he ·didn't ˋroar || at ˇplaytime | the ˉlittle ˏgirl | and the ˏlion | went ·into the ˋplayground || ˉall the ˍchildren | stopped ˎplaying | to ˋstare at the ˎlion || ˋthen they ·went on ˋplaying a·gain || the ˉlittle ˏgirl | ˉstood in a ˎcorner of the ˏplayground | with the ˇlion | beˎside her || ˋwhy don't we ˍplay | like the ˋothers ^ the ·lion ·asked || the ˉlittle ˍgirl ˍsaid | I don't ˋlike ˏplaying | be·cause some of the ˇbig boys | are so ˋbig | and ˎrough || they ˉknock you ˋover | without ˋmeaning to || the ˬlion | ˋgrowled || they ·wouldn't knock ˊˇme over ^ he ·said || there's ˉone ˏbig ·boy | the ˋvery ˬbiggest ^ said the ·little ·girl | his ˋname is ·Jack ˬTall | he ˉknocks me ˏover | on ˋpurpose || ·which is ˎhe ^ said the ·lion || ˉpoint him ˎout to ·me || the ˉlittle ˏgirl | ˋpointed ·out Jack ˏTall | to the ˎlion || ˎah ^ said the ·lion | so ˋthat's ·Jack ·Tall || ˉjust ˏthen | the ˎbell ·rang a·gain | and ˉall the ˏchildren | went ˍback to their ˋclassrooms || the ˇlion | went with the ˍlittle ˋgirl | and ·sat beˋside her || ˉthen the ·children ˏdrew | and ·wrote until ˋdinnertime || the ˬlion | was ˋhungry | so ˇhe wanted to ·draw | a ˉpicture of his ˋdinner || ·what will it ·be for ˋdinner ^ he ·asked the ·little ·girl | I ˋhope it's ˬmeat || ˇno ^ said the ·little ·girl | it will ·be ^ ˉfishˋfingers | be·cause toˍday is ˋFriday || ˉthen the little ˍgirl | ˉshowed the ˏlion | ˋhow to ·hold the ˉyellow ˏcrayon | ˉin his ˏpaw | and ·draw fishˎfingers || ˋunderneath his ˬpicture | she ·wrote ^ ˋI like ˎmeat | ˋbetter than ˏfishfingers || ˉthen | it was ˎdinner ·time || the ˉlion sat ·up on his ˏchair | at the ˏdinner ·table | ˋnext to the ˉlittle ˎgirl || the ˋlion ·ate ˋvery ˬfast | and ˋat the ˬend he ·said | ˋI'm still ˋhungry | ↑and I ˍwish it had ·been ˬmeat || ↑ˇafter ·dinner | ˉall the ˏchildren | went into the ˋplayground || ˉall | the ˉbig ˍboys | were ˉrunning aˏbout | and the ˉvery ˇbiggest ·boy | ·Jack ˬTall | came ˉrunning toˏwards | the ·little ˋgirl || ↑he was ·running in ˎcircles | ˋcloser | ·and ˋcloser | to the ·little

ˋgirl || ·go a ˎway ‸ said the ·lion | you ˋmight knock my ˋfriend ·over || ˉgo a ˎway || ˋshan't ‸ said Jack ·Tall || the ˋlittle ˇgirl | got beˋhind the ˇlion || Jack ˋTall was ·running | ˊcloser | and ˏcloser | and ˋcloser || the ˇlion | ˎgrowled || then ˉJack ˏTall | saw the ˉlion's ˋteeth | as ˉsharp as ·skewers and ˎknives || he ˉstopped ˋrunning || he ·stood ˋstill || he ˎstared || the ˉlion | ·opened his ˍmouth ˎwider | ˇso wide | that ˋJack Tall could ·see his ˎthroat | ˋopened | ˉwide | and ˉdeep | and ˎdark | like a ˋtunnel to go ·into || ˉJack ˇTall | went ˋpale || ˉthen | the ·lion ˎroared || he ˎroared | and he ˋroared | and he ↑ˋroared || ˉall the ˎteachers | came ˉrunning ˏout | ˉall the ˍchildren stopped ˏplaying | and ·stuck their ˉfingers in their ˎears || and the ˇbiggest ·boy | Jack ˇTall | ˉturned ˏround | and ˉran | and ˉran and ˎran || he ˉnever ˋstopped ·running | un·til he ˉgot ˎhome | to his ˎmother || the ˉlittle ˏgirl | ˉcame ˎout | from beˎhind | the ˎlion || ˆwell ‸ she ·said | I ˋdon't think ·much of ˇhim | I shall ˋnever be ·scared of ˇhim a·gain || ˉI was ˎhungry ‸ said the ·lion | I could ˉeasily have ˋeaten him | only I'd ˋpromised you || ˋand his ˋmother | ˎwouldn't have ˋliked it ‸ said the little ·girl || ˉtime for ˋafternoon ·school ˏnow || I'm not ˋstaying for ·afternoon ˏschool ‸ said the ·lion || ˋsee you on ˇMonday ·then | ·said the little ˏgirl || but the ˉlion did not ˋanswer || ↑he just ˍwalked ˋoff || ˉon ˏMonday | the ·lion did ˋnot ·come to ˏschool || ˉat ˇplaytime | in the ˇplayground | the ˇbiggest boy | came ˋup to the little ˋgirl || ˉwhere's your ˎfriend | that ·talked so ˋloudly ‸ he ·said || he's ·not ˋhere toˏday | said the little ˏgirl || ˋmight he ·come aˇnother ·day | ·asked the ·biggest ˏboy || he ˇmight ‸ said the ·little ·girl || he ↑ˉeasily ˎmight || so ˉyou just watch ˋout | Jack ˏTall ||

028 SPOKEN ENGLISH CORPUS TEXT G02
Listening and Reading: 'Lion at School'
Broadcast notes: Radio 4, 2.20 p.m., 28th January, 1987
Overlap passage

Transcribed by BJW

ˉN | ˍO | ˉI | ˬL | ˋNoil || the ˉteacher ˍwrote the name ˍdown | in the ˋregister || ˋNoil || and then she ˋfinished ˋcalling the ˋregister || ˉBetty ˏSmall | she •said || ˉyes | said the little •girl || ˇNoil | said the ˏteacher || ˋyes | said the •lion || he ˋmumbled | ˋopening his ˋmouth as ˋlittle as ˋpossible | so that the ˋteacher should ↑ˉnot ˍsee his ˋteeth as ˋsharp as ˋskewers and ˋknives || ˉall that ˏmorning | the ˉlion sat up on his ˍchair ˉnext to the little ˍgirl | like a ˉbig ˎcat || with his ˉtail •curled ˍround his front ˎpaws | as ↑ˉgood as ˎgold || he didn't ˋspeak unˋless the ˋteacher ˋspoke to ˋhim || he didn't ˏgrowl | he didn't ˋroar || at ˇplaytime | the ˉlittle ˍgirl and the ˏlion | went into the ˋplayground || ˉall the ˍchildren •stopped ˋplaying | to ˋstare at the ˋlion || ˋthen they went on ˋplaying a•gain || the ˉlittle ˏgirl | stood in a ˇcorner of the •playground | with the ˋlion beˋside her || ˋwhy don't we ˉplay | like the ˋothers | the lion •asked || the ˉlittle girl ˍsaid | I don't ˇlike •playing | because ˋsome of the ˋbig •boys are so ˋbig and ˋrough || they ˋknock you ˋover without ˋmeaning to || the ˋlion ˋgrowled || they ˋwouldn't knock ˋme •over | he •said || there's ˉone ˏbig •boy | the ˋvery ˇbiggest | said the little ˏgirl || his ˋname is •Jack ˇTall ||

Transcribed by GOK

ˉN ˍO ˋI ˇL | ˋNoil || the ˋteacher •wrote the name ˏdown | in the ˎregister || ˎNoil || and •then she ˋfinished | ˎcalling the ˋregister || ˉBetty ˊSmall ‸ she said || ↑ˉyes | said the •little ˏgirl || ˬNoil ‸ said the •teacher || ˍyes | said the ˏlion || he ˋmumbled | •opening his ˬmouth | as ˋlittle as ˎpossible | so that the ˉteacher | should ˉnot ˎsee | his ˎteeth | as ˋsharp | as ˎskewers | and ˎknives || ˉall that ˏmorning | the ˉlion sat up on his ˏchair | ˋnext to the •little ˏgirl | like a ˉbig ˎcat | with his ˉtail | ˋcurled •round his ˉfront ˎpaws | as ↑ˉgood as ˎgold || he ˉdidn't ˎspeak | un•less the ˋteacher ˋspoke to ˬhim | he ˉdidn't ˏgrowl | he •didn't ˋroar || at ˇplaytime | the ˉlittle ˏgirl | and the ˏlion | went •into the ˋplayground || ˉall the ˍchildren | stopped ˎplaying | to ˋstare at the ˎlion || ˋthen they •went on ˋplaying a•gain || the ˉlittle ˏgirl | ˉstood in a ˎcorner of the ˏplayground | with the ˇlion | beˎside her || ˋwhy don't we ˍplay | like the

ˋothers ‸ the ·lion ·asked || the ˉlittle ˍgirl ˍsaid | I don't ˋlike ˏplaying | be·cause some of the ˇbig boys | are so ˋbig | and ˎrough || they ˉknock you ˋover | without ˋmeaning to || the ˬlion | ˋgrowled || they ·wouldn't knock ˊˇme over ‸ he ·said || there's ˉone ˏbig ·boy | the ˋvery ˬbiggest ‸ said the ·little ·girl | his ˋname is ·Jack ˬTall |

029 SPOKEN ENGLISH CORPUS TEXT G03
Streamline English - Unit 10
'A funny thing happened to me'
Transcribed by BJW

a ¯funny _thing ˇhappened to me ·last ˋFriday || I'd ¯gone to ˎLondon | to do some ˋshopping || I ·wanted to get some ˇChristmas ·presents | ¯and I _needed to find some ˋbooks | for my ˋcourse at ˋcollege | you see I'm a ˋstudent || I _caught an ˋearly train to ˇLondon | so by ¯early afterˏnoon | I'd ˋbought every·thing that I ˋwanted || ˋanyway I'm ·not ˇvery fond of ·London | all the ˏnoise | and ˏtraffic | and I'd ˋmade some aˋrrangements for that ˋevening || so I took a ˋtaxi to Waterloo ˋstation || I can't ˋreally aˇfford taxis | but I ˋwanted to ·get the three thirty ˋtrain || unˏfortunately | the ˇtaxi got ¯stuck in a ˇtraffic ·jam | and by the ˋtime I got to Waterˇloo | the ˋtrain had just ˋgone || ↓I had to wait an ˋhour for the ˋnext one || I ·bought an ¯evening ˎnewspaper | the ˋStandard | and ¯wandered _over to the ·station ˋbuffet || at ¯that time of _day it's nearly ˋempty || so I ·bought a ˊcoffee | and a ·packet of ˬbiscuits | ˋchocolate biscuits || I'm very ˋfond of ˋchocolate ˋbiscuits || there were ˋplenty of ˋempty ˇtables | and I ˋfound one near the ˋwindow || I ¯sat ˏdown | and be¯gan doing the ˎcrossword || I ˋalways en·joy doing ˇcrossword ·puzzles || ¯after a ·couple of ˎminutes | a ˋman | ˋsat down ˋopposite me || there was ˋnothing ˇspecial about him | exˋcept that he was ˋvery ˋtall || in ˋfact | he ˋlooked like a ˋtypical ˋcity ↑ˋbusinessman | ˋyou ·know | ˇdark suit | and ˇbriefcase || I ¯didn't ˏsay anything | and ¯I carried _on with my ˋcrossword || ˇsuddenly | he ¯reached across the ˏtable | ¯opened my ·packet of ˏbiscuits | ˇtook one | ¯dipped it into his ˏcoffee | and ¯popped it into his ˋmouth || I ˏcouldn't be·lieve my ↑ˋeyes || I was too ˋshocked to ˇsay anything | ˋanyway I ˋdidn't want to make a ˋfuss || so I deˋcided to igˋnore it || I ˋalways a·void ˋtrouble | if I ˋcan || ˋI just ·took a ·biscuit myˋself | and went ·back to my ˋcrossword || ˋwhen the ·man took a ˇsecond biscuit | I ¯didn't look ˏup | and I ¯didn't make a ˎsound || I preˋtended to be ¯very _interested in the ˋpuzzle || ¯after a couple of _minutes | I ¯casually put out my _hand | took the ¯last _biscuit | and ˋglanced at the ˋman || he was ˋstaring at me ˋfuriously || I ˋnervously ˋput the ·biscuit in my ˇmouth | and de¯cided to ˎleave || I was ¯ready to get _up | and ˋgo | when the ˋman | ˇsuddenly | ¯pushed back his _chair | ¯stood _up | and ¯hurried out of the ˎbuffet || I ·felt ˋvery reˋlieved | and deˋcided to ˋwait two or three ˋminutes | before ·going myˋself || I ¯finished my ˏcoffee | ¯folded my ˏnewspaper | and stood ˋup || ↓and ˇthere | on the ˏtable | where my ˇnewspaper had been | was ˏmy ˏpacket of ˋbiscuits ||

030 SPOKEN ENGLISH CORPUS TEXT G04
Streamline English - Unit 19
'Night Flight'
Transcribed by GOK

↑it was •Christmas ˎEve | •nineteen•fifty-ˎnine | ↑and the be•ginning of a•nother rou_tine ˎflight || the ˇhostesses | •started preˇparing | the ˋfood •trays || a ↑ˇfew of the •passengers | were ˬtrying to •get some ˋsleep | but ˬmost of them | were ˎreading || there was ¯nothing to ˎsee from the ˏwindows | ex•cept the ¯vast ˎblackness | of the Au•stralian ˋdesert | beˎlow || ↑there was ˋnothing uˇnusual a•bout the •flight | ex•cept per•haps that the •plane was •nearly ˇfull || a ↑ˇlot of the •passengers | were ¯travelling ˋhome | to •spend ˋChristmas | with their ˎfamilies || the ↑ˇhostesses | •started _serving ˎdinner || it was a ˋsmooth | and ˬquiet •flight || the ˇhostesses | had •finished co_llecting the ˎtrays | and ↑they were in the ˎgalley | ˋputting •things aˎway | when the ¯first ˋbuzzers •sounded || ↑ˇone of the •hostesses |¯ went a•long the ˏaisle to ˎcheck || ¯when she came ˏback | she •looked surˋprised || it's a↑^mazing ‸ she •said | ˋeven on a ¯smooth •flight like ˏthis | ¯two ˏpeople | have been ˋsick || ˋtwenty •minutes ˇlater | nearly ˇhalf the •passengers | were ˋill | draˋmatically •ill || ˇseveral | were ˋmoaning | and ˎgroaning || ˇsome | were ¯doubled •up in ˋpain | and ˇtwo | were unˎconscious || ˇfortunately | there was a ˋdoctor on •board | and ¯he was ˋhelping the •hostesses || he ˋcame to the ˬgalley and •said | •I'd ˇbetter •speak to the ˋcaptain || •this is a se¯vere ˎcase of ˋfood •poisoning || I ˇthink | we'd •better ˎland | as •soon as ˋpossible || what ↑ˋcaused it ‸ asked •one of the •hostesses || ↑ˋwell ‸ re•plied the •doctor | ˇI had the ˋbeef for •dinner | and •I'm ˋfine || the ˋpassengers who •chose the ˇfish | are ˋill || the ˇhostess | ˋled him to the ˋflight •deck || she ˇtried | to •open the ˋdoor || ↑I _think it's ˋjammed ‸ she •said || the ¯doctor _helped her | to ¯push it ˎopen || the ˇcaptain | was ˇlying | beˋhind the •door | he was unˎconscious || the ˋco-pilot was ˋslumped a•cross the conˇtrols | and the ↑ˇradio •operator was •trying to reˎvive him || the ˇdoctor | ¯quickly eˎxamined | the •two ˎpilots || ↑they just coˋllapsed ‸ said the •radio •operator || I ˋdon't feel ˇtoo good | myˋself || can ˇyou •land the •plane | said the ˏdoctor || ↑ˋme | ↑ˋno | ˬI'm not a •pilot || we've ˋgot to reˋvive them ‸ he re•plied || the ˋplane's on •auto•matic ˎpilot | we're ˋOK for a ˇcouple of •hours | •I don't ˎknow ‸ said the •doctor | they ¯could be ˎout | for a ¯long ˎtime || ¯I'd better ˏcontact | •ground conˋtrol ‸ said the •radio •operator || the ˇdoctor | ¯turned to the ˎhostess | per¯haps you should •make an aˎnnouncement | ¯try to find ˎout | if there's a ˋpilot on •board || ↑we _can't do ˏthat ‸ she said | it'll •cause a _general ˋpanic || well •how the

ˋhell | are we ·going to ·get this ·thing ˋdown ^ said the ·doctor || ˇsuddenly | the ˉhostess reˎmembered ·something || ·one of the ↑ˋpassengers || I ˋoverheard ˇhim saying | that ˇhe'd been a ·pilot | in the ˋwar || I'll ˋget him || she ˬfound the ·man | and ˇasked him | to ·come to the ˎgalley || ˋdidn't you ·say | you ˋused to be a ˬpilot ^ she ·asked || ˋyes ... ↑ˋwhy || the ˋpilot's all ˬright | ˏisn't he || she ˬled him | to the ˋflight ·deck || they exˋplained the situˎation to him || you mean you want ˊme to ·fly the ·plane ^ he ·said | ↑you ˍmust be ˋjoking || I ˇwas a ·pilot | but I flew ·single-ˋengined | ˋfighter ·planes | and ˋthat was ·fifteen ˋyears a·go || ˇthis thing's got ˋfour ·engines || ˋisn't there ·anybody ˊelse ^ he ·asked || I'm aˋfraid ˋnot ^ said the ·hostess || the ˋman sat ·down at the conˎtrols || his ˋhands were ˎshaking ·slightly || the ˉradio ˏoperator | coˇnnected him | to ˍAir ·Traffic Conˎtrol || they ˇtold him | to ˉkeep ˏflying | on ˉautomatic ˬpilot | towards ˋBrisbane | ·and to ˋwait | for ˉfurther inˏstructions | from an ex·perienced ˎpilot || an ˉhour ˏlater | the ·lights of ˋBrisbane | aˋppeared on the hoˎrizon || he could ˋsee the ˎlights | of the ˋrunway | ·shining ˋbrightly | be·yond the ˋcity || ˉAir Traffic Conˍtrol | ˉtold him to keep ˇcircling | until the ˇfuel ·gauge | ˍregistered ·almost ˎempty || ˇthis gave him a ·chance | to get ·used to ·handling the conˋtrols || ˉin the ˏcabin | the ˉhosˬtesses | and the ˬdoctor | were ˋbusy | a·ttending to the ˋsick || ˇseveral ·people | were unˋconscious || the ˉplane ˏcircled | for ·over ˉhalf an ˎhour || the ˇpassengers | had beˉgun to ˇrealize | that ˬsomething | was ˎwrong || ↑ˉwhat's going ˎon | ˉwhy don't we ˎland ^ ·shouted a ·middle-aged ·man | my ˋwife's ˋill | we've ˇgot to ·get her to ˋhospital || a ˇwoman | be·gan ˋsobbing | ˎquietly || at ˋlast | the ·plane ˎstarted | its deˎscent || ˬsuddenly | there was a ˋbump | which ˋshook the ·plane || we're ˬall going to ˋdie ^ ·screamed a ·man || ˉeven the ˋhostesses ·looked ·worried | as ˋpanic be·gan to ˋspread through the ·plane || it's ˉall ˎright ^ ·someone ·said | the ·pilot's ˋjust ·lowered the ˎwheels | ˉthat's ˍall || ˋas the ·plane a·pproached the ˇrunway | they could ·see ˋfire ·trucks | and ˋambulances | ˉspeeding aˍlong | be·side the ˇrunway | with their ˇlights | ˎflashing || there was a treˉmendous ˎthump | as the ˋwheels hit the ˋtarmac | ·bounced ˊtwice | ˋraced a·long the ˏrunway | and ˋscreeched to a ˎhalt || the ˉfirst ˬairport ·truck | was ·there in ˋseconds || ˋthat was ˇnearly | a ˉperfect ˋlanding || ˉwell ˎdone ^ ·shouted the con·trol ·tower || ˋthanks ^ said the ·man | any ·chance of a ˊjob ||

031 SPOKEN ENGLISH CORPUS TEXT G05

Morning Story: 'What shall we do if it rains'
(First part)
Broadcast notes: Radio 4, 10.30 a.m., 26th November, 1986
Transcribed by GOK

↑you ·simply ·have to be ‸ ·philoˋsophical a·bout it ‸ said ·Mr ·Henshaw | ˉrubbing the ˏwindow | and reˉgarding | a ˉrural ˏlandscape | diˇssolved | in ˎrain || it's ˋnot a ·bit of ˋgood | ˋmooching aˬbout | and ˇmoaning | and ·saying ‸ ˉthis ˬweather | ˉwhat a ˬclimate ‸ and ·so on || ·this is ↑ˋEngland | and ˉthat's ˎthat || I can't re·member ˇus making a ·fuss about the ·weather | when ˬwe were ·children || it was eˉnough | ˉsimply to be on ˎholiday || when ˋI woke ·up in the ˍmorning | my ˉfirst ˍthought was | ˍI'm on ↑ˋholiday || and I'd ·feel ˉhappy | and ˉwarm | and ˋsnuggle ·down in ˍbed a·gain | and ˎlie there | ·listening to the ˎrain ·falling || all ˎright | ·read a ˋbook || ·let me ˎsee now | ˋwhat was I ·reading at ˎyour ·age || ˎwell | adˋventure ·books ˏmostly | ˊHenty | ˊKipling | ·Rider ˊHaggard | ·King ·Solomon's ˊMines | ˏthat ·sort of ·thing || ˎhuh | ˎyoung ·people toˬday | ·simply ˋdon't ·read || ˋnever ·pick up a ˎbook || it's ·all ˋvideos | and ˎmusic || ˊwhat is it | ˊrock || ˎyes | ˎrock || ˎrubbish || but ˋas to ·actually ˋturning a ˬpage | ↓ˋoh ˎno || and ˋwhat ·happens to the i·magiˇnation | as a reˋsult I should ·like to ·know || it ˎrots || of ↓ˋcourse it ·rots || when ˇI read a ·book | I ˋlived it | ·never ˋnoticed the ˏweather || ↑ˉoh ˏno | ˋI was ·out ˏthere | ˋhacking my ·way through the ˍjungle | ·facing ˉdeath | in ˉburning ˍdeserts | ·riding to the ˍrescue | of some ˉdamsel down a ·leafy ˍlane | ˉjousting with || ˉwhat ˏtime is it || I ‸ I ·don't ˋknow ‸ said his ·son | ˇsorry ||ˋ well you've ·got a ˏwatch ·haven't ·you || ˋyes ·dad | but it's in ˋpieces || ˋwhen Mr ·Henshaw ˬturned | he could ˋsee | that ·this was ˎso || ↑well ˋwhy do you ·want to ·take a ˉperfectly good ˎwatch to ·pieces || it'll ˏnever go aˋgain || I ˉwant to find ˏout | ·how it ˋworks || it'll ˋbe all ˇright | I've ˋhad it to ˬpieces | beˋfore || ˎhuh | ˍfiddling | ˎfiddling ‸ said ·Mr ·Henshaw || when ˉI came ˋin here | you were ˉdoodling | ·silly ˉfaces | on the ·steamy ˊwindows | and ˋnow you're ˇfiddling | with a ˋwatch || you're ˇclearly | at a ˉloose ˎend || when ˇI was ·your age | on ˉwet ˍdays | I'd ˋsettle ·down to ·something ˋmeaningful | creˋative | a ˋproject | would ˋshape it·self | ˉquite ˎclearly in my ·mind || he ·turned ˋrestlessly a·way from the ˎwindow || ˉhas the ˏpost been ·yet || I ˍdon't ˋknow || ·Mr ˎHenshaw | ·ran an ˉirritable ˎeye | over a ˉshelf of ˎbooks || ˋhuh | what a ˉterrible seˎlection || they ·must have ˇbought ·this lot | by the ˋfoot || I ˋcan't see ·anyone ·actually ˇchoosing such ·rubbish || ˇmother's ·brought some ·books with ·her | if you ·want something to

ˏread || ↑ˋoh don't ·worry about ˬme | ·I can find ˎplenty to ·do || the ¯day's | ˋnever ·long e·nough for ˬme || I may ¯read | I may ˋnot || ˋpeople are ·too reˋliant on ˏbooks || as ˋsoon as they've an ¯idle ˏmoment | their ¯fingers | ¯reach ˍout | they ·read ˎanything || it su¯ggests | ¯inner ˎemptiness || now ˋstop ·fiddling with that ˎwatch for a ·moment | and ˏlisten | to ˏwhat I ˋsay | ·this is ˍvery imˋportant || ¯people | ˋshouldn't be so deˬpendent | on ˇother people's | iˎdeas || we should ·find our ˇown ·worlds | he ·tapped the ·side of his ˋhead | ¯up ˎhere || oh ˋsurely the ·post should have ·been here by ˬnow || ·rural ineˏfficiency || the ˋpostman's ˋprobably ‸ being deˬlayed | by the ˋweather ‸ said his ·son || he's ·got to keep ·covering his ˋbag | and ·drying his ˋhands I suˏppose || he ·lifted ·out the ˍflywheel from the ˎwatch | with ˇfrowning | ·concenˎtration || ¯keep ˍoff | the ·subject of the ˍweather || ˋtalking a·bout the ˬweather | and di·scussing our diˇgestive ·system | is the ¯national ˋsickness || ¯what are the ˎtwins ·doing || ↑I ˍthink they're ·still in ˋbed || preˎcisely ‸ said ·Mr ·Henshaw | that's e¯xactly what I ˎmean || the ˋhappiest ˋdays of their ¯lives | and they just ¯roll ˎover || when ˋI was a ·lad in the ¯country | it was ˋup with the ¯lark | and ¯on with the ˋwellies || ˋI thought | you ˋsnuggled ·down in ˋbed || Mr ·Henshaw ˋglared || if ↑we're ˍall just ·going to ˋhang around the ˬhouse | we ˋmight as well have ·stayed at

ˋhome || he ·pulled a ·book from the ˋshelf | and ·started ·flipping the ˎpages || ˋhuh | what ¯utter ˎrubbish || ˋwhy don't you | ·take it aˋway with ·you ‸ said his ·son | ·seeing that Mr ˇHenshaw | had ·started ˇreading | in ˋearnest || ·Mr ˍHenshaw | reˋplaced the ˬbook | and ·left the ˎroom || ¯in the ˏhallway | he en·countered a ˇfigure | in a ¯floating ˎrobe | ad·vancing toˎwards him || its ˇeyes | were ·tightly ˬclosed | its ˬarms | outˎspread || be¯ware Macˋ Beth || Mac¯Beth | doth ¯murder ˋsleep || ¯what | ·bloody ˊman is ˋthis || ·two ˎeyes | ·opened ˎsuddenly || ˋoh | ↑heˍllo ˏdad || ˇyou should have | ·something on your ˋfeet ‸ said ·Mr ·Henshaw || what ˍare you ˋdoing || I'm being ·Lady Macˋ Beth ‸ said his ·daughter || ˎwell | you've ¯got ˍShakespeare | ˋthoroughly ˎgarbled || if you're ˇgoing to ·act him | ¯get it ↑ˋright || when ˇwe were ·children | we ·used to go ¯over our ˏplays | with ·great ˋcare | and we ˬdid them | toˎgether || ˋpeople don't ˎdo things toˏgether any ·more | that's ·half the ˍtrouble with the ˋworld || you should ·all get to·gether ‸ in ¯one ˋroom | not ·wander a·bout ‸ ·draughty ˏcorridors | in your ·bare ˊfeet || ˎah | I'd ·better get ·hold of that de·structive ˇbrother of ·yours | ˋfetch ·down the ˋRip Van ·Winkle ˇtwins | and ·get you ¯all ˬstarted | on the ¯right ˎlines || we can ·use the ˋlounge | or per·haps the old ˋbarn || ¯mayˍbe | we should ¯start ˍoff | with a chaˋrade || and ˋwe were ˋvery keen on cha • rades when • I was a ˏlad || we ˋonce ˇacted out | a ¯seven • syllable ˋword || well ˇactually ˆ said his • daughter | I would ˇrather | act aˋlone if you don't ˏmind || but ˆ if you ˇreally want to • act in a cha • rade | I ˋdon't mind • fetching • down the ˇothers || I'm ˋnot doing • this for ˇmy • sake ˆ said • Mr • Henshaw | ˇI don't • want to • act in a cha • rade || be • lieve ˎme | I've got ˋtoo much on my ¯plate alˎready || the ¯day is • simply not ˎlong e • nough || ↑¯what on ˍearth | is that ˋnoise || I ¯think the ˎtwins | are • getting ˋup || ˎoh | • this is an ˎage | which can ¯only exˎpress it • self | in ˍviolence ||

031 SPOKEN ENGLISH CORPUS TEXT G05
Morning Story: 'What shall we do if it rains'
(Second part)
Broadcast notes: Radio 4, 10.30 a.m., 26th November, 1986
Transcribed by BJW

_well you've ˉgot ˎShakespeare ˋthoroughly | garbled || if you're ˇgoing to •act him | get it ↑ˋright || when ˇwe were children | we used to go ˋover our ˋplays with ˉgreat ˋcare | and we ˋdid them toˋgether || ˋpeople don't do things toˉgether any •more | that's ˉhalf the •trouble with the ˉworld | you should ˋall get together in ˉone ˉroom | not _wander about •draughty •corridors in your •bare ˊfeet || _ah I'd better get hold of that des•tructive ˇbrother of yours | ˋfetch down the ˋRip Van Winkle ˇtwins | and •get you ˉall _started on the right ˎlines || we can use the ˎlounge || or perhaps the old ˋbarn || ↑ˋmaybe we should ˋstart off with a chaˋrade || we were ˋvery keen on cha•rades when I was a ˉlad || we •once ˋacted out a ˋseven •syllable ˋword || well ˇactually | said his ˏdaughter | I would ˇrather | act aˋlone | if you don't ˏmind | but | if you ˇreally want to act in a cha•rade | I ˉdon't mind •fetching down the ˋothers || I'm ˋnot doing this for ˋmy •sake | said Mr ˏHenshaw | ˋI don't want to •act in a chaˏrade | beˉlieve ˎme I've got ˋtoo much on my ˋplate alˋready | the ˉday is simply not ˎlong enough || ↑ˉwhat on ˏearth is that ˋnoise || I think the _twins are getting ˋup || oh this is an ˉage which can only ex_press itself in ˋviolence || ↑Mr _Henshaw ˋwandered about the ˉhouse | ˋpoking into empty ˉrooms || ↑in the ˏkitchen | his ˇwife | was making ˋbread || ˉthis ˏhouse is in ˋtotal ↑upˎheaval | he •said || ˉno one can ˎsettle to •anything || ˋoh | ˋI thought they were •doing rather ˋwell | conˋsidering it's been ↑ˋraining for a ˋweek || if ˉdoing _well is disˋmembering a ˉperfectly good ˇwatch | ˉwandering the •corridors in _bare ˉfeet and ˋmutilating ˇShakespeare | or ˋfighting in ˇbedrooms | then the ˋfuture of the ˉworld is in ˎjeopardy || ˋI told •Sarah she could ˉdress up in my old ˇclothes | and ˋthat watch is ˋfinished || the ˉtwins | said last _night they're having a terˋrific ˋtime || ↑why are _you making ˎbread | said Mr •Henshaw || there's ˋperfectly good ˉbread in the ˋvillage || ˇmaking your own is •simply | ˉdoing something to •fill in the ˋtime || like _half these •daft ˋyouth opportunity •projects they ˉfoist off on the ˎyoung | building ˎwalls | no one ˎneeds | making ˋfoot•paths | we never ˋwalk on || ˋwhat they should ˇteach is ˇinner reˋsourcefulness || ah this is a ˋrestless gene•ration it ˉcannot sit _still || if we were _all to sit ˋquietly for an •hour every ˇmorning we might ˉchange the ˋworld || ↑em has the ˏpost been yet || it's so _long since I've ˋmade my own •bread said Mrs ˏHenshaw | and I ˋcouldn't reˋsist the ˇAga || ˉwhy | you're not exˇpecting any •post are you | you ˋtold them not to ˇforward any || ˉwell _naturally I | ˋmade exˊceptions | there is this _Asian ˊcrisis || I'm ˋsure the ·paper can manage withˋout you for ·three ˇweeks || if you ˋwant something to ˇdo | you can | ˉknead this ˋdough || ˋI don't want ·anything to ˊdo | it's the ˋrest of this ·household that should con·cern ˋyou || ↑we ˉdon't seem to have | _taught them ˋanything || ↓well I ˉthink I'll go for a ˎwalk || it's ˋterribly ˋwet || ˋtalking about the ˉweather | is the ˉnational ˎsickness | said Mr ·Henshaw || he ˋput on ˉwaterproofs | and _wellies | and ˋset off a·cross the ·sodden ˋfields || like a ˉblasted ·great ·green ˎsponge | he said || ˋcows | ˉhuddled under ˏtrees | ·watched him ˉplunge he_roically through a ·small ˎbog || oh it's ˇall right | ˋonce you get ˏstarted | he ˏtold them || ↑when he ˎreached the village | ˋrain | was ˋtrickling down his ˋchest || he ˉwent into the ˎpub | just a _quick one while I dry ˊoff | he ·thought || he _dropped his ·sodden outer garments in a ˎcorner | and ˉclapped his _hands ˋbriskly || ↑ah good ˋmorning | good ˎmorning | a ˇdouble whisky I ·think | and and yourˊself || ˋI don't usually ·drink this ˉearly but | ↓aye | it's the ˋweather | said the ·landlord | ˋthank you I ˋwill || huh | be ˋbuilding an ˇark ·soon || ˋcheers || oh ˋcheers || the ˋweather | oh no _no | doesn't bother ˋme || I _simply don't ˋnotice it || no ˋwhat bothers ˋme | is my ˉrestless ˋfamily || can't ˎsettle to ·anything || we've ˋrented this ˋcottage in the ˇcountry | for ˋpeace and ˋquiet | and ˋall they do is ˋwander about | _fiddling with ˋthis | _fiddling with ˋthat | and ˋfighting || oh when ˋI was ˉyoung ˇI wasn't like ·that || ˋI never had the ˋslightest ·trouble | ˋfilling in a rainy ˊday || ↓but not ˋthem || and ˋwhen I try to get them ˇstarted on ·something | ·give them the ˋbenefit of my ex↑ˉperience | they just _don't want to _know || the ˉtrouble ˎis | the ˉworld's got _used to disˋtractions | that's ˉall it ˎknows || he ˋhoped that the ˋlandlord might posˋsess a philoˋsophical ˋtemperament | and re·ply in ˎkind | but the ˋlandlord was enˋgrossed in drying ˋglasses and holding them ˋup to the watery ˋlight || ↑Mr _Henshaw ˉdrummed his _fingers on the ˋcounter | and ·looked ˋaround || it's eh | very ˋquiet || ah ˋwell | it's ˋearly ·yet sir | ˋlocals ˉdon't come in for another ˋhour || ˇthey'll give you some conver·sation || ↑oh ˋno | I'm just _here for a ˉnip | I've got to get _back | ·too much to ˋdo | the day's not ˋlong enough for me || he surˋveyed his empty ˋglass || ˋwell | perˋhaps | ˋone | for the ˊroad || it's | ˋraining all ˇover | ↓said the ˏlandlord || ˋtalking aˋbout the ˉweather | is our ˉnational ˎsickness || if ·we didn't have the ˇweather to ·talk about | a ˋsilence would ·fall | a ·great | ˋhush would des·cend || ˋfolk would turn ↑aˋway from each ·other in ˉanguished ˎsilences || I have ˉnothing to say to this ˋperson | their _faces would ˉsay || ↓Mr ˇHenshaw | ˋemptied his ·glass | ˎsadly ||

031 SPOKEN ENGLISH CORPUS TEXT G05

Morning Story: 'What shall we do if it rains'
Broadcast notes: Radio 4, 10.30 a.m., 26th November, 1986
Overlap passage

Transcribed by BJW

ˍwell you've ˉgot ˎShakespeare ˋthoroughly | garbled || if you're ˇgoing to •act him | get it ↑ˋright || when ˇwe were children | we used to go ˋover our ˋplays with ˉgreat ˋcare | and we ˋdid them toˋgether || ˋpeople don't do things toˉgether any •more | that's ˉhalf the •trouble with the ˉworld | you should ˋall get together in ˉone ˉroom | not ˍwander about •draughty •corridors in your •bare ˊfeet || ˍah I'd better get hold of that des•tructive ˇbrother of yours | ˋfetch down the ˋRip Van Winkle ˇtwins | and •get you ˉall ˍstarted on the right ˎlines || we can use the ˎlounge || or perhaps the old ˋbarn || ↑ˋmaybe we should ˋstart off with a chaˋrade || we were ˋvery keen on cha•rades when I was a ˉlad || we •once ˋacted out a ˋseven •syllable ˋword || well ˇactually | said his ˏdaughter | I would ˇrather | act aˋlone | if you don't ˏmind | but | if you ˇreally want to act in a cha•rade | I ˉdon't mind •fetching down the ˋothers || I'm ˋnot doing this for ˋmy •sake | said Mr ˏHenshaw | ˋI don't want to •act in a chaˏrade | beˉlieve ˎme I've got ˋtoo much on my ˋplate alˋready | the ˉday is simply not ˎlong enough || ↑ˉwhat on ˏearth is that ˋnoise || I think the ˍtwins are getting ˋup || oh this is an ˉage which can only exˍpress itself in ˋviolence ||

Transcribed by GOK

ˎwell | you've ˉgot ˍShakespeare | ˋthoroughly ˎgarbled || if you're ˇgoing to •act him | ˉget it ↑ˋright || when ˇwe were •children | we •used to go ˉover our ˏplays | with •great ˋcare | and we ˬdid them | toˎgether || ˋpeople don't ˎdo things toˏgether any •more | that's •half the ˍtrouble with the ˋworld || you should •all get to•gether ‸ in ˉone ˋroom | not •wander a•bout ‸ •draughty ˏcorridors | in your •bare ˊfeet || ˎah | I'd •better get •hold of that de•structive ˇbrother of •yours | ˋfetch •down the ˋRip Van •Winkle ˇtwins | and •get you ˉall ˬstarted | on the ˉright ˎlines || we can •use the ˋlounge | or per•haps the old ˋbarn || ˉmayˍbe | we should ˉstart ˍoff | with a chaˋrade || and ˋwe were ˋvery keen on cha•rades when •I was a ˏlad || we ˋonce ˇacted out | a ˉseven •syllable ˋword || well ˇactually ‸ said his •daughter | I would ˇrather | act aˋlone if you don't ˏmind || but ‸ if you ˇreally want to •act in a cha•rade | I ˋdon't mind •fetching •down the ˇothers || I'm ˋnot doing •this for ˇmy •sake ‸ said •Mr •Henshaw | ˇI don't ·want to ·act in a cha·rade || be·lieve ˎme | I've got ˋtoo much on my ˉplate alˎready || the ˉday is ·simply not ˎlong e·nough || ↑ˉwhat on ˍearth | is that ˋnoise || I ˉthink the ˎtwins | are ·getting ˋup || ˎoh | ·this is an ˎage | which can ˉonly exˎpress it·self | in ˍviolence ||

032 SPOKEN ENGLISH CORPUS TEXT H01

'Eunice'

From: 'Betjeman Reads Betjeman'

Transcribed by BJW

¯with her _latest /roses | ¯happily en/cumbered | ¯Tunbridge _Wells /Central | ¯takes her from the /night || ¯sweet _second /bloomings | ¯frost has ·faintly /umbered | ¯and some _double /dahlias | ¯waxy ·red and ˇwhite || ¯shut again till /April | ¯stands her little /hutment | ¯peeping over _daisies | ¯Michaelmas and ¯mauve | ¯lock'd is the ˇElsan | in its ¯brick a/butment | ¯lock'd the little /pantry | ¯dead the little /stove || ¯keys with Mr ˇGroombridge | but ¯nobody will /take them | to her ¯lonely _cottage | by the ¯lonely ¯oak || po¯tatoes in the _garden | but ¯nobody to _bake them | ¯fungus in the ˇliving room | and ¯water in the ˇcoke || ¯I can ·see her _waiting | on this ¯chilly /Sunday | for the ¯five /forty | ¯twenty minutes ˇlate || ¯one of many /hundreds | to ¯dread the coming /Monday | to ¯fight with influ/enza | and ¯battle with her ˇweight || ¯tweed _coat and _skirt | that with ᵛsuch antici·pation | on a ¯merry _spring time | a ¯friend had ·trimm'd with _fur || _now the friend is \married | ¯and oh \desolation | ¯married to the _man | who ¯might have _married ᵛher || ¯high in _Onslow /Gardens | where the ¯soot ·flakes /settle | an ¯empty _flat is ᵛwaiting | her ¯struggle up the \stair || and ¯when she puts the \wireless on | the ¯heater and the _kettle | it's ¯cream and _green and \cosy | but ¯home is never ˇthere || ¯home's here in \Kent || and how ¯many _morning \coffees | and ¯hurried little ˇlunch hours | of ¯planning will be \spent || through the ¯busy ·months of _typing in the \office | until the ·days are ¯warm enough | to _take her back to \Kent ||

033 SPOKEN ENGLISH CORPUS TEXT H02
'The Last of Her Order'
From: 'Betjeman Reads Betjeman'
Transcribed by GOK

with ¯one con·suming _roar a·long the ˏshingle | the ¯long _wave | ¯claws and _rakes | the ·pebbles ˎdown | to ·where its ˇbackwash | and the ˇnext wave | ·mingle ^ a ˋmounting ·arch of _water | ¯weedy-ˏbrown | a¯gainst the ˏtide | the ¯off-shore _breezes ˏblow | oh ¯wind and ˏwater | ·this is ˎFelix·stowe || in ˇwinter | when the ¯sea _winds | ¯chill and ˇshriller | than ¯those of ˏsummer | ¯all their _cold unˏload | ¯full on the _gimcrack ˏattic | of the ˏvilla | where I am ˏlodging | ·off the Orwell ˏRoad | I ˋput my ·final _shilling in the ˎmeter | and ˎonly ·make my ¯loneliness comˎpleter || in ¯eighteen _ninety-ˏfour | when we were ˏfounded | ¯counting our _Reverend ˏMother | we were ˎsix || ˋhow full of ˎhope we ·were | and ˎprayer-su·rrounded | the ¯Little ˎSisters | of the ¯Hanging ˎPyx || we ¯built our ˏorphanage | ↑we _ran our ˎschool | now ¯only ˎI am ·left ^ to ·keep the ·rule || ¯here in the ˏgardens | of the _Spa Paˏvilion | ¯warm in the _whisper of a _summer ˏsea | the ¯cushioned ˏscabious | a ·deep verˏmilion | with ¯white ˏpins | _stuck in it | ¯looks ˎup at ·me | a ¯sun-lit _kingdom | ·touched by ˎbutterflies | and ¯so my _memory of _winter ˎdies || a¯cross the _grass | the ¯poplar _shades | grow ˏlonger | and ¯louder _clang the _waves | a·long the ˏcoast | the ¯band packs ˎup | the ¯evening _breeze is ˏstronger | and ¯all the _world | goes ˏhome | to ↓¯tea and ˎtoast || I ¯hurry past a _cakeshop's | ¯tempting _scones | ¯bound for the _red brick | ·twilight of St ˎJohn's || thou ¯knowest my down ˏsitting | and mine upˎrising | ↑ˋhere where the ·white light ˊburns | with ·steady ˎglow | ¯safe from the _vain world's | ¯silly ˎsympathising | ¯safe with the _Love | that I was ¯born to ˏknow | ¯safe from the _surging | of the ¯lonely ˏsea | my ¯heart finds _rest | my ˋheart ·finds ¯rest in ˎThee ||

034 SPOKEN ENGLISH CORPUS TEXT H03

'Harrow-on-the-Hill'
From: 'Betjeman Reads Betjeman'
Transcribed by BJW

when ¯melancholy _Autumn comes to ˏWembley | and e¯lectric •trains are _lighted after ˬtea | the ¯poplars near the _Stadium are _trembly | with their ˋtap and ˋtap and ˇwhispering to •me | like the ¯sound of little ˎbreakers | spreading ¯out along the ˎsurf-line | when the ¯estuary's •filling with the ˎsea || ↓then _Harrow-on-the-¯Hill's | a •rocky ˎisland || and ¯Harrow ˬchurchyard | ¯full of •sailors' ˎgraves || and the ˋconstant ˋclick and ˋkissing of the ˋtrolley •buses ˎhissing | is the ¯level to the •Wealdstone | ↑turned to ˎwaves || and the ¯rumble of the _railway is the ¯thunder of the ˎrollers | as they ¯gather up | for ˋplunging into ˋcaves || there's a ˋstorm •cloud to the ˋwestward over ˋKenton || ↑there's a ¯line of harbour _lights | at PeriˋVale || is it ¯rounding rough Pen_tire | in a ¯flood of •sunset _fire | the ¯little fleet of •trawlers under •sail || ↓can those _boats | be only ˊroof tops | ↓as they ˋstream along the ˊskyline | ↓in a ¯race | for ˋport and ˊPadstow | ↓with the ¯gale ||

034 SPOKEN ENGLISH CORPUS TEXT H03
'Harrow-on-the-Hill'
From: 'Betjeman Reads Betjeman'
Transcribed by GOK

when ¯melancholy _Autumn ·comes to _Wembley | and e¯lectric _trains are ·lighted after ˏtea | the ¯poplars near the _Stadi·um are _trembly | ·with their ·tap and ·tap and ˬwhispering to ·me | ·like the ¯sound of ·little ˎbreakers | ·spreading ¯out along the ˎsurf-line | when the ¯estuary's _filling with the ˎsea || then ˏHarrow-on-the-·Hill's a ·rocky ˋisland | and ↑ˋHarrow ·churchyard | ¯full of ·sailors' ˎgraves | and the ˋconstant ˋclick and _kissing | of the ˋtrolley ·buses ˎhissing | is the ·level to the ·Weald·stone ¯turned to ˎwaves | and the ˋrumble of the _railway | is the ˋthunder of the ˎrollers | as they ·gather up ˄ for ˋplunging into ˎcaves || there's a ˋstorm cloud to the ˋwestward over ˎKenton || ↑there's a ¯line | of ¯harbour ˎlights | at ¯PeriˎVale || ↑is it ·rounding ·rough Penˏtire | in a ¯flood of ·sunset ˏfire | the ·little ·fleet of ·trawlers under ˏsail || ↓can those ˏboats | be only ˏroof tops | as they ·stream along the ˏskyline | in a ¯race for ·port and ˏPadstow | with the ˊgale ||

035 SPOKEN ENGLISH CORPUS TEXT H04
Time for verse: 'The Linnet's Nest'
Broadcast notes: Radio 4, 3.47 p.m., 26th November, 1986
Transcribed by BJW

ˉo what has ˍwrought aˋgain the ˋmiracle of ˋSpring || this ˉold ˍgarden of ˍmine that was ˉso ˎbeautiful and ˉdied ·so ˍutterly || ↑what ˍpower of ˉearth or ˍsky from ˉdead ˍsticks and ˉdead ˎmould | has ˉraised up ˎParadise || the ˉflow'rs we ˍknew we ˋwelcome aˋgain in their ˋturns | ˏprimrose | aˏnemone | ˏdaffodil and ˬtulip || ˉblossom of ˍcherry | ˉblossom of ˍpear and ˋapple || ˉiris and ˎcolumbine || and ˉnow the ·white ˎcistus || in a ˉround ˎbush it ·grows | this ˉcistus of deˎlight || a ˉmound of ·delicate ˍpure ·white ˍcrinkled ˇpetals | in the ˉheart of the ˍgarden where the ˉgreen ·paths ˍcross | where the ˉold ·stone ˍdial throws its ˉmorning ˎshadow || ·come ˋnearer | and ˉspeak ˎlow || ˋwatch while I ˉput aˎside this ˉthickly ˍflow'ring ˉspray || and ˋstoop till you can ˉsee | ˉthere in the ˍshadowy ˇcentre | a ˉtiny ˎnest || and ˋon it ˋfacing us a ˋbright-·eyed ˋbird ˋsitting || she has ˉfive ˎeggs | ˉshaped and ˍspeckled most ˋdaintily || but ˋthis she ˋcannot ˋknow || ˋnor how they are ˋquick'ning with ˋthat which ˋsoon will be on the ˋwing || and ˉsinging the ˍancestral ˋlinnet-song of ˋthoughtless ˋrapture || ˍno ˋthis she ·cannot ˋknow | ˉnor indeed ˋanything that ˋwe call ·knowledge || ˉnor such ·love and ˋhope as ours | yet ˉshe for her ˏtreasure will enˉdure | and ˬtremble | and ˉso find ˉpeace | that ˋpasseth our underˋstanding || you ˋwonder at my ˏwonder || the ˉbird has ˋinstinct || the ˋlaw by ˋdust orˉdained | for ˉthat which ˍdust creˉates || what then ˋis beauty | and ˋlove || my ˉheart is ˋrestless | to ˋknow what ·love and ˋbeauty are ·worth in the ˋend || the ˉbird I ˍknow will ˇfly | ˉnest | ˉbrood | ˉcistus | ˉgarden | will ˋall be ·lost || when ˋwinter takes the ˋworld again || yet ˉin my ˍmind ˉtheir ˋloveliness will surˋvive | till ˉI ˍtoo in my ˋturn | oˍbey the ·laws of ·dust || are ˉwe then ˎall || is there ˋno ·Life | ↓in whom ˉour ·nests | ·our ˉtrembling ˍhopes | and ·our ˋunintelligent ˉloves | may ˋstill | for the ˋbeauty they ˋhad | the ˋfaith they ˋkept || live ˋon as in a ˋvast eˋternal ˇmemory || yet ˉso for ˍus would ˉbeauty ˋstill be ·meaningless || ˉmortal and ˎmeaningless || our ˋhearts are ˋrestless ˋstill | to be ˋone with that ˉspirit | from whom ˉall ·life ˎsprings || and ˉtherein to beˍhold ˋall ·beauty for ˋever || perˉhaps the ˍlinnet ˋtoo | is ˏmore than ·dust || perhaps ˋshe though so ˇsmall | of so ˋquick-·perishing ˇbeauty | is ˉnone the ˋless | a ˋpart of ·His immortal ·dream || and beˉneath her ˍbreast | ˋcherishes the diˉvine ˋlife ||

035 SPOKEN ENGLISH CORPUS TEXT H04
Time for verse: 'The Linnet's Nest'
Speaker: Isabel Dean
Broadcast notes: Radio 4, 3.47 p.m., 26th November, 1986
Overlap passage

Transcribed by GOK

the ¯bird I ˎknow will ˏfly | ˊnest | ˊbrood | •cistus •garden will ˋall be •lost | when ˋwinter •takes the •world aˏgain || yet ¯in my ˍmind | •their ˋloveliness | will surˋvive | till ¯I ˋtoo in my ˏturn | o•bey the •laws of ˍdust || are ¯we then ˬall || is there ¯no ˍLife | in •whom our ˍnests | •our •trembling ¯hopes | and •our •unin•telligent ¯loves | may ˋstill | for the •beauty they ˋhad | the •faith they ˋkept | ¯live ˎon | as in a ¯vast | e¯ternal ˍmemory || yet ¯so | for ¯us | would ¯beauty ˎstill be •meaning•less || ¯mortal and ˎmeaning•less || our ¯hearts | are ¯restless ˋstill | to be ˋone with that ˍspirit | from •whom ¯all ˋlife •springs | and there¯in to beˍhold | ¯all ˎbeauty | for ˎever || per¯haps the •linnet ˎtoo | is •more than ˍdust || per¯haps ˋshe | though ¯so ˬsmall | of so ˋquick-•perishing ˇbeauty | is ¯none the ˋless | a •part of •His i•mmortal ˏdream | and be¯neath her ˎbreast | ˋcherishes the di•vine ˎlife ||

Transcribed by BJW

the ¯bird I ˍknow will ˋfly | ¯nest | ¯brood | ¯cistus | ¯garden | will ˋall be •lost | when ˋwinter takes the ˋworld again || yet ¯in my ˍmind ¯their ˋloveliness will surˋvive | till ¯I ˍtoo in my ˋturn | oˍbey the •laws of •dust || are ¯we then ˎall || is there ˋno •Life | ↓in whom ¯our •nests | •our ¯trembling ˍhopes | and •our ˋunintelligent ¯loves | may ˋstill | for the ˋbeauty they ˋhad | the ˋfaith they ˋkept || live ˋon as in a ˋvast eˋternal ˋmemory || yet ¯so for ˍus would ¯beauty ˋstill be •meaningless || ¯mortal and ˎmeaningless || our ˋhearts are ˋrestless ˋstill | to be ˋone with that ¯spirit | from whom ¯all •life ˎsprings || and ¯therein to beˍhold ˋall •beauty for ˋever || per¯haps the ˍlinnet ˋtoo | is ˏmore than •dust || perhaps ˋshe though so ˇsmall | of so ˋquick-•perishing ˇbeauty | is ¯none the ˋless | a ˋpart of •His immortal •dream || and be¯neath her ˍbreast | ˋcherishes the di¯vine ˋlife ||

036 SPOKEN ENGLISH CORPUS TEXT H05
Time for verse: 'The Nightjar'
Broadcast notes: Radio 4, 3.47 p.m., 26th November, 1986
Transcribed by GOK

we ˋloved our ˏNightjar | but she •would not ˍstay with •us || we had ˇfound her | ˉlying as ˬdead | but ˉsoft and ˬwarm | •under the ˋapple •tree | be•side the ˉold thatched ˎwall || ˉtwo ˍdays | we ˋkept her in a ˎbasket | by the ˬfire | ˇfed her | and ˇthought she ˉwell might ˋlive | till ˇsuddenly | in the •very ˉmoment | of ˉmost con•fiding ˍhope | she ˋraised her•self ˉall ˍtense | ˇquivered | and ˉdrooped | and ˎdied || •tears ˍsprang into my ˋeyes || why ˋnot | the •heart of ˬman | ˋsoon sets it•self to ˋlove a •living comˏpanion | the ˋmore so if by ˇchance | it •asks some ˋcare of him || and ˋthis one had the ˋkind of ˇloveliness | that •goes ˉfar ˎdeeper | than the ˋoptic ˬnerve | •full fathom ˎfive | to the ˉsoul's ocean ˎcave | where ˉWonder and ˏReason | ˉtell their alˇternate •dreams | of •how the ˬworld was •made | ˉso ˬwonderful she •was | her ˉwings | the •wings of ˋnight | but ˋpowdered | ˉhere and ˍthere | with ˉtiny •golden ˎclouds | and ˉwave-line ˎmarkings | like ˉsea ˎripples | on the ˋsand || ˋo how I ˉwish | I might ˉnever forˏget | ˉthat ˎbird || •never ^ but even ˎnow | like ˉall ˉbeauty of ˏearth | she is ˉfading ˎfrom me | into the ˉdusk of ˎTime ||

037 SPOKEN ENGLISH CORPUS TEXT J01
Review of the Year
(Second part)
BBC World Service
Transcribed by BJW

[Speaker: Kevin Geary]

well ˋlet's turn our a·ttention now to ˉnorth of the ˇborder | ·where | alˋthough it was | ˉCeltic and Aberˋdeen | who ·ended up with the ˇtrophies | the ˋstory was ˋreally about ˉMartin the | ˋdesperate ˉluck of poor ·Heart of Midˎlothian ||

[change of speaker: Martin Fookes]

yes they ˇdid have some desperate ·luck || they ˉlost the league ˎchampionship || I ·think on the ˋlast day of the ˋseason when they were ˋbeaten at Dunˏdee | having had a ˉlong unbeaten ˎrun | ˋCeltic by scoring ˋfour goals on the same ˎday | ˉmanaged to ·clinch | the league ˎchampionship | and ˉthen | I think the ˋheart had gone ˋout of ˉHearts | by the ˍScottish cup ·final and they ·lost | ˋheavily | ˉthree nil to Aberˎdeen ||

[change of speaker: Kevin Geary]

well ˋthank you very ·much for that | ˊMartin | that's ˉfootball | ↓in the year nineteen eighty-ˉsix | but aˋway from ˉfootball | the ·year's ˋother ·major ·sporting ˊgathering | was the ˍthirteenth ˋCommonwealth ·Games in ˊEdinburgh || the ˉGames have long ˋstriven to mainˋtain their ˋfeel of ˉinternational ˇharmony | through a ·joyous celeˋbration of the deˉlights of ˍfriendly compeˋtition || ·sadly ˋthis year ˉpolitics suˆcceeded in ˉtainting | ˉone more iˎdeal || but ·those ˊathletes | left ˉfree to comˇpete by their ·governments | still ˏmanaged | some ·memorable ˏmoments | and there to enˏjoy them | as ˉever | was Paddy ˉFeeny | ·Paddy your ˎthoughts ||

[change of speaker: Paddy Feeny]

well as you were ˉsaying Kevin | the ˇthirteenth Games | unˇlucky thir·teen | ˇdefinitely because | ·more than ˉfifty per ˎcent | of the ·countries that ˇcould have turned ·up | in fact ˇdidn't || and they ˇalso had these fiˇnancial problems | and the Games' ˋchairman Robert ˋMaxwell said that the ˋboycott ·certainly hadn't helped ˎhim ||

[statement by Robert Maxwell omitted]

aˋpart from the ˇcash | in ˇsporting terms | they made the ˇboxing ·virtually ·meaningless | the ˋbadminton and the ˋweightlifting they suffered ˋbadly from the lack of the ˉAsians | ˉtrack and ˍfield | again | the ˉabsence of the ˇWest ·Indians | and ˋalso the ˇAfricans | meant that there ˉwasn't | the ˋstrength and ˋdepth that there ˋshould have been || having ˇsaid that | there were some ˇvery good per·formances | the Caˇnadians took | ˉthree out of ˍfour | of the ˇsprint gold ·medals | and ˉthen of ·course | there was the ˉman of the ˋmoment on the ·track | ·Steve ˇCram | he ·won the ˋeight hundred metres | and then ˇtwo days ·later | he was in the ˉfinal of the ˎfifteen hundred ||

[live coverage omitted]

but ˋCram wasn't the ˋonly one of ·course to a·chieve a ˉdouble | Kirsty ˋWade of ˇWales became the first ˉwoman to take the ˇeight hundred and the ˇfifteen hundred | and in ˇmy opinion | even ˇmore meritorious in a ·way | Debby ˋFlintoff of Auˋstralia | 'cause ˋshe won both the ˋfour hundred ˇflat and ↑ˋalso | that | ˋabsoˋlutely ˇkilling event | the ˉfour hundred metres ˎhurdles || but the ˇbiggest | and most ˋpopular | ˬwin | as ·far | as the ˇlocal crowd was con·cerned | was of course ˉthat | of the ˍScottish lass | Liz ˋLynch | in the ˍten thousand ˎmetres ||

[live coverage omitted]

in the ˋCommonwealth ˉpool | well the ˋcelebrating ˉthere | was for ˉEngland's ·Sarah ˋHardcastle | who came ·very ˋvery close inˋdeed to the world ˏrecord | in the ˍeight hundred metres ˇfreestyle | ↑ˋalso for the ˉfact that the Auˍstralians | and the Caˍnadians managed to beˋhave themselves | for a ˇchange | after the | disˋreputable ˋantics in both ˉEdmonton | and ˇalso | in | eh ˇBrisbane | but to ˉme ˋthe man | in the ˇpool | just as Steve ˇCram was | on the ˍtrack | ·was | the the ˉworld ˎclass one | the the ˉman from ˍCanada | ˉAlex ˍBowman | ˉwinning | a·mongst ˍother things | the ˉfour hundred metres ˎmedley ||

[live coverage omitted]

but of ˉcourse | the | ˋCommonwealth Games weren't | unˇfriendly | and they ˉweren't | unˋhappy ˋeither | exˋcept for one or ˇtwo people of ·course | I ˋdon't think that ˋFatima ˋWhitbread was | too ˏhappy she | conˉtinued her ˍrivalry | in the ˉwomen's ˬjavelin with | ·Tessa ˇSanderson | once aˉgain she looked the | more conˇsistent | once a·gain ˍFatima | was

ˋbeaten ˇinto second ·place | by an inˋcredible third ·throw | by ˍTessa which ¯nobody exˎpected ||

[change of speaker: Kevin Geary]

Paddy ˋnot long ˇafter that | the ˋtears of ¯grief | and fruˍstration | turned to ·tears of ˇjoy for Fatima | in the Euroˇpean Championships | which were of an exˋceptionally high ˋstandard ˋweren't they ||

[change of speaker: Paddy Feeny]

ˋyes inˋdeed || yes inˋcredible | and of ·course she ˇalso | in ·nineteen eighty- six ¯beat the world ˋrecord | so it was a ˇgood year for her || but the ↑but the ˋEuropean ˋChampionships | inˋcredible ˋweren't they ||

[change of speaker: Kevin Geary]

yes a ·world ¯record | for ·Fatima ¯Whitbread | in ¯Stuttgart | and ˍalso | the gold ˊmedal || as exˊpected the ·Soviet ˊUnion and East ˊGermany ˍdominated the ·field e¯vents || but on the ¯track | it was a different ˊmatter with | ˇBritish runners | exˋcelling themselves || and ˋnone was ¯happier | than ·Seb ¯Coe | in the ˇeight hundred metres | finally ˇlaying | a ·personal ˎjinx ||

037 SPOKEN ENGLISH CORPUS TEXT J01
Review of the Year
(First part)
BBC World Service
Transcribed by GOK

[Speaker: Kevin Geary]

ˊso | ¯what was ˎyour ·sporting _highlight | of ·nineteen eighty- ˎsix || per·haps it was Di¯ego Maraˎdona's | ˋbreathtakingly ˇbrilliant ·goal | against ˏEngland | in the ¯World _Cup finals | in ˎMexico || or ¯India's deˎlight | at ·winning a ¯test match at ˏLord's | for the _first ˎtime || maybe for ˊyou | the ·moments to ¯savour | in·volved a ¯string | of re¯markable Au·stralian ˋvictories | in ·just about ˋeverything ex¯cept | he ·added wi·thout a ˇhint of ·gloating | ˋcricket || or ¯could it ˎbe | that ·when you look ¯back | at the ¯sporting _year | ˋnineteen eighty- ¯six | ·etched inˋdelibly on your ¯memory | will be the ¯frighteningly | dra¯matic ˎmoment | when ·Nigel ¯Mansell's | ˋtyre ·burst | at ¯two hundred ·miles an ˎhour | to deˇny him | the ·World _Motor Racing ˋChampionship || or ·those _classic enˋcounters | be·tween ·Dancing ˊBrave | and ¯Shahraˋstani | in the ·sport of ˋkings || or ¯Boris ˋBecker's | ·thrilling ¯march | to aˇnother | ¯Wimbledon ˋtitle || ¯or | ˋwell the ˋlist just ·goes | _on and ˋon || it's ·only when you ·stop to ˋthink about | all the ˋfeasts | laid ˋon for us | by the ˎworld's | ˋsportsmen and ˏwomen | that you ˇrealise | that ·nineteen eighty- ˇsix | was ↑in_deed | a ¯vintage ˎyear | for some ˋhugely enˇjoyable | _overinˋdulgence || but ˋwe've ·got just ¯half an ˋhour | in ·which to a¯ttempt | to ·reˊlive it ·all | and to ·help us ·do just ¯that | we've ·gathered in the ¯studio | just ·some of the ˇmany re·porters | who've ˋbrought the ·year's ·sporting ˇnews to ·you | on the _World ˎService || ¯so | _where to ˋstart || with ·so much to ˊchoose from | I'm ·feeling like a ·wide-eyed ·kid in a ˋsweet ·factory || ↑but a deˏcision | _has to be ˎmade || and as ˋfootball is the ·world's most ˇpopular ·sport | and as it proˊvided us | with the ·year's ˇcentrepiece | the ·world ¯cup | we'll be¯gin | with ˇMexico | and ·Martin ˎFookes || well ˊMartin | as a ·compeˏtition | did it live ¯up to your expecˎtations ||

[change of speaker: Martin Fookes]

well I reˎcall ·saying at the ˋtime | that I ·think the ˋgood ·outweighed the ˎbad || we ˋcertainly ·did have some ˋdire matches in ‸ ˏMexico | and ·one that ·comes to ˏmind is | Moˋrocco a·gainst West ˋGermany | where ·we were ‸ ¯all ˎpraying | for the ¯final ·whistle to ˎgo || but a¯gainst _that | we had some ˋexcellent ·matches | ˋFrance a·gainst the ·Soviet ¯Union |

·finished one ˏone | an inˉcredible game | be·tween ˉBelgium | and the ·Soviet ·Union ·four ˏthree | and ˋFrance a·gainst Bra˯zil | de·cided on ˎpenalties || ˉthose were the ˋhighlights I ·felt | of the ·World ˎCup || and of ˉcourse | the ˋfinal itˎself | was ˋexcellent || ·Argenˏtina | ˏcoasting a·long there | ˉtwo goals ˍup | through ˉBrown and Valˍdano | and ·then the ·West ˉGermans came ·back | through ˊRummenigge | and ˊVoller | just a ˉfew minutes to ˍgo | and ˋthen there was ·that fanˉtastic ˋclimax ||

[live commentary omitted]

[change of speaker: Kevin Geary]

·and as ˎhistory will reˉcord | it ˉwas inˋdeed the ˏwinner || ·Martin ˄ do you ˋthink that the ˄ ˉbest side ·won it in the ˊend ||

[change of speaker: Martin Fookes]

ˋyes | I ·think there's ˋno question that ·Argentina deˇserved to ·win | they beat ˇUruguay | and ˉEngland | and ˯Belgium | on their ·way through the ˇknockout ·part of the ·compe·tition | ↑and in ˉMaraˎdona | without ˋdoubt | they ·had the ˋstar of the ˄ ·compe·tition || he ˋscored one ·rather ˋdubious ·goal | which ·irks us ˄ eh ˄ ˎsomewhat ·here in ·England | a ˉhandˎball ·goal | the ˋfirst one | in the ˋmeeting with ˏEngland | but the ˇsecond one | was ˋtruly miˋraculous ||

[change of speaker: Kevin Geary]

yes in·deed a magˇnificent ·goal | and I reˋmember | ˋPaddy ·doing an ˋinterview | on ˋSports Interˇnational | ˋnot long ˇafter the World ·Cup | with ·Bobby ˎRobson | the ·England ˇmanager | eh ˄ when ·Bobby said he ·felt that ˋif England had ˇbeaten Argen·tina | they ˋcould have gone ·on to ˄ eh | to ˇwin the World ·Cup | ˋPaddy ˇFeeny | is ˋactually ·sitting alongˋside me | now ˋPaddy | ˋyour ·views on ·that || [Laughter over last sentence]

[change of speaker: Paddy Feeny]

ˋyes | I ·think if ˄ er ˄ ·Bobby ·Robson was being ˍhonest | he'd a·gree as ˋwell || there ˋwas a ·problem ˋalso | as ·far as ˇEngland was con·cerned | was that they ˉhadn't ˍhad | any ·Euroˋpean compe·tition | at ˋclub ·level | which ˉcan't have ˎhelped ||

[change of speaker: Kevin Geary]

which ˋleads us ˋnicely ˬon ·Paddy | ·thank you very ·much inˊdeed | to eh ^ the ¯European ·club compeˊtitions | eh ^ ˇin ·Europe last ·season | and of ·course as ˇPaddy was ·saying | ˋno English represenˇtation ·there | ·em ^ ¯Martin deˇspite ·that | in at least ˇtwo of the three ·finals | I ·think we ·saw ^ some ¯fine ˋfootball ||

[change of speaker: Martin Fookes]

¯yes we ˋdid || ˋSpain | ·funnily eˏnough | was ·repre·sented in all ˋthree Euro·pean ˏfinals | ·and er ^ ˋSteau ˇBucharest | be·came the ˋfirst team from ˇEastern ·Europe | to ˋwin the ·European ·Cup || and ˋI think de¯servedly ˎso || the ˋgoalkeeper ¯Helmut ˎDucherdam | is a ^ a ˋfigure we will re¯member for some ˎtime || of ·course ¯Dinamo Kiˋev | won the ˇCupwinners' ·Cup | and ˋthey were | a magˋnificent ·side | without ¯any ˋdoubt | they're ˋstill going in the ·Euroˋpean Cup ˇnow | and they suˋpplied most of the ˋSoviet ·team for the World ˋCup || but ˋthey gave a ^ magˋnificent per·formance to ·beat | Atˋletico Maˬdrid | in ˇLyons | and ˇReal Ma·drid | ·won the ^ UˋEFA ·Cup | ·for the ¯second ˎtime || so ˇSpanish ·clubs | did ¯very ˎwell | in the ¯European compeˎtitions ||

[change of speaker: Kevin Geary]

doˇmestically | I ¯hate to ˎmention ·this | with ˋPaddy alongˇside ·me | it was ˋvery much | ˋLiverpool's ˏyear | ·here in ˏEngland | with the ˊdouble ||

[change of speaker: Martin Fookes]

ˎyes it ˋwas || em ^ ¯they surˎprised me | ˋgreatly | be·cause ˋeven in the ˋdying ·weeks of the ˎseason | I ¯did ˏfeel | that ˋEverton were ^ a ·better ˋteam || ·and I ˋthink ·Everton | ˋblew the ·league ·championship | ·one ˋmidweek ·night at ˎOxford | when they ˋlost || ·up until ^ ˇthat ·point | they were ·in the ¯box ˎseat as it ·were | but ˋLiverpool were ·then in coˎmmand | and to their ¯very great ˎcredit | they ˋreally | ·took a ˋgrip on ·things then | and of ˋcourse | in the ˇfinal ·match | ·very ˋfittingly at ˇStamford ·Bridge | ˋKenny Dalˬglish | ·scored the ¯winning ˍgoal | to ·wrap up the ·league ˋtitle || ↑ˋeven in the ·FA ˋcup | I'd ˋstill ·had that ·sneaking suˬspicion | that ˬEverton | were ˍgoing to ˋwin | but of ·course I was ˋwrong a·bout ·that as ˇwell | and the ˋFA ˇcup final | was ˋreally ˋall a·bout | a ˋgentleman ·called | ¯Ian ˎRush ||

[live commentary omitted]

[change of speaker: Kevin Geary]

well ˋlet's turn our aˋttention ·now | to ˋnorth of the ˇborder | where alˋthough it was er | ˋCeltic and Aber↑ˋdeen | who ·ended ·up with the ˋtrophies | the ˋstory was ˇreally a·bout ·Martin | the ‸ ˋdesperate ˏluck | of poor ¯Heart of Midˋlothian ||

[change of speaker: Martin Fookes]

yes they ˋdid have some ·desperate ˏluck | they ¯lost the league ˋchampionship || I ·think on the ·last _day of the ˋseason | when they were ·beaten at Dun_dee | having ·had a ˋlong unbeaten _run | ·Celtic by ·scoring ˋfour goals on the ·same ˎday | ·managed to ·clinch ‸ the ·league ˎchampionship || and ¯then | I ·think the ˋheart had gone ˋout of ˏHearts | by the ‸ ˋScottish ·cup _final | and they ·lost ¯heavily 3-ˎ0 | to ·Aberˎdeen ||

[change of speaker: Kevin Geary]

well ˋthank you very ·much for ˏthat ·Martin | that's er ‸ ˋfootball in the ·year ·nineteen eighty- ˊsix | but aˇway from ·football | the year's ˇother ·major ·sporting ·gathering | was the ·thirteenth ·Commonwealth ˏGames | in ˊEdinburgh || the ¯Games | have ¯long ˋstriven | to main·tain their ·feel of ·international ˇharmony | through a ¯joyous celeˋbration | of the de¯lights of ·friendly compeˋtition || ·sadly ˇthis year | ˊpolitics | sucˋceeded in ¯tainting | ·one more iˎdeal || but ¯those ˏathletes | left ˋfree to com¯pete | by their ˊgovernments | still ¯managed | some ·memorable ¯moments | and ·there to enˊjoy them | er ‸ as ˊever | was ·Paddy ˊFeeny || ¯Paddy ·your ˎthoughts ||

037 SPOKEN ENGLISH CORPUS TEXT J01
Review of the Year
BBC World Service
Overlap passage

Transcribed by BJW

[Speaker: Kevin Geary]

well ˋlet's turn our a·ttention now to ˉnorth of the ˇborder | ·where | alˋthough it was | ˉCeltic and Aberˋdeen | who ·ended up with the ˇtrophies | the ˋstory was ˋreally about ˉMartin the | ˋdesperate ˉluck of poor ·Heart of Midˎlothian ||

[change of speaker: Martin Fookes]

yes they ˇdid have some desperate ·luck || they ˉlost the league ˎchampionship || I ·think on the ˋlast day of the ˋseason when they were ˋbeaten at Dunˏdee | having had a ˉlong unbeaten ˎrun | ˋCeltic by scoring ˋfour goals on the same ˎday | ˉmanaged to ·clinch | the league ˎchampionship | and ˉthen | I think the ˋheart had gone ˋout of ˉHearts | by the ˍScottish cup ·final and they ·lost | ˋheavily | ˉthree nil to Aberˎdeen ||

[change of speaker: Kevin Geary]

well ˋthank you very ·much for that | ˊMartin | that's ˉfootball | ↓in the year nineteen eighty- ˉsix | but aˋway from ˉfootball | the ·year's ˋother ·major ·sporting ˊgathering | was the ˍthirteenth ˋCommonwealth ·Games in ˊEdinburgh || the ˉGames have long ˋstriven to mainˋtain their ˋfeel of ˉinternational ˇharmony | through a ·joyous celeˋbration of the deˉlights of ˍfriendly compeˋtition || ·sadly ˋthis year ˉpolitics suˆcceeded in ˉtainting | ˉone more iˎdeal || but ·those ˊathletes | left ˉfree to comˇpete by their ·governments | still ˏmanaged | some ·memorable ˏmoments | and there to enˏjoy them | as ˉever | was Paddy ˉFeeny | ·Paddy your ˎthoughts ||

Transcribed by GOK

[change of speaker: Kevin Geary]

well ˋlet's turn our aˋttention ·now | to ˋnorth of the ˇborder | where alˋthough it was er | ˋCeltic and Aber↑ˋdeen | who ·ended ·up with the

ˋtrophies | the ˋstory was ˇreally a·bout ·Martin | the ‸ ˋdesperate ˏluck | of poor ¯Heart of Midˋlothian ||

[change of speaker: Martin Fookes]

yes they ˋdid have some ·desperate ˏluck | they ¯lost the league ˋchampionship || I ·think on the ·last ˍday of the ˋseason | when they were ·beaten at Dunˍdee | having ·had a ˋlong unbeaten ˍrun | ·Celtic by ·scoring ˋfour goals on the ·same ˎday | ·managed to ·clinch ‸ the ·league ˎchampionship || and ¯then | I ·think the ˋheart had gone ˋout of ˏHearts | by the ‸ ˋScottish ·cup ˍfinal | and they ·lost ¯heavily 3-ˎ0 | to ·Aberˎdeen ||

[change of speaker: Kevin Geary]

well ˋthank you very ·much for ˏthat ·Martin | that's er ‸ ˋfootball in the ·year ·nineteen eighty- ˊsix | but aˇway from ·football | the year's ˇother ·major ·sporting ·gathering | was the ·thirteenth ·Commonwealth ˏGames | in ˊEdinburgh || the ¯Games | have ¯long ˋstriven | to main·tain their ·feel of ·international ˇharmony | through a ¯joyous celeˋbration | of the de¯lights of ·friendly competˋtition || ·sadly ˇthis year | ˊpolitics | sucˋceeded in ¯tainting | ·one more iˎdeal || but ¯those ˏathletes | left ˋfree to com¯pete | by their ˊgovernments | still ¯managed | some ·memorable ¯moments | and ·there to enˊjoy them | er ‸ as ˊever | was ·Paddy ˊFeeny || ¯Paddy ·your ˎthoughts ||

038 SPOKEN ENGLISH CORPUS TEXT J02

Streamline English - Unit 16
'Inside Story'
Transcribed by BJW

¯Julian | ¯can you ˍtell us | ¯how you were ˍcaptured in the ˋfirst ·place ||

[change of speaker]

¯well | I was ˋon my ˋway to ·visit a ˋvillage near the ·front ˋline || I ˋcame round a ˋbend in the ˇroad | and ·there was a ˋtree lying aˋcross the road || I only ˋjust managed to ·stop in ˋtime || ˇsuddenly | ·armed ˍmen a·ppeared on all ˋsides ||

[change of speaker]

what did you ˋdo ||

[change of speaker]

what would ↑ˋyou do || I just ˍsat there with my ˋhands in the ·air || ˇanyway they | ˋmade me get ˋout of the ˇLand Rover and | made me ·lie on the ˏground || I ˇthought | this is ˋit | they're going to ˋshoot me || I started ¯saying my ˋprayers ||

[change of speaker]

what ·happened ˋnext ||

[change of speaker]

ˏwell || they ˇsearched me || of ˋcourse I ˋdidn't have any ˊweapons | just a ˋcamera || ↑it's ˋfunny they let me ˋkeep it || ↓then they ˋtied my ˇhands together and | ˋblindfolded me || then they ˋmade me get in the ˋback of a ¯truck and | ˍlie under some ˋsacks || I've ˋno iˋdea where they ˇtook me | ex¯cept that | it was ˋquite a ·large ˋtraining camp || I was ¯there for ·ten ˋdays ||

[change of speaker]

were you ¯treated ˊwell ||

[change of speaker]

ˏyes | I su·ppose I ˏwas || they ¯let me ˍwalk about the ˊcamp | and they ˍlet me take ˇphotographs | but they ˋwouldn't let me ˋphotograph any ↑ˋfaces || I ˋwas able to ˋinterview ·some of the ˋleaders ||

[change of speaker]

¯how did you eˎscape ||

[change of speaker]

I ˋdidn't || they put me ¯back in the ˍtruck | ¯blindfolded me aˏgain | ¯drove for a ·few ˏhours then | ¯made me get ˏout | ¯pointed me in the direction of ˏtown and | ¯let me ˎgo ||

[change of speaker]

and ˋwhat e·xactly did the gue·rrilla leaders ˋsay | a·bout the situ·ation ||

[change of speaker]

ˎah || ˋwell if you ˋwant to know ˇthat | you'll ˋhave to buy toˋmorrow's ·Daily ↑ˋNews ||

038 SPOKEN ENGLISH CORPUS TEXT J02
Streamline English - Unit 16
'Inside Story'
Transcribed by GOK

·Julian ‸ ¯can you ˍtell us | ·how you were ˏcaptured | in the ˏfirst place ||

[change of speaker]

ˎwell | I was ¯on my ˍway | to ·visit a ˋvillage | ·near the ·front ˎline || I ˋcame round a ˋbend in the ˬroad | and there was a ¯tree lying aˋcross the ·road || I only ˋjust ·managed to ·stop in ˋtime || ˬsuddenly | ·armed ˋmen a·ppeared on ·all ˋsides ||

[change of speaker]

·what did you ˋdo

[change of speaker]

ˎhuh | ·what would ˋyou ·do || ↓I just ˏsat there | with my ˋhands in the ·air || ˋanyway they | ˋmade me get ·out of the ˇLand Rover and | ·made me ·lie on the ˏground | I ˋthought | this is ˋit | they're ˍgoing to ˋshoot me | I ¯started ·saying my ˋprayers ||

[change of speaker]

¯what happened ˋnext ||

[change of speaker]

ˎwell || they ˇsearched me || of ˋcourse I ·didn't have any ˊweapons | just a ˋcamera || it's ↑ˋfunny they let me ˋkeep it || ·then they ‸ ˋtied my ˇhands to·gether and | ˋblindfolded ·me || ·then they ˋmade me ·get in the ¯back of a ˊtruck | and ‸ ¯lie under some ˋsacks || ↑I've ˋno i·dea ˋwhere they ˇtook me | ex·cept that ‸ it was ‸ ·quite a ˎlarge ˋtraining ·camp || I was ¯there for ten ˋdays ||

[change of speaker]

were you ·treated ˊwell ||

[change of speaker]

ˊyes | I su·ppose I ˏwas || they ˋlet me ·walk about the ˏcamp | and they ·let me take ˇphotographs | but they ˋwouldn't let me ·photograph any ˋfaces || I ^ ˋwas ·able to ·interview ·some of the ˋleaders ||

[change of speaker]

¯how did you eˎscape ||

[change of speaker]

ˋhuh | I ˋdidn't || they ·put me ¯back in the ˏtruck | ¯blindfolded me aˏgain | ·drove for a ¯few ˏhours | then ¯made me get ˏout | ˋpointed me in the di·rection of ˏtown | ↑and ^ ˍlet me ˎgo ||

[change of speaker]

and ˋwhat e·xactly did the gue·rrilla ·leaders ˋsay ^ a·bout the situ·ation ||

[change of speaker]

ˋah || ·well if you ˋwant to know ˇthat | you'll ˋhave to ·buy toˋmorrow's ·Daily ˋNews ||

039 SPOKEN ENGLISH CORPUS TEXT J03
Streamline English Course - Unit 25
'Murder at Gurney Manor - Part 2'
Transcribed by GOK

where ˎis everybody ˏSergeant

[change of speaker]

they're ˉall in the ˋdrawingroom ·sir | ·Constable ˋDickson's ·with them | ˉwhat do you ˎthink sir ||

[change of speaker]

it ˉcould have been any ˋone of them | ˋcouldn't it || we ˋdon't know ˋwhat ·skeletons are in the ˏcupboard | ↑it ·may have been ˉtwo of them toˋgether || it might ˉeven have been | ˋall of them || ↑ˋnobody ·seems very ˏsad ||

[change of speaker]

ˋno sir || Lord ˉGurney | was a ˉvery un·popular ˋman in the ˏvillage || ·nobody ˋliked him || it ˇcould have been an outˋsider ||

[change of speaker]

↑no ˎno ·Watts | it ˋmust have ·been ·one of ˋthem || ˉlet's look at the ˎevidence ||

[change of speaker]

it ˋseems to ˬme | that ˋeverybody has ·got a ˇmotive ·sir | and ˉnobody's got an ˋalibi || they ˉall ˏsay | they were aˬlone | when it ˋhappened ||

[change of speaker]

ˎyes | and there are ˋno ˎfingerprints | on the ˎgun ||

[change of speaker]

it ˋcouldn't have ·been ˇher ·sir ||

[change of speaker]

ˉwhy ˎnot ·Watts ||

[change of speaker]

ˋwell | she's ˍin a ˋwheelchair || she ·can't ˋmove very ·fast || ˋanyway | they've been ˋmarried for ·thirty-five ˋyears | it ˋcan't have been ˬher ||

[change of speaker]

¯most ˏmurders | are ¯inˏside | the ˋfamily ˏWatts | and there ¯is a ˎdoor | be·tween ¯her ˏroom | and the ˋlibrary ||

[change of speaker]

ah ↑ˋyes sir | but it was ˋlocked ||

[change of speaker]

·doors have ˋkeys ˏWatts ||

[change of speaker]

↑but ˇwhy would she ·want to ˋkill him ||

[change of speaker]

¯Miss ˍSmart's | a ¯very aˬttractive | ·young ˋwoman || we ·don't know ˍwhat was going ˋon | she ˍcould have been ˋjealous ||

[change of speaker]

but ˎsir | ·he was over ˋsixty | ·he was ˏold e·nough to ·be her ˋfather ||

[change of speaker]

ˎah ˋwell ·Watts | he was a ˋgood-·looking ˋman | and ¯very ˎrich ||

¯what about the ˎMajor | ˏWatts | ¯he's a ˍstrange ˋfellow ||

[change of speaker]

↑I've been ˇthinking about ·that | it ˋcan't have been ˬhim ·sir ||

[change of speaker]

ˊreally | ¯why ˎnot ||

[change of speaker]

¯why would he _need to ˇfire | ¯five ˋtimes || he was an ¯army ¯pistol ˋchampion | he could have ˏkilled him | with ¯one ˋshot ||

[change of speaker]

·maybe he ^did ·Watts | ·maybe he ^did

[change of speaker]

¯I don't underˎstand sir ||

[change of speaker]

there are a ˋlot of things ·you don't underˏstand ·Watts | per·haps he's more ·clever than he ˋlooks ||

[change of speaker]

↑but there's _no ˋmotive sir ||

[change of speaker]

there ˇmay have ·been || I ¯mean | there ˋwas ·that ˇscandal | with the ˬproperty ·company ||

[change of speaker]

but ˋhe was at the ˋlake sir ||

[change of speaker]

he ·might ˇnot have ·been ·Watts || he's a ^pistol ·champion | he ·could have ·shot him from the ˋtrees | and ·thrown the ·gun into the ˋroom ||

[change of speaker]

ˎoh | ↑do you ¯really ˏthink so ·sir ||

[change of speaker]

↑ˋI don't ^know ·Watts | it's ¯just a ˎtheory ||

040 SPOKEN ENGLISH CORPUS TEXT J04
Streamline English Course - Unit 72
'Getting things done'
Transcribed by BJW

ˋTim || that ˋbathroom ·tap's ↑ˋstill ˋdripping || ↑it's ˋgetting on my ˋnerves || I ˉthought you ˍsaid you were ·going to ˋfix it ||

[change of speaker]

↓oh ·yes || the ˍwasher needs reˋplacing ||

[change of speaker]

ˍwhy don't you reˋplace it ·then ||

[change of speaker]

it's ˋnot as ˋeasy as ˊthat || I'll ˋtry and do it ˋnext ·week ||

[change of speaker]

but you ˉsaid ˏthat | ˋlast ·week ||

[change of speaker]

I ˋknow || I ˋthink you'd better ˉphone for a ˍplumber and get it ˉdone || I'm not ˇreally quite ·sure how to ·do it ||

040 SPOKEN ENGLISH CORPUS TEXT J04
Streamline English Course - Unit 72
'Getting things done'
Transcribed by GOK

↑ˋTim | that ˋbathroom ·tap's ↑¯still ˎdripping | it's ↑ˋgetting on my ˋnerves || I ↑¯thought you ˏsaid | you were ·going to ˋfix it ||

[change of speaker]

oh ˎyes | the ˋwasher needs reˎplacing ||

[change of speaker]

ˏwhy don't you reˋplace it then ||

[change of speaker]

it's ˋnot as ˋeasy as ˏthat | ↑I'll ¯try and ˍdo it next ˎweek ||

[change of speaker]

but you ↑¯said ˏthat | ˋlast ·week ||

[change of speaker]

I ˋknow || I ˋthink you'd ·better ·phone for a ˬplumber and ·get it ·done | I'm ¯not ˇreally quite ·sure how to ·do it ||

041 SPOKEN ENGLISH CORPUS TEXT J05
Streamline English Course - Unit 75
'Messages'
Transcribed by BJW

good ˏmorning A·manda | could you come ˏin for a ·minute please ||

[change of speaker]

good ˏmorning Mr ·Dawson | ¯did you have a good ˎtrip ||

[change of speaker]

ˋyes ˏthank you || ¯were there any ˏmessages for me ·yesterday ||

[change of speaker]

ˎyes || ¯quite a ˎfew || ↑shall I just ·run ˇthrough them ||

[change of speaker]

ˋplease ||

[change of speaker]

ˋJenny ·phoned || she ¯said she wouldn't be _in till ˋFriday ||

[change of speaker]

ˎoh || why's ˎthat ||

[change of speaker]

she ˋsaid she had ˋ'flu || she'd ¯seen the ˇdoctor ||

[change of speaker]

ˏright || ˇgo on ||

[change of speaker]

then Mr ˋWatkins ·called || ↑ˋhe said he ·couldn't make the ˋmeeting this afterˋnoon | but would ¯ring you on ˎWednesday ||

[change of speaker]

↓o´kay ||

[change of speaker]

ˇGodfrey | came in ˋlooking for you || he ¯said he wanted ˋFriday off ||

[change of speaker]

^did he ||

[change of speaker]

ˋyes || he ·told me his ˋgrandmother had ·died | and he'd ¯have to go to the ˎfuneral ||

[change of speaker]

oh ˎdear || I'd better ˋsee him ˋlater ||

[change of speaker]

and ¯Wadley's ˎGarage ·called || they ¯said your new ˎcar wasn't ·ready ||

[change of speaker]

¯oh ˍno || ¯why on earth ˍnot ||

[change of speaker]

they said there was a ˋstrike at the ˋfactory ˋyesterday ||

[change of speaker]

a¯gain ||

[change of speaker]

¯after lunch Miss ˋDobson ·phoned || she ˋsaid that ¯Western ˬVideo ·Systems | had to ˋcancel their ·last ˋorder | because their ˋcustomers had changed their ˋminds ||

[change of speaker]

ˬpity ||

[change of speaker]

Mr GonˬZalez called from ˋMexico | to say he ˋmight be in ˋLondon from the ˉtwenty-ˎfirst | to the ˉtwenty-ˎfifth || he ˉsaid he wanted to ˍsee you ˎthen ||

[change of speaker]

ˋoh | ˋgood || I ˋhope he can ˇmake it ||

[change of speaker]

then a ·lady ˬphoned | Saˉmantha ˋEllis || she ˋasked you to ˉphone her as ˍsoon as ˋpossible | she ˋsaid it was ˋurgent ||

[change of speaker]

ˋah | Saˋmantha || I wonder what ˋshe ·wants ||

[change of speaker]

ˋoh | and ˉjust before ˬfive | Mr ˋBerry phoned || he ˉtold us ˍnot to supply ˇMason and Co until ·further ˋnotice || he ˋsaid it was imˋportant | and that he would exˉplain ˎlater ||

[change of speaker]

·anything ˊelse ||

[change of speaker]

ˎno || that's ˎit || ˏcoffee ||

[change of speaker]

ˋplease || ˉthat would be ˎnice ||

042 SPOKEN ENGLISH CORPUS TEXT J06
Kempson and Green dialogue
(First part)
Recorded at MSU Lancaster University
Transcribed by GOK

[RG] ˋhere's a good ˏjob | ˉSaudi Aˋrabia ||

[HK] ˋBrian was in ˏSaudi ||

[speech extract omitted]

[RG] and ˉwhat did he ˋthink of ·Saudi A·rabia ||

[HK] I re·member he ·told me that he ·absolutely ˎhated it || there was no ˏfraternising | ˏobviously | with ˇfemale ·teachers | ˋeven with ·Euroˇpean teachers | and of ˋcourse they ·lived in ‸ ·segregated ˬquarters | which was ˋmaybe O·K in the beˇginning | but ‸ ˋlater there was a ˇdoorman | on the ‸ ˇwomen's building | ·and they ‸ just ˉweren't a·llowed to ‸ ·visit at ˋall ||

[RG] and ˋthat was | Euroˋpean women ||

[HK] ˋyes even ·Euroˋpeans | as ˬI under·stood it ||

[RG] and ˏwhat was the i·dea be·hind ˋthat || iˉllicit ˊsex ||

[HK] I suˇppose so | I think ˇSaudi's too exˋtreme || but ˉwhat about ˋEgypt || Aleˊxandria ·schools || do you think ˊthat would be ·very ·interesting ||

[RG] ˋhmm | it's for ˇchildren ·though | ˋisn't it || ˉwhat about the ˎsalary ||

[HK] ˉah the ˎsalary | ·let's have a ˎlook || it's ˋonly a ˇlocal ·salary | of ˋthree ·hundred and ˊsixty E·gyptian ·pounds a ·month | that's ˋnot ·really very ˎmuch || it's ˇmore or ·less subˆsistence ˏreally ||

[RG] ˉthat's the ˎtrouble | with ·these small ˬads || they don't ˎreally offer very ˋmuch || I ·mean ‸ ˋhere's one for ˎZambia || now ˉI'd ˋquite like to ·go to ˏZambia | haven't ˋbeen to ˏAfrica | I think it would be ·very nice to ˋwork there || but ‸ you ˉhave to ˍhave | a ˉlocal ˏsalary | ·and ˋthis one has | ˋfour thousand US ·dollars a ˋyear || so ‸ ¯what's ˎthat || a¯bout | ¯two thousand ·five hundred ˊpounds || it's ¯not ˎreally very ˋmuch ||

[HK] ˎno I suppose ˋnot || ¯there's ‸ ˋone here for ·Bangˋkok | ·that's a ˎPrincipal || ˎno | I ˋdon't think ˋthat's a very ·good iˏdea || ↑·er ‸ ·Addis ˊAbaba || an ˊEnglish co·mmunity ·school || ↓I ˎdon't think I'd like ˇthat very ·much || ↑¯what about ‸ ·teaching adviser in ˎParis ||

[RG] ˋah | ˎnow || ·that's a ˋgood one || ¯but | you ¯have to be ˏfluent in ˋFrench ||

[speech extract omitted]

[RG] ˇI thought | it ˋmight suit someone ¯more like ˎGill | because ↑she ˋstudied ˏFrench | as a ¯first deˋgree | ˏdidn't she ||

[HK] ˎyes she ˋdid || I ˋthink I ˋmentioned it ·to her | the ·other ˋday | but ‸ she ˇmay be ·staying in this ·country | ˋanyway ||

[RG] ˎnow you could ·go for an ˇinterview || ¯how about ˋthat ||

[HK] ˏyes | I su·ppose you ˎcould || they're ·paying ˎwhat | a ˊhundred pounds ex·penses || ˋyes | an ˇinterview wouldn't be a ·bad i·dea || you could take the ˏboat | and stay ·on for a ·few more ˏdays ||

[RG] ˎyes | you'd ¯have to ˎtake the ·boat | be·cause they're ‸ they're only ˋpaying a ·hundred ˎpounds | in reimˇbursement ||

[HK] ˎhm || ˋah | ˋhere's one for ˋcyprus | but ˎthat's ·teaching ˋchildren a·gain ||

[RG] ↑have you ˇever taught ·children ||

[HK] ¯only ˎonce | ·that was in ˋLondon | in a ˋprivate ·school ||

[RG] did you ˊlike it ||

[HK] ˇyes | it was ˋmore or ·less a ˋprivate ˇlesson | I had ˋtwo young Iˇtalian ·brothers | I ·used to ·take them ‸ ·down to the ˏmarket | and ·get them to ·do ˏshopping ·for me | and ˊˇthey seemed to ·like it | and their ˋEnglish ‸ ·actually im·proved | as ˋwell | ·much to my surˏprise || I ˋdon't know whether | ˇI had ‸ any e·ffect | or ‸ ·whether it was ·just because they were ·living in ‸ ¯London itˋself ||

[RG] ˋwell that ˉmakes a big ˋdifference | ˋdoesn't it | when you're ·actually ˋliving in the ·country where | you ·have to ·learn the ·target ˎlanguage || ˇmy only ·inex... ‸ ex·perience in ·teaching ‸ ·children is in Indoˋnesia || ˋI had to ·teach some ·Indonesian ˋgirls | in the afterˎnoon | and I ˉmust adˎmit | they were ˋvery ˎquiet || but beˉsides ˍthat | ↑ˉIndoˋnesia | is a ·nice ·place to ˋwork || the ˬmoney is very ·good | ·em ‸ not ˋonly | if you ·have your ˋown salary ˇfrom the ·job | but you can ˎalso pick up a lot of ˋprivate ·teaching | as ˋwell || for exˍample | ˋI had | ˉtwo Japanese ˋcooks ‸ whom I ·used to ·teach ||

[HK] did you ˊcharge them very ·much ||

[RG] ˋwell | ˋas it worked ˇout in ·fact | ˋthey didn't ·pay themˇselves | it was the ˋcompany that | they ˋworked ·for | you ·see ˋthey worked at the ·Hotel ˬHilton | ·and it was ˋin their ˇinterests | for them to ˋlearn ·English | so the ˋcompany ˇsponsored them | to ˍcome | and have ˍlessons with ˎme || ˎso I | I ˉwasn't ˎreally exˇploiting them | but I ˋused to ·make them ˎpay | whether they ˉcame or ˎnot ||

[HK] ˊreally | but I su·ppose if the ˇcompany paid then | I su·ppose that's acˏceptable ||

[RG] I ˋworked for a ˇprivate ·company ·there | ˉInt... ‸ ˉInternational ˋLanguage ·Programs | I ˉdon't su·ppose you've ˎheard of it ||

[HK] ˎno | I've never ˉheard of ˏthat ||

[speech extract omitted]

[HK] (had you ever) ˊtaught ES·P be·fore || (* bracketed words erased *)

[RG] ˎno | ·that was my ˉfirst ‸ exˋperience of ·teaching ES·P || ˇfortunately | we ·had a ‸ Diˋrector of ˬStudies ·who | ˋconcentrated on pro·ducing ma·terials ˋfor the ˬcourse | so ·that ‸ ˋall we ·had to ·do was | ˉread ˎup | ˉwhat we ·wanted to ˎdo | ˇwith the ma·terials | we ˋdidn't ·actually ·have to pro·duce ma·terials ourˋselves ||

[HK] ·and ˉwhat were the ma·terials ‸ in themˋselves ·like || did you have a ·set ‸ ˊtext ·book | or ‸ ˊhandouts ||

[RG] ↑ˉmainly ˎhandouts | ·er ‸ be·cause we ˉwanted to ·look at ·different ˎstudy ·skills | ˋand we ·also used ˏfilms | with ·cartoon

ˏcharacters | which were quite ˏfun and | ˋI managed to ·learn something about ˏoil and ·engineering ·English ˋtoo ||

[HK] so I su·ppose you were ·just more or less ·staying ¯one step aˋhead ||

[RG] ¯very ˎmuch so | ˎyes | ¯very ˎmuch so ||

[HK] and ¯how long were you ˋthere for ||

[RG] ↑ˋhm | ¯just a ˎyear | ˎyes | ¯just a ˎyear || ↑I ˇcould have re·newed my ·contract | but ˇsomehow | I ˋwasn't very ·keen on ·staying ˍlonger | the ˋjob itˬself | ˋdidn't give much ·scope for ‸ em | proˏmotion | or ·doing something ·very much ·different from ·what I ·had already ˋdone || but on the ˋsocial side of ·things | it's a ˋlovely ˋcountry to ˬgo to | if you ·like ‸ ¯outdoor ˏsports | and ˏswimming | and ˏsnorkelling || I ¯must adˎmit | the ˋone thing my | ˋlanguage ·school | ¯could ˎdo | was ˋorganise | the ·weekends ·out to the ·thousand ˎislands || ·they were ˋreally ·good || and ˏalso | it's a ·good place if you ·want to ·travel to ˋother countries like | ·er ‸ Bangˏkok | Maˏlaysia | or ·Singaˋpore ||

[HK] ˎah | ˋRomy was in ·Singaˏpore || ·I ‸ ˋdon't think she ˇliked it very ·much ||

[RG] well it ˋis a very orgaˇnised country and it | it ·sort of de·pends what you ˋwant | ˏreally ||

[HK] I'm beˍginning to ·wonder what I ˋdo want || are there ¯any ˏmore ads ·here in the ·paper ||

[RG] ˋwell I ·think they're only ˇsmall ads ·now | ↑but ↑you ˏknow | I ˋlook at these ·small ˍads | and I ·think ‸ ↑well ‸ am I ˋnot overˋqualified ·for them ||

[HK] ˬyes | but ·can you ever ˍreally be | ˇoverqualified to ·teach ||

[RG] ↑ˋwell | I su·ppose I ·think I'm ˏhere | I'm ·doing an MˏA | for ·one ˏyear | and ·taking a ·year ˏoff ·working | em ‸ ˋnobody's making any ˇmoney during this ·course | ·so ‸ if I've ˋgone to the ·trouble of ˇgetting the M·A | I'd ˋlike to be ·able to ˋuse it | in my ˋjob ||

[HK] ˬyeah | I su·ppose you've ·got a point ˬthere ||

[RG] ·and on the ˇother hand | ↑if ‸ you are ·going to ·work for a ·lower ˏsalary | or in a less dyˋnamic ˬatmosphere | I ˋreally ·do think | it's ˉbetter to work for a ˋvoluntary ·organi·sation | like ·VSˋO | ·rather than ·work for a ·private ˬcompany | who just ˏsits there and | ·laps up the ˋmoney ||

[HK] that's ˏtrue || ˋah | there's ·something ·here for ˊˇLibya || ˋI had a ‸ Sudaˋnese friend who ·went to ˏLibya || I met him ˋhere | the other ˎday | he's on ·one of the ‸ sh...short ˋstudy skills ·courses || ˋhe went to ·Libya while ˋI was in Su·dan || he was ‸ iˇnitially | on a ‸ ˋthree year ˋcontract | but in the ˊend | he only ˋstayed about six ˏmonths || ˋhe said it was a ˋterrible place | he ·absolutely ˋhated it || he said there were ˊshortages | in the ˊshops all the ·time | he said there were reˋstrictions on ˊtravel | and the ˋschools were ˋvery poorly eˎquipped | ˋjust like in Suˬdan | if not ˋworse || ˋand I suppose ˇalso | ˎlife for a Euroˇpean wouldn't be too ·pleasant | ·and if ‸ ˋhe as a ·practising ˇMuslim didn't ·like it | then I ˋdon't really ·think that a | ˉwhite female Euroˋpean would ‸ a·dapt very ·well ||

[RG] ˎhmm | I'm ˋsure you're ˎright || so he ˉdidn't ˋfinish the ·three year ·contract ||

[HK] ˍno | he went ˉback to Suˏdan | and ·then came ·here in | ˋJanuary ||

[RG] and they ˉdidn't cause any ˋproblems about ·not com·pleting the ·contract ||

[HK] I ˋdon't ˬthink so | I ·think the Suda·nese ·more or less ·left en ˋmasse ||

[RG] ˋyou worked in the Suˏdan | ˋdidn't you ||

[HK] ˋyes | I ˎdid | I was ·there for ‸ ˊthree years || I ·went in ·nineteen eighty-ˊthree | and ·stayed un·til about ·nineteen ‸ eighty-ˎsix || alˇthough | the ·academic ˋyear in Suˬdan | is ˋnot very ·long | in ˋfact you ·don't get ˋstarted un·til | ˉAugust Sepˊtember | ˉthen you have a ˏbreak of | ˋup to four ˏweeks | ·sometime in Deˊcember | ↑and ˍthen | ↑you ·finish ˍteaching | ↑aˍround the ·end of ˎMarch || there are ˋno hard and | ˎfast | ˇdeadlines | ˉso | you've got about ˉtwenty ˍweeks | to ‸ ·cover your ˋsyllabus | and ˋI found it | ·just wasn't ˋlong e·nough || you ˋjust couldn't get ·anything ˋdone ||

[RG] i... ‸ ↑does ˋthat happen ·both in ‸ uni·versities ˇand schools | or is it ↓¯just the uni ˎversity ||

[HK] I ˋthink the uniˇversity is | ˬpossibly | even ˎworse || while ˬI was ·there with | the ‸ poˬlitical situ·ation | the ·university was on ˎstrike | for ‸ ·much of the ˎtime ||

[RG] so between ¯March and Sepˎtember | there is no ˋschooling as ·such ||

[HK] ¯no | not at ˎall || I ˋthink this is beˎcause | ˋpartly ˇanyway | be·cause of the ‸ ˋheat in Su·dan | and of ·course there's ¯no ˬair-conditioning | be·cause it's such a ‸ ¯poor ˬcountry | and it ˋis ¯very ˋdifficult ‸ to ·work ‸ under con·ditions like ·that | when the ·temperature's ˎwhat | ˊfifty de·grees ·centigrade | ˊsometimes ||

[RG] it's as ¯high as ˋthat ||

[HK] ˎyes | ¯very ˍhot inˎdeed ||

[RG] ˎhm | so ¯what do the ·children ˋdo during that ·time || do they ·do any sort of agriˊcultural ·work | or they ·just stay at ˋhome ||

[HK] I ˎthink the ‸ maˏjority | stay at ˆhome ||

[RG] ↑ˋthat seems ‸ fairly ˋboring

[HK] ˇyes | but ˋlife in Suˎdan is | ·very very ˋdifferent to | ·life in ˋthis country || a ˋlot of children ‸ ·finish ·school | ·after they've ·done ·six years ˋprimary | in ˎany case || ↑·I suppose the ˎchildren who come | from the ‸ mainly ˇrural ·districts but | the ·whole of Suˋdan is | a ˬrural district | I suppose ˎthey must ·do some ·work in the ˏfields ||

[RG] ˍyes | ↑I ‸ ↓I just paraˋllel that situˏation | with ˋChina where | as ˎsoon as the ·children are ¯out of ·school | or they have a ˬholiday | if they're ˋfrom the ˬcountryside | and ·still ·eighty per ·cent of the ·people ˋwork ˋin the ˏcountry | ·then ‸ they iˋmmediately go ˋinto working | ˋon the | ˏfarm | ·em ‸ ˋeven ˋif the ·temperature is quite ˋhigh || it ˋdoesn't get so ·high as the Suˬdan | but it ¯gets pretty ˇcold | and it gets ¯minus ˋtwenty ·in er | the ˎwinter | ·in Peˋking ||

[HK] and ¯how long were ˋyou there ·for ||

[RG] ·er ‸ ¯I was in _China | for ·nearly ¯five ˎyears || ·em ‸ ¯we _have | a ˋdifferent ·system | we ˋalso have ·two ˋterms | like ˎyou do in the Su˯dan | but ‸ ˋour terms are ·twenty weeks ˋlong | so in ·fact ‸ the ˋschooling is ˎtwice | what ˎyours ·is || ·em ‸ and alˋthough I have ·ample ˋtime to ·get through the ·work I ˇwant to get ·through | I have aˋnother ·problem | in ·that ‸ the ·students just cannot ˋconcentrate for ·twenty ·weeks | _nor can the ˋteachers | it's ·just too ˋlong || ·so ‸ ·like the ˎterm starts in Sepˇtember | and ·runs through till ˏJanuary | when we ·have ‸ Spring _Festival | which ·is the ‸ ·Chinese New ˏYear || now ˋschools and uni·versities will ·close for three ˋweeks | and that ·is a parˋticularly ˋcold time of the ˏyear | in the ˎNorth || and then the ·term starts a_gain | ·finishing at the ·end of ˋJune || ·and the ‸ ˋstudents will | ·have ¯two months ˏoff | in the ˋsummer || ↑but ‸ the ˋterms are just ¯really too ˎlong || by the ˋtime you hit ˇmidterm | ·after about ‸ the ¯tenth | or ¯eleventh ˎweek | the ˋstudents are ˯really | at an ¯all-time ˎlow | and it's ¯very ˎdifficult | to ˋmotivate them | ·into ‸ into ˎstudies a·gain ||

[HK] and ¯what do they ·do er | when they're ‸ on ˎholiday | during the ˎsummer | these two ˎmonths || do they ·work on the ˊland | do they ‸ (* unfinished tone group *)

[RG] ˏwell | ·em ‸ ˋthose that ˎcome from agri·cultural ˇfamilies | ˋwill work ˇon the ·land | ¯others | will ·probably just ·help the ˏfamily | ↑ˋquite a ˯lot of them | e·specially ¯at uni_versity | will ˎstudy || they ‸ ˇwill have to ·study | in ·order to ·get through the eˋxams | in ·order to ·get ‸ a good ˋjob || ·em ‸ the ˋpeople them˯selves | ˎdon't ·actually ¯get | ˇmany more ·days | than ˋsix | a ˎyear || they ˋjust get the ·national ˋholidays | they ¯don't ˋhave | ·er ‸ an ‸ an ·actual ·separate ˏholiday | un·less ‸ _em ‸ ·someone has ˏdied | or they're getting ˏmarried | in ¯which case they are a·llowed | some _extra time ˎoff ||

042 SPOKEN ENGLISH CORPUS TEXT J06
Kempson and Green dialogue
(Second part)
Recorded at MSU Lancaster University
Transcribed by BJW

[RG] does that ¯happen both in | _universities ˇand ·schools | or is it ·just the uni ˎversity ||

[HK] I ˋthink the uniˇversity is | ˇpossibly | even ˎworse || while ˇI was there with | the poˇlitical situ·ation | the ˋuniversity was on ˋstrike || ↓for ˋmuch of the ˋtime ||

[RG] so between ˋMarch and Sepˋtember there is no ˋschooling as such ||

[HK] ¯no | not at ˋall || I ˋthink this is be¯cause | ˋpartly ˇanyway because of the | ˋheat in Su·dan || and of ¯course there's no ˬair-conditioning because it's such a | ¯poor ˎcountry | and it is ˋvery ˋdifficult | to ·work | ↓under conˋditions like ˋthat | when the ˋtemperature's ·what | _fifty degrees ˊcentigrade sometimes ||

[RG] it's as ·high as ¯that ||

[HK] ˋyes | ˋvery ˋhot inˋdeed ||

[RG] ¯hm || so ¯what do the children ˋdo during that time do they | do any sort of | agri¯cultural work or they _just stay at ¯home ||

[HK] I ˋthink the ma¯jority stay at ˋhome ||

[RG] ↑that _seems | fairly ˋboring ||

[HK] ˇyes | but ¯life in Su_dan is ¯very very ˋdifferent to | ¯life in ˇthis country || a ˋlot of children | ˇfinish ·school | ¯after they've done ·six years ˋprimary | in ˋany case || I su¯ppose the children who _come | from the | mainly ˇrural districts but | the ˋwhole of Suˋdan is | a ˇrural district | I suppose ˎthey must | _do some work in the ˇfields ||

[RG] _yes ↑I | I just paraˋllel that situ·ation | with ˋChina where | as ¯soon as the ˎchildren are | out of ¯school | or they have a ¯holiday | ˋif they're from the ˋcountryside and | ↓still ·eighty per·cent of the people ↑¯work | ˇin the ·country | then | they iˋmmediately go into ¯working | ˇon the | ˇfarm | em | even ˋif the temperature is quite ˋhigh || it ˋdoesn't get so ˋhigh as the SuˋSudan | but it ¯gets pretty ˇcold | and it gets minus ˋtwenty in er | the ˋwinter || in Pe¯king ||

[HK] and ¯how long were ˋyou there for ||

[RG] er || ¯I was in ˍChina for nearly ¯five ˍyears || ¯em | ¯we ˍhave | a ˋdifferent | system we ˋalso have two ˋterms like ˋyou do in the Suˋdan || but ˋour terms are ˋtwenty weeks ˋlong so in fact | the ˋschooling is ˋtwice what ˋyours is || em | and al·though I have ·ample ↑ˋtime to get through the ·work I ˋwant to get through I have aˋnother problem | in that | the ·students just cannot ↑ˋconcentrate for twenty ·weeks || ˍnor can the ˋteachers | it's just too ˋlong || ˍso | ·like | the ˋterm starts in Sepˇtember | and ˍruns through till ˏJanuary | when we ˍhave | Spring ˍFestival which is the ¯Chinese New ·Year || now ¯schools and uni·versities will ·close for three ˋweeks || and that is a parˋticularly ˋcold time of the ·year | in the ˋNorth || and then the ·term starts again ·finishing at the end of ↑ˋJune || and | the ˋstudents will have ˋtwo months off in the ˋsummer || ↑but | the ˋterms are just ˋreally too ˋlong || by the ˋtime you hit ↑ˋmid·term | after about the ¯tenth or e·leventh ¯week || the ˋstudents are ˋreally at | an ˋall-time ˋlow || and it's ˋvery ˋdifficult to ˋmotivate them | ˇinto | into ˎstudies a·gain ||

[HK] and ¯what do they ·do | ˍwhen they're | on ˋholiday during the ˋsummer these two ·months | do they ·work on the ¯land | do they |

[RG] ˊwell | ˍem | ˋthose that ˋcome from agricultural ˋfamilies ˋwill ·work | ˇon the ·land || ¯others ˍwill | probably just ˇhelp the family || ¯quite a ˋlot of them | e¯specially at uniˍversity will ˋstudy || they | ˋwill have to ·study in order to get through the eˋxams in order to get | a good ˋjob || em | the ˋpeople themˋselves | ¯don't actually ˍget | ˋmany more ¯days than ˋsix | a ˋyear || they ¯just ·get | the ˍnational ˋholidays they don't ˋhave | er | an an actual ˇseparate holiday un·less | em | someone has ¯died | or | they're getting ¯married | in which ¯case they are a·llowed | some ¯extra time ˎoff ||

[HK] so they ˋdon't have any reˋligious holidays in ·China ||

[RG] ˋno | ¯em || ˋmost of the country is ˋnot | a reˋligious country obviously it being a ·Communist ˋstate || ¯some allowances ↑¯are ˍmade for those miˇnorities | ·such as over | in the southˇwest of ·China | around Yuˇnnan province | ·where | there are a lot of ˋBuddhists || but | ¯no particular reˍligious holidays are held as ˎsuch ||

[HK] ah that's ˋtotally unlike Suˋdan | because ·obviously Suˇdan is | ·by and large a ˇMuslim country | and of course ˇthere you | don't have ˇvery many ·holidays | but | the month of ˇRamadan | when people are ˉfasting | from ˋsunrise to sunˉset | every ·day | then ˋvery little work ˋdoes get done || and ·then there are the ˉtwo | ˉIids ↓or | reˇligious festivals | and alˇthough these | ·only | ·last a few ˇdays | in fact ˇtravelling time | to get ·back to see your ˇfamily | can ·add on another ˋweek or ·more || because of course ˋtravelling in the Suˋdan is extremely ˋdifficult || for ˉone thing | there are no ˉroads || and for a_nother the | public ˋtransport system is ·very very | ·poor || there ·are ˉbuses | but ·these are | usually conˋverted ·Bedford ˉtrucks || and | ↑ˋmost people in ·fact | travel by ˋlorry ||

[RG] so | did you enˋjoy working in the Su·dan | on the ·whole ||

[HK] oh very ˋmuch so ·yes | ·yes I ˋdid deˋspite the | ˋdifficult conˉditions | and of ˉcourse having to a_dapt to a Muslim ˋculture | was not ˋeasy || parˋticularly being a ˋwoman || I _found that | I ˋwas treated | ˋreasonably ˉwell | and I was ·treated ˇmore or less | as an ·honorary ˋmale || er ||

[RG] in ˉwhat _ways did you have to ˋchange | in ·order to | get ˋused to that kind of ·culture ||

[HK] ↑well I su_ppose | ˏdressing | was quite an imˏportant | ˏfactor || _obviously you couldn't ·walk around with bare ˉarms | and _also you ·had to have | a ˉskirt of a reasonable ˏlength || ↑but | ·strangely eˋnough this was | ˋmore or less the ·same for | European ˋmale teachers || I remember ˋonce | there was one ˋyoung teacher in El Oˋbeid | who went ˉout to the | ˋcorner shop | wearing his ˋshorts | and | he was given a ˋreal dressing-·down | ↓by ·someone | for | ˋflaunting his ˋbody || because ˉbodies are _not considered to be very ˋnice ·things ||

[speech extract omitted]

[RG] ↑by comˋparison in Afghaniˋstan | the ˉwomen _there had to ˉwear | the ˋveil || from ·head to ˋtoe | eˉspecially the women from _outside | the ˋcapital || ˉonly my ˋstudents there were a·llowed to wear European ˋdress || so that | if I went ˋout into the ˋvillages just outˋside the ·capital | I would ˉalways find the ·women ˋcovered in the | what was called the 'chadaˋree' | ˋcovered from ˉhead | to ˎtoe || in fact ˉI | ·tried one of them ˎon | just to ˉsee what it was ˉreally ˋlike | to be beˋhind one of those ·things || and in

Afghaniˎstan | what they ˎwear | it ˉhas this small ˋgrille-like ˉfeature over the ˬeyes | so that ˉyou can see ˍout and | ˉother people of ·course can't see ˋin || but ˋwhat was really quite aˋmusing is that the ˋwomen who ˇwore them | would ˉoften ˍwear ˋvery nice ˋshoes | at the ˋbottom | to sort of ˉshow that they | were ˋtrying to be | more ˋWesternised even though their ˋhusbands and ˋfamily didn't aˋllow them || ↑did ˉyou have that | ↑situ·ation at all | outˊside the main ·cities ||

[HK] ˋno | not ˇreally || it was | the ˋtobe was | ˇmore or less | uniˋversal || and it was ˋawfully ˋhot || ˇmost of them were made of ˋnylon | and imˋported | which ˋI found ˋvery ·very ˋstrange || ˇI tried one on ·once | and I found it ˋquite unˋbearable || ˉwhat was it ·like in·side this | ˋchador ||

[RG] em | it | it ˉwasn't very ˎhot | because of ˉcourse we didn't have the ˎheat | problem in ˋAfghanistan that | ˋyou have in the Suˋdan || em | I ˉfelt | like | ˉother people couldn't ˎsee me | but ˉI could see ˎthem || it's a ˉvery very ˍstrange ˋfeeling || em | but ˉany European who ·tried to ˋwear ·one | actually ˋout in the ˋstreets | could be ˋrecognised iˉmmediately from the way they ˋwalked || because the way a Euroˋpean woman ·walks | is quite ˋdifferent from how the ˋAfghan women | ·walked || but it was ˋpart of the Muslim ˉlaw ˍthere that the ˉwomen | ˍwore | ·those | ˉthings to cover themˍselves ||

[HK] it was ·actually ˉlaw did you have anything ·like | Iˍslamic Shaˊria Law ||

[RG] ↑ˉwell | it ˉwasn't particularly | ˍnoticeable in the ˋcapital as I ˋsay | but I'm sure ˋout in the ˋcountryside | you would never ˋsee women | unless ˉyou ˍwere re·lated to the ˎfamily || if ˉyou were a | a ˉEuropean ˎman | and you ˉwent to visit a ˍstudent you would not ˋsee | that student's ˉwife | or | ·that student's ˋsister ||

[HK] ˉdid they have | Iˉslamic ˬpenalties | for | oˊffending | ·such as | ˏflogging || I ˉknow in Suˎdan | they ·brought in | Shaˋria Law | ˋsoon after I aˋrrived in | September nineteen eighty-ˋthree || and of ˉcourse this ˎmeant that there was | no ˏalcohol | there was ˉno | ˍdriving with a | ˉmember of the ·opposite ˎsex || ˋthis was for | Sudaˋnese people | but of ˉcourse | ˋyou as a ˋforeigner | could ˋnot be seen | in the ˇsame car | with a ˉSudanese ˎman || it was a ˋvery ·strange | ˋperiod in ·fact || ˋvery very faˋnatical in the beˋginning || but | of ˍcourse there were | ˉways and ˍmeans of | ˉgetting ˍround these ·things ||

[RG] ˉwas it like | the | faˉnaticism we ˍhear about | in Iˋran was it ˋthat kind of thing ||

[HK] ˉnot | ˍreally I don't ˉthink ˍso because in Suˋdan | the maˇjority of the ·Muslims are | ˋSunni Muslims || and I beˋlieve in Iˋran they're ˋShiah || I | ˋdon't know the eˋxact difference between the ˋtwo || but | Shaˉria ˎLaw | was ˉcertainly very ˎstrong in | Suˉdan nevertheˎless ||

[RG] in Afghaniˋstan they were mainly ˋSunni as ˋwell just like in the Suˉdan | ·very few ˎShiah || unˉlike | ·neighbouring Iˋran || em | we ˋdidn't have ˋany Christians at ˋall there || ˉjust | the Euroˇpeans | who were ˋworking there ||

[speech extract omitted]

[RG] ↑how did you ˋget that ·job in the ˋfirst ·place ||

[HK] ˉI ˍsaw an adˋvertisement | in the | ˋGuardian || I beˋlieve that they | ·advertise every ˋyear || they ˉask ˍfor | ˋgraduates || native ˋspeakers of ˏEnglish || ˇany discipline | it doesn't ˉreally ˍmatter || and | that's ˋit || you don't ˉhave to ˍhave ˉany ˏteaching qualifi·cations || and a ˋlot of young ˋpeople | ˎgo || either beˍcause | they don't ˉquite know what they ·want to do | or they ˍcan't find a ˊjob | and unˇfortunately there ˇare some | who have ˉabsolutely ˍno commitment to ˉteaching whatsoˎever || they are ˉthere because it's | an ˍeasy thing to ·do | it's ˍinteresting | it's ˉsomething to ˍtell your ˍfriends a·bout | because ˇmost of them | only ˍstay for | one ˎyear || which | doesn't ˋreally do ˇthem any ·good | and ˍcertainly doesn't do Suˋdan any good || I ˇreally think that | the ˋgovernment ·policy there is quite ˋwrong || well it's ˉnot ˎgovernment | it's the ˋMinistry of Eduˋcation || but | I ˍdon't think they'll be ˋtold ||

[RG] ↑unˍfortunately ·that situ·ation o·ccurs in ˉmany ˎcountries ˋdoesn't it || for eˍxample even in ˋChina | well e↑ˆspecially in China I think because ˉnow that ˍChina | ˇhas opened up to the ·West | ˉlots of ˍteachers want to ˇgo there | to ˍwork | and ˉlots of people want to ·go there just as ˋyou have said er | just for a ˋholiday || em | ˋeven in my own uniˋversity where | ˋI worked in Shangˇhai | ˍI would say | probably ˋthree out of the ˋten teachers that were ˇthere | were | coˇmmitted | to ˏteaching || whereas the other ˋseven were very ·much more ˋinterested in | ˉwhere they could ˍgo on their ˉweekends | on their ˉholidays | how many ·days they could take ˉoff without | ·causing any ˍproblems | and | aˉgain | ˉmany of them were _there just for the one `year || they didn't `stay very long `I was unˇusual in | in ¯staying as long as I `did ||

[HK] I `see || ↑what about `travelling in ·China || was ´that easy ||

[RG] `actually it `was || ↑`not at the beˇginning || but | em | ¯after a_bout ¯eight ˎmonths || I'd ·been there ¯eight ˎmonths | _and | the ·law `changed || you see when ˇI arrived | ¯foreigners were ·not allowed to travel ˇanywhere in ·China | without a `permit ||

[HK] and was it ´easy to get a ·permit ||

[RG] ´well you _had to ·ask your | Foreign Aˇffairs Office || that ¯means you had to go to somebody `in your university and ask ˇthem || and if they a¯greed | then you could go ·down to the poˇlice station | and ¯they would give you a `permit || to _travel | to a ¯certain place which you ·named | on a _certain _day | by a ¯certain type of `transport || in ¯other _words they wanted to ·know the e¯xact ˎdetails | of ¯where you would _be at any given `time || now I `think it was in Oc`tober eighty-`two that ·policy suddenly `changed || it's _something to do with the ¯open door ¯policy || _and | `after that ˇtime | you could ¯travel to `twenty-seven cities without a `permit || so you could ¯actually ·walk _down to the `railway station and ↑ˇbuy a ticket and _jump on a `train | and you ¯can't be`lieve || I _know we take this for `granted | in ˇEngland | that | `oh I'll just go `home for the week`end | but in `China | `you were just not `able to ↑`do that || you're not a`llowed to ·do that || and `suddenly to be `given that ↑`freedom ||

[speech extract omitted]

[HK] _very different to Suˇdan || ¯travel is | not a ˇproblem there | admittedly `foreigners were suˇpposed to have ·travel permits | but ˇI | `never got one | in ¯all of my three `years || and I ˏtravelled the ·length and ¯breadth of the `country || ¯no policemen ever _stopped me and ¯asked me || ↑po`licemen ˇstopped me | when they ¯saw me in ˇvillages | _asked me what I was ¯doing and | _where I was ˇfrom || but they ·never ˏasked to see | ¯even so _much as a `passport ||

[RG] did you ¯have to _carry | like er | an `internal ´residence ·card ||

[HK] ˇyes | I ¯had ˬthat | that was _stuck inside my `passport || but I ˇnever | ¯took my | `passport when I was ·travelling with me || I just ˏused to ex·plain | who I ¯was | what I was ´doing | why I was ´there | and they'd

ˋlove just sort of | ·sitting ˋround and ˅chatting and | bringing ¯cups of ˏtea | ˋand of course ˅some of them had | ·little | ¯stashes of ˎalcohol || ˋso we would ˋsit in the po¯lice station and | ·have a few ˋdrinks ||

[RG] and ¯you were talking to them in ˅English ||

[HK] ˎwell || ¯broken ˎArabic || ·not par˅ticularly fluent but | ¯I could ˎmanage || and ¯that | I ˅also | I ˋthink made it a lot ˋeasier || had I ˅not spoken any ·Arabic | then their ·attitude towards this ·strange ˅foreign woman | ˋmight have been totally ˋdifferent ||

[RG] that was | eˋxactly the same ·case in ˋChina || ¯speaking Chi_nese | you could ¯get | ˋlots of things that you ˋwouldn't be able to get | you'd be ·able to go to ¯lots of _places that | the ˅normal | ¯tourists wouldn't be able to ˋgo to || in ¯China we had ·two _cards | a ˅residence card | and | a ˋwork card || now the ˋwork card that ˋI carried was the same as ¯every _Chinese ˎcitizen || ¯every ·Chinese _citizen has | a ¯work _card | it's ˬred | and it ¯shows your ˋunit | ¯this is the _place where you ˋwork | and it's ¯sort of | like the ˋinternal passport for Chiˋnese an iˋdentity ·card if you ·like || and | theo˅retically we were su·pposed to carry a·round | the ˋresidence card which is ˋgreen | ˋand the ·red card as ˋwell || but ¯most people who | could ˅speak Chi·nese | just ·showed the ˋred card || but you ˋhad to show these unlike ˋyour situation | if you ·wanted to go to a hoˊtel to stay | if you ·wanted to buy a ˊtrain ticket | or a ˊbus ticket | you had to ¯show these _things if you ¯wanted to change ¯money or ˋanything like that || you had to ¯show those ˬcards || and if you ¯didn't ˎhave them | then you had to be ˋvery very good at ˋarguing in Chiˋnese || in _order to | ˅you know | get a¯way with | not ˋhaving the ˋdocuments || of ↑ˋcourse || it | ¯did lead to a _growth of | ˎfalse cards || the ¯tourists that came _in from ¯other parts of ˎAsia | you know _travelling on a ˊshoestring | they ¯soon _learned that if you ˋhad these ˋcards | it eˋnabled you to get a reˋduction on the ˋtrains || you see ˋI didn't ·pay the full ˋprice on the ·trains || I didn't pay the Chiˋnese price ˋeither | I paid ¯somewhere in beˋtween || so ˋprobably I had ˋthirty percent ˋoff | ↓the ˋtrain | er ˋticket ||

[HK] and was | ¯travelling very exˊpensive | ↓or | ˎnot ||

[RG] ↑I su·ppose in com_parison to ˋEngland | ˋnot very ·much | ˋno || em | the ˋtrains there were ·very ˋgood | I must adˋmit | very e˅fficient || er | the ¯problem was _getting | the ˎtrain ticket ||

[HK] ¯I ˍsee || I suˍppose that was the ·problem too in Suˋdan || they ˋdid have ˇtrains | they ¯might | ˍcome and they might ˇnot || they could be a ¯day late | or ·five ¯hours late | or ˬtwelve hours late || but they ˋusually came in the ˇend || you ˋhad to buy your ˋticket before | the ·train ˋcame a few ↑ˋdays before || and ˍbook a ˋseat || but | the thing ˍwas you often ˋfound | that al·though you had | a reˋserved seat | ↑that | there ˍjust wouldn't be ·room on the ˋtrain || but as a ˇforeigner | aˇgain | ˍpeople would often | ¯make ˍway for you || ↑which | I ¯didn't | ˍlike in ˎsome respects || ˋobviously it was | very conˋvenient | but | to be ˋtreated ˋdifferently simply be¯cause | you were a ˇforeigner | is | ↑¯quite unˎpleasant ||

042 SPOKEN ENGLISH CORPUS TEXT J06
Kempson and Green dialogue
Recorded at MSU Lancaster University
Overlap passage

Transcribed by BJW

[RG] does that ˉhappen both in | ˍuniversities ˇand ·schools | or is it ·just the uni ˎversity ||

[HK] I ˋthink the uniˇversity is | ˇpossibly | even ˎworse || while ˇI was there with | the poˇlitical situ·ation | the ˋuniversity was on ˋstrike || ↓for ˋmuch of the ˋtime ||

[RG] so between ˋMarch and Sepˋtember there is no ˋschooling as such ||

[HK] ˉno | not at ˋall || I ˋthink this is beˉcause | ˋpartly ˇanyway because of the | ˋheat in Su·dan || and of ˉcourse there's no ˬair-conditioning because it's such a | ˉpoor ˎcountry | and it is ˋvery ˋdifficult | to ·work | ↓under conˋditions like ˋthat | when the ˋtemperature's ·what | ˍfifty degrees ˊcentigrade sometimes ||

[RG] it's as ·high as ˉthat ||

[HK] ˋyes | ˋvery ˋhot inˋdeed ||

[RG] ˉhm || so ˉwhat do the children ˋdo during that time do they | do any sort of | agriˉcultural work or they ˍjust stay at ˉhome ||

[HK] I ˋthink the maˉjority stay at ˋhome ||

[RG] ↑that ˍseems | fairly ˋboring ||

[HK] ˇyes | but ˉlife in Suˍdan is ˉvery very ˋdifferent to | ˉlife in ˇthis country || a ˋlot of children | ˇfinish ·school | ˉafter they've done ·six years ˋprimary | in ˋany case || I suˉppose the children who ˍcome | from the | mainly ˇrural districts but | the ˋwhole of Suˋdan is | a ˇrural district | I suppose ˎthey must | ˍdo some work in the ˇfields ||

[RG] ˍyes ↑I | I just paraˋllel that situ·ation | with ˋChina where | as ˉsoon as the ˎchildren are | out of ˉschool | or they have a ˉholiday | ˋif they're from the ˋcountryside and | ↓still ·eighty per·cent of the people ↑ˉwork | ˇin the ·country | then | they iˋmmediately go into ˉworking |

ˇon the | ˇfarm | em | even ˋif the temperature is quite ˋhigh || it ˋdoesn't get so ˋhigh as the Suˋdan | but it ¯gets pretty ˇcold | and it gets minus ˋtwenty in er | the ˋwinter || in Pe¯king ||

[HK] and ¯how long were ˋyou there for ||

[RG] er || ¯I was in _China for nearly ¯five _years || ¯em | ¯we _have | a ˋdifferent | system we ˋalso have two ˋterms like ˋyou do in the Suˋdan || but ˋour terms are ˋtwenty weeks ˋlong so in fact | the ˋschooling is ˋtwice what ˋyours is || em | and al·though I have ·ample ↑ˋtime to get through the ·work I ˋwant to get through I have aˋnother problem | in that | the ·students just cannot ↑ˋconcentrate for twenty ·weeks || _nor can the ˋteachers | it's just too ˋlong || _so | ·like | the ˋterm starts in Sepˇtember | and _runs through till ˏJanuary | when we _have | Spring _Festival which is the ¯Chinese New ·Year || now ¯schools and uni·versities will ·close for three ˋweeks || and that is a parˋticularly ˋcold time of the ·year | in the ˋNorth || and then the ·term starts again ·finishing at the end of ↑ˋJune || and | the ˋstudents will have ˋtwo months off in the ˋsummer || ↑but | the ˋterms are just ˋreally too ˋlong || by the ˋtime you hit ↑ˋmid·term | after about the ¯tenth or e·leventh ¯week || the ˋstudents are ˋreally at | an ˋall-time ˋlow || and it's ˋvery ˋdifficult to ˋmotivate them | ˇinto | into ˎstudies a·gain ||

[HK] and ¯what do they ·do | _when they're | on ˋholiday during the ˋsummer these two ·months | do they ·work on the ¯land | do they |

[RG] ˊwell | _em | ˋthose that ˋcome from agricultural ˋfamilies ˋwill ·work | ˇon the ·land || ¯others _will | probably just ˇhelp the family || ¯quite a ˋlot of them | e¯specially at uni_versity will ˋstudy || they | ˋwill have to ·study in order to get through the eˋxams in order to get | a good ˋjob || em | the ˋpeople themˋselves | ¯don't actually _get | ˋmany more ¯days than ˋsix | a ˋyear || they ¯just ·get | the _national ˋholidays they don't ˋhave | er | an an actual ˇseparate holiday un·less | em | someone has ¯died | or | they're getting ¯married | in which ¯case they are a·llowed | some ¯extra time ˎoff ||

Transcribed by GOK

[RG] ‸ ↑does ˋthat happen ·both in ‸ uni·versities ˇand schools | or is it ↓¯just the uniˎversity ||

[HK] I ˋthink the uniˇversity is | ˬpossibly | even ˎworse || while ˬI was ·there with | the ‸ poˬlitical situ·ation | the ·university was on ˎstrike | for ‸ ·much of the ˎtime ||

[RG] so between ˉMarch and Sepˎtember | there is no ˋschooling as ·such ||

[HK] ˉno | not at ˎall || I ˋthink this is beˎcause | ˋpartly ˇanyway | be·cause of the ‸ ˋheat in Su·dan | and of ·course there's ˉno ˬair-conditioning | be·cause it's such a ‸ ˉpoor ˬcountry | and it ˋis ˉvery ˋdifficult ‸ to ·work ‸ under con·ditions like ·that | when the ·temperature's ˎwhat | ˊfifty de·grees ·centigrade | ˊsometimes ||

[RG] it's as ˉhigh as ˋthat ||

[HK] ˎyes | ˉvery ˍhot inˎdeed ||

[RG] ˎhm | so ˉwhat do the ·children ˋdo during that ·time || do they ·do any sort of agriˊcultural ·work | or they ·just stay at ˋhome ||

[HK] I ˎthink the ‸ maˏjority | stay at ˆhome ||

[RG] ↑ˋthat seems ‸ fairly ˋboring

[HK] ˇyes | but ˋlife in Suˎdan is | ·very very ˋdifferent to | ·life in ˋthis country || a ˋlot of children ‸ ·finish ·school | ·after they've ·done ·six years ˋprimary | in ˎany case || ↑·I suppose the ˎchildren who come | from the ‸ mainly ˇrural ·districts but | the ·whole of Suˋdan is | a ˬrural district | I suppose ˎthey must ·do some ·work in the ˏfields ||

[RG] ˍyes | ↑I ‸ ↓I just paraˋllel that situˏation | with ˋChina where | as ˎsoon as the ·children are ˉout of ·school | or they have a ˬholiday | if they're ˋfrom the ˬcountryside | and ·still ·eighty per ·cent of the ·people ˋwork ˋin the ˏcountry | ·then ‸ they iˋmmediately go ˋinto working | ˋon the | ˏfarm | ·em ‸ ˋeven ˋif the ·temperature is quite ˋhigh || it ˋdoesn't get so ·high as the Suˬdan | but it ˉgets pretty ˇcold | and it gets ˉminus ˋtwenty ·in er | the ˎwinter | ·in Peˋking ||

[HK] and ˉhow long were ˋyou there ·for ||

[RG] ·er ‸ ˉI was in ˍChina | for ·nearly ˉfive ˎyears || ·em ‸ ˉwe ˍhave | a ˋdifferent ·system | we ˋalso have ·two ˋterms | like ˎyou do in the Suˬdan | but ‸ ˋour terms are ·twenty weeks ˋlong | so in ·fact ‸ the

ˋschooling is ˎtwice | what ˎyours ·is || ·em ∧ and alˋthough I have ·ample ˋtime to ·get through the ·work I ˇwant to get ·through | I have aˋnother ·problem | in ·that ∧ the ·students just cannot ˋconcentrate for ·twenty ·weeks | ˍnor can the ˋteachers | it's ·just too ˋlong || ·so ∧ ·like the ˎterm starts in Sepˇtember | and ·runs through till ˏJanuary | when we ·have ∧ Spring ˍFestival | which ·is the ∧ ·Chinese New ˏYear || now ˋschools and uni·versities will ·close for three ˋweeks | and that ·is a parˋticularly ˋcold time of the ˏyear | in the ˎNorth || and then the ·term starts aˍgain | ·finishing at the ·end of ˋJune || ·and the ∧ ˋstudents will | ·have ˉtwo months ˏoff | in the ˋsummer || ↑but ∧ the ˋterms are just ˉreally too ˎlong || by the ˋtime you hit ˇmidterm | ·after about ∧ the ˉtenth | or ˉeleventh ˎweek | the ˋstudents are ˬreally | at an ˉall-time ˎlow | and it's ˉvery ˎdifficult | to ˋmotivate them | ·into ∧ into ˎstudies a·gain ||

[HK] and ˉwhat do they ·do er | when they're ∧ on ˎholiday | during the ˎsummer | these two ˎmonths || do they ·work on the ˊland | do they ∧ (* unfinished tone group *)

[RG] ˏwell | ·em ∧ ˋthose that ˎcome from agri·cultural ˇfamilies | ˋwill work ˇon the ·land | ˉothers | will ·probably just ·help the ˏfamily | ↑ˋquite a ˬlot of them | e·specially ˉat uniˍversity | will ˎstudy || they ∧ ˇwill have to ·study | in ·order to ·get through the eˋxams | in ·order to ·get ∧ a good ˋjob || ·em ∧ the ˋpeople themˬselves | ˎdon't ·actually ˉget | ˇmany more ·days | than ˋsix | a ˎyear || they ˋjust get the ·national ˋholidays | they ˉdon't ˋhave | ·er ∧ an ∧ an ·actual ·separate ˏholiday | un·less ∧ ˍem ∧ ·someone has ˏdied | or they're getting ˏmarried | in ˉwhich case they are a·llowed | some ˍextra time ˎoff ||

043 SPOKEN ENGLISH CORPUS TEXT K01
Week's Good Cause
Broadcast notes: Radio 4, 8.50 a.m., 18th January, 1987
Transcribed by GOK

·good ˎmorning || ^every ·three ˏmonths | ˉhere on Radio ˏFour | I preˉsent a ˏprogramme ·called ‸ ˋWork·force || it's a ˋquarterly ˉbulletin | ·on emˎployment | ˉnot ˬunemployment | emˋployment || and I'm ˋalways ·careful to exˎplain | that the ˇworkforce consists of | ˉone | ·those who are emˬployed | ˉtwo | ·those who are ˇself em·ployed | and ˉthree | ·those who are ˋunemployed || ˏlast ·year | the ˏworkforce ˋgrew || at the ·end of the ˊyear | there were ·more of ˊone | and of ˉtwo | and ˉfewer of ˎthree | ↓·not ˇmany ·fewer | but ˉnonetheˍless | ˉsome of ˍthose | who'd been ˉseeking ˍwork | had ˎfound it || and ˇone of ·them | was a ˉboy called ˋStephen || ↑ˉStephen left ˎschool ·last ·year || now ˉunemˍployment | a·mong school ˎleavers | as I'm ˉsure you ˍknow | is ˉvery ˎhigh || ˉone in ˬfour ·teenagers | over the ˉcountry as a ˏwhole | is ˍout of ˎwork || ·that's the ˋnational ˋaverage || and of ·course the proˋportion is ˇhigher | in ·areas of ˍhigh unemˋployment || it's even ˋworse if you're ˎblack || it's ·almost ˉone in ˋtwo || ˉevery ˍother | ˋblack ·teenager in ˎBritain | is ·out of ˋwork || and al·though ‸ ·unem·ployment at ˋany age | is a ˋtribuˇlation | it ·does seem e·specially ·un·fair to the ˋyoung || ·after all ˉthey ˎcan not be ·blamed in any ↑ˋway | for a·llowing it to ˋhappen || and it is ·such a ·rotten ˎstart to ·life || a ·job ˋmay not ·be | the ˋbe-all | and the ˋend-all | but it ˋdoes make you ·feel ˋuseful || ˋanyway | ˉStephen deˍcided | that he was ˋgoing to ·get a ˎjob || and he ˋhit u·pon the iˏdea | of ˋleaving ·school at ˇEaster | in·stead of ˋwaiting un·til Juˬly | so that he would be aˉpplying for ˏjobs | be·fore ˉall his conˏtemporaries | came ˍonto the ˎmarket || he ˉhadn't ˋtaken his ·final eˇxams | but he's ˎbright | and he deˉcided | that he would ˋjob hunt ·during the ˉday | ˉswot at ˏnight | and ·hope to ·organise ·things so that he could ˉstart ˍwork | the ·moment he'd ·finished his eˋxams || there was ˉonly one ˎproblem || he had ˉno ˎmoney || he ˋdidn't ·want to ·sponge off his ˏmother | be·cause there ˋwasn't much ·coming into the ˋhome || so he ˉwent to the ˍlocal | ·DHSˋS ·office | ˊtold them | that he'd ˉleft ˏschool | had a·pplied for ˉten ˏjobs | and ˏplease | was he enˍtitled to any ˋmoney | to help ·pay for his ˋfares to the ˎinterviews | and a ·new ˋshirt | and ·so that he could give ˍsomething to his ˋmother | for his ˋkeep || ˉnot ‸ un·til Sepˎtember ‸ they ·said || and ˋthis was ˋApril || but the ˉDHSˏS | was ˋwrong || ˉStephen was enˏtitled | to ˉeighteen ˏpounds | ˉtwenty ·pence a ˎweek | to ·help him ˋlook for ·work | ˉas he diˏscovered | when ↑he ·sought the adˍvice | of ˉYouthˎaid | which is an ˉorgani·sation | which ·helps ·young

ˉunemployed ˎpeople || ˊso | he ˉgot the ˏmoney | he ˉfound a ˏjob | ·albeit a ˉpart-ˇtime ·job | he ˉstarted ˏwork | he ˉstopped ·claiming ˏbenefit | and as he ˋsaid ·somewhat ˇruefully | he ˋnow had a ˇlittle ·money | and ˉstill the ˍtime | to ˋlook | for a ˋbetter ·job || ·oh and he ˋdid pass his eˬxams || ˉYouthˏaid | is a ˉsmall | ·national ˎcharity | ˉnow | ˉten years ˏold | ˉdedicated | as I ˎsaid | to ·helping ˉunemˍployed | ·young ˎpeople || ˊlast year | it ·helped ˋthousands of ·young ·people | ˉlike ˏStephen | to ˉget some ˏmoney | so that they could ˋlook for ·work | ·during the ˋsummer || ˇYouthaid | ·can't of ·course help ˋeverybody indiˇvidually | al·though it ·does its ˋbest | so it ˉalso camˏpaigns | for ˉchanges in the ˏrules | to ·help the ˏyoung | in their ˉhunt for ˏwork | get ·rid of ·some of the ˋbureau·cratic ˇhurdles | and it is ˋnow deˇveloping | the ˉfirst | ·national ˇdatabase | of ˉall | the ˉlocal | ·indeˇpendent ·groups | who ˇhelp ·young ·people | ·find an alˏternative | to ·YTˏS | or the ˋdole || it ˉalso | ˉargues the ˋcase for the ·young | in the ˉnational deˋbate | aˋbout em·ployment || and ˋall ·that | ˊhelping | adˏvising | perˏsuading | ˉcosts ˎmoney || ˉYouthˎaid | I can aˋssure you | is a ˇvery ·tightly ·run | ˋcharity || it never ·wastes a ˋpenny || it gets ˍnothing from ˏgovernment | ·nor would it ˋwant to | it ˋis indeˋpendent || but it ˉdoes ˍneed ˎmoney || and ˉif | like ˋme | you ·came onto the ˋlabour market | in the ˉdays of ˋfull em·ployment | when it ˋwasn't a ·matter of | ˋwill I ·get a ·job | but ·which job ·offer will I acˋcept | then I'm ˉsure you would ˍlike to con·tribute to its ˎwork || and ˉif | by ˉchance | you had a ˋstruggle your·self | ·finding a ·first ˏjob | you ·may be ·all the more ˬanxious | to ˎhelp || ˇeither ·way | ˉplease | will you ·send a doˉnation to ˎme | ˉBrian ˎRedhead | ·at ˆ ˉYouthˎaid | it's ˉall one ˎword | ˉYouthˎaid | ˉ9 | ˎPoland ˆ ·Street | ˉ9 | ˎPoland ˆ ·Street | ˉLondon | ˋW1ˬV | ˉ3 | ·DˎG | ˉLondon | ˋW1 | ˉV for ˍVictor | ˉ3 | ˉD for ˍDavid | ˉG for ˎGeorge || you'll ˉfind the aˍddress | on to·day's ˆ ˋRadio ·Four ˉpage | in the ·Radio ˊTimes | and if you have ˉCeefax on the ·telly | on the aˎddress page of ·Ceefax | which is page ˉone eight ˎnine || ˎso | ·please ˆ ˉsend ˎsomething || per·haps you would ·like to ·pop it in the ˋpost | on your ·way to ˎwork | in the ˎmorning ||

044 SPOKEN ENGLISH CORPUS TEXT K02
Week's Good Cause
Broadcast notes: Radio 4, 8.50 a.m., 25th January, 1987
Transcribed by BJW

↓good ˋmorning | I'd ¯like to _draw your aˏttention | to something a ˋlot of us · take for ˋgranted | our ˋhearing || we _set our aˊlarms | to wake ¯up | we _listen to the ¯radio | as _you are doing ˏnow || when the ˊkettle · whistles | we know the ˏwater has ˏboiled || we hear a ˋcar · coming | and its ¯warning ˋhorn or the ˋtelephone · ringing | and en_joy a · chat with our · friends and ˋfamily || ˏjust to ˏkeep in ˋtouch || wiˋthout our a¯bility to _hear | we would be ˋcut off from ¯many of our _everyday acˋtivities || ˋchildren ¯need to ˇhear · properly | so that · they can _learn to ˋspeak || ˋpatterns of ¯words and _speech de¯velop from ˋinfancy | as they try to ˋimitate | what they ˋhear || ˇdeafness | and ¯damaged ˏhearing | preˋvent them from coˋmmunicating · properly | and en_gender fruˋstration | and ˋanger || ↑be¯cause it's not ˎseen | ˋdeafness is ˋtruly the in¯visible ˎhandicap | ↓which ˋisolates · people || we're ˋlucky in ˇthis · country | that ¯many ˬspecialist services | are a¯vailable to iˋdentify · deafness | at an _early ¯age | ˋand to proˏvide | a¯ppropriate ˏtreatment | eˏquipment | and ¯special eduˇcational fa · cilities | if ˋneeded | to a¯ssist the _deaf to lead as ¯normal _life as ˋpossible || ˋsadly there are a ˋgreat number of ˏdeaf people ¯living in the de_veloping ˋworld | who're ˋnot so · lucky || many ˋdeaf children's conˏdition goes unˋrecognised | and they're ˏoften ˏtreated as being ˋmentally subˋnormal || Me¯nata ˏMalik | a ¯six-year-old ˇIndian · child | has been ˏdeaf since ˋbirth || her ˋparents are ¯very _poor | but are ¯sending Me_nata to a · special ˋschool for the · deaf || but they ¯can't a_fford a ˋhearing aid for her || ˋso | through a ˎscribe | her ¯mother wrote a ↑¯very _touching re_quest | to the ¯Common_wealth Soˏciety | for the ˋDeaf || ˏsaying | ¯please ex_tend your ¯helping _hands to¯wards my ↑¯deaf ˏdaughter | and ¯help her into the _world of ˋhearing | by doˋnating a ˋhearing de · vice || Meˋnata is · now ¯happily _using her ¯new ˏhearing aid at ˋschool || it is in preˋcisely ˋthese ˏareas | that the ¯Commonwealth Soˏciety for the ˏDeaf | has been ¯working for the _past twenty-five ˋyears || a¯ssisting ˏparents to · set up ˬschools for the · deaf | and enˏcouraging the ˏtraining for ¯teachers | of the ¯deaf | providing ¯much needed eˏquipment | and a¯bove _all | coˋoperating with ¯government deˏpartments | and ˋlocal ˇvoluntary organi · sations | to run ˋsurveys to iˋdentify the ˋcauses | and ˋprevalence | of ˎdeafness || ¯as a reˎsult | of ˋsurveys | · carried out in ¯West _Africa | ¯many _cases of ¯childhood ˏdeafness | were _found to be preˋventable || almost ¯twenty _children in ¯every _hundred | ¯under _fourteen · years of _age | ¯suffer from ˋear in·fections || ¯simple ˏtreatment | by ¯non-ˬmedical people | would preˋvent ·permanent ·deafness in ˇmany ·cases || the soˋciety has de¯vised | an ¯easy-to-_use diag¯nostic _chart | and a ¯simple ˎtreatment kit | costing ¯fifty _pounds | for ˋdistri·bution to help preˋvent ·deafness || ↑¯each _kit can treat ¯sixty in_fected ˋears | and has ¯helped to ·save the ˎhearing | of ˋmany ¯African ˎchildren || ˋso | ¯I'm here this ˏmorning | to ¯ask you to eˏnable | the ¯Commonwealth So_ciety for the ˏDeaf | to ¯give a _chance to ¯deaf ˏchildren in ·these ˏcountries to live ˋnormally || to be ˏeducated | to be able to coˇmmunicate | ↑and to be ˎtrained | so they can ¯earn their own ˎlivings || ¯ten _pounds can ·mean ¯so _much || ¯it can ˏpay | for a ¯small pack of ˏteaching aids | or ¯twelve ˎhearing aid ·cords || ˇfifty ·pounds | pays for a ˇtreatment ·kit | which ¯could _save the _hearing | of ¯sixty ˎchildren || and a ˋthousand ·pounds ˋcould pay for an ¯audi_ometer | to measure ˋhearing ·loss || ˋso | ¯if you'd ˬlike to send a do·nation | ¯send it to ˎme || ˏSusan ˏHampshire | the ¯Commonwealth So_ciety for the ˏDeaf || ¯Susan ˬHampshire | the ¯Commonwealth So_ciety for the ˏDeaf || ¯one o ˏfive | ˇGower Street | ¯one o ·five ˏGower Street | ¯London | ¯WC_1ˇE | ¯6AˎH || ˋLondon || ¯W_C¯1_E | ¯6_AˋH || the aˇddress | is on to¯day's _page of the ·Radio ˋTimes | so ¯don't ˎworry if you can't ·manage to write it ·down || ˇAccess | and ˇVisa donations | are ˇalso a·cceptable | ¯through the ˏcoupon | in the adˏvertisement in the ·Radio ˋTimes || ˋthank you ||

045 SPOKEN ENGLISH CORPUS TEXT M01
‘An unpleasant Nursemaid’
From: ‘Betjeman reads Betjeman’
Transcribed by BJW

the ¯sunlit ·weeks beˏtween | were ¯full of ˎmaids || ˋSarah | with ¯orange _wig and ¯horsy ˎteeth | was ˋso ·bad-tempered that she ¯scarcely ˎspoke | ¯Maud was my _hateful _nurse who ¯smelled of ˎsoap | and ¯forced me to eat _chewy bits of ˎfish | ˋthrusting me back to ˋbabyhood | with ˋthreats of ˋnappies ˋdummies and the ˋfeeding bottle || you’re ¯late for ˇdinner ·John || I ¯feel again that _awful ·feeling || ¯fear con_fused with ˎthrill || as I would ¯be un_buttoned | ¯bent a·cross her _starchy ·apron ¯screaming ˋdon’t ·Maud ˋdon’t | till ¯dissolution | ¯bed | and ˋkindly ¯fur | of ¯aged _uncomplaining ˎArchibald ||

045 SPOKEN ENGLISH CORPUS TEXT M01
'An unpleasant Nursemaid'
From: 'Betjeman reads Betjeman'
Transcribed by GOK

the ¯sunlit ·weeks be/tween | were ¯full of \maids | ↑\`Sarah | with ¯orange /wig | and ¯horsy _teeth | was ¯so _bad-/tempered | that she ¯scarcely \spoke || ¯Maud | was my ¯hateful \nurse | who ¯smelled of \soap | and \`forced me to ·eat ¯chewy bits of \`fish | ¯thrusting me ·back to \babyhood | with ·threats of /nappies | /dummies | and the \feeding ·bottle || ↑you're ¯late for ˇdinner ·John || I ¯feel a\gain | that ¯awful \feeling | ↑¯fear con_fused with \thrill | as ¯I would be un_buttoned | \`bent a·cross her ·starchy _apron | ¯screaming ↑\`don't Maud | \don't | till ↓¯disso\lution | ˇbed | and ¯kindly /fur | of \`aged | ¯uncom_plaining \Archibald ||

046 SPOKEN ENGLISH CORPUS TEXT M02
Motoring News
Broadcast notes: Radio 4, 8.55 a.m., 18th January, 1987
Transcribed by BJW

in ˋspite of the ·low | of the ˉslow ˬthaw | conˋditions are ˋprobably more ↑ˋdangerous on the ˉroads this ˏmorning | because ˋyesterday's ˋslush and ↑ˇsnow | is this ˍmorning's ˋice || in ˊKent | the ˉA ˍtwo six ˋfour is still ˋclosed at ↑ˇBlackham | as are ˉmany ˎside ·roads || and about a ˋdozen of the more ˋisolated ˇvillages | reˋmain cut ˋoff || aˍpart from the ˊweather | ˋgas and ˇwater main re·pairs | toˍgether with | ˋscheduled ˋweekend ˉwork | are ˋalso going to aˋffect the roads toˋday || and in ˇLondon | ex·pect ˋlong delays in ↑ˋChiswick || where the ˋwest·bound ˋelevated section of the Mˋfour | is ˉclosed for ˋmost of toˉday | and only a ˋsingle ˋeastbound lane is ˋopen || in ˋLancashire | ˋnorthbound traffic on the ·Mˋsix | will be reˋstricted to the ˋcentre lane ˇonly | between ˋjunctions ˇthirty-·one | and ·thirty-ˋtwo from ↑ˋPreston || to the ˉM fifty-ˍfive ˏintersection until ˍfour pˋm || and ˋyou can expect ˋlong ·queues ˋthere || at ˉten o'clock this ˏmorning | the ˉThames Valley poˏlice are diˉverting ·all ˋnorthbound ˋtraffic ˋoff the Mˋone || and are ˉleaving only ·one ˋsouthbound lane ˇopen | between ˋjunctions ˇfourteen and ˋfifteen | while a rather ˋcomplicated reˋcovery ope·ration is being carried ˋout || so ex·pect very ˋlong delays ˋthere || that's between ˋjunctions ˇfourteen | and ˇfifteen | on the Mˋone this ·morning ||

047 SPOKEN ENGLISH CORPUS TEXT M03
Weather Forecast
Broadcast notes: Radio 4, 18th January, 1987
Transcribed by BJW

ˋnow the ˋweather •forecast | ↓ until dawn toˋmorrow || over ˋEngland and ˇWales | ˋmany places will be ˉcloudy but ˎdry || but in ˉparts of ˏCornwall and west ˏWales | a ˉlittle •light ˇrain is •likely | ↓which will exˉtend into parts of ˍCumbria overˎnight || ˋeastern ˇScotland | will have a ˉdry | ˇcloudy •day | ˍfollowed by •rain or ˋsleet | toˎnight || over •Northern ˇIreland | and ˋwestern ˊScotland | ˋrain will exˉtend from the ˇsouthwest | reaching •Northern ˇIreland | ˍearly this ˇmorning | and ˉwestern ˏScotland soon ˎafter || ˍoutbreaks of ˉrain | ↓will perˉsist | ↓into the ˊnight || but ˉafter ˬmidnight | they're exˉpected to ˬclear | from ˍNorthern ˎIreland || ˇeastern •areas will aˍgain be ˊcold | but in the ˉwest it'll beˍcome ˋless •cold than ˋrecently || and the ˉoutlook for ˍMonday and ˇTuesday | ˇmainly | ˉdry and ˍcold in the southˇeast | but reˇmaining •areas will be ˇmilder | with | a little ˎrain || ↑so ˍthings are im•proving slightly ˎthere ||

048 SPOKEN ENGLISH CORPUS TEXT M04
Programme News
Broadcast notes: Radio 4, 18th January, 1987
Transcribed by GOK

ˋnow let's •look at our ˋprogrammes | •coming up on ‸ •Radio •Four this ˋmorning || ˏwell | in a ˇmoment | in ‸ ↑ˋtwo-and-a-•half ˏminutes or therea•bouts | •there's the ˎnews | ˊfollowed | by our ˏbrowse | through the •Sunday ˋpapers || then at ˉnine fifˍteen | ˉAlistair ˎCooke | pre•sents this •week's ‸ ˉLetter from Aˎmerica || our ˉmorning ˏservice | at •nineˏthirty | •comes ˊthis week | from ˋEnfield | in ˎMiddlesex || and it's ˏfollowed | at •ten fifˊteen | by ‸ aˉnother ˍchance | to catch •up with the •week's go-ings •on at ˋAmbridge || •Margaret ˊHoward | will be •here with her ‸ •Pick of the ˎWeek | at a •quarter past eˇleven | and ˋthis week | we'll be •hearing a•bout ‸ ˉcamel •wrestling in ˏTurkey | •nights •spent in the ˋGreat •Pyramids at ˇCairo | ˊHamlet | in ˬElsinore | and ˉtales | from ˉwildest ˏCanada | and ˋEcuador || •add some ‸ •do-it-your•self •Gilbert and ˇSullivan | and a reˋminder of the •comedy of ˍAl ˏReid | and ˋthat's our •Pick of the ˍWeek | •at e•leven fifˎteen || the ˇcastaway | in •Desert Island ˏDiscs | •one hour ˇlater | is •silly-ass •actor ˉJeremy ˋLloyd | who's ˉalso ˍknown | •as a ˋscriptwriter || he's ˋone half of the ˏwriting •team | that cre•ated ‸ •Are You Being ˊServed | and ‸ 'A•llo 'Aˎllo || he'll be •chatting a•bout ‸ •chatting a•bout his caˊreer | to ˉMichael ˋParkinson | and •picking his ˉeight favourite ˍrecords | at ↑a ˍquarter •past ˎtwelve || and •that takes us to ↓ˉlunchtime | and ‸ The •World at ˎOne || ˇfinally | I've ˋjust ˍtime | for a ˏword a•bout our ˍSunday ˋfeature | which is a ˇpoetry •programme | with a ˋdifference | ˉGardens of ˎEden | by ˉMicheline ˋWonder || ˉMaureen ˏLipman •plays ˎEve | •Adam's first ˎwife | aˉccording to the New ˎTestament | and ‸ ˉMiriam ˏMargolis | •plays ˋLillith | who is ˉAdam's first ˏwife | aˉccording to the ˍalphabet | of ˍBen ˋSeurat || their ˉmeeting inˏvolves | a •kind of ˋlife swap | ˉLillith | •journeys to the Old ˇTestament | and takes ˍtea with the ˋLord | while ˇEve de•cides | she's ˉhad eˎnough | of •being ˍeveryone's ˎmother ||

049 SPOKEN ENGLISH CORPUS TEXT M05
Nelson Mandela speech
Recorded at MSU, Lancaster University
Transcribed by BJW

your ¯Royal _Highness and ˎChancellor | ↑it is my _privilege to preˏsent to you | on be¯half of the ˬSenate | the ¯name of Dr _Nelson Manˎdela || the im¯prisoned ˏleader of the ¯African • National ˎCongress | as one ¯eminently _worthy of the de¯gree of • Doctor of ˎLaws || ¯Dr Mandela's ˏlife | has been de¯voted to the _effort to seˏcure | for ¯all the _citizens of his ¯native South ˏAfrica | re¯gardless of their ˏcolour | ¯certain _simple yet • basic ˎrights || the most ¯fundamental of _which is the right of ¯each of those who must o¯bey the ˬlaw | to an ¯equal _voice within the po¯litical ˬsystem | under ¯which the • law is creˎated || ¯those who live in ˏcountries | where the ¯basic ˏrights | that Dr • Man¯dela seeks for his _people have been ˏwon | ¯owe • at the very _least | a ¯duty of ˎsympathy | for ¯those who have • no such ˎrights || and they ¯owe ˏtoo | a ¯duty of res_pect to _those ¯who | like ¯Dr Manˏdela | have un¯ceasingly _striven in the • face of ¯hardship and ˏdanger | to ¯claim those ˎrights || but in aˋddition to what is ¯owed to • Dr Manˏdela by the ¯citizens of ˇany free • nation | ¯any uniˇversity in a • free society | ¯owes him a special ˋtribute || for ¯in his _speeches and ˏwritings | ¯Dr Manˏdela has un¯swervingly aˏsserted the cenˋtrality of an ¯open eduˎcation | to the ¯cultural _life of any ˎnation || he has inˊsisted | as the ¯Charter of the ¯African • National Congress ˎputs it | that the • doors of ¯learning and ˏculture | shall be ˋopen || he has ¯emphasised | that in a ¯healthy soˏciety | ¯young _scholars are to be ¯thought of as a ˋcredit to their ˋnation | and • not ¯merely as a _threat to its ˋrulers || he has in¯sisted upon the pro¯foundly • liberalising eˎffects | of the ¯meeting of the world's ˎpeoples | in ¯open institutions of ˎlearning || and to use his ¯own _words | he has re¯soundingly aˏffirmed | that for ¯centuries uniˎversities have ¯served | as ¯centres | for the di¯ssemination of ¯learning and ˎknowledge | to ¯all ˏstudents | irre¯spective of • colour and ˎcreed || in ¯multi-racial so_cieties he continues | they ˋserve as the ˋcentres for the deˋvelopment of the ˋcultural and ¯spiritual ˎaspects | of the ¯life of the ˎpeople || ↑the ¯Charter of this uni_versity coˏmmands | that ¯no _test re•lated to ¯sex | ˏrace | ¯colour | or ˏcreed | shall be imˏposed upon any ˏperson | in ¯order to entitle ¯him | to be ad¯mitted | as a ¯member | _teacher | or ˎstudent || ↑for the • members of this uniˏversity | this ¯charter en•shrines a vic¯torious ˎprinciple || and the ¯fruits of that _victory can i¯mmediately be ˏseen | in the ¯international co¯mmunity of ˏscholars | that has ¯graduated •here toˎday || their ¯presence has en¯riched this uni_versity and this ˎcountry || and ¯many will return ˏhome | to en¯hance their own ˎnations || but ¯those who · live by the ˍprinciples of such ˏcharters as our ˏown | owe a ¯special duty of ˎtestimony | to ¯those | for whom the ¯fight to achieve a recog¯nition of those ˇprinciples | has ¯not been ˎwon || whose a¯llegiance to the ˍprinciple of an ¯open educational ˏsystem | in an ¯open soˏciety | is a con¯fession and a ˍproclamation to be ˊpaid for | in the · coin of im¯prisonment | sepaˏration | and even ˎdeath || and ¯Nelson Manˏdela has of ¯course been · willing to pay that ˎprice || ↑your ¯Royal Highness and ˎChancellor || at ¯all ˏtimes | there have been ¯women and ˏmen | whose ¯lives and ˏwords have taken on a ¯special ˏmeaning | to i¯nnumerably ˏmany of their ¯fellow human ˎbeings || their ¯lives emˏbody | and their ¯words ar˅ticulate | the le¯gitimate aspiˍrations of the de¯prived | the ¯suffering | and the ˎslighted || ¯Nelson Manˏdela | has be·come ¯one ˎsuch || and I can ¯think of no better ˍway to commend him ˏto you | than to use his ¯own closing ˏwords | ¯spoken in ˏcourt | at the ¯end of his final ˏtrial | when he ¯was indeed ˍfacing the possiˍbility of a ¯sentence of ˎdeath || ¯during my ˏlife I have ¯dedicated myˏself to the ¯struggle of the ¯African ˎpeople || I have ¯fought against ˏwhite domi·nation | and I have ˍfought against ˎblack domi·nation || I have ¯cherished the iˍdeal of a demo¯cratic and ¯free soˎciety || in which ¯all persons live toˍgether | in ¯harmony | and with ¯equal opporˎtunities || it is an ¯ideal which I · hope to ¯live for and aˎchieve | but if ¯needs ˏbe | it is an ˋideal for which I am pre¯pared to ˇdie || a ¯life that has indeed been ˍlived in the ¯spirit of these iˏdeals | ¯cannot but coˍmmand our reˎspect || and I ¯therefore preˍsent to you the name of Nelson Manˏdela | a¯las in abˍsentia | as one ¯eminently ˏworthy | of the a¯ward of the deˍgree | of ¯Doctor of ˏLaws | ho¯noris ˎcausa ||

050 SPOKEN ENGLISH CORPUS TEXT M06
Tom Stephenson speech
Recorded at MSU, Lancaster University
Transcribed by GOK

Your ¯Royal _Highness | and ˎChancellor ||

it ¯is my _privilege to preˏsent to you | ¯Tom ˎStephenson | to ·whom ¯all _those | who ·walk for ·recre¯ation in this ˎcountry | ·owe an in¯estimable ˎdebt || ¯Tom ˏStephenson | was ˏborn | in ¯eighteen_ninety-ˬthree | in ˇChorley | in ˬLancashire | the ˋson of an en¯graver | in a ¯calico ˋprinting ·works || al¯though at that ˏtime | the ˋhalf-time ˋsystem of ¯edu_cation | still e¯xisted in ˎschools | he was a¯llowed by his _father | to ¯study full-ˏtime | un·til the ¯age of thirˎteen | which ¯meant that he _had | for ¯those ˏdays | a ¯relatively ·full eduˎcation | for a ¯working class ˎboy || at ¯thirˏteen | he ¯went to _work | in a ¯textile ˋprinting ·works | ·walking ¯two ˏmiles | in ·order to ·work an i¯llegal ·twelve hour ˬday | from ¯six aˏm | until ¯six pˎm || he would ˋthen ·walk a ¯further two ˏmiles | from his ˇwork-place | to ˋClitheroe | in ¯order to ·spend the ˏevening | in the ¯town ˎlibrary | and would ¯then _walk | the ˎfour ·miles ˋhome || the ¯first book he ·took from the ˏlibrary | was ¯Darwin's ‸ ·Origin of ˎSpecies | which inˋspired him with the ˏdream | of be·coming a geˋologist || ·so at ¯eighˏteen | he a·ttended ˇnight ·classes | at ¯Burnley ˋTechnical ·School | and for ¯four _years | ·covered the ¯eight miles ˏthere | and ¯eight miles ˏback | by ˎbicycle || ˇfinally | in ¯nineteen fifˏteen | ·after a ¯taxing ˏprogramme | of ¯study and e·xamiˏnation | he ·won a ¯scholarship in geˏology | to the ¯Royal ·College of ˎScience | ·now Im¯perial ˎCollege || ¯this ca·reer was inteˏrrupted | ·when in ¯nineteen sixˏteen | he was im¯prisoned in ·Wormwood ˎScrubs | for ¯three ˏyears | as a ¯consci·entious obˎjector || on his re¯lease in ·nineteen nineˏteen | his ˇcollege | re¯fused to ·take him ˎback | and he re¯turned to his _work | as a ¯block ˏprinter | ¯running a ˏbranch | of the ¯Independent ˋLabour ·Party | in ˋKent | which was a¯ddressed | by such ˬnotables | as ¯Russell and ˋShaw || in ¯nineteen ·twenty- ˏtwo | he ·moved to the ˋLabour ·Party ·national ˋoffice || ↑the ¯love of the ˏcountryside | had been ¯one of Tom ˏStephenson's | ¯earliest exˎperiences || re¯calling his _boyhood a_pprenticeship he ˏsaid | ↑with the ·country all ˏround me | ·I would ¯stand at the _top of the ·steps of the ˏwork ·shop | and ˋlook up to ·Waddington ˏFell | ¯Pendle ˏHill | and ·Longridge ˎFell || he be¯gan ˋwalking | ¯always aˎlone || and ¯when he was fourˏteen | he ·walked ·through the ¯Trough of ˎBowland | to the ˋLake ·district || it ¯just ·over-ˎpowered me ‸ he ·wrote || in ↑¯nineteen ·thirty-ˏone | he be¯gan to _write | for a ¯small ˏjournal | ·called the ¯Hiker and ˎCamper | ¯urging in an ·early ˏnumber | that the ¯Forest of ˏBowland | should be ·one of the ¯first ·national ˎparks || in ¯nineteen ·thirty-ˏthree | ¯no less a _figure | than ¯Ernest ˎBevin | ·offered him the ˇeditorship | of the ¯Hiker and ˎCamper | and the ˋjob of ·correˇspondent | on the ¯outˏdoors | to the ¯Daily ˎHerald || it was ↑¯through the ·Daily ˏHerald | that ·what is ·probably the ·most out¯standing of his ·contriˏbutions | was ·first to ·see the ·light of ˎday || ¯two Aˇmerican ·girls | ˋhaving ·walked the ·Appa¯lachian ˏWay | in the U¯nited ˏStates | ¯wrote to ·ask Tom ˏStephenson | whether ¯any such _walk | could be ·done in ˋEngland || ↑ˋin a ·famous ·middle page ˏarticle | in the ˏHerald | he ¯sketched a ˎroute | ·starting at ¯Edale in ˏDerbyshire | ¯northward to·wards the ·Yorkshire ˏPennines | ¯so across ˏDurham | to ·Hadrian's ˏWall | and e¯ventually to the ˏCheviots | and the ·Scots ˎborder || and he ˏwrote | ¯none could ·walk that ·Pennine ˏWay | wi¯thout being imˎproved | in ¯mind and ˎbody | and ˋfilled | with a deˎsire | to ex·plore ¯every ˎcorner | of this ¯lovely ˎisland || ¯that ˏarticle | ·started an ¯agiˎtation | ·that was to ˇculminate | in the ¯National ˏParks | and ¯Access to the ˎCountryside ·Act | of ¯nineteen ·forty-ˎnine || and ˇlater | ·sixteen ·years after ˏthat | his most ¯glorious ˏmonument | the ¯Pennine ˏWay | be¯came a reˎality || a¯bout that aˏchievement | ·one of the ·greatest of ˇall writers on ·walking | ·Arthur ˇWainwright ˆ ·said | oˇfficially | ¯WhiteˋhalI cre·ated the ·Pennine ˏWay | but ¯those who ˏwalk it | should reˇmember | that it was ¯one man who inˎspired | in his ¯mind | and by his ¯patience and ˎeffort | the ¯freedom they enˎjoy || his ¯name will be reˎvered | for his i¯maginative conˎception | of a con¯tinuous ·way for ˎtravellers | ¯on ˎfoot | across ¯half of ˎEngland || ↑in ¯nineteen ·forty-ˏeight | ¯Tom ˏStephenson | be·came ˋsecretary of the ˋRambler's A·ssoci·ation | a ¯post he was to ˏhold | for ¯twenty- one ˎyears || he ¯was in this caˏpacity | a ¯main _force | in a¯chieving | the ¯National ˋParks ·Act | of ¯nineteen ·forty- ˎnine | and the ˋCountryside ·Act | of ¯nineteen ·sixty-ˎeight || and he ·helped ˇstrengthen | the ¯legal ˎframework | ·guarding our ˇfootpaths | and ¯uncultivated ˎuplands || ¯one who _walked with ·Tom _Stephenson ˏwrote | I ˇwalked with ·him | a·long his be¯loved ·Pennine ˎWay | ·last ˋautumn || ¯everywhere we ˏwent | he ·knew ¯each ˇdetail | of the ˎlandscape | ˋwhy an ·outcropping of ˎlimestone | was ·thrust ¯high in the ˎair | e¯xactly where a ˋpath ·went | that ¯disappeared ·off to the ˎright || there ↑was a ·splatter of ˏrain | and a ¯greying ˏsky | and a ¯rising ˎwind | but ↑there was a ·magˎnificence | a·bout the ¯vast ˎemptiness | and the ¯blurred | ·distant

↘hills | and ¯even the ·rocky deso↘lation | ¯all a↘bout us || and ¯Tom ↗said | it's been a ¯long ↘walk ||

your ¯Royal _Highness | and ↘Chancellor || ↑for ·Tom ↗Stephenson | ·from the ¯step of the ↗mill | from ¯which as a ↗boy | he ¯longingly ·viewed the ·open ↗countryside | un¯til ↗now | ·some ¯eighty years ↗later | a re¯vered _figure | among ¯those | who ¯love the ·English ↗countryside | it ·has in¯deed ↗been | a ¯long ↘walk || a·ccomplished with te´nacity | ↗courage | ↑and ↘love || ↑and the ↘consequence of that ·long ↗life | has been that ¯countless of his ·fellow men and ↘women | have ·had their ¯spirits `lifted | because he has ·made it ∨possible for them | to ·walk in the ¯wild places of ↘England | ¯under the ·wide ↘sky | and ˇafter·wards | to re¯turn | to a ¯more mun¯dane e↘xistence | ↓¯heartened and re↘stored || ↑¯that ex↗perience | has `not merely ·given so ·very ↗many | what that ¯great ·walker of the ↗countryside | ∨Wordsworth | re¯ferred to | as the re¯membered _landscapes | of the ¯inner ↗eye | which pro¯vide | a con¯tinual ↗source | of inspi¯ration and conso↘lation || for to ¯many | he has ·also given ·something ↘deeper | what ·Wordsworth ¯also de↗scribed | when he ¯said | that to ¯nature he owed ↗something | of ¯aspect more su↘blime | ´namely | as he ↘put it | a ¯blessed ↘mood | in which the ¯burthen of the ↘mystery | in which the ¯heavy | and the ¯weary ↗weight | of ·all this ¯unin·telligible ·world is ↘lightened | and in ¯which | in the ¯presence of ↘nature | with an ¯eye made ↗quiet | by the ¯deep power of ↗harmony | and the ¯rich power of ↗joy | we ·see into the ¯life of ↘things || ¯one who has ·made this ↗possible | for ¯so ↗many | has in¯deed earned the ↗gratitude | that ¯millions ·feel to↘wards him || ¯Tom ↗Stephenson | was by ¯conscience de·prived of a de↗gree | for ·which he had ¯laboured long and ↘hard || to´day | we make ¯good that o↘mission || it is ¯therefore my ·very great ↘privilege | on be¯half of the ↘Senate | to pre`sent to you ¯Tom ↘Stephenson | whose ¯many a_ccomplishments | in his ¯long _life | make him most ¯eminently ↘worthy | of the de¯gree | of ¯Doctor of ↘Laws | ho↓¯noris ↘causa ||

050 SPOKEN ENGLISH CORPUS TEXT M06
Tom Stephenson speech
Recorded at MSU, Lancaster University
Overlap passage

Transcribed by BJW

your ˉRoyal ˍHighness | and ˎChancellor || ↑for ˍTom ˇStephenson | from the ˉstep of the ˍmill from ˉwhich as a ˍboy he ˉlongingly ˍviewed the open ˇcountryside || unˉtil ˍnow | some ˉeighty years ˍlater | a reˉvered ˍfigure among ˉthose who ˉlove the •English ˏcountryside | it has inˉdeed ˍbeen a ˉlong ˎwalk || aˉccomplished | with teˊnacity | ˍcourage | and ˎlove || and the ˋconsequence of that •long ˍlife | has been that ˉcountless of his •fellow men and ˏwomen | have ˉhad their spirits ˎlifted | because he has ˉmade it ˍpossible for them to •walk in the ˉwild places of ˎEngland | under the ˉwide ˎsky | and ˉafterˍwards to re•turn to a •more munˋdane e•xistence | ˏheartened | and reˎstored || ↑that exˏperience has ˉnot merely ˍgiven so very ˏmany | what that ˉgreat •walker of the ˇcountryside | ˇWordsworth | reˋferred to as the reˋmembered •landscapes of the •inner ˏeye | which proˉvide a conˉtinual ˍsource of inspiˉration and consoˎlation || for to ˉmany he has ˍalso given something ˎdeeper || what •Wordsworth ˋalso de•scribed when he ˉsaid | that to ˉnature he owed •something of ˉaspect more subˎlime || ˉnamely | as he ˏput it | a ˉblessed ˎmood || in which the ˉburthen of the ˎmystery | in which the ˉheavy and the •weary ˍweight of all this ˉunintelligible •world is ˎlightened || and in ˋwhich in the ˉpresence of ˇnature | with an ˉeye made ˍquiet | by the ˉdeep power of ˇharmony | and the ˉrich power of ˍjoy | we ˉsee into the •life of ˎthings || ↑ˉone who has made this ˏpossible | for so ˏmany | has inˉdeed earned the ˍgratitude | that ˉmillions feel toˎwards him || Tom ˍStephenson was by ˉconscience de•prived of a deˍgree for which he had ˉlaboured long and ˎhard || toˉday we make •good that oˎmission || it is ˉtherefore my very great ˍprivilege on beˉhalf of the ˎSenate | to preˉsent to you Tom ˎStephenson || whose ˉmany aˍccomplishments | in his ˉlong ˍlife | make him most ˉeminently ˎworthy | of the deˉgree | of ˉDoctor of ˎLaws | hoˉnoris ˎcausa ||

Transcribed by GOK

Your ˉRoyal ˍHighness | and ˎChancellor || ↑for •Tom ˏStephenson | •from the ˉstep of the ˏmill | from ˉwhich as a ˏboy | he ˉlongingly •viewed the •open ˏcountryside | unˉtil ˏnow | •some ˉeighty years ˏlater | a reˉvered ˍfigure | among ˉthose | who ˉlove the •English ˏcountryside | it

·has inˉdeed ˏbeen | a ˉlong ˎwalk || a·ccomplished with teˊnacity | ˏcourage | ↑and ˎlove || ↑and the ˎconsequence of that ·long ˏlife | has been that ˉcountless of his ·fellow men and ˎwomen | have ·had their ˉspirits ˋlifted | because he has ·made it ˬpossible for them | to ·walk in the ˉwild places of ˎEngland | ˉunder the ·wide ˎsky | and ˇafter·wards | to reˉturn | to a ˉmore munˉdane eˎxistence | ↓ˉheartened and reˎstored || ↑ˉthat exˏperience | has ˋnot merely ·given so ·very ˏmany | what that ˉgreat ·walker of the ˏcountryside | ˬWordsworth | reˉferred to | as the reˉmembered ˍlandscapes | of the ˉinner ˏeye | which proˉvide | a conˉtinual ˏsource | of inspiˉration and consoˎlation || for to ˉmany | he has ·also given ·something ˎdeeper | what ·Wordsworth ˉalso deˏscribed | when he ˉsaid | that to ˉnature he owed ˏsomething | of ˉaspect more suˎblime | ˊnamely | as he ˎput it | a ˉblessed ˎmood | in which the ˉburthen of the ˎmystery | in which the ˉheavy | and the ˉweary ˏweight | of ·all this ˉunin·telligible ·world is ˎlightened | and in ˉwhich | in the ˉpresence of ˎnature | with an ˉeye made ˏquiet | by the ˉdeep power of ˏharmony | and the ˉrich power of ˏjoy | we ·see into the ˉlife of ˎthings || ˉone who has ·made this ˏpossible | for ˉso ˏmany | has inˉdeed earned the ˏgratitude | that ˉmillions ·feel toˎwards him || ˉTom ˏStephenson | was by ˉconscience de·prived of a deˏgree | for ·which he had ˉlaboured long and ˎhard || toˊday | we make ˉgood that oˎmission || it is ˉtherefore my ·very great ˎprivilege | on beˉhalf of the ˎSenate | to preˋsent to you ˉTom ˎStephenson | whose ˉmany aˍccomplishments | in his ˉlong ˍlife | make him most ˉeminently ˎworthy | of the deˉgree | of ˉDoctor of ˎLaws | ho↓ˉnoris ˎcausa ||

051 SPOKEN ENGLISH CORPUS TEXT M07
Travel Roundup
Broadcast notes: Radio 4, 8.55 a.m., 25th January, 1987
Transcribed by GOK

↑ ¯five to ˎnine ·now | and er ˆ ˋhere's this ·morning's ˇtravel ·roundup | ˋweekend engiˇneering ·work | will cause ˏproblems | for both ¯road | ·and ˎrail ·travellers to·day I'm aˏfraid || deˊlays can be ex·pected | on the ˋM eight in ˋGlasgow | where there are ˋlane closures in ↑ ˋboth di·rections | between ¯Kingston _Bridge | and ˋCharing ·Cross ˋtunnels || at ·junction ˇten | the ˇon ramp is ·closed | from ¯Barty _Beeth ˎroad | to·gether with ·two ˋwestbound ·lanes | on the ¯motorway itˎself || at ↑ ˇManchester | ˋwork on the M·sixty-ˋtwo | has ·closed the ·nearside ˏlane | and ·hard ˊshoulder | of ˇboth ·carriageways | at ˋjunction sevenˋteen | to·wards ˋPrestwich || and there are ˋalso | ˇeastbound ·lane ·closures | on the ¯M fifty-ˋsix ·leading from ˇCheshire | be·tween ·junction ·three and ˊfour | at ˋAltrincham || near ˇWorcester | ˋboth ·carriageways of the Mˋfive are still ¯closed | ·following ·overnight ¯work | be·tween ·junctions ·five and ˇsix | ·and diˋversions are a·long the A thirty-ˇeight | until ˋten this ·morning || on the ↑ ˇrailways | engiˏneering ·work | is ˋwidespread | with ˋbuses ·operating in·stead of ˋtrains | on ˎsome routes || ˏeastern ·region ·trains | will be de¯layed | on the ·London ·King's ¯Cross to ˋPeterborough ·line | as will ˋwestern ·region ·services | on the ˋPaddington | to ˋExeter ·route || I ·hope you ·get there in the ˋend ||

052 SPOKEN ENGLISH CORPUS TEXT M08
Weather forecast
Broadcast notes: Radio 4, 25th January, 1987
Transcribed by GOK

•here's the ˋweather •forecast for the U•nited •Kingdom until | ˉdawn to↓ˎmorrow || in ˉsouthern ˏcounties | of •England and ˏWales | it'll be ˏdull | but ^ ˋearly •patches of ˉmist and ˏdrizzle | will ↓ˋclear during this ˎmorning || over ↑ˉnorthern ˏEngland | and •Northern ˏIreland | it'll •stay ˉmainly ˬcloudy | but ˬdry | during toˏday | and toˎnight || in ˋsouthern ↑ˇScotland •after •early ˇsunshine in •places | it'll be ˋmostly ˇcloudy | but ˬdry | al•though toˉnight there ↑ˋmay be some •light ˎrain || ˋnorthern ˏScotland | will have oˉccasional light ˏrain | which will be ˉfollowed during the ˏday | by ˉcolder | but •still ^ ˉmainly ˎcloudy •weather | with a •few ˉsleet and ˎsnow •showers || ˇtemperatures to•day | will •be ^ ˉmuch as ˏyesterday | ex•cept in ˉnorthern ˎScotland | where it'll •turn ˉnoticeably ˎcolder || and the •outlook for •Monday and ˊTuesday | it'll be •rather ˬcold | in ˇmost •places | with southˇwestern •areas | •staying ˎdry | but ˬelsewhere | some ˋlight rain or ˍsleet | is ˎlikely ||

053 SPOKEN ENGLISH CORPUS TEXT M09
Programme News
Broadcast notes: Radio 4, 25th January, 1987
Transcribed by BJW

we'll just _check | some of today's ˇprogrammes | on ·Radio ˋFour | ↑¯for you | for our Morning ˇService | at half past ˇnine | we'll join the congreˏgation in the parish ˏchurch of St ˋFaith in Great ˋCrosby || and then at a ˋquarter past ˇten | some ¯Ambridge ˋbell-ringing to en·joy || ↓just one ˋhighlight in the ·lives of the ˋArchers this week || ¯after that ·Margaret ˋHoward | with ˇher se·lection | of ¯listening _highlights | from the ¯past week's ˎbroadcasting ||

[change of speaker: Margaret Howard]

↑the ¯chief _constable of Greater ˋManchester | James ˋAnderton has been ·much in the ·news this ¯week || ˋmany interpreˋtations have been put on his ˋstatements about being an ˋinstrument of ↑ˋGod || on ·Pick of the ¯Week | you can _hear | what he ·actually ˋsaid || ˋNigel ˇHawthorne | temporarily deˋserts ˋYes ·Prime ¯Minister | for a ˋnew role | on ˋOne Man and His ˋDog || ˋhe plays the ·part of a ¯five year old ·border ˋcollie || we reˋcall the ¯day that King ·George the ¯Sixth | ·kept the ·Empire ˋwaiting || David ¯Frost | e_licits a cure for ˊsnoring | ˋand we take a ·ride out with a ˋBicester | in pur¯suit of the ˎfox ||

[change of speaker: male]

Margaret ˋHoward || that's ·all in Pick of the ¯Week | at a _quarter past eˋleven || an ¯hour ˬlater | Baroness ¯Ryder of ˎWarsaw | joins Michael ˇParkinson | for a ¯stint on the old desert ˎisland || the ¯Baroness ·heads the Sue ˋRyder foun·dation | which ¯looks after the sick and diˋsabled in ·many parts of the ˋworld || and in ¯past years has ˋfrequently driven ¯lorries full of ˬmedical supplies and proˋvisions | to dis¯tressed _areas of ·central ˋEurope || ¯all she has to do toˇday | is to pick her ¯eight desert island ˋdiscs so | ˇjoin her | and enˋjoy her musical se¯lection | at a _quarter past | ↓ˎtwelve || ↑this ¯evening at a quarter past ˬsix | the ¯first of _two Actuˇality profiles | of some ˋmen and ˋwomen recently reˇcruited | ↑to do | ¯voluntary _overseas ˋservice || over the ˋnext two ˇweeks | we'll ˋjoin them | as they're pre¯pared for | not only the exˋcitement of ˋliving in ˋstrange and eˋxotic ˇclimes | but ¯also | the ˎdown side of ·things ||

[speech extract omitted]

well they all sound ˍcheerful eˏnough | but for ˇmost ·VSO re·cruits | the ˉtraining ˍperiod is a mixture of ˉfears | ˍfantasies | and expecˎtations || as you can ˉfind out through Actuˋality toˋnight at a quarter past ˉsix || and ·just a reˊminder | that it's ˇBurns ·night || ↓if you're not ·planning to go ˋout for a ·Burns night ˊsupper | then ·stay ·in and en·joy The ˉMiller's ˋReel | which beˍgins at a quarter past ˋseven | this ˋevening || The ·Miller's ˊReel | takes the ·form of a ˋlove story | ˏwoven | from the ˉletters | ˍpoems | and ˇsongs of Robert ·Burns | and features the ˉsinging of Jean ˍRedpath and Rod ˋPatterson || that's The ˉMiller's ˎReel | eˉspecially for ˎBurns ·night | ↓ˍhere on Radio ˎ4 ||

Appendix 1: The CLAWS1 tagset

.	punctuation tag - full stop
...	punctuation tag - ellipsis
(	punctuation tag - left bracket
]	punctuation tag - exclamation mark
&FO	formula
&FW	foreign word
**'	punctuation tag - close quotes
*-	punctuation tag - dash
*'	punctuation tag - open quotes
)	punctuation tag - right bracket
;	punctuation tag - semicolon
___	punctuation tag - new sentence marker
,	punctuation tag - comma
?	punctuation tag - question mark
:	punctuation tag - colon
ABL	pre-qualifier
ABN	pre-quantifier
ABX	pre-quantifier/double conjunction (both)
AP	post-determiner
AP$	post-determiner + genitive
APS	plural post-determiner (others)
APS$	plural post-determiner + genitive (others')
AT	singular article (a, an, every)
ATI	singular or plural article (the, no)

BE	be
BED	were
BEDZ	was
BEG	being
BEM	am
BEN	been
BER	are
BEZ	is
CC	coordinating conjunction
CD	cardinal
CD$	cardinal + genitive
CD-CD	hyphenated pair of cardinals
CDS	plural cardinal
CD1	one
CD1$	one's
CD1S	ones
CS	subordinating conjunction
DO	do
DOD	did
DOZ	does
DT	singular determiner
DT$	singular determiner + genitive
DTI	singular or plural determiner
DTS	plural determiner
DTX	determiner/double conjunction (either/neither)
EX	existential there
HV	have

HVD	had
HVG	having
HVN	had(past participle)
HVZ	has
IN	preposition
JJ	adjective
JJB	attributive adjective
JJR	comparative adjective
JJT	superlative adjective
JNP	adjective with word-initial capital
MD	modal
NC	cited word
NN	singular common noun
NN$	singular common noun + genitive
NNP	singular common noun with word-initial capital
NNP$	singular common noun with WIC and genitive
NNPS	plural common noun with WIC
NNPS$	plural common noun with WIC + genitive
NNS	plural common noun
NNS$	plural common noun + genitive
NNU	abbreviated unit of measurement unmarked for number
NNU$	abb. unit of measurement unmarked for number + genitive
NNUS	abb. plural unit of measurement
NNUS$	abb. plural unit of measurement + genitive
NP	singular proper noun
NP$	singular proper noun + genitive
NPL	singular locative noun with WIC

NPL$	singular locative noun with WIC + genitive
NPLS	plural locative noun with WIC
NPLS$	plural locative noun with WIC + genitive
NPS	plural proper noun
NPS$	plural proper noun + genitive
NPT	singular titular noun with WIC
NPT$	singular titular noun with WIC + genitive
NPTS	plural titular noun with WIC
NPTS$	plural titular noun with WIC + genitive
NR	singular adverbial noun
NR$	singular adverbial noun + genitive
NRS	plural adverbial noun
NRS$	plural adverbial noun + genitive
OD	ordinal
OD$	ordinal + genitive
PN	nominal pronoun
PN$	nominal pronoun + genitive
PP$	first possessive personal pronoun
PP	second possessive personal pronoun
PPL	singular reflexive personal pronoun
PPLS	plural reflexive personal pronoun
PP1A	I
PP1AS	we
PP1O	me
PP1OS	us
PP2	you
PP3	it

PP3A	he, she
PP3AS	they
PP3O	him, her
PP3OS	them
QL	qualifier
QLP	post-qualifier (enough, indeed)
RB	adverb
RB$	adverb + genitive
RBR	comparative adverb
RBT	superlative adverb
RI	adverb (homograph of preposition)
RN	nominal adverb (here, there, now, then)
RP	adverb which can also be a particle
TO	infinitival to
UH	interjection
VB	verb
VBD	verb past tense
VBG	present participle
VBN	past participle
VBZ	verb 3rd person singular
WDT	wh-determiner
WP	wh-pronoun, neutral between nomin. and obj.
WP$	possessive wh-pronoun
WPA	nominative wh-pronoun (whosoever)
WPO	objective wh-pronoun (whom, whomsoever)
WQL	wh-qualifier
WRB	wh-adverb

XNOT	not or n't
ZZ	letter of the alphabet

Total number of tags = 134

Appendix 2: Complete version of *Through the Tunnel* by Doris Lessing

Going to the shore on the first morning of the holiday, the young English boy stopped at a turning of the path and looked down at a wild and rocky bay, and then over to the crowded beach he knew so well from other years. His mother walked on in front of him, carrying a bright striped bag in one hand. Her other arm, swinging loose, was very white in the sun. The boy watched that white, naked arm, and turned his eyes, which had a frown behind them, towards the bay and back again to his mother. When she felt he was not with her, she swung around. 'Oh, there you are, Jerry!', she said. She looked impatient, then smiled. 'Why, darling, would you rather not come with me? Would you rather—' She frowned, conscientiously worrying over what amusements he might secretly be longing for, which she had been too busy or too careless to imagine. He was very familiar with that anxious, apologetic smile. Contrition sent him running after her. And yet, as he ran, he looked back over his shoulder at the wild bay; and all morning, as he played on the safe beach, he was thinking of it.

Next morning, when it was time for the routine of swimming and sunbathing, his mother said, 'Are you tired of the usual beach, Jerry? Would you like to go somewhere else?'

'Oh, no!' he said quickly, smiling at her out of that unfailing impulse of contrition – a sort of chivalry. Yet, walking down the path with her, he blurted out, 'I'd like to go and have a look at those rocks down there.'

She gave the idea her attention. It was a wild-looking place, and there was no one there; but she said, 'Of course, Jerry. When you've had enough, come to the big beach. Or just go straight back to the villa, if you like'. She walked away, that bare arm, now slightly reddened from yesterday's sun, swinging. And he almost ran after her again, feeling it unbearable that she should go by herself, but he did not.

She was thinking, Of course he's old enough to be safe without me. Have I been keeping him too close? He mustn't feel he ought to be with me. I must be careful.

He was an only child, eleven years old. She was a widow. She was determined to be neither possessive nor lacking in devotion. She went worrying off to her beach.

As for Jerry, once he saw that his mother had gained her beach, he began the steep descent to the bay. From where he was, high up among red brown rocks, it was a scoop of moving bluish green fringed with white. As he went lower, he saw that it spread among small promontories and inlets of rough, sharp rock, and the crisping, lapping surface showed stains of purple and darker blue. Finally, as he ran sliding and scraping down the last few yeards, he saw an edge of white surf and the shallow, luminous movement of water over white sand, and, beyond that, a solid heavy blue.

He ran straight into the water and began swimming. He was a good swimmer. He went out fast over the gleaming sand, over a middle region where rocks lay like discoloured monsters under the surface and then he was in the real sea – a warm sea where irregular cold currents from the deep water shocked his limbs.

When he was so far out that he could look back not only on the little bay but past the promontory that was between it and the big beach, he floated on the buoyant surface and looked for his mother. There she was, a speck of yellow under an umbrella that looked like a slice of orange peel. He swam back to shore, relieved at being sure she was there, but all at once very lonely.

On the edge of a small cape that marked the side of the bay away from the promontory was a loose scatter of rocks. Above them, some boys were stripping off their clothes. They came running, naked, down to the rocks. The English boy swam towards them, but kept his distance at a stone's throw. They were of that coast; all of them were burned smooth dark brown and speaking a language he did not understand. To be with them, of them, was a craving that filled his whole body. He swam a little closer; they turned and watched him with narrowed, alert dark eyes. Then one smiled and waved. It was enough. In a minute, he had swum in and was on the rocks beside them, smiling with a desperate, nervous supplication. They shouted cheerful greetings at him; and then, as he preserved his nervous, uncomprehending smile, they understood that he was a foreigner strayed from his own beach, and they proceeded to forget him. But he was happy. He was with them.

They began diving again and again from a high point into a well of blue sea between rough, pointed rocks. After they had dived and come up, they swam around, hauled themselves up, and waited their turn to dive again.

They were big boys – men, to Jerry. He dived, and they watched him; and when he swam around to take his place, they made way for him. He felt he was accepted and he dived again, carefully, proud of himself.

Soon the biggest of the boys poised himself, shot down into the water, and did not come up. The others stood about, watching, Jerry, after waiting for the sleek brown head to appear, let out a yell of warning; they looked at him idly and turned their eyes back towards the water. After a long time, the boy came up on the other side of a big dark rock, letting the air out of his lungs in a sputtering gasp and a shout of triumph. Immediately the rest of them dived in. One moment, the morning seemed full of chattering boys; the next, the air and the surface of the water was empty. But through the heavy blue, dark shapes could be seen moving and groping.

Jerry dived, shot past the school of underwater swimmers, saw a black wall of rock looming at him, touched it, and bobbed up at once to the surface, where the wall was a low barrier he could see across. There was no one visible; under him, in the water, the dim shapes of the swimmers had disappeared. Then one, and then another of the boys came upon the far side of the barrier of rock, and he understood that they had swum through some gap or hole in it. He plunged down again. He could see nothing through the stinging salt water but the blank rock. When he came up the boys were all on the diving rock, preparing to attempt the feat again. And now, in a panic of failure, he yelled up, in English, 'Look at me! Look!' and he began splashing and kicking in the water like a foolish dog.

They looked down gravely, frowning. He knew the frown. At moments of failure, when he clowned to claim his mother's attention, it was with just this grave, embarrassed inspection that she rewarded him. Through his hot shame, feeling the pleading grin on his face like a scar that he could never remove, he looked up at the group of big brown boys on the rock and shouted, '*Bonjour! Merci! Au revoir! Monsieur, monsieur!*' while he hooked his fingers round his ears and waggled them.

Water surged into his mouth; he choked, sank, came up. The rock, lately weighted with boys, seemed to rear up out of the water as their weight was removed. They were flying down past him now, into the water; the air was full of falling bodies. Then the rock was empty in the hot sunlight. He counted one, two, three . . .

At fifty, he was terrified. They must all be drowning beneath him, in the watery caves of the rock. At a hundred, he stared around him at the empty hillside, wondering if he should yell for help. He counted faster, faster, to hurry them up, to bring them to the surface quickly, to drown them quickly – anything rather than the terror of counting on and on into the blue emptiness of the morning. And then, at a hundred and sixty, the water beyond the rock was full of boys blowing like brown whales. They swam back to the shore without a look at him.

He climbed back to the diving rock and sat down, feeling the hot roughness of it under his thighs. The boys were gathering up their bits of clothing and running off along the shore to another promontory. They were leaving to get away from him. He cried openly, fists in his eyes. There was no one to see him, and he cried himself out.

It seemed to him that a long time had passed, and he swam out to where he could see his mother. Yes, she was still there, a yellow spot under an orange umbrella. He swam back to the big rock, climbed up, and dived into the blue pool among the fanged and angry boulders. Down he went, until he touched the wall of rock again. But the salt was so painful in his eyes that he could not see.

He came to the surface, swam to shore and went back to the villa to wait for his mother. Soon she walked slowly up the path, swinging her striped bag, the flushed, naked arm dangling beside her. 'I want some swimming goggles', he panted, defiant and beseeching.

She gave him a patient, inquisitive look as she said casually, 'Well, of course, darling.'

But now, now, now! He must have them this minute, and no other time. He nagged and pestered until she went with him to a shop. As soon as she had bought the goggles, he grabbed them from her hand as if she were going to claim them for herself, and was off, running down the steep path to the bay.

Jerry swam out to the big barrier rock, adjusted the goggles, and dived. The impact of the water broke the rubber enclosed vacuum, and the goggles came loose. He understood that he must swim down to the base of the rock from the surface of the water. He fixed the goggles tight and firm, filled his lungs, and floated, face down, on the water. Now, he could see. It was as if he had eyes of a different kind – fish eyes that showed everything clear and delicate and wavering in the bright water.

Under him, six or seven feet down, was a floor of perfectly clean, shining white sand, rippled firm and hard by the tides. Two greyish shapes steered there, like long, rounded pieces of wood or slate. They were fish. He saw them nose towards each other, poise motionless, make a dart forward, swerve off, and come around again. It was like a water dance. A few inches above them the water sparkled as if sequins were dropping through it. Fish again – myriads of minute fish, the length of his fingernail, were drifting through the water, and in a moment he could feel the innumerable tiny touches of them against his limbs. It was like swimming in flaked silver. The great rock the big boys had swum through rose sheer out of the white sand – black, tufted lightly with greenish weed. He could see no gap in it. He swam down to its base.

Again and again he rose, took a big chestful of air, and went down again. Again and again he groped over the surface of the rock, feeling it, almost hugging it in the desperate need to find the entrance. And then, once, while he was clinging to the black wall, his knees came up and he shot his feet out forward and they met no obstacle. He had found the hole.

He gained the surface, clambered about the stones that littered the barrier rock until he found a big one, and, with this in his arms, let himself down over the side of the rock. He dropped, with the weight, straight to the sandy floor. Clinging tight to the anchor of stone, he lay on his side and looked in under the dark shelf at the place where his feet had gone. He could see the hole. It was an irregular, dark gap but he could not see deep into it. He let go of his anchor, clung with his hands to the edges of the hole, and tried to push himself in.

He got his head in, found his shoulders jammed, moved them in sideways, and was inside as far as his waist. He could see nothing ahead. Something soft and clammy touched his mouth; he saw a dark frond moving against the greyish rock, and panic filled him. He thought of octopuses, of clinging weed. He pushed himself out backwards and caught a glimpse, as he retreated, of a harmless tentacle of seaweed drifting in the mouth of the tunnel. But it was enough. He reached the sunlight, swam to shore, and lay on the diving rock. He looked down into the blue well of water. He knew he must find his way through that cave, or hole, or tunnel, and out the other side.

First, he thought, he must learn to control his breathing. He let himself down into the water with another big stone in his arms, so that he could lie effortlessly on the bottom of the sea. He counted. One, two, three. He counted steadily. He could hear the movement of blood in his chest. Fifty-one, fifty-two . . . His chest was hurting. He let go of the rock and went up into the air. He saw the sun was low. He rushed to the villa and found his mother at her supper. She said only, 'Did you enjoy yourself?' and he said, 'Yes.'

All night the boy dreamed of the water filled cave in the rock, and as soon as breakfast was over he went to the bay.

That night, his nose bled badly. For hours he had been underwater, learning to hold his breath, and now he felt weak and dizzy. His mother said, 'I shouldn't overdo things, darling, if I were you.'

That day and the next, Jerry exercised his lungs as if everything, the whole of his life, all that he would become, depended upon it. Again his nose bled at night, and his mother insisted on his coming with her the next day. It was a torment to him to waste a day of his careful self-training, but he stayed with her on that other beach, which now seemed a place for small children, a place where his mother might lie safe in the sun. It was not his beach.

He did not ask for permission, on the following day, to go to his beach. He went, before his mother could consider the complicated rights and wrongs of the matter. A day's rest, he discovered, had improved his count by ten. The big boys had made the passage while he counted a hundred and sixty. He had been counting fast, in his fright. Probably now, if he tried, he could get through that long tunnel, but he was not going to try yet. A curious, most unchildlike persistence, a controlled impatience, made him wait. In the meantime, he lay under water on the white sand, littered now by stones had had brought down from the upper air, and studied the entrance to the tunnel. He knew every jut and corner of it, as far as it was possible to see. It was as if he already felt its sharpness about his shoulders.

He sat by the clock in the villa, when his mother was not near, and checked his time. He was incredulous and then proud to find he could hold his breath without strain for two minutes. The words, 'two minutes', authorized by the clock, brought close the adventure that was so necessary to him.

In another four days, his mother said casually one morning, they must go home. On the day before they left, he would do it. He would do it if it killed him, he said defiantly to himself. But two days before they were to leave – a day of triumph when he increased his count by fifteen – his nose bled so badly that he turned dizzy and had to lie limply over the big rock like a bit of seaweed, watching the thick red blood flow on to the rock and trickle slowly down to the sea. He was frightened. Supposing he turned dizzy in the tunnel? Supposing he died there, trapped? Supposing – his head went around, in the hot sun, and he almost gave up. He thought he would return to the house and lie down, and next summer, perhaps, when he had another year's growth in him – *then* he would go through the hole.

But even after he had made the decision, or thought he had, he found himself sitting up on the rock and looking down into the water and he knew that now, this moment, when his nose had only just stopped bleeding, when his head was still sore and throbbing – this was the moment when he would try. If he did not do it now, he never would. He was trembling with fear that he would not go; and he was trembling with horror at that long, long tunnel under the rock, under the sea. Even in the open sunlight, the barrier rock seemed very wide and very heavy; tons of rock pressed down on where he would go. If he died there, he would lie until one day – perhaps not before next year – those big boys would swim into it and find it blocked.

He put on his goggles, fitted them tight, tested the vacuum. His hands were shaking. Then he chose the biggest stone he could carry and slipped over the edge of the rock until half of him was in the cool, enclosing water and half in the hot sun. He looked up once at the empty sky, filled his lungs once, twice, and then sank fast to the bottom with the stone. He let it go and began to count. He took the edges of the hole in his hands and drew himself into it, wriggling his shoulders in sideways as he remembered he must, kicking himself along with his feet.

Soon he was clear inside. He was in a small rock bound hole filled with yellowish grey water. The water was pushing him up against the roof. The roof was sharp and pained his back. He pulled himself along with his hands – fast, fast – and used his legs as levers. His head knocked against something; a sharp pain dizzied him. Fifty, fifty-one, fifty-two . . . He was without light, and the water seemed to press upon him with the weight of rock. Seventy-one, seventy-two . . . There was no strain on his lungs. He felt like an inflated balloon, his lungs were so light and easy, but his head was pulsing.

He was being continually pressed against the sharp roof, which felt slimy as well as sharp. Again he thought of octopuses, and wondered if the tunnel might be filled with weed that could tangle him. He gave himself a panicky, convulsive kick forward, ducked his head, and swam. His feet and hands moved freely, as if in open water. The hole must have widened out. He thought he must be swimming fast, and he was frightened of banging his head if the tunnel narrowed.

A hundred, a hundred and one . . . The water paled. Victory filled him. His lungs were beginning to hurt. A few more strokes and he would be out. He was counting wildly; he said a hundred and fifteen, and then, a long time later, a hundred and fifteen again. The water was a clear jewel-green all around him. Then he saw, above his head, a crack running up through the rock. Sunlight was falling through it, showing the clean, dark rock of the tunnel, a single mussel shell, and darkness ahead.

He was at the end of what he could do. He looked up at the crack as if it were filled with air and not water, as if he could put his mouth to it and draw in air. A hundred and fifteen, he heard himself say inside his head – but he had said that long ago. He must go on into the blackness ahead, or he would drown. His head was swelling, his lungs cracking. A hundred and fifteen, a hundred and fifteen pounded through his head, and he feebly clutched at rocks in the dark, pulling himself forward, leaving the brief space of sunlit water behind. He felt he was dying. He was no longer quite conscious. He struggled on in the darkness between lapses into unconsciousness. An immense, swelling pain filled his head, and then the darkness cracked with an explosion of green light. His hands, groping forward, met nothing; and his feet, kicking back, propelled him out into the open sea.

He drifted to the surface, his face turned up to the air. He was gasping like a fish. He felt he would sink now and drown; he could not swim the few feet back to the rock. Then he was clutching it and pulling himself up on it. He lay face down, gasping. He could see nothing but a red-veined, clotted dark. His eyes must have burst, he thought; they were full of blood. He tore off his goggles and a gout of blood went into the sea. His nose was bleeding, and the blood had filled the goggles.

He scooped up handfuls of water from the cool, salty sea, to splash on his face, and did not know whether it was blood or salt water he tasted. After a time, his heart quietened, his eyes cleared, and he sat up. He could see the local boys diving and playing half a mile away. He did not want them. He wanted nothing but to get back home and lie down.

In a short while, Jerry swam to shore and climbed slowly up the path to the villa. He flung himself on his bed and slept, waking at the sound of feet on the path outside. His mother was coming back. He rushed to the bathroom, thinking she must not see his face with bloodstains, or tearstains, on it. He came out of the bathroom and met her as she walked into the villa, smiling, her eyes lighting up.

'Have a nice morning?' she asked, laying her hand on his warm brown shoulder a moment.

'Oh yes, thank you,' he said.

'You look a bit pale.' And then, sharp and anxious, 'How did you bang your head?'

'Oh, just banged it,' he told her.

She looked at him closely. He was strained; his eyes were glazed-looking. She was worried. And then she said to herself, Oh, don't fuss! Nothing can happen. He can swim like a fish.

They sat down to lunch together.

'Mummy,' he said, 'I can stay under water for two minutes – three minutes, at least.' It came bursting out of him.

'Can you, darling?' she said. 'Well, I shouldn't overdo it. I don't think you ought to swim any more today.'

She was ready for a battle of wills, but he gave in at once. It was no longer of the least importance to go to the bay.

References and bibliography

Knowles, G., A. Wichmann, & P. R. Alderson (1996) *Working with Speech: the computational analysis of formal British English speech.* London: Longman.

Francis, W. & H. Kucera (1982) *Frequency Analysis of English Usage, Lexicon and Grammar.* Houghton Mifflin Company, Boston.

Garside, R., G. Leech, & G. Sampson (1987) *The Computational Analysis of English: A corpus-based approach.* London: Longman.

Johansson, S., G. Leech & H. Goodluck (1978) *Manual of information to accompany the Lancaster - Oslo/Bergen Corpus of British English, for use with digital computers.* Department of English, University of Oslo.

Johansson, S., E. Atwell, R. Garside, & G. Leech (1986) *The Tagged LOB Corpus Users' Manual.* Norwegian Computing Centre for the Humanities.

Leech, G., R. Garside, & E. Atwell (1983) *The Automatic Grammatical Tagging of the LOB Corpus.* In: *ICAME News*, 7:13-33.

O'Connor, J. D. & G. F. Arnold (1973) *Intonation of Colloquial English.* London: Longman.

Quirk, R., S. Greenbaum, G. Leech, & J. Svartvik (1985) *A Comprehensive Grammar of the English Language.* London: Longman.

Newsletter of the International Computer Archive of Modern English. The Norwegian Computing Centre for the Humanities, P.O. Box 53, N-5014 Bergen University, Norway.